VAMPIRES, GATORS, AND WACKOS

A FLORIDA NEWSPAPERMAN'S LIFE

FRANK STANFIELD

WILDBLUE
PRESS

WildBluePress.com

VAMPIRES, GATORS, AND WACKOS published by:
WILDBLUE PRESS
P.O. Box 102440
Denver, Colorado 80250

ISBN 978-1-957288-20-8 Hardcover
ISBN 978-1-957288-19-2 Trade Paperback
ISBN 978-1-957288-18-5 eBook

Interior Formatting/Cover Design by Elijah Toten
www.totencreative.com

VAMPIRES, GATORS, AND WACKOS

Table of Contents

Introduction

We slumped back in the plush, high-back conference room chairs as if we had been shot. Glassy-eyed, we looked down at the severance packages.

"More than 30 years in the business," I thought, "and it's come to this.'"

"This is not about you," the editor said. Our jobs at the 50,000-circulation daily *Ocala Star-Banner* in central Florida had simply been eliminated, like so many other newspaper jobs across the nation in 2008.

Ad sales had plummeted. The only demand for anything, it seemed, came from management—for cost-saving ideas.

Sections were dropped or slashed. One of the first things to be cut was community pages, filled with features and what journalists call "chicken dinner" news, and then it was the stock pages and the Sunday TV listings magazine—all popular features, especially among our oldest, most loyal readers.

The stock listings were outdated the moment they were printed, editors noted. Readers should go online, they said. TV sections are money losers with few ads.

A slick magazine was created and then killed. Free weeklies were dropped, including one for the nationally known mega retirement community of The Villages.

The *Star-Banner* shrank the size of its pages and sold advertising on the front page.

Single-sale boxes were taken off the streets. Circulation routes to outlying areas were dropped. Even worse, if a subscriber didn't get his paper that day, we would not bother to redeliver, even in our prime area.

We had meetings to talk about new products, new circulation areas, partnering with Craig's List for classifieds, and on and on, often without even trying to produce a prototype or a solid plan.

Steps were taken to combine some operations with our sister paper in Gainesville. Some of those moves seemed to make some sense moneywise, though it caused the first of many painful layoffs. News operations were combined, too, despite the fact that the two papers serve very different markets.

I wondered, "What kind of business stops providing basic services to its customers in order to stay afloat?"

For me, it wasn't just the loss of a job but the end of a career, I figured. I was fortunate to be able to get back into the game later, at the *Daily Commercial* in Leesburg. But what a ride it had been!

I remembered, for example, the first time I wrote the phrase "vampire cult murders" in a lead paragraph for the *Orlando Sentinel.* A conservative person by nature, I found my hands hovering over the keyboard thinking, "Is this for real?" Not only was it "for real," but it was vintage Lake County, where real events are often too unbelievable for a Stephen King novel.

How else do you explain cattle rustlers throwing ranchers' bodies into a "bottomless pit" so they could be eaten by alligators? What was the woman thinking when she wrote a love note on her husband's chest after she stabbed him to death? How did the cops bungle the case of a missing millionaire, allowing the killer to get away with murder? In what other job can you write investigative stories to pressure authorities to dig up a dead man to prove he was a murder victim?

Before Casey Anthony became "the most hated woman in America" in her 2011 trial for the death of her 2-year-old daughter, Caylee, another mom killed herself before revealing what happened to her toddler. The child's grandfather, a former cop. is on death row for killing another child.

Fortunately, some stories are funny. There was the drunk, for example, who insisted at the jail that his name was Osama Bin Laden. There was a planeload of naked people buzzing houses, and then there was a stir caused by a nude man walking down the road who told cops, "It's not as bad as it looks."

Some of the wackiest characters of all are in the news business.

Few tales are as titillating as the story of Debra Lefave, a teacher who had sex with one of her middle school students, yet was too pretty to go to jail, according to her lawyer.

There is also a chapter on the stuff of Florida legend: attacks by alligators, snakes, bears, and sharks. Another chapter details coverage of a deadly tornado, hurricanes, and sinkholes.

Vampires, Gators, and Whackos: A Newspaperman's Life tells these stories and more and raises the question whether newspapers are headed for the grave or a digital resurrection.

Chapter 1

Vampires

Jennifer Wendorf crept into her home on cat paws, slipping quietly through the darkness past her father, Richard, stretched out on the couch. It was 10:30 p.m., on Nov. 25, 1996. It was a school night and she had gone to see her boyfriend after leaving her part-time grocery store job. She was 15 minutes late and the 17-year-old cheerleader didn't want to have to explain herself.

But when she entered the kitchen, she forgot all about curfew and her dad. There, on the floor, was her mother, sprawled out, face down in a sea of blood. Jennifer spun around and ran toward her father. She tried but could not rouse him. Then, in the dim light, she could finally see that his head had been beaten beyond recognition. His face, in the words of the first deputy on the scene, looked like "hamburger."

Amazingly poised but with her voice quaking, she called 911 to report that Richard Wendorf and Ruth Queen, had been killed.

"What makes you think that they have been killed?" the operator asked.

"There is blood everywhere. Please, as fast as you can," Jennifer said.

Asked if she was alone Jennifer replied: "My sister is gone. She should be here. She's only 15 years old and she's gone."

Lake County sheriff's deputies swarmed the quiet neighborhood, turning the rural area near Eustis, Fla., into a carnival of flashing lights and long stretches of yellow crime scene tape. It would be a normal thing for a late-night TV crime drama or a bad neighborhood in Orlando 40 miles away, but not here.

The three-bedroom brick house with a swimming pool and a big yard sat on a rise overlooking other middle-class homes with big lots, fences, and a dead-end road that created the illusion of mini-ranches. It had certainly given a false sense of tranquility to the Wendorfs.

The first question on investigators' minds was: Where was Jennifer's sister, Heather? Had she been kidnapped or killed, or was she responsible for this heinous crime?

The questions wouldn't go away, but the first thing deputies had to face was horror of the crime scene.

Jennifer's mother had been beaten so severely her brain stem was exposed. Some deputies speculated that she had been shot. Others thought she may have been attacked with an ax.

She had fallen near a doorway between the kitchen and the dining room. Crime scene technicians found bloody boot prints where the attacker pursued her. Blood spatter was on the kitchen walls and the ceiling. Pieces of her skull were in the dining room. Ruth's growling little white poodle wouldn't let authorities near her body. A golden retriever wandered aimlessly outside.

There was no sign of the weapon.

Jennifer passed the point of being brave or rational, yet still had to fight the impulse to be hysterical. She told deputies that the family's 1993 blue Ford Explorer was also missing.

Shortly after sheriff's deputies arrived, family friend Suzanne Leclaire, drove up to the house with a warning for the Wendorfs.

Moments earlier, she discovered her 16-year-old daughter, Jeanine, hiding in the woods near her home, waiting for a ride. She was supposed to run away with Heather, a former classmate named Rod Ferrell, and a handful of teens from Murray, Ky. Ferrell, 16, had a nasty reputation at Eustis High School when he eventually moved with his family to Kentucky. He dressed in black, carried a walking stick, and wore an inverted cross, typically a sign of devil worship.

Almost a year earlier, he had convinced Jeanine to "cross-over" and become a vampire in a ceremony in which they sucked each other's blood. The following month he moved away.

He stayed in touch with Heather, however, running up an expensive long-distance phone bill that angered her parents. It was the three teens' interest in vampirism that kept the phone lines humming, and there were consistent themes, Jeanine recalled in a deposition.

"Killing?"

"He might have mentioned some of that."

"Taking over your soul?"

"Some of that, also," she said.

Suzanne had discovered a letter from Ferrell that mentioned his mother. "It sounded like violence and blood and murder," she said.

News coverage was immediate and intense.

"5 sought in bludgeoning," read the headline in the Lake County edition of the *Sentinel*. "Officials: Missing teens include daughter of victims (*Sentinel* Nov. 27, 1996)."

Shock waves rippled through the community. Richard Wendorf was a respected manager at a container company. Ruth was a volunteer at the girls' school.

"It's absolutely appalling and unbelievable to those of us who knew them," said Richard's father, James Wendorf, 75, a former attorney for the Billy Graham Crusade. Heather is "a demure little girl," he said. "I'm almost believing that she's a victim (*Sentinel,* Nov 27, 1996)."

The public was getting a different perspective in a story headlined "Parents' murders: Ultimate shocker?"

While Jennifer was a popular cheerleader, Heather, or "Zoey" as she liked to be called, was a talented artist who dyed her hair purple, wore bizarre outfits with fishnet stockings and carried a backpack with a Barbie doll dangling off the back with a noose.

Investigators tore through Heather's room looking for clues. Besides the things one would expect, like notes passed in class and a journal entry confessing that she could not sleep without her teddy bear, they also found ceramic gargoyles, drawings of demons, Anne Rice's best-selling vampire novels, and a video of *Interview with the Vampire.*

I was beside myself. Because little happens in a courthouse during holidays, I had taken a week's vacation to help care for my father-in-law, who was recovering from surgery. The entire staff of the Lake bureau, it seemed, was getting a piece of the biggest story in memory. I needn't have worried. Because it was so crazy, the *Sentinel* would report on every motion, every hearing, and every scrap of paper that came through the courthouse. It would largely become my story after some very fine reporting by staffers, especially Mary Murphy, Jerry Fallstrom, and Lesley Clark.

"There's plenty for everyone," County Editor Lauren Ritchie said, trying to cool my competitive jets. "No there's not," I replied. This kind of story doesn't come along every day, even in scenic but often bizarre Lake County. The story would not just be about the occult or a terrible crime, it would become a rare opportunity to peer into people's souls and see the unfathomable depth of mankind's depravity.

Investigators found a journal entry in which Heather said there were two sides to her personality: one, which is "nonresistant, passive, nonaggressive," and the other "is the essence of vengeance, hate and destruction. Purely chaos modeled into a hideous monster, writhing and tearing the inside of me to ribbons."

She also wrote: "Blood would taste really good right about now. Or maybe ice cream. Hey! What am I saying? Blood is good all the time."

She wrote that she was "stoned" while writing the note.

In another note, she wrote of Ferrell's plan to start a vampire "family," that she would be one of the queens and would be paired with a boy from Kentucky.

Investigators also learned that after making his surprise visit to Central Florida, Ferrell met Heather after school and took her to a nearby cemetery where she "crossed over" in the blood-drinking ceremony.

That was on Monday. That night a panicked Heather called Jeanine saying they had to leave right away. Even more distressing, "Rod is talking about killing my parents," she said in comments later revealed in court records.

Through luck or by the grace of God, Jeanine missed the ride that could have ended up with deadly consequences for her family.

"He mentioned about [how] he was going to have to kill my parents and take everything out of the house and I said, 'No, you're not going to kill my parents and take everything out of the house,'" Jeanine said in a deposition.

"He was like, 'Fine, we'll tie them up and take everything out of the house.' I was like, 'No, I'll empty my bank account, but you're not going to do that either.'"

It wasn't just Ferrell who talked about murder.

Jennifer told investigators about a disturbing question that Heather had asked one night: "Jen, have you ever plotted Mom and Dad's death?"

Nor would it be the only incriminating statement. Once, when she was having trouble with a boyfriend, Heather told Jennifer: "Rod Ferrell would be a person to ask if you wanted someone killed."

Information began to pour in after the slayings. The first person Ferrell visited in Central Florida was a 16-year-old former classmate named Shannon. He told her that he planned to kill Heather's parents and take their vehicle. Ferrell and his friends were traveling in a battered, cramped 1987 Buick Skyhawk that was on the verge of breaking down.

"I didn't understand why they wanted to kill them, so I didn't believe them," the girl told *The Sentinel*.

Ferrell's mother told the *Sentinel* that Heather "was saying she was going to kill her parents for a long time (Nov. 30, 1996)."

Authorities in Kentucky were not surprised that Ferrell was at the center of a manhunt.

"You've got one wild bunch on the loose," Callaway County, Ky., Sheriff Stan Scott, told the *Sentinel*, referring to Ferrell, his girlfriend, Charity "Shea" Lynn Keesee, 16, Howard Scott Anderson, 17, and Dana L. Cooper, 19. Ferrell was suspected in a horrific cult mutilation of 60 dogs at the local animal shelter. He was also building gasoline bombs, reports said.

Authorities were also familiar with Ferrell's mother, Sondra Gibson.

She was caught writing "lurid" letters to a 14-year-old boy while trying to engage him in sex acts while "crossing over" to become a vampire, prosecutors said.

"I longed to be near you for your embrace. Yes ... to become a vampire, a part of the family, immortal, and truly yours forever," the 34-year-old wrote.

Later, in an exclusive interview with me, Gibson and her parents defended her son, and she denounced her involvement in vampirism, calling it "stupidness" and "Hollywood idiocy."

"This is not Rod," she said of the allegations (*Sentinel*, Jan. 21, 1998), and she denied that he had anything to do with animal abuse.

Ferrell's father had abandoned him at an early age after failing to work out visitation with Gibson after their divorce.

As a teen, Rod and his friend, Matt Goodman, spent countless hours playing dark fantasy games that they created. Eventually, Rod hung out with teen vampire enthusiasts, sometimes all night in mausoleums and cemeteries. One night, his mother discovered him cutting his arms for blood drinking.

Another evening, neighbors saw Rod and his mother wearing all-black clothing. Because they were holding hands, some thought they were boyfriend-girlfriend. When the two moved out, the landlord found a pentagram emblazoned on the floor.

Ferrell wasn't the only one in the cult who came from a wildly dysfunctional family. Scott Anderson's father was an alcoholic on welfare. The family lived in a house with garbage bags for windows, which did a poor job of keeping out the cold during Kentucky's fierce winters.

Cooper, who was trying to live on her own with a low-paying job, said she threw in with the group because she was lonely.

Charity's father wanted her to stay away from Ferrell, but she was wowed by his long hair and crazy stories. Yet it would be Charity whose actions would lead to the group's downfall in Baton Rouge, La.

***

The vampires were a sorry looking sight in the Baton Rouge police detective's squad room. Greasy-haired, smelly and exhausted, they sat across the room from each other as far as detectives could manage.

Capture was inevitable but capture without bloodshed was no sure thing. The group had burglarized a home after leaving New Orleans, stealing a handful of items, including a shotgun that Ferrell vowed to use if police tried to capture him.

Charity had called her mother, a corrections officer, asking her to book a motel room in Baton Rouge for her and her friends. When they arrived, they received handcuffs, not a stack of clean towels. Inside the stolen SUV were several items, including a book of magic spells and Anne Rice's vampire novel, *Queen of the Damned*. Heather's teddy bear was also inside with her mother's pearls draped around its neck.

Louisiana officers did some interrogations on this third day of the short-lived vampire reign, but much of the heavy lifting would be done by Lake County sheriff's detectives Al Gussler and Sgt. Wayne Longo. What they found was surprising.

Heather was eating pizza and joking with Ferrell across the room.

"How can you stand to be in the same room with him and laugh and joke and smile at each other?" Longo asked her. "Do you know what he did to your parents? Tell me, tell me."

"He killed them," she replied.

He kept pressing her, asking her how he had killed her parents, until she said he had used a crowbar or tire iron.

"…we're trying to understand why you didn't defend your mom and dad who are no longer here to do it theirselves (sic) but you chose to go with the man who killed your parents. We're trying to find out why. You don't seem to think that there is anything wrong with that other than an hour-and-a-half being upset for a day," the detective said, relying on information passed along to them.

"You don't know how upset I am inside," she said. "I didn't know he was gonna kill my parents."

Ferrell, clearly exhausted, his swagger gone, held nothing back when the detectives put him in the interrogation room. It was "a rush," he admitted.

"To feel that fact that I was taking a life, because that's just like the old philosophy about if you can take a life, you become a god for a split second, and it actually kind of felt that way for a minute, but if I was a god, I wouldn't exactly be here, would I?"

He said he was confronted in the kitchen by Heather's mother, and he became enraged when she struggled and threw coffee at him, so he literally beat her brains out.

He said Scott, who was in the house with him, was "almost like a kid at an amusement park for the first time." Scott said he "froze" when Ferrell began beating his victims.

Ferrell told officers that he would tell them what they wanted to know under one condition: He wanted to see Charity. He said she was two months pregnant (she was not, apparently), and she was the only thing he cared about.

Officers put the two together inside an interview room, alone but for a hidden camera.

"Take care of the … kid," he said, using a profanity.

He also talked about the possibility of ending up in "Old Sparky," Florida's electric chair.

The 16-year-old, who told his followers that he was a 500-year-old immortal vampire, told detectives: "I wanted to kill myself, and when I met her, I wanted to live. Now that she is being taken away, I will find a way to kill myself. No matter if it's in a little padded room or what."

Keesee began her interview by saying, "I got one question. Why are you guys questioning me? I didn't do anything."

Later, however, she said of Ferrell: "He said he was gonna kill something. He didn't say who or what or why or anything."

Asked when he said it, she replied: "All the way down there and after we got to Florida …. He's like, 'I want to kill something. I want to kill something. I want to kill somebody. I want to kill something.' I had thought about it and I thought maybe that was what he was doing when we dropped him off [at the Wendorfs]."

Ferrell talked about killing Jeanine's parents, "and then he was like no, all they have is a *hoopdee* for a car," Keesee said. "He goes, 'We'll definitely kill Zoey's [parents] because I guess he knew that they had two brand new cars.'"

She also said that she witnessed Ferrell and Anderson breaking a large stick in two so they would both have a weapon.

Ferrell told Heather to go inside her house and get some clothing and to slip back outside. He then told Cooper and Keesee to drive Heather to her boyfriend's house so she could say goodbye to him. They also stopped by Jeanine's house, but she told Heather she couldn't slip out because her parents were still awake. Heather told her they would be back.

It was shortly after that that Heather began to realize something was terribly wrong. She spotted her parents' Explorer, Keesee said, "and she's like, 'Oh my God. That's my parents… that's my parents' car, they stole it.' I'm like, 'I don't know Zoey,' you know. Because I didn't think they'd actually kill them. I mean, he's always talking like that, so I figured oh, he killed -- maybe he killed a dog or something, you know and maybe he just stole the car."

He stopped the car and he got out to speak with Keesee. He didn't have to tell her, she said. He had blood all over his face. He and Scott had also stripped off their shirts.

Later, after they ditched Anderson's little Buick, Ferrell placed the bloody crowbar under the seat by Keesee's feet.

Cooper, in her interview with the Lake County sheriff's detectives, said that she and Keesee tried to talk Ferrell and Anderson out of killing the Wendorfs.

"They was like, well there's no other way [to get the Explorer]. It was like talking to a brick wall ...."

Cooper told detectives it was her idea to leave the Wendorf home before Ferrell and Anderson launched their deadly strike. "Shea and I didn't want to be any part of it, so we got in the car, and we said we was gonna take Heather to see her boyfriend."

Cooper also said that when Heather first saw her parents' car, she slid down to the floor because she thought her parents were looking for her.

Gussler asked Cooper about the moment Heather learned that her parents had been killed.

"She started freaking out real bad." Cooper said she had to get in the back seat and lay on top of her to get her to settle down. Heather finally went to sleep.

Asked how long it took Heather to start acting normal, Cooper said it was about a day-and-a-half later. "She was talking and laughing ...."

Later, she would get quiet and "sort of space out," Cooper said.

Cooper said she didn't think Ferrell was really a vampire but she "crossed over" in the cult's blood-drinking, "because for one it would give me somebody to be with, somebody to hang out with. As it was, I was alone by myself in my apartment. The only people that came over were my parents. Nobody else. And once I crossed over and, through Rod, I had people calling me, checking on me, coming over to pick me up and take me out places ...."

* * *

When detectives finished their questioning, the Louisiana court system lurched into slow motion. Prosecutors in Florida had assured Baton Rouge investigators there was no problem interviewing the teens without their parents being present. Louisiana judges, citing a much different law in their state, weren't so sure. Finally, on Dec. 6, the teens were taken back to Florida.

I was among a crowd of reporters and photographers who greeted the caravan outside the Lake County Jail. Whisked into a closed sally port behind steel doors, Ferrell stuck his tongue out at photographers. He smooched a glass partition in the booking area.

On Dec. 17, a Lake County grand jury indicted all but one of the teens—Heather. Her lawyer told me she would be testifying before the closed-door panel. "I think the grand jury is an excellent forum for a person who wants to tell the truth and does not fear the truth," James Hope said (*Sentinel,* Jan. 17, 1997). Hope said he was convinced of her innocence, in part, because of a greeting card Heather had left for her father. "To my dad, the best father any daughter ever had. Love, Heather."

Not to be outdone, Ferrell responded to an interview request I had made at the jail. I had already left the office when he called, but two other reporters pounced on the opportunity.

The next morning, the *Sentinel* landed like a bombshell on driveways with the headline "Interview with the 'vampire."

Ferrell denied killing the Wendorfs and blamed a rival vampire clan. He then claimed that he had multiple personalities and fell into "special blackout moments" (*Sentinel,* Dec. 19, 1996). He said his rival vampire leader in Murray was trying to get him to do "totally immoral" things like killing animals. He also implicated Scott Anderson in the killings, claiming he was outside and dozing when his friend drove up in the Wendorf's Explorer.

Reaction was swift.

State Attorney Brad King said it was the first time anyone had heard any story about multiple personalities, not to mention 10, as Ferrell claimed.

The Lake Sheriff George Knupp also fired back. "We've got the right people in jail (*Sentinel,* Dec. 20, 1996)."

Ferrell's attorney, Assistant Public Defender Candace Hawthorne, was furious at the paper for publishing the interview, insisting he was a "disturbed child" who had been taken advantage of by the news media. All I got out of it was the threat of a subpoena, which worried me because if I became part of the story, I wouldn't be allowed to cover the trial.

Psychiatrists I interviewed said multiple personalities are so rare some mental health professionals doubt the condition even exists.

Assistant State Attorney Bill Gross joked that it didn't matter to him which personality did the killings, as long as all of them were in jail.

The Public Defender's office, worried about pretrial publicity, urged reporters to refer to the slayings case as "the Wendorf case" instead of vampire cult murders.

The state attorney also worried that the trial would have to be moved because of publicity. "This case has nothing to do with vampirism," Brad King said.

Heather and her attorney were running a risk. Most defendants facing a grand jury invoke their Fifth Amendment right not to incriminate themselves.

Heather would testify that while she planned to run away from home, she did not want her parents harmed and had no warning or participation in their deaths. If the grand jury believed her, she would not be charged with murder or with being a principal.

Heather had earlier written to Jennifer from the jail in Baton Rouge claiming her innocence.

"I want to believe that that's true because she's my little sister, and I love her to death," Jennifer told authorities. "Maybe she's just putting all the blame on Rod just so she won't get in trouble."

Heather faced tough questions for two hours, sometimes breaking down under the strain, Hope said.

The other defense attorneys, who were not allowed to hear the testimony, were sweating. Soon, their worst fears were realized when the state attorney told the grand jury that statements by two witnesses against Heather were false. The first was a statement by a 15-year-old girl who told police that Heather had confessed to planning the murders. She later recanted and said she didn't even know Heather. The second was from Ferrell's mother, who claimed Heather had planned to kill her parents for "a long time."

Although grand jury testimony is sealed, it was clear that Heather insisted that she had been tricked into going off with the girls to see her boyfriend before her parents were killed.

After deliberations, the panel decided all charges against her should be dropped.

"While she certainly acted inappropriately in planning to leave home, and arguably so in remaining with the others after learning what had been done, we acknowledge that these acts are not crimes," the grand jury wrote in its report. "We also wish to unequivocally state that these actions were wrong."

The panel scolded her for her choice of friends but also wished her well with "God's mercy and grace in the recovery …."

Lake County Sheriff George Knupp said he was "mad as hornet" and would later demand a new grand jury. Ferrell's attorneys were especially put out. The time-honored strategy of taking the spotlight off a client and shining it on someone else was suddenly in jeopardy. She could even become a star witness for the state.

The public at the time didn't know what to think, and many still don't, but Heather was sticking to her statements to detectives.

A: "I remember telling him flat out, 'Don't even go near my parents.'"

Q: "Why would you tell him not to even go near your parents?"

A: "Because he asked me not too long ago if I wanted my parents dead or alive, and I said straight out I wanted them alive."

The "not too long ago" was just a few hours before the slayings when she met Ferrell and the other cult members after school in a cemetery. It was there, Heather said, that she "crossed over" to become a vampire.

Cooper described the cult initiation in her interrogation.

"You make three incisions on either arm and you put blood into a cup from each of the people that are present. You add a little water to it and the person who's being crossed over then drinks the whole contents of that cup."

Cooper also talked about "feedings."

"If someone gets weak in the group you make two incisions on one arm, one on your hand, one on the arm."

***

The months leading up to Ferrell's trial were filled with the taking of depositions. Motions were filed, lab results reviewed, and psychologists were lined up.

The defense lawyers kept trying to peel layers off Heather. In one deposition, in October of 1997, one of the first questions was: "How many times have you visited your parents' graves?"

Cooper's lawyer, Mary Ann Plecas, wanted to know how Heather, who described herself as "hysterical," could be "comfortable enough, or your mind was at ease enough, that you were able to not once, but twice, fall off to sleep?"

"I'm not saying I passed out, but you can get hysterical enough to exhaust yourself, and that's what happened. I was exhausted," she replied.

Ferrell's co-counsel, Bill Lackay, asked if she had written letters to friends saying she wished her parents were dead.

"I have always wanted them alive. I loved them," she said.

Every piece of evidence from Heather seemed to bolster her claim that she had no knowledge her parents were going to be killed. In a letter to her sister from the juvenile detention center in Ocala, Heather said she fainted when she learned what happened. Ferrell insisted on telling her every graphic detail.

"I know she was afraid of Rod," Jennifer said in her deposition. "I believe he had some hold over the other three."

Heather still said some very questionable things, Jennifer said. Once, Heather asked Jennifer if she ever thought about plotting their parents' deaths ("I just blew that off"), and there was also Heather's statement that Ferrell was a "hit man."

Heather tried to clarify that statement in her deposition by saying that Jennifer once had an abusive boyfriend. One night, Heather asked her sobbing sister, "Do you wish he was dead?"

"Yes, I really wish he was dead."

"I mean, if you really do, I mean, it might could happen. It might could happen."

Heather explained that she thought Ferrell might not kill the boy, but that he might "beat him up or something. I don't know. Just make him pay for what he did to my sister."

Despite being set free, not everything was quiet and peaceful for Heather. She was alienated from her family, especially her father's twin brother. Almost a year to the date of the murders, Heather had a self-described breakdown while staying with her maternal grandmother. After the two had argued, Heather collapsed to the ground and her grandmother fired a pistol in the air to try and get her to stop screaming. Heather moved into the home of a lawyer who was not connected to the case.

One defense attorney asked the judge for a copy of Heather's secret grand jury testimony. It's not unheard of, but attorneys must have a good reason to believe a witness was lying or telling a contradictory tale. The judge denied the motion.

By January, lawyers were locked in a crucial battle over Ferrell's videotaped confession.

It is hard to imagine that Ferrell would not be convicted, even if Circuit Judge Jerry Lockett ruled that the confession should not be played for the jury. A bloody boot print on the kitchen floor matched Ferrell, according to a crime lab report, and DNA material beneath Ruth's fingernails belonged to both her and Ferrell. But the confession was dynamite. "When the jurors see it, they're going to want to throw the switch themselves," one of the teen's defense attorneys told me.

Confessions can be thrown out if a defendant had been coerced, tricked, or not given his Miranda rights explaining that he has the right not to incriminate himself.

Ferrell claimed he had downed a big bottle of wine in 10 minutes about an hour before his arrest. It had "a disorienting effect," he said, and he claimed a detective threatened "to put me under the jail."

The officer denied it. Ferrell said on the videotape, "You didn't beat my ass or anything."

The state attorney pointed out that there was no evidence in the video that Ferrell was drunk.

Ferrell's attorney, Hawthorne, insisted he had been "hot-boxed" in the tiny interrogation room while being chained to a chair.

After listening to testimony, the judge ruled that the videotapes of all of the defendants were admissible.

As the time drew closer to the trial, emotions began to simmer. The lawyers worked long nights and the Wendorfs were steeling themselves to hear the terrible details. Ferrell's grandparents also tried to prepare themselves.

Harrell Gibson was a thin, harried-looking man who transported automobiles for a living.

"There hasn't been any drinking, tobacco or abusive language in our house since 1958," he said, referring to the year the couple joined a Pentecostal church.

Ferrell's grandmother, Rosetta, worked in food service at Murray State University. Looking like a grandmother right out of central casting, with her glasses and her gray hair pinned up in a bun, she was Ferrell's fiercest champion.

"Rod is a good boy and has always been a good boy," Rosetta told me (*Sentinel,* Jan. 11, 1998). "He never met a stranger," she said, which may have led him to "fall in with the wrong crowd."

After moving back to Kentucky from Eustis in 1995, Ferrell became interested in the undead and began playing fantasy games.

"I thought it was a kid's game," she said.

Months before the murders, Ferrell ran away to Florida in an attempt to "rescue" Heather from "hell."

"I don't know if you understand or even care how close I was to being the happiest I've ever been," Heather wrote in a letter to a friend. "I've been so close that I could feel Rod's life all around me," she wrote.

"He didn't come to Florida to kill those people. He was coming to Florida on a trip with his little girlfriend," Rosetta said.

As for his confession, he was probably on drugs or acting crazy to throw investigators off the trail, the grandparents said.

Harrell said his grandson had "the potential for being a great spiritual leader," and predicted Ferrell would be set free.

But if he wasn't, and he was sentenced to die in the electric chair, "I've always told him no man knows when a heartbeat will be his last. Be ready to meet the Lord."

***

Ferrell's family might have believed in him, but he wasn't helping his case. Besides granting the newspaper interview, he boasted to a jail guard that he had been thinking of ways to escape with a hostage.

"You get an innocent person and the cops won't do anything to you. They don't want to shoot the innocent person."

A corrections officer also quoted Ferrell as saying, "I don't know why Heather got off. She had it done."

Ferrell said he heard that a man named "Tyme," had committed the murders.

As the clock ticked down, Ferrell's attorneys went over their limited options and came up with one thin hope: Their client was borderline psychotic and "suffers from the influences of vampirism and practices of the occult," they wrote in a pretrial motion.

It would be an especially tricky defense because it was not an insanity defense per se. To plead not guilty by reason of insanity, a defendant must not have been able to tell the difference between right and wrong. Unlike some states, Florida does not allow a "diminished capacity" defense. The best the attorneys could hope for was to get psychologists to say that his bizarre beliefs should be considered a mitigating factor in his sentencing.

The defense also claimed that he was under the influence of drugs during the crime, that he had been sexually abused as a child, that his mother had not exercised parental control, and that he suffered from "divorced kid syndrome."

Divorce does not cause crime, the state countered.

Once the state understood what the defense was trying to do, they knew they would be able to talk about all of the macabre vampire details to the jury.

Now, pretrial publicity was a bigger issue than ever. A questionnaire was sent out to hundreds of prospective jurors.

One woman wrote: "I am so convinced that Ferrell killed the Wendorfs that I almost feel you could skip the trial part and just go to the death penalty. I can't forget the image of the little sick jerk sticking his tongue out when arrested."

One man insisted, however: "I don't believe everything I see on TV or read in the papers. I believe guilt should be proved in a court of law."

Knowing something about a case doesn't exclude someone from jury duty. It's whether the person can set aside the information and be impartial.

King was confident a jury could be picked without moving the trial to another city. Four years earlier, a local jury was selected in the case of two teens who carjacked and raped a young widow, Dorothy Lewis. They shot her, left her for dead, and killed her two young children in one of the most heinous crimes in the history of Florida.

That's not to say picking a jury would be easy. One woman broke down in tears during questioning. Others recalled hearing about vampire "oaths," described the crimes as "gruesome," and talked about whether they agreed with the state's death penalty law, especially since the defendant was only 16 when the crimes were committed.

Ferrell's long hair was gone by this time. He wore glasses, a white shirt, tie, and a sweater, and sat doodling and drawing vampire figures at the defense table. His image had been transformed from a menacing looking freak to a harmless-looking nerd.

Finally, after three days, the attorneys managed to pick 12 jurors and a handful of alternates.

Court TV arrived with miles of cable. A Miami-based German TV crew also showed up. British papers had done extensive coverage of the crime. An adjoining courtroom had been set up as a press room, with monitors for the TV news crews and phone hookups for The Associated Press.

While all eyes were turned toward the trial, another judge told me that the Wendorfs' life insurance company wondered if Heather should get half of her father's $20,000 benefit, or did she have a role in their murders? Records showed that wise investments, including Disney stock, meant that each girl could end up with as much as $350,000.

The trial began on Feb. 5. Brad King was making his opening statement with a standard speech about how people make choices every day when defense attorney Bill Lackay suddenly interrupted.

"Mr. Ferrell has indicated … he may want to do something to change things."

The judge cleared the courtroom, and after reporters scurried to call their editors, they settled in for a three-hour wait while Ferrell talked with his lawyers.

A plea deal could change everything. In theory, Ferrell could testify against Anderson, the only other defendant who was in the house that night.

King told reporters that he didn't need Ferrell's testimony and he didn't want it. Left unsaid was the obvious fact that Ferrell was the main guy. Why would anyone give him any kind of deal?

Sondra Gibson, who had said that her interest in vampirism had been "stupidness," approached the restroom, stopped, turned toward a group of reporters and said: "We live forever!" You could almost hear the *Twilight Zone* theme song playing in the background.

When court reconvened, the world would learn that Ferrell decided to plead guilty in hopes that he would not be sentenced to death.

King was not deterred. The prosecutor insisted and the judge granted permission to start the sentencing part of the trial.

The first moments were gut-wrenching for the Wendorf family. They wept as King recited the facts of the case.

Rosetta Gibson, who seemed tough and broken at the same time, cried when Ferrell pleaded guilty.

"I want to touch him," she said, reaching her arm out toward her grandson as bailiffs cleared the courtroom. She never got the chance. Ferrell was fingerprinted and led off to jail.

A week later, lawyers began the penalty trial.

The day began with testimony of a former classmate in Eustis who described Ferrell as "a regular, dorky kid." He got her attention, however, because she was interested in witchcraft. When he showed up again in 1996, he had been "transformed" into a vampire, she said. He asked her to run away with the cult, and said he was fleeing authorities in Kentucky because he had been building bombs. She refused to go. The next day, the Wendorfs were dead.

The medical examiner's testimony was gruesome. Richard Wendorf had been struck 20 times in the head.

King warned the Wendorfs that they might want to leave the courtroom, but they stayed, choking back tears as the pathologist used a photo to point out each blow.

The next day, a psychiatrist testified that Ferrell claimed that Richard was dead and that Ruth was dying when he entered the house.

"I had the feeling it was like a game to him," Dr. Wade Myers III testified.

Ferrell was suffering from depression, had a schizotypal personality, and hallucinations about seeing and hearing angels and demons. Sometimes he imagined smelling burning sulfur, the University of Florida psychiatrist said.

It was all caused by a chaotic, abusive childhood, abandonment by his father, and a psychotic mother, he said.

King pointed out that Ferrell's psychological test scores showed that he was more likely to have conduct disorder, characterized by lying, stealing, running away from home, robbing people and being cruel to animals.

Meyers admitted that that he may have scrapped one test because Ferrell lied.

Longtime mental health expert, Harry Krop, called Ferrell's kin "one of the most dysfunctional families I have ever encountered."

Ferrell told him he had been sexually assaulted at age 6 when his grandfather took him to a black magic cult gathering.

"I don't know anything about any cult," Gibson told me during a break.

Krop testified that Ferrell never believed he was a vampire. It was a way to get attention.

He also talked about troubles in Kentucky, including the time he threatened to slit a teacher's throat.

The psychologist said it was probably an empty threat and just "bravado."

King said that for the Wendorfs, "it wasn't bravado. He said what he was going to do and did what he said he was going to do."

Jurors that day also heard about the genetic evidence, but it would be the following day when jurors would see the real Ferrell.

Jurors looked over at Ferrell as they watched the obscenity-laced videotape, and they were no longer able to keep a poker face when they heard him talk about killing Wendorf.

"… I didn't stop because he was still like breathing and stuff. I just kept beating him, and beating him, and beating him, and beating him, taking pleasure at that."

Rosetta Gibson put her head on her husband's shoulder, wept, covered her eyes, and then walked out of the courtroom.

There would be a lot more tears that day, including those of Ruth's daughter from another marriage, who said she would miss her mother's advice on how to raise her three children.

Most telling was the testimony of Ferrell's father, who never looked at his son.

The next day, if a casual visitor walked in, he might think that he was witnessing a child neglect case, with Sondra on trial.

She admitted she had no control over him and said she approved of the way he decorated his all-black room with an altar, a book of witches' spells, candles, and satanic symbolism.

She also conceded she had not had her son treated for abusing drugs, including LSD.

King impeached defense reports saying Ferrell's umbilical cord was wrapped around his neck at birth, possibly causing brain damage, and a report claiming he had suffered from a bout of encephalitis. Medical records did not support the claims.

Jennifer testified about Heather asking her if she had ever thought about killing their parents.

But the most colorful testimony came from a vampire.

I had never met vampire Steven "Jaden" Murphy, the so-called "Prince of the City" of Murray, but I had talked to him extensively over the phone. With his dark hair swept back past his earrings and his tongue pierced with a silver ball, the charismatic 19-year-old practically strutted into the courthouse. When I identified myself, it was as if he had just found his long-lost brother. The commotion caught the attention of the Court TV people, who immediately set up an impromptu press conference outside.

"I still love Rod," he said (*Sentinel*, Feb. 20, 1998). He said he had no bitterness over Ferrell's attempt to blame him for the slayings. He also said he knew right away that the murders were not about vampirism because Ferrell "did not bleed the bodies."

He told the growing crowd that Ferrell once told him that if he ever did kill someone, it would be by "cutting them up into little pieces or bludgeoning."

On the stand, he told jurors that vampirism is "a lifestyle."

"I'm 19, not thousands of years old. I know I can die," he said.

He also opened his mouth and stuck out his tongue to show that he had no fangs.

He then pulled out a Valentine's Day card from Sondra, signed "Dark Angel, eternally, Star, aka Mistress of the Dark."

After testifying, he stepped down from the stand and blew a kiss to Ferrell. Ferrell blew one back.

It was great theater but not as important as the next day's testimony of psychologist Elizabeth McMahon, Ph.D. Animated, brilliant, and articulate, she could be a prosecutor's worst nightmare if taken lightly.

Ferrell was living in an uncontrollable rage, frustrated by his dysfunctional family, and obsessed with fantasy, she testified.

Ferrell believed he was going to Florida to "rescue a damsel in distress. He began to see Heather's parents as bad. It never occurred to him that he was not getting the whole story."

King, in cross-examination, got her to admit that Ferrell was able to stop himself from committing other crimes, if he thought he might be tripped up by a burglar alarm, for example.

She also conceded that Ferrell told her he felt no remorse and didn't even consider the couple to be real people until he saw Richard's twin brother in the courtroom.

Rebuttal witnesses testified that Ferrell did not keep his court-ordered appointment in Kentucky, nor did he write a mandatory paper saying how the occult had impacted his life. On that day he was in Florida murdering the Wendorfs.

But it was the witness that King didn't call that stirred grumbling from the reporters and planted even more distrust within the family. Heather never testified, and because of that, defense attorneys couldn't conduct a withering cross-examination, sowing seeds of doubt and just generally making her look bad.

The state's strategy wasn't without risk. Curious jurors had to wonder why she wasn't called.

***

A life sentence was certainly what Hawthorne wanted. A death sentence would make him the youngest prisoner on death row. It would be especially tragic, the defense attorney argued, since his chaotic upbringing prevented him from making good decisions.

The jury had just one request. It wanted to see Ferrell's videotaped confession again.

What they saw was a long-haired, cigarette-smoking, remorseless, bored teenager using the term *"splack"* to describe the sound of a crowbar mashing an innocent person's skull. They also heard him say what a "rush" it was to kill someone and how it made him feel like "a god."

When the jury came back, Ferrell stood awaiting the recommendation. The Wendorfs held hands, put their arms around each other, or held their breath. The Gibsons braced themselves, too.

The judge warned everyone to keep their emotions in check.

The recommendation was death.

"A life sentence would have brought closure to this case today," Hawthorne said (*Sentinel* 2/24/1998).

King said the 12-0 vote was a clear signal of "holding people accountable for things they do."

Bill Wendorf said he was happy with the jury's recommendation, but he had doubts about Heather. He wanted to hear convincing testimony from her. At the same time, he had been bristling at defense hints that his brother and sister-in-law were somehow to blame for the tragedy.

"Richard and Ruth's honor were restored," he said.

The next day brought another hearing. The defense argued that because he was only 16 at the time, an execution would violate the Constitution's ban on cruel and unusual punishment.

On Feb. 25, Ferrell took the stand.

He said he told Heather that Anderson's Buick wasn't running very well. "I asked her if it was cool if we stole her parents' car. She said she didn't have a problem with that."

Then he said, "You spoke so much about killing your parents. You still want me to? She said yes."

He testified that Heather told him the keys to the Explorer were probably in her parents' dresser drawer. Instead, they were in the ignition.

"I wondered why she had told me that," he said, adding that he would not have even needed to go into the house.

He said Heather asked him to retrieve her father's pocketknife and a string of pearls belonging to her mother. He said she used the knife to carve her initials and his first name on a tree in Baton Rouge. She draped the pearls around the neck of her teddy bear.

Hawthorne presented Heather's "split personality" journal entry to the court.

"Heather's not on trial," an angry James Wendorf told the judge when it was his turn to speak about the impact the crime had had on his family.

Keesee took the stand to try and blame drugs for Ferrell's behavior.

"Usually, he was pretty normal … sensitive," she testified.

Her attorney, Tommy Carle, stood by her side, occasionally advising her to plead the Fifth as to whether she had also taken drugs or was ever afraid of Ferrell.

The saddest testimony came from Rosetta.

He was not the "monster" the public perceived, she said. As a little boy, he was loving and sensitive, so sensitive that he once went fishing, buried a fish too small to eat, then dug it up to see if it was OK.

She also denied that anyone had ever abused him at a satanic cult gathering.

Bill Wendorf's heart was also broken.

"They were really good to those girls," he said of his brother and his wife, "good to everyone."

"He killed a part of all of us," said his wife, Gloria.

Tears came to Hawthorne's eyes, too.

Ferrell has changed, she said. He was no longer the remorseless killer seen in the videotape. "It's unfortunate that people in this courtroom cannot see his pain," she said.

"The death penalty is not about revenge," she told me outside the courtroom. "It's about punishment, and we believe the appropriate punishment is consecutive life sentences (*Sentinel* Feb.28, 1998)."

But it was Judge Jerry Lockett's decision to make, and he based it on the jury's recommendation.

"There is genuine evil in the world. There is a dark side and a light side competing in each of us," he said, staring down at Ferrell from the bench.

He agreed with the defense's claim that Ferrell was "disturbed," but said it was no excuse. He knew what he was doing was wrong.

"I hope, Mr. Ferrell, you search the light side and ask forgiveness."

He also blasted Gibson for not getting help, allowing him to smoke, drop out of school, and play fantasy games until he became engrossed in the occult.

"In some respects, Ms. Gibson should be on trial," he said.

Ferrell turned to vampirism to have structure in his life, the judge said. "Suddenly one day you wake up to find *this*."

Ferrell and his attorneys stood to receive the sentence: Death, not just one, but two sentences of death for the murders, and two life sentences for armed robbery and armed burglary.

Ferrell, trying to stay cool, betrayed himself for a split second by raising one eyebrow in surprise.

Then, the judge raised everyone's eyebrows in the courtroom. "It is the strong suggestion of this court for Mr. King to reconvene the grand jury."

Lockett didn't have the power to order a new grand jury, but he was holding court in the court of public opinion.

He noted that Heather did not testify and said her actions raised "significant questions."

King was angry. Outside the courtroom, he said there was no evidence to convict Heather of anything.

"I wouldn't want to go court based on what Mr. Ferrell says." Ferrell lied to everyone, even the psychologists trying to help him, he noted.

King, bowing to public pressure, convened another grand jury. Heather could not be reached for comment, but she had told me in an exclusive interview that she worried about just such a thing.

"Even if I live to be 99 years old, I'll be turning and looking over my shoulder. I hope and pray that it doesn't happen (*Sentinel,* Aug. 15, 1998)."

The sheriff claimed he had "new evidence," so prosecutors sent him a subpoena and asked him to share his findings.

Knupp blamed prosecutors for not giving his detectives a chance to lay out their theories. That was the reason Heather wasn't indicted, he figured. "A good prosecutor can indict a ham sandwich (*Sentinel,* Dec. 12, 1998)."

That comment angered Assistant State Attorney Bill Gross.

He later confronted the sheriff in the grand jury room, pulled out his sack lunch and said: "You said a prosecutor could indict a ham sandwich, well here it is."

King kept his cool.

"If being stupid was a crime there would be no problem. But when it comes to proving the elements of a crime, if you don't prove all of the specific things you don't get a conviction."

He said the public made "moral judgments" about Heather's interest in vampirism, her choice of friends, and her failure to warn her parents when Ferrell talked about killing them. "They're looking at it from a commonsense point of view," King said (*Sentinel,* Aug. 15, 1998).

"Of course, he [Knupp] didn't have any new evidence," Gross said.

The other defendants, seeing the writing on the wall, pleaded guilty. Anderson did so in exchange for a life sentence without the possibility of parole.

In an interview after the sentencing, reporters asked him if Heather wanted her parents to be killed.

"Not a clue," he said (*Sentinel* April 2, 1998).

Cooper's lawyer vowed to go to trial. Cooper gave an interview on *America's Most Wanted* TV show saying, "I didn't do anything. I'm still paying for a crime I didn't commit. I'm guilty by association."

She ended up entering a plea and was sentenced to 17-and-a-half years in prison.

Keesee, thin, frail, and looking even younger than her 17 years, wept when she pleaded guilty and was sentenced to 10 ½ years in prison. Among the pieces of evidence against her had she gone to trial, was a diary with notes written in big, loopy letters. The cover of the children's diary depicted a colorful little horse nibbling grass. The notes were about normal teenage things, but there was also plenty of talk about blood, sex, vampires, and death.

"I don't even know if I believe in vampires. Oh well, I guess I really wouldn't mind being one one day since I like the taste of blood anyway. Well, better go. C-ya. Shea."

Keesee and a fellow inmate were later caught drinking each other's blood in prison.

After sentencing, she told *Sentinel* reporter Kathryn Quigley: "I didn't really believe he would do it."

In Baton Rouge, she only had one thing on her mind: "I just don't want to be separated from Rod."

Now, they are separated forever.

Someone else who was learning about forever was Heather. In her interview with me, accompanied by author Aphrodite Jones, who wrote a book on the case called *Embrace,* Heather denied that she wanted her parents to be harmed. She even called for the release of Cooper and Keesee, saying they also did not know what was going to happen.

Asked if Ferrell had some kind of supernatural hold over her, she said he was the cult members' "maker." She described Keesee as "the dark mate (*Sentinel* Aug. 14, 1998)."

"We were one blood, like kin," she said.

Ferrell talked of being immortal for hundreds of years, of being a monster, killing police officers, dying and coming back to life, and rival clans killing children in his group.

"It was like a fairy tale. So much more interesting than getting up, going to school, going home and going to bed," she said.

She said she just wanted to go on a "road trip." Once she realized her parents were dead, she was "too terrified" to try to get away.

"I feel so guilty for even knowing Rod. I feel so bad I was so naive. Everyone tells you, 'It's not your fault. It's not your fault.' But he came to Florida. He left Kentucky to pick me up."

Four months later, King's office was conducting the second grand jury probe. This time, she would not testify.

The sheriff said he had had a letter from Heather saying she wanted to get rid of her parents, and a phone conversation overheard by another teen in which she allegedly asked Ferrell to "kill them." He also had a 4-inch stack of court records and transcripts, including statements by Ferrell saying she wanted her parents killed.

But the panel rejected all of it, saying it was not credible. Grand jurors did put King on the stand to find out how the first grand jury reached its conclusion.

"We share the opinion of the first grand jury," the foreman wrote, "that the actions of Heather Wendorf were inappropriate and wrong. We also share its conclusion that while wrong, her actions did not rise to the level of criminal activity."

No one would ever say that Ferrell's actions were not criminal, but he did get a break from the Florida Supreme Court. He was too young for the death penalty, the court ruled, and he was sentenced to life without parole.

People still talk about the case more than two decades after the murders. Many still have questions about Heather, who moved to North Carolina to attend an art school.

Deputies searching for evidence found a poem she wrote entitled "The Problem."

"Do I try to be different? Do I try to be the same?
What does my life come to? Am I to blame?
These are the questions that go through my mind.
The answers to them, someday I may find.
I walk the street. This is how it goes.
No one comes with me. I cry as the wind blows.
I hold myself, to keep myself warm.
The full moon is soon covered by a storm.
As the rain falls, it hides away my tears.
But the cold, wet drops open up my fears.

I drop to my knees filled up with pain.
And I hope it will be washed by the oncoming rain.
So I cry and plea, in a pool I lay.
To the unseen God, I beg and pray.
Then I stop and get up to go.
I'll have to explain something I don't even know.
My parents ask questions throughout the night.
They think to themselves, 'Is she all right?'
We all know the answer but they don't give aid.
'It's her problem,' they say. 'The problem she made.'"

Was Heather sincere in her interview about blaming herself, at least partially? Was she telling the truth when she made statements under oath that she did not want her parents to be harmed? Only Heather and Ferrell know what was said in the hours leading up to the slayings, and because of Ferrell's history of lying, he has no credibility.

Heather was found to be not guilty of committing a crime, but she may carry with her for the rest of her days the knowledge that in part, the tragedy was "the problem she made."

Ferrell, dysfunctional family and mental health issues aside, was responsible for the problems he made. However, in 2019, he got a second chance with a resentencing hearing.

"I know nothing I say or do can bring them back," he told his victims' skeptical family members. "I hope you know just how truly sorry I am," he said, choking back tears. (*Daily Commercial,* Nov. 20, 2019).

But Jennifer begged the judge presiding over the trial to keep him locked up.

"May I have a place that's not traumatized by looking over my shoulder? If he ever gets out, I'll be destroyed. I'll be back that lonely little girl nearly 23 years ago." (*Daily Commercial*, Nov.18, 2019).

By April of 2020, the judge had made up his mind. Ferrell is "irreparably corrupt," he said.

Chapter 2

Beauty and the boy

Blonde, blue-eyed, beautiful, and bewildered-looking with her unblinking, Barbie-like stare, 24-year-old middle-school teacher Debra Lafave was exposed in the white-hot glare of news camera lights. She was charged with having sex with one of her 14-year-old students. She allegedly had a tryst with him in her Tampa townhouse and in a classroom in 2004. She even romped with him in the back seat of her SUV while his 15-year-old cousin drove along some busy roads in Ocala.

Wild, crazy, and sounding like a pornographic novel, the story caught fire on the Internet and attracted the attention of people across the globe.

The question everyone was asking was: Why would this beautiful, married woman do something this stupid?

The question not posed in news stories but widely discussed by cynical men (including many in newsrooms) was whether the boy was a victim of sex abuse or a "winner" in a pubescent male fantasy come true?

It wasn't a question up for debate among serious Christians, therapists, or the boy's mother, however. In fact, nobody knows how the boy felt about it, since he was a minor. We never published his name, let alone interviewed him.

Adding to the clamor was the fact that she had done some professional modeling in some sexy poses, including sitting astride a motorcycle while wearing a bikini. There are no marketing figures on whether her figure boosted motorcycle sales, nor were there any guesses about how many 10-car pileups she would have caused had she actually been riding on a bike wearing that provocative outfit.

Her husband, Owen, divorced her, saying he was "crushed" and "shocked." He wrote a non-fiction book, *Gorgeous Disaster,* which added to the drama (*Star-Banner*, Oct. 15, 2006).

The case against her was divided into two parts: charges filed by the Tampa-area State Attorney's Office, and the charges filed by Ocala prosecutors.

Her attorney, John Fitzgibbons, negotiated a no-jail plea in the Tampa case, but then ignited a firestorm when he told reporters: "To place Debbie into a Florida state women's penitentiary, to place an attractive young woman in that kind of hell hole, is like putting a piece of raw meat in with the lions (*Star-Banner*, Dec. 25, 2006)."

In other words: My client is too pretty to go to jail.

She didn't do herself any favors, either. When interviewed by Matt Lauer on NBC's *Dateline,* she blamed the boy for being the aggressor and cited mental problems stemming from bipolar disorder.

She said he consented "but I should have been the one to say, 'Look. You are a kid. And this is not a good idea, whether you want it or not.'"

She also said she was not a sexual offender, though she had been classified as such by the law. The way she saw it was, "I made a really, really, really bad choice."

The boy's mother was not happy with the TV interview and said so in an e-mail to *Star-Banner* reporter Mabel Perez.

"While she could have taken this opportunity to show even the slightest bit of remorse, instead, she chose to ... lie and accuse my son of being aggressive (*Star-Banner*, Dec. 25, 2006)."

She also said her son was doing well, was playing on his high school's basketball team, and was surrounded by good, supportive friends.

But if the stories proved to be entertaining, if not titillating, the judge handling the Ocala case was not amused. Circuit Judge Hale Stancil refused to go along with a no-jail plea.

Behind the scenes, reporters frequently joked that Lafave always seemed to have the look of "the porch light is on but nobody's home." But the day she learned of the judge's decision, she blinked and turned to her attorney with a look of confusion and panic. Could a beautiful woman really be thrown into a den of lionesses?

Fortunately for her, she had an unlikely ally in her effort to stay out of jail—the boy's mother. She didn't want the case to go to trial, not because Lafave didn't deserve punishment, but what it might do to her son's self-esteem and reputation.

"I strongly feel it would further victimize my son if he was forced to testify in court," she said in the *Star-Banner* e-mail. "The added intense media coverage from around the world, along with Court TV airing the trial live [the network told prosecutors they would cover the trial], would further expose him so much more than he already has been."

She said United Kingdom news outlets had already published his high school yearbook picture (the *Star-Banner* was not about to publish his name or his mother's name, which would identify him). "If this were to go to trial, his current picture and name would be posted around the world, and then it would follow him forever. He deserves to have a chance to live a normal life, graduate high school, and then move on to college without everyone knowing him as the 14-year-old boy in the Lafave case. That is why I agreed to the plea deal, to avoid the 'media circus' this trial would bring, for the sake of my son."

She said she also feared what she said would be a "humiliating" cross-examination of her son by Lafave's defense attorney.

When Judge Stancil refused to allow a plea deal, Ocala prosecutors were forced to drop the charges.

She could have faced up to 30 years in prison if convicted by a jury. Because the boy's mom didn't want the case to go to trial, she was allowed to plead guilty to two counts of lewd and lascivious battery in the Tampa case, serve three years of community control (a more highly supervised form of probation) and seven years of sexual offender probation. She was also ordered not to have any unsupervised visitation with children.

It wasn't the end of the story, however. No longer allowed to teach school, she went to work at a restaurant where she ran into trouble with her probation officer for talking about her case to a teenage girl coworker. She got out of that scrape, however.

In 2012, as the mother of twins and engaged to be married, Lafave asked to be released early from probation. The judge, who was about to retire, agreed to it but prosecutors objected.

The 2nd District Court of Appeal overturned the judge's ruling, saying it was "an abuse of judicial power resulting in a gross miscarriage of justice (tampabay.com, Feb. 25, 2013)."

Was the boy's mom correct in not wanting her son exposed to unwanted publicity? Absolutely! Under the law a minor is incapable of giving consent. Even if he was "aggressive," Lafave was right when she said that she was the adult and she should have said no. Besides, that was her story. Because the boy never ended up testifying, we can't know for sure, but she had plenty of aggression to go around.

Then, there is the too-pretty-to-go-to-jail defense. Are beautiful people exempt from the law? People getting a plea deal are usually required to take some responsibility and acknowledge wrongdoing. Yet not only did she blame the kid but she seemed to be in denial about being a sexual offender.

As for her mental illness defense, prisons are packed with people with mental problems.

What about the media's role? It would be hard to argue that the story wasn't newsworthy. Obviously, a lot of people were interested. Was it because of its salacious nature? No doubt it played a huge role. The newspaper's web page, Ocala.com, had a huge number of hits on the story. But there was also the injustice, the idea of a predatory teacher and human failings that made it the top story of 2006 for the *Star-Banner*. Would the website light up like a pinball machine today if you again posted her name and photos? Two words, one concept: *Cha Ching!*

***

If Olympic athletes' feats are spectacular (and they are), they are nothing compared to a sex offender's mental gymnastics, with denial, justification, and self-pity.

Take the case of a Leesburg High School social studies teacher and girls' softball coach, who was batting a thousand in stupidity when he had sex with a 15-year-old student.

First, he got caught taking her to a motel in August 1997. The girl told her mother she was spending the weekend with a friend in St. Augustine. However, mom was suspicious and when she began digging through her daughter's room she found love letters from Peter Paul Yates, 27, and plans for their getaway.

He was arrested and charged with two counts of sexual intercourse with an unmarried person younger than 18, a law that took the place of the state's old statutory rape law. The charges were for two incidents at his house. He also took her to a no-tell motel on the west coast of Florida, where he was charged with interfering with custody and contributing to the delinquency of a minor.

Yates resigned his teaching job. The school superintendent said he would have been fired anyway, and he asked the state to revoke Yates' teaching certificate.

Yates posted a $3,500 bond and was told to stay away from the girl.

When the girl started whispering into the phone one night, mom decided to place a hidden microphone in the phone and taped the conversation.

"It talked about them being together Saturday evening (9-20) and Monday afternoon (9-22) and plans to see each other this Saturday," she said of the tape in a sworn statement to police on Sept. 24.

"It talked about tapes that Yates had given [to her] to listen to, expressing his feelings and love for her," she said.

Yates also asked the girl to write a note to her mother asking her to "calm down" the prosecutor "and not get him any jail time," she noted in the affidavit. "He also told her of an incident he heard about where a 15-year-old got her dad to sign for her to marry or she would tell everyone he had sex with her."

The letters were signed "Petey Pooh" and "AP Pooh."

The girl later admitted that she had taken a taxi to Yates' house where they "laid together on a blanket in the woods."

Yates was arrested, his $3,500 bail was revoked, and a new amount set at $150,000. Authorities said they were afraid he was trying to leave the state. He had slipped her directions and a map to a place in Georgia.

Now, prosecutors were talking about boosting the charges to sexual battery by a person in a custodial position, a charge that could result in a prison sentence of more than 20 years.

Prosecutor J.J. Dahl offered 16 years if he pleaded guilty.

Yates was smart enough to know he was in trouble but thought he could talk his way out of it in a letter to Circuit Judge Jerry Lockett, a "hanging judge," he acknowledged, who had a nickname of "Lock 'em up Lockett."

He said he deserved a second chance because he was a nonviolent first-time offender and that he feared for his life if sent to prison as man who had sex with a minor.

His case had "political overtones," he said.

"Teachers, policemen, religious figureheads and several other occupations are put on pedestals by society at large. When we screw up (and mind you, we're not supposed to somehow, we are above that), we seldom get second chances. However, a politician, movie star, sports person, or rock star can wham-bam the babysitter all they want. Society isn't shocked by it; in fact, they expect it.

"My case had little to do with sex. Two people hit it off and fell in love. Many high school girls hit on me, and I never crossed any lines. This relationship happened innocently, slowly, and subtly. I never saw it coming until I was knee-deep in the hoopla. Subsequently, I made a few poor choices and bad judgments.

"I can tell you that regardless of how the state attorney or a vindictive parent tries to distort things, [she] is intellectually mature, cognitively sound, and emotionally stable."

He complained about a police officer who told her "horror stories" about a niece who was "ruined" by an older man who got her pregnant and then left.

She won't be "scarred for life," Yates insisted, referring to the student.

"Most of the damage comes from the sex-starved, sensationalistic media and the police," he said.

Maintaining again that the case was about "politics" and also about "revenge," he asked: "What good does it do anyone for me to go to prison? Will I get … rehabilitation? Not hardly. I'll probably get raped, beaten up, or killed.

Then, I will have an impossible task of trying to reassimilate myself back into society someday."

He told the judge that despite his harsh reputation, "You are a human being that is as capable of good or bad as the next person..."

"Only God is perfect," Yates said, and maintained that he deserved a second chance just as much as the next guy.

"I will leave you with one final thought: Maybe one day you will be standing in front of the bench instead of sitting behind it. (Yeah, I know it could never happen. That's what I thought, too). However, anyone can make a wrong turn or have life deal us a bad blow. The bottom line is this: Would you want a second chance? I think so."

He wisely did not sign it "Petey Pooh," nor did he mention his note to her about the girl who threatened her father with extortion.

He also did not mention the fact that he got caught trying to send a note to 17-year-old vampire cult member Charity Lynn Keesee in the jail. Keesee's boyfriend, cult leader Rod Ferrell, was already cooling his heels in prison. She was awaiting trial or a plea deal.

Yates had at least one supporter out in the world, though he never knew it because the letter to the editor was not published. The letter writer, who said he married a 16-year-old when he was 21, blasted the authorities for taking action against Yates "due to the *warped* [his emphasis] perspective of our overly-concerned society & our overly-protective courts."

He would have made a good juror for the defense had the case gone to trial, but Yates thought better of trying to go that route. He entered a plea of no contest to the lesser charge of sexual battery on a person younger than 18 with no physical harm.

Lockett sentenced him to five years in prison, counseling, then probation with all kinds of restrictions, including no contact with anyone younger than 18.

Does it matter if you express remorse? It would seem so in the case of a Umatilla High School math teacher, especially if the school superintendent speaks up for you.

Like the Yates' case, the girl's mother found love notes from Norris Bonds, 27, addressed to her daughter. Bonds, who had been a teacher for several years, admitted having sex with the 15-year-old girl several times, saying he "made a mistake and did not know how to fix it."

Jerry Cox, the assistant superintendent of schools, had known Bonds' family for years.

"Obviously, he made a very serious error here. One of the things he wanted to do is apologize to the School Board and to the girl's parents (*Sentinel,* June 17, 1999)."

According to court records, he carried on the affair with the girl for five months until his fiancée became "suspicious."

Unlike Yates, who came back for more trouble after he was told to stay away, Norris was contrite. He entered a guilty plea. He was sentenced to five years in prison, but that sentence was suspended, pending completion of probation, including counseling.

***

Lafave's and Yates' behavior was inexcusable. They betrayed their students and their profession. But as bad as those cases were, it's even worse when the students are younger, and it's an outrage when the school fails to act quickly to stop the abuse.

John R. Townsend, 48, was one of those teachers in 1996 that "was either loved or loathed by students and staff," Umatilla Elementary School's guidance counselor told authorities (*Sentinel,* Oct. 12, 1997).

There were enough complaints about the 21-year teacher, however, for Florida Department of Law Enforcement investigators to start looking into the complaints of girls who said he was "mean," snapped their bra straps, talked about "horny" little boys and girls, and touched them—in one case by reportedly slapping a girl on the buttocks. Two parents complained that he left bruises on their children when he grabbed their arms to discipline them.

Investigators looking into the girls' complaints discovered that Townsend had been convicted of molesting a 9-year-old boy at a camp in North Carolina in 1989. He agreed to a negotiated plea that included counseling and probation.

Lake County authorities didn't know about the arrest. Umatilla's police chief would end up admitting that he hit the wrong key on a computer while attempting to do a background check.

Townsend dug himself a deeper hole by lying on his teaching recertification paperwork in 1994 when he said he had never been arrested. That act resulted in misdemeanor perjury charges being filed against him.

When news of the North Carolina case and the girls' complaints became known, the parents of a young boy notified authorities that their son had been molested, too.

The boy said that when he was in the fourth grade Townsend had grabbed his genitals while "tickling" him during an after-school tutoring session. Later, as he prepared to drive him home, Townsend said, "Oh, I'll cut that little penis off ...." The boy said he was "scared," according to court documents.

Townsend also took him on a youth camping trip. After that campout ended, Townsend allegedly took him swimming and insisted that he change out of his swimming suit in front of him in his car. "Don't worry, I won't look," Townsend said. The boy wanted to change in the dressing room, just as he did before he went swimming.

The boy said Townsend also asked him if he wanted to drive the car. When he said yes, Townsend said, "Hop on my lap," according to court records. The boy said Townsend grabbed his hands and placed them on the steering wheel, then placed his own hands on the boy's shoulders.

Townsend denied any wrongdoing in the complaints.

At first the boy's parents didn't believe their son. According to court records: "when [he] was in the fourth grade, he disclosed to them that Mr. Townsend had touched him on his penis, but because they knew Mr. Townsend's reputation as a good teacher, they chose to discount the information thinking that [he] may have misinterpreted a friendly gesture. After seeing the recent newspaper article concerning Mr. Townsend's out-of-state arrest, they knew they were mistaken and should have believed their son …." He ended up in Townsend's classroom again as a fifth grader.

Court records indicate that not only did the parents not believe him, but when the boy threatened to tell someone at school about the alleged abuse, they told him not to tell anyone. "…his parents told him that if he did, or if Mr. Townsend lost his job, [he] would be grounded."

The boy told a guidance counselor anyway. He was called out of physical education class one day and told to go to the office. Once he arrived, he discovered to his horror that Townsend and the principal were sitting in the office. They asked him about his allegations. Neither the guidance counselor nor the parents were present.

As he was about to leave, the principal asked him "not to spread this around the school." He said Townsend treated him as if nothing had ever happened.

Lake County school officials said they were shocked by the allegations and had no idea there was any problem. The principal had given Townsend excellent annual reviews. However, the girls' parents sued school officials, including the principal, saying they should have known and that they failed to protect their children.

In October 1997 prosecutors took the boy's case to trial, with Townsend charged with lewd and lascivious acts on a child.

Circuit Judge Mark Hill, in a tough ruling against the defense, said the young man who was the victim in North Carolina would be allowed to testify.

That man, who was by this time 19, had just finished a hitch in the U.S. Marine Corps. He testified in a pretrial deposition that Townsend fondled him all night. He said he was frozen with fear and so traumatized he was unable to speak.

"Why?" asked Assistant State Attorney Hugh Bass.

"Embarrassment and fear," he said (*Sentinel,* Oct. 12, 1997).

He testified that Townsend tried to get him to touch him, but he moved his hand away.

He said it was weeks before he could tell his parents.

When a jury was picked and the trial got under way, it was the defense's turn to win some battles. Because of evidentiary rules, jurors were kept in the dark about Townsend's conviction in North Carolina. Nor were they allowed to learn of the girls' complaints, which led to the discovery of the boy's allegations.

There was also a lack of physical evidence, something that Bass talked about in his closing remarks to jurors.

"Touching doesn't leave fingerprints," he said (*Sentinel,* Oct. 16, 1997).

The man from North Carolina testified that he awoke to find that Townsend was fondling him.

Townsend, who took the stand in his defense, said the weather had turned damp and chilly and he was merely touching the boy's abdomen to make sure he was not suffering from hypothermia.

A fellow camp counselor testified that Townsend was following proper procedures.

"Is touching someone's penis the way to check for hypothermia?" Bass asked on cross-examination.

"No," he conceded.

Defense attorney Michael Graves, knowing he was dealing with an abhorrent allegation and a young, alleged victim, was treading lightly in his remarks.

"I'm not suggesting they were lying. They have been given an interpretation and they have run with it."

The six-member jury was obviously disturbed when they learned that the lewd and lascivious charge was not filed until three years after the boy's initial complaint. Shortly after beginning their deliberations, they came back with two questions for Judge Hill: What kind of work is Townsend doing now, and why did the FDLE wait until 1996 to contact the boy?

Hill, following strict court guidelines, said he could not answer their questions. The jury, he said, would have to decide on the evidence presented in the trial.

After deliberating for an hour and 15 minutes they came back with a not-guilty verdict.

The boy sobbed loudly. The ex-Marine, who was stone-faced, did not utter a sound.

In May 1999, Lake County schools settled the lawsuit filed by the parents of the girls and the boy for a total of $241,250. The school district was not admitting any fault, its lawyer said, which is standard in such cases.

The boy's family got $50,000. The other families received $111,250, $45,000 and $35,000. The suit claimed the boy suffered bodily injury, pain and suffering, disability, mental anguish, loss of capacity for enjoyment of life and emotional pain and suffering. It also claimed the alleged incidents damaged his relationship with his parents and that he was deprived of his right to an education and civil rights, including "his right to be a child of innocence (*Sentinel*, May 13, 1999)."

Regrettably, there was not a comment from the families in the settlement story, but the boy's mother was furious when the not-guilty verdict came back in the criminal trial.

"We have so many pedophiles today because nobody believes the victims," she said.

Chapter 3

Lambs

The Post-it note attached to the arrest affidavit said, "Frank, here is one to make you puke," and it was initialed with the letters K.Q. My colleague, Kathryn Quigley, wasn't trying to be funny. She knew I would be outraged and sickened, just as she was. All child and animal abuse cases make me sick. The victims are not only helpless but depend upon adults to love and take care of them.

The case she was referring to, on May 21, 1999, was a 41-year-old truck driver who was charged with 400 counts of sexual battery of a child under 12 and 300 counts of sex with a child younger than 18.

The man lived in the house with the child and the girl's guardian. The abuse allegedly started when she was 8 and morphed into full intercourse when she turned 14. It only stopped when she moved to Pennsylvania and told a guidance counselor about the abuse.

It included accounts of the man videotaping her and the two of them engaging in sex acts. But the real punch to the gut came a year later when the state agreed to drop the 700 sexual battery charges in return for a no-contest plea to "use of a child in a sexual performance."

The judge withheld adjudication of guilt, which meant that he could truthfully say on a job application form that he had never been convicted of a felony. He was placed on four years of sex-offender probation, which was followed by four years unsupervised probation.

The problem, the prosecutor said, was that the only tape that could be found was a 90-second segment in which she exposed herself. There were no images of anyone touching her or engaging in sex acts with her. Plus, to take a sexual battery case to trial, prosecutors must have dates, locations, and other information. To make matters worse, she was being directed by nonverbal signals, so his voice was not on the tape.

It was an especially egregious miscarriage of justice in a system filled with half (if even half) measures for such offenses. Anyone convicted of sexual battery on a child less than 12 years old must serve a mandatory life sentence (real life, with no chance of parole).

Often, the young victims are afraid to tell anyone about what happened to them.

In another case, it took two years for a girl younger than 16 to tell the woman who was her guardian because she was afraid that she "wouldn't want her anymore."

When her guardian confronted her boyfriend, he threatened to "kill them all," according to court records.

Often it is the boyfriend who either molests or harms a child left in his care when the child's mother is at work.

***

One of the most heart-breaking cases involved a dad molesting and then raping his two daughters, starting with the oldest girl when she was only 4.

Howard R. Johnson, 53, had already made headlines in *National Enquirer* in 1985 when he traded his pickup truck and 20 acres of farmland to the father of a 13-year-old girl so he could marry her.

"Joann's my child bride and I love her," he said of his new wife in Parrotsville, Tenn., in an interview with the tabloid. "I call her my own Dolly Parton because she's the sweetest and most loving little thing on earth."

The girl said she was up for it.

"I know I'm very young to be married, but I've put away my dolls and I'm determined to be a good wife (*National Enquirer*, Jan. 22, 1985)."

Three months after they celebrated their honeymoon breakfast by eating cupcakes and drinking Dr. Pepper, they were divorced.

"We had little in common," Johnson told the tabloid. "It was driving me crazy trying to find something for us to talk about (April 2, 1985)."

In fact, the articles pointed out that he may have married her in the first place because the girl's father was thinking about pressing statutory rape charges against him.

The court files in the Florida rape case included a copy of his marriage license to the child and copies of the tabloid articles.

Normally, such cases are filled with expert witnesses, some physical evidence in the form of DNA extracted from clothing or bed linens, and maybe some corroborating witness testimony. But this time it was marked only by painful, pitiful testimony by the sisters, who by this time were adults, in their 20s and 30s respectively. They marked with X's places on the floor plans of buildings and homes where they said they had been raped.

"Why are you doing this?" the oldest sister asked.

"I'm getting you ready," he replied.

What was he getting her ready for? He would later tell the younger girl, at age 9, that he was getting her ready for marriage so that she would be a good wife. They were forced to undergo sexual intercourse, oral sex, and sodomy and he would not stop until they claimed to have enjoyed it.

The girls felt such shame they didn't tell each other about the abuse for years. Going into the trial, the older woman said she had lost "trust, dignity, self-esteem, relationships, and security."

I don't know what has happened to the women since I interviewed them for the *Sentinel*. The younger woman was happily married with children.

The women testified that their mother urged them to record the abuse in diaries as she prepared to divorce him in 1982. The mom testified that she didn't tell the girls what to put in the diaries. She said she later burned at least one of the diaries.

"What was in the diary?" asked Assistant State Attorney Larry Houston.

"I don't remember," she said (*Sentinel*, May 29, 1997).

The testimony angered the woman's coworkers. The woman worked for the clerk of court's office (not in the felony division) and more than one clerk told me they felt like pushing her down the stairs.

The final straw for the sisters came in 1987 when Johnson came back to Florida and married their mother again. They finally came forward in 1995.

Three days after the trial began, the jury took less than an hour to find Johnson guilty of 12 counts or raping the girls in the 1970s and 1980s.

The six-member jury hugged the two women on their way out the door.

"I'm very relieved," the younger woman said when it was over. "I was afraid of what would happen if they didn't believe us."

"I'm ecstatic, relieved," the older sister said (*Sentinel*, Mary 30, 1997)."

Circuit Judge Mark Hill, who glared at Johnson as the verdict was being read, imposed 12 consecutive life sentences on Johnson.

***

It's almost impossible for normal, decent people to understand just how sick and disgusting the defendants are in these cases. Take the case of the 45-year-old man who was sentenced to 10 years in prison (at least he got a prison sentence) for two counts of sexual battery of a child between the ages of 12 and 18 and possession of a pornographic performance by a child.

It was revolting, but even worse was the fact that it was the girl's mother who was doing the videotaping. To top it off, she sobbed and begged the judge not to send him to prison.

"It will never, never happen again," she said. She described the three of them as "good people."

She was sentenced to two years of house arrest for her role, followed by five years of probation. The greatest punishment was that she was forbidden to see her daughter, who was 17. The girl was placed in foster care.

The judge complained that he could not send the man to prison for a longer term. Before sentencing guidelines were imposed by the Legislature, a 30-year sentence would have been possible.

One rapist did get a long prison sentence—35 years— when his victim became pregnant. He still faced 13 more charges for sexual abuse against the same girl, starting when she was 7.

He apologized. "I was the adult. I'm sorry."

But he didn't take any responsibility in a secretly taped phone conversation with the girl that the prosecutor played for the jury. "You took advantage of the situation on several occasions when you were old enough to know better," the man told the girl.

Occasionally the bad guy does pay the price, but the victims keep on suffering.

"This was a great tragedy," a 15-year-old girl said in a letter read to the court in another case. "He hurt me not only physically but also mentally."

Her suffering included fear, nightmares, flashbacks, and a desire for vengeance. She said her attacker should be sentenced to life in prison, "or be raped ... so that he may feel the pain, heartache, fear, and shame that I felt."

Her 7-year-old sister was also traumatized by what she witnessed. She held her older sister's hand while she was being threatened with death.

Trodd Buggs, 33, closed his eyes, bit his lip, and tilted his head back when he learned his fate: life without parole. He was sentenced as a habitual offender. His lawyer bitterly accused the court of favoritism for the girl's family because her dad worked for the Public Defender's Office. Prosecutors denounced the accusation.

The dad, whose job was to help defend people, suddenly found himself in new, dark territory. "It has been very hard for me to sit back and let justice be done," he said in a letter to the judge.

***

Every day, it seems, a new arrest and criminal complaint reaches the clerk's office about someone touching, fondling, committing lewd acts, or having intercourse with children—both male and female victims.

Prosecutors say the cases are difficult to deal with. For one thing, it puts young victims face-to-face with the abuser in court, which is both traumatic and problematic.

Jurors do not want to believe that a parent or guardian could do something so harmful to a child. Nor do jurors want to think about the possibility of a parent harming or killing their child. The Casey Anthony case in Orange County is just one example. After listening to days of testimony and reviewing a mountain of evidence the jury declared that there was no proof the young mother killed toddler Caylee. Nor was there any evidence of child abuse or neglect, even after admittedly lying about leaving her with a babysitter and failing to report her missing for days, they decided.

The case was worrisome for jurors because the state was seeking the death penalty. They were also obviously enthralled with defense attorney Jose Baez's charge that Casey's dad, George, had sexually abused her as a child. He denied it.

Meanwhile, the everyday garden-variety sex abuse case becomes a kind of seller's market for a plea bargain. It's not unusual to find cases of molestation plea-bargained down to a misdemeanor battery. That's the kind of charge that a man might be charged with, for example, if he just simply touched another person during an argument. And jail time? Forget it. The offender in such a case might get probation— if anything. If the victim is lucky, the offender will be told to have no more contact. The prevailing theory seems to be that it is better than nothing, that the offender gets a warning to stay away. Plus, prosecutors can chalk up another number in the conviction column.

Even when juries concede that a parent or guardian did harm a child, they often can't seem to find it in their hearts to find guilt in the highest degree felonies, including murder one, which could result in the death penalty.

Judges can fall into this category, too.

Maybe it's because if you're a parent you recognize the possibility that you might "lose it," one day and harm a child.

That is apparently what happened, for example, when a 29-year-old dad drowned his son in a lake while trying to teach him how to swim.

"No, please, I don't want to do this," the 6-year-old boy pleaded as his dad repeatedly dunked him below the surface over an hour's time.

The dad's defense? He said he was drunk.

The State Attorney's Office originally charged him with manslaughter. Later, prosecutors dropped that charge and upped it to first-degree murder. In the end, he was sentenced to about 12 ½ years in prison.

In another case, a 45-year-old man was arrested after his girlfriend told police he dragged her son through a small swimming pool with his head under water because he had wet his pants. The child was not even quite 2 years old.

Bathroom accidents are frequently a trigger for child abuse. It was soiled underwear that set Richard Adams off on his homicidal rampage against his 6-year-old daughter, Kayla Mackean, in a case that made national headlines.

Sometimes a kid gets lucky and doesn't get hurt. Police in Mount Dora ended up arresting and charging a 32-year-old woman with trying to run over her 14-year-old son with her car one evening.

Police found her sitting behind the wheel of the car in her driveway. She said her son was trying to keep her from leaving.

Neighbors said the boy was on the hood of the car and holding on for dear life as she moved the car, then hit the brakes. At one point he was in front of the car when she drove forward. He shouted, "No! No! No!"

The neighbors videotaped the incident and turned it over to police. Once they entered the home, police found a filthy house with dirty clothing "all over the house," moldy food, and insects.

Court records indicate the 32-year-old bookkeeper had a troubled life, with child abuse and neglect charges, animal abuse, paternity and domestic violence injunctions and other signs of a tumultuous life, which usually indicates drug or alcohol abuse or mental illness. At one point, she was placed on probation and was released from it ahead of time. Hopefully, she eventually got her act together.

Neglect is another issue.

A 5-year-old boy was critically injured in Eustis when he suffered second and third-degree burns in a fire that erupted at his grandfather's house. The grandmother left him alone but took a 3-year-old child with her to the convenience store so she could buy cigarettes and a loaf of bread.

"I used poor judgment sure," she told the *Sentinel* (April 10, 1995), "but I don't think I should be condemned for it."

At least she didn't blame it on the victim. Still other cases involve shaken-baby syndrome, where a mother (or often a boyfriend), shakes the crying baby until it suffers brain damage or dies.

These are the kinds of cases that make misguided punishment or sheer stupidity look relatively harmless. One idiot, for example, put 1 or 2 ounces of beer into a baby bottle for his 2-year-old boy at a street festival. He told police the boy needed something for his "fever," but paramedics said the child was not sick—at least not until he had the beer. Another man was charged with two counts of child abuse when he smeared heat rub and Tabasco sauce on the genitals of two children, ages 9 and 11, when he caught them "playing doctor."

Sometimes the state, in trying to remedy an issue, ends up making things worse. It is not clear why, but the state Department of Children and Families removed one toddler from his parents, put him in a foster home and terminated parental rights. Then, the 23-month-old wandered through an unlocked gate at the foster home, climbed into an above-ground pool and drowned.

DCF waited a week to tell his parents. On top of that, officials said the parents were not allowed to attend the funeral. DCF wasn't obligated to tell the parents, since parental rights have been terminated, an administrator said.

"They said we weren't fit to take care of Austin, but if he was with us, he would still be alive," the boy's father told the *Orlando Sentinel* (May 9, 2002).

Sometimes it seems that even when the state tries to do the right thing it ends up moving too slowly to save a child.

When a father killed himself and his 10-month-old son by running a hose from his car tailpipe to the interior, the child's mother sued DCF, claiming the agency should have known the child was in danger.

The woman, who had obtained a temporary injunction for protection against her estranged husband, Billy Lynn Casey, 33, said he sometimes snatched the child out of her hands and threw things when he was drunk. There were times that he struck Nickolas when he was trying to hit her, Crystal Casey said in a sworn statement.

"He gets aggravated when my son cries, and starts yelling at him," she wrote in her court petition (*Sentinel, July* 23, 1999).

He yelled at her, saying, "I'll kill you if you take me to court."

Lake County Sheriff's spokesman Lt. Nick Pallitto summed it up when he said, "I think he felt he was losing control of his life."

Crystal was granted custody of the child, but he would go to the babysitter's house and pick up the child after she dropped him off on her way to work. She said she tried to work out some custody arrangement. She had refused to sign divorce papers. He set fire to the child's car seat so she could not take him away. In one fit of rage, he destroyed everything in Nickolas' room, including his crib, clothing, and stroller.

They were married in February 1988 and were in a whirlwind of turmoil and violence almost immediately, according to court records. Casey had a record of things like possession of marijuana, drunk driving, and resisting arrest.

One call in October was weird, even for them.

Casey told deputies Crystal struck him in the eye "for no apparent reason." She said she was in bed and writing down all the names he was calling her when he snatched the pen out of her hand and "poked *himself* in the eye."

Concerns about violence between the adults led to three reports being filed with the Florida Abuse Registry in the month leading up to the deaths. Because neither parent had a telephone, the abuse investigator had to leave messages with the child's grandmother. Casey was scheduled to meet with a child abuse investigator with DCF in the days before the deaths.

When the child was reported missing, DCF said caseworkers repeatedly tried to find him. He hadn't gone far. He was spotted by a taxi driver sitting in front of his house in a junked out 1973 Lincoln. Not only had he run a hose into the car so he and Nickolas would die of carbon monoxide poisoning, but he had also placed a garden hose in the radiator so the engine wouldn't overheat and quit running.

The child protective investigator was placed on desk duty. "It will be important to know whether the risk to this child was adequately assessed by the staff—and whether there was any action that could have been taken to protect him from harm's way," said Katherine Kearney, secretary of DCF.

It wasn't the only time caseworkers found themselves in the white-hot glare of news cameras. In 1994, the death of a 2-year-old boy was blamed on infections stemming from neglect and filthy living conditions. When he was taken to a hospital, doctors found lice crawling all over his scalp and his feet were covered in feces.

"In 30 years of law enforcement it's one of the most appalling things I've ever seen," said Sumter County Chief Deputy Bill Farmer.

Richard Day had been removed from his family's home two years earlier. The child protective case made its way through the system, with the parents ordered to take a parenting class and clean up their house. A judge then cleared the case. The boy went back to live with his parents. With no new complaints over the past year, caseworkers stopped making visits to the home. Case closed.

A grand jury was called to investigate the way the then-Health and Rehabilitative Services department had handled the case, and that of an 8-month-old child, who died in an unrelated case.

"HRS had provided supervision to the home in the form of day care for the children, parenting classes and mental health evaluations for the parents and an in-home training program for the family, the grand jury noted in its report.

"In fact, it appears that no substantial changes had occurred in the routine of the Day household as evidenced by an HRS contact with the Day home in March of 1994 where the same deplorable conditions were found to exist but were ignored by HRS."

A review by HRS itself found that counseling and parenting classes were inadequate and psychological evaluations ordered by the court were never carried out.

After HRS was notified of Richard's death, the surviving children were still not removed from the home for 24 hours, the grand jury reported.

The parents were arrested and charged with manslaughter.

The grand jury's report on the death of 8-month-old Brian Eslinger was also critical of the agency.

HRS responding to a complaint found "obvious bruising to the child's head, arms, and back," the grand jury noted. "Family members denied observing injuries. HRS did not remove the child from the home, but rather, recommended the parents make an appointment to have the child examined by a physician. Another abuse complaint to HRS went unheeded apparently due to faulty in-house communications. In less than three months of the initial complaint and within six days of the follow-up complaint that was unheeded by HRS, the Eslinger child was dead."

The grand jury made several recommendations about beefing up documentation, accountability, getting rid of "boilerplate" counseling programs in favor of addressing specific needs, and including law enforcement in the investigations. They also urged the inspector general of HRS to investigate both the Day and Eslinger cases.

HRS Director Jim Towey defended his agency, saying caseworkers didn't do "a perfect job," but denied there was any "gross negligence (*Sentinel*, Aug. 24, 1994)."

Sumter County Sheriff Jamie Adams also made recommendations, including follow-up visits to homes in cases cleared by HRS and a judge–like Day's case.

"If they [social workers] don't have the authority to go back a year later and check on these people, who they know have had past problems, then the law needs to be changed," he said.

On Aug. 26, Brian's parents, Brian Eslinger, 22, and Tarea Boom, 19 were indicted on charges of third-degree murder and child abuse.

***

Sheriff Adams' department was faced with another tragic case that year (the fifth child fatality of the year for the rural, 32,000-resident county) when they received a report of a 2-year-old girl who had been shot. When deputies arrived, they found Savannah Lang dead from a gunshot wound to the back of her head. Investigators surmised that the girl's 3-year-old brother had been handling a Winchester 30-30 rifle when it when it discharged. She was shot in the back of the head while napping.

Some officials were skeptical, however. The lever-action rifle would be heavy and hard to handle for a toddler, who supposedly dragged it from one bedroom to another, aimed it, and pulled the trigger.

"We have some serious, serious doubts about this," Adams told the *Sentinel*. "I'm not saying the child did this or did not do this, but we're looking at a different angle (Dec. 9, 1994)."

He classified the case as "a full-blown murder investigation."

Witnesses gave differing accounts of what happened. Deputies were already familiar with the family, which Adams described as "bizarre."

The sheriff's office said there was a standing feud between two half-brothers, Marvin Allen Lang, the children's father, and Sean Brown, 20, the children's uncle and the new boyfriend of the children's mother.

One witness said Brown was in the mobile home at the time of the shooting. Another said he was outside washing a car.

Brown, who was under community control probation, was forbidden to have a gun because he was a convicted felon.

Deputies charged him with tampering with evidence, possession of a firearm by a convicted felon, and failure to safely store a firearm.

Brown, who went to trial five months later, denied bringing the rifle into the house. He blamed it on his mother's boyfriend. Brown's mother and her boyfriend also lived in the home.

"David borrowed the rifle," Brown testified at the trial, referring to his mother's boyfriend, David Williams.

Williams disputed the allegation. "He [Brown] said he wanted to go hunting with his daddy."

The owner of the rifle said Brown borrowed it on Dec. 2, five days before the shooting.

A neighbor testified that he ran to the house when he heard Brown's mother screaming. Once inside, he saw Brown. "He said, 'I'm wiping my prints off because I'm not supposed to be around guns," the neighbor testified (*Sentinel,* May 2, 1995).

Brown, who said he carried both the child and the rifle into the living room, said he panicked.

"I didn't know what to do," he testified. "I wiped off my fingerprints so no one would think I had shot the baby."

Williams again took the stand, this time to say that Brown begged him to tell prosecutor Hugh Bass that he had borrowed the rifle and brought it into the house. "I wouldn't do it."

But Brown's mother came to the aid of her son and testified that it was Williams who had borrowed the weapon.

In the end, the State Attorney's Office had to give up on charging Brown with the possession of a firearm, and there was no proof but that the boy didn't shoot his sister.

Was the child blamed for an act of negligence on the part of an adult? If so, it would be the worst form of child abuse.

Unfortunately, we may never know.

Chapter 4

In the beginning

The Augusta National Golf Club, bordered by dazzling azaleas and shaded by majestic oaks waving strands of Spanish moss at the best players in the world, is a picture of perfection. In the weeks after the Masters Golf Tournament visitors leave town, the sizzling Georgia sun comes out to fry streets like bacon, blister paint on battered bars, and steam residents in neighborhoods, including some with nicknames like "Pinch Gut."

This was my view—at least partially—in 1976 of the town dominated by *The Augusta Chronicle,* its building squatting regally between downtown buildings in the shadow of a tall Confederate monument.

The paper had hired me for my first full-time journalism job, and I was excited.

I had done some freelance work for my hometown paper in Jacksonville, Fla., and I wrote copy for the 11 o'clock news at a TV station there. I had also been an editor at the University of North Florida student newspaper. These combined experiences prompted the editors to offer $5 more per week than for the completely clueless rookie, for the gaudy sum of $155.

The *Chronicle*, which had a respectable circulation of 50,000, boasted a slogan on its masthead: "The South's Oldest Newspaper—Established 1785."

The jokesters in the newsroom used to pretend to insert parentheses with the words: "and still paying the same wages," but I wasn't complaining.

Hired by the managing editor because the city editor was out of town, I was misled from the beginning.

"She's a great lady," he said of my future boss. What he didn't say was, "I should know, I'm sleeping with her."

Nor did he say that she was in over her head as city editor. That was bad, because so was I.

Schizophrenic by design, the long, rectangular newsroom was shared by both the morning *Chronicle* and the afternoon *Herald*. Though the papers were owned by the same publisher, we competed for stories, which forced us to whisper into the phone so the afternoon guys couldn't hear what we were saying eight feet away.

Along the back wall, wire service teletype machines clattered away at the speed of 60 words per minute and wire photo machines would spin until photographs magically appeared. Occasionally the wire services would send out an urgent message and a bell would ring. Often, it was to announce the death of an editor at some obscure paper, which was not exactly urgent or news.

In the back corner was the newspaper "morgue," which in those pre-online days consisted of rows of little boxes of clippings and file cabinets filled with photos. The morgue was run by a retired Army man who had a unique take on filing. For example, the city had been struck by a major blizzard a few years earlier, and when an editor looked for the clips for an anniversary story, he couldn't find them under "S" for snow or storm or even "W" for weather. Finally, he finally found it under B—not for blizzard—but for "Big Snow."

The city desk got a lot of strange calls, including those from people who apparently think they are calling the reference desk at the public library. One night, two guys were in the middle of arguing about a bar bet when they called. One man said Georgia was bordered by four states and the other said five. It wasn't clear how much money had been wagered. A friend of mine told the caller that the answer was four.

"It makes you feel good that people put their trust in the newspaper," said my friend, who was the education writer.

"It's five," an editor said.

The next day the two men visited the morgue to see a map for themselves. My friend, however, was hiding.

Margaret Twiggs, a columnist for the *Herald,* was the queen. Margaret, who was 57, was royally portly, charming, with an aristocratic Georgia drawl, and had eyes and ears that missed nothing when it came time to collect political tidbits for her column. If you were lucky enough to be her pal you were in, but if you were on her bad side, she might just bludgeon you to death with her pen.

A longtime writer, she didn't bother with social fluff. She was a journalist when women just didn't do that kind of thing, and she was a scrapper like the rest of her family, who had fought in every war since the Revolution.

Georgia cities and counties, which had terrible open meeting laws, could shut reporters out of meetings with the flimsiest of excuses, which just added to the rich tapestry of corruption.

Once, Margaret got down on her hands and knees and put her ear to the air vent on the door. When someone opened the door on the other side, she fell into the conference room.

"Come on in, Margaret," the county commission chairman boomed.

One time, commissioners had a sheriff's deputy escort her out of a room when she refused to stub out her cigarette before entering a no-smoking zone.

One of her archenemies was the newsroom's own receptionist and operator. One day, when someone called for Margaret, the woman announced: "She's not at her desk. She's on the toilet."

One of Margaret's best sources was a favorite for all of us. As the county's chief building official, Willie Watkins not only knew about new developments that were coming, but also every juicy bit of political gossip and intrigue in the courthouse.

He didn't smoke his cigars so much as he chewed them, pausing in mid-sentence sometimes to remove a soggy wad from his mouth so he could toss it into a trash can across the room.

His coffee was strong enough to float a horseshoe, but reporters lined up to get a cup and pretend to drink it.

Not only did Watkins know where all the "bodies were buried," but he liked to needle his bosses on the county commission.

One day, one of the commissioners, holding a cup of the gut-destroying coffee and taking a load of abuse in Watkins' office, threatened to fire him. Watkins, whose nickname was "The Judge," removed the soggy cigar stump from his mouth and pointed it at the commissioner like a weapon.

"Go ahead," he said. "The next day I'll have a press conference on the front steps of the courthouse and tell *everything* I know."

The commissioner stomped out. Willie put the soggy cigar back in his mouth. There was no more talk of firing the 60-year-old.

It wasn't just the politicians' egos that he punctured.

When one of the major TV sports networks showed up to broadcast the Masters, one of the engineers from New York City puffed out his chest and said he didn't have to buy a permit.

"Go ahead," Watkins said. "It doesn't matter to me if you don't get any electricity to those cameras."

The man bought the permit.

"I don't understand it," Willie joked. "Everybody in this courthouse gets free tickets to the Masters but me."

Sometimes even his enemies had to laugh. Once, he wore an Army helmet to a budget meeting. When it came time for him to defend his requests, he took off the helmet and placed it over the seat of his pants and said, "I'm ready."

Not everyone had a sense of humor. I once caught a planning and zoning board member voting for a proposal that he had a financial interest in instead of abstaining. He blasted me during the next meeting, as if I was the one who had violated ethics laws. I guess I didn't know how to play. The paper also got a photo one day of the board's high-priced attorney sleeping through a meeting.

I also got wind of a City Council member voting for the city to buy property that he owned. I called him for a comment. "I don't care," he said.

The next time I saw him, however, he was contrite. A 70-year-old-plus Southern gentleman, he had been chided for his remark.

"My mother always told me never to say, 'I don't care.'"

Augusta, like a lot of cities in those days, had a racist undercurrent that occasionally raised its ugly head, and nothing is uglier than a pointy-headed Klansman.

The imperial potentate-whatever had chosen a remote area outside of town one Saturday night as the site for a rally. The editors, to their credit, didn't want to give any ink to the hate group, but someone needed to keep an eye on things. This was especially true since a man had just used his car to plow through a Klan rally in Jimmy Carter's hometown of Plains, Ga.

I was assigned to go to the rally, but I was only to file a story if there was any violence.

I didn't know what to expect. I didn't want anyone to think I was going undercover, or "under sheet," so to speak, so I decided to identify myself as a reporter, hang around no longer than necessary, and then leave. The guard I talked to scurried off to find the grand *pooh bah*. He apparently thought I wanted an interview. I proceeded to wander around.

The crowd of young men milled about aimlessly, trying not to inhale large clouds of pungent mosquito spray. Speakers began making virulent remarks about "protecting the white race" from blacks, Jews, and communists. Particularly galling for this crowd this day was the fact that a black man was serving on the county commission. Eventually, the haranguing stopped long enough for an ominous robed figure to ignite a wooden cross draped in a burlap bag that was soaked in kerosene. Hooded figures encircled the cross. I left, sickened by the sight. It was bad enough to hear the hateful words; it was even worse to see the cross set ablaze.

On Monday morning, one of the hooded heroes called the city desk demanding to know the name of the reporter who had attended the rally without giving it a "glowing" (no pun intended) write-up. To her credit the city editor not only did not give out my name, but she also did not disclose my address, home phone number, serial number, or the exact time that I would be walking through a dark alley to get to my car after work. In 1978, I would cross paths with another fanatic, J.B. Stoner. Stoner, his supporters, and his *Thunderbolt* propaganda flyer, had spewed a nasty racist message across the region. This time he was announcing his candidacy for governor.

I covered the press conference on the front lawn of a small, old house converted to a campaign headquarters on a busy highway. I didn't stand too close, however. If there's anything I hate, it's an angry drive-by gunman with sloppy aim.

Stoner would later be convicted of charges relating to the bombing of a church in Alabama.

Not every story was upsetting. One day I prepared to knock on the mayor's office door when it suddenly opened, and I found myself standing face-to-face with soul music legend James Brown. As a fan, I was so surprised I forgot I was a journalist and just mumbled something inane. Later, I wished I had said: "Just scream something for me."

Not surprisingly, Brown was in trouble. He was upsetting his upscale white neighbors. He had turned his home into a giant, holly, jolly, jukin' Christmas display, with dancing and singing robotic Santas, and lights so bright they were visible to airline pilots. Cars were lined up and blocking traffic to get inside the gates.

"The hardest working man in show business" was apparently a nice guy when he wasn't upsetting his neighbors, attacking one of his wives, or trying to run a highway patrolman off the road.

Often, the news was grim, especially on Saturdays, when it was my job to do the police beat.

My first death story was the drowning of a drunken man who had climbed over a fence to swim in a pond. With his left arm bent upward and locked into place by rigor mortis, he looked like he was still trying to swim to the surface.

There was also a section of town where people sat on the front steps of their homes drinking, harboring old grudges, and stewing in the smothering heat. By nightfall, there would be an argument, a fight maybe. Witnesses would recall seeing the glint of a knife blade under a dim streetlight or hearing gunfire that "sounded like firecrackers."

I happened to be driving by one of these neighborhoods once when one of these grim calls came in over my hand-held police scanner.

Here's a tip for young reporters: Don't beat the cops to a homicide. Crowds at murder scenes are sometimes angry, drunk, high, confused, and looking at a face that is decidedly out of place in their neighborhood. In those days, we wore nice clothes, even ties, if not jackets, to a crime scene. "Who are you?" they asked, figuring I must be a cop, because surely, no sane person would show up unarmed in the middle of a melee.

On the other hand, cops tend to shoo witnesses away from reporters, so sometimes it's good to arrive early. Years later, while working for the *Orlando Sentinel,* I went to the scene of a police-involved shooting. I rushed up to the witness, who was standing in the doorway of a house, and began asking questions quickly because I knew officers would be especially eager to toss me from a scene where one of their own was under investigation.

While taking notes, I kept looking over my shoulder and I wondered why they had not ordered me to hit the road. Then, I noticed they were stretching out crime scene tape and that I was inside the barrier.

They ignored me. I got my information and turned to leave when I realized why I had been so lucky. I was wearing a black windbreaker like the ones the officers were wearing.

Another time I came close to being locked up for my unwillingness to leave a crime scene. I respect the badge, but it was minutes to deadline and the call heard over the police scanner had been intriguing: "Burning body found in a ditch near cemetery."

"Get out of here!" said the freaked-out cop, who was single-handedly trying to preserve an important crime scene in his little town.

"Just tell me if it's true," I shouted as he was putting up crime scene tape along the road.

"I'll lock you up if you don't leave!"

"Just confirm it, yes or no," I said.

With veins sticking out on his forehead, he pointed his finger at me and began walking toward me.

I threw up my hands and hurried to my car so I could figure out a way to drive up to the scene from a different angle. I found a way, thanks to an editor who lived nearby. I was pushing up against the crime scene tape when friendly faces from the sheriff's office emerged out of the gloom. I called in two brief paragraphs. Detectives were less talkative the next day. They had some clues that would have helped my readers identify the victim, including the fact that he had a wooden leg and was allegedly torched by a drug dealer with a severe anger management problem.

I learned early on that timing is everything. Once, while making a routine trip to pick up arrest records at the jail in Augusta, I found myself in the middle of a riot. Glass was flying, some spectacular strands of curse words were flying, and frankly, I was afraid to find out what else was flying between the bars. Corrections officers locked down everything and everyone. I found myself locked up with a few visitors and a handful of inmates.

I was tempted to try and defuse the tension with humor by saying, "I hope none of you are in jail for assaulting a reporter." I thought better of it, though. Some people are in jail precisely because they do not have a sense of humor.

Supposedly, the copy desk pulled my picture and was prepared to put in the paper, in case I was injured or killed.

The copy desk chief, nicknamed "Sand Man," was a legendary drunkard.

He sat every night at a horseshoe-shaped copy desk doling out pages, copy, photos, and gas created by cheap beer.

He did things that made sense only to him, like randomly putting the word *Caramba!* in photo captions, including one depicting President Gerald Ford's daughter, Susan, skiing in Colorado.

Once, he laid out the front page with a one-column picture of a man getting off an airplane with a briefcase. Because the photo was so tall and narrow, he looked like the comic book superhero, Plastic Man.

Months later, the publisher held up the page to journalism students at a seminar and said that that edition was an embarrassment—because it didn't include an important business story.

Sand Man could recognize a major story sometimes. I was writing a routine city council story one day when I noticed the newsroom was buzzing. Sand Man suddenly stood up, threw down a metal print measuring stick, and exclaimed: "Hot damn, I've got a front page now!"

Elvis had "left the building" for good. He had died at his home in Memphis.

Color newspaper photos were in their infancy. Wire services transmitted different colored copies of the picture so production departments could put them together and produce a normal-looking image. I picked up one with a greenish tint and joked, "No wonder he died. He looked terrible."

One night after work, Sand Man fell off a bar stool at a saloon across the street and rolled out of sight under a table. The bartender locked up and turned off the lights. Sand Man woke up in the middle of the night. He was disoriented and babbling something about being dead when he called a friend to come rescue him.

One day, editors fearing the worst, sent me to his apartment when he didn't come to work. I knocked and waited until the door opened a crack. Suddenly, I was looking at an eyeball so bloodshot it looked like a road map of Atlanta. An ice pack, which I thought only existed in cartoons, was sitting atop his head.

The paper also had a food editor who liked recipes with wine. There was much speculation however, that the wine never made it into the mixing bowl.

At an office Christmas party, she observed an editor's wife coming in the door and exclaimed in a stage whisper: "There's Mrs. ... as big as ever!" We all scooted down a space, trying to pretend we didn't know her.

Later, she hunkered over a drink at the bar and said: "You know what's great about being old? You can say anything you want."

But if the food editor thought she could say anything, and Margaret acted like a queen, the publisher, William S. Morris III, was king. One night, editors sent a hapless reporter to his home with a copy of a particularly sensitive story. He drove through the gate and was greeted by a pack of snarling watch dogs. He rolled his window down just far enough to slide the papers through to Morris and waited until the great man read the story and sent him on his way.

The city editor, who wouldn't have recognized news if it hit her in the face, believed noteworthy items could only be found in government meetings.

One day a month, which I called "black Tuesdays," I had to cover five meetings, the first at 8 a.m., and the last at 5 p.m. The last was particularly painful. It was an airport board, and it was chaired by Morris. Occasionally he would turn around and say in front of everyone: "This part isn't newsworthy." And it certainly wasn't if it wasn't getting into the newspaper.

Morris had inherited the Augusta paper and a chain of others from his father. He liked to tell people that he had been a "printer's devil" in his youth, performing odd jobs around the plant. Staffers doubted that he ever spent much time mixing ink in the press room. He liked the newsroom but preferred the opinion department, writing ultra conservative editorials and promoting the Augusta National, where he was a board member.

Though rarely in the newsroom, there was one night he could not resist seeing the latest news on the wire service teletypes. It was election night, and he did not enjoy learning that the man he did not want in the White House—fellow Georgian Jimmy Carter—was winning.

The paper's editorial cartoonist had won brief national fame for depicting Carter as a grinning, giant peanut. Now, Morris was eating crow, not peanuts.

To ease his stress, Morris turned to his treasured reserved parking spot, his helipad on the roof, and the corporate jet.

The rest of us had to run downstairs every few hours to feed parking meters.

I learned as much about human frailties as I did about journalism in those two years.

One day I came into the office and asked my coworkers what was going on that day.

"Not much," one of them replied. "They're carrying the managing editor out of his office," he said, pointing to an ambulance crew.

And they were. Apparently, he had an ulcer as big as a dinner plate, though he wouldn't be eating much of anything for dinner until they could stop the internal bleeding.

Eventually, his city editor/lover resigned for unknown reasons, and it was all we could do to keep from jumping up and clicking our heels. But one day, the managing editor held an emergency staff meeting. The city editor's husband had died, we were told, but there was some good news, too, he said. The city editor was coming back. Fortunately for me, I was leaving.

I had been hired to replace a reporter who was leaving to go to law school. Now, the University of Georgia journalism school was offering me a teaching assistantship and the Veterans Administration had extended my education benefits so I could get a master's degree.

I made a lot of silly rookie mistakes in Augusta, like writing "billion" instead of "million" in a local budget story. The managing editor, who really was a nice guy, and apparently a good college professor at his last job, said something that I never forgot as I began learning how to be accurate under deadline pressure.

"Doctors bury their mistakes," he said. "We put ours on the front page for the whole world to see."

"I may be an extrovert," I thought, "but I am not an exhibitionist."

Chapter 5

Missing millionaire

No one knows what Neil Haber was thinking in the moments he got out of his car and walked into the garage of his home in the early morning hours of Aug. 1, 1981. Maybe the 51-year-old millionaire developer was glad to be home. Maybe he was dreading seeing the only family member that was expected to be in the house.

He was respected and liked by his business associates, and he was charming—maybe too charming. He had been gone for several days on a trip to Mexico with his 26-year-old girlfriend while his wife was away.

It was about 2 a.m. on that Saturday by the time he made his way through one of Leesburg's oldest, tree-lined, lakefront neighborhoods, and approached his unassuming ranch-style home. What happened next would end his life, tar reputations, shake up a police department, spark a long list of suspects, and spur finger-pointing, changing stories, false leads, and a titillating investigation. It would end with a killer getting away with murder.

It would start with one of the most bizarre tales ever told by a supposed eyewitness. Robert W. Ford was Haber's 29-year-old stepson. Divorced and unemployed, he was staying at his mom and dad's house on 9th Street.

He didn't tell anyone what he allegedly saw for two days. When he did decide to talk, he dictated a statement to Haber's secretary, Pat Parent, who called police.

The statement, complete with misspellings and punctuation, read: "About 2 a.m., I went outside to smoke a joint, stayed out a pretty good while, I was sitting in a lawn chair in the grass when Dad drove up. And as soon as he did another car drove up at the same time. Somebody said, 'Neil.' They walked up to each other, they talked but [I] couldn't understand the words. The garage door opened and they all went in (I think) and the door shut. Only sound heard thru the door was a funny strange pop sound. After a while longer the door opened and closed. I heard someone open the trunk of the Mercedes. The garage door opened and closed again. Nothing else heard from Dad. Man & woman talked, not understandable, maybe "Follow me." Then both cars started up and drove off. Stayed laying till maybe 5:30 a.m. in grass. Got up and walked looked in driveway went back to pool area and entered house by family room door.

"Then went to the garage, opened door, turn on lite and looked around. Saw a stream of blood on wall from lite switch to floor …."

He said he opened the door and walked outside to a trash bin he described as a "dumster" (sic). He said he noticed the lid was not on properly. It was then, he said, that he noticed a tarpaulin. When he moved the tarp, he saw rolled up plastic sheeting that was "all bloody and messed up."

"Came back into house and sat down. Smoked a joint. Afraid to call the police. Sat around awhile. Wiped off wall blood."

He said he then took the tarp and plastic sheeting to a nearby apartment complex that was being built by his father's company, and placed them in a large commercial trash bin. "Then came home and did nothing."

If police asked why he thought it was a good idea to "do nothing," and to hide evidence, there is no record of it in the handful of cardboard boxes that now serve as the final resting place for the case reports, partial transcripts, hand-scrawled notes, and scraps of paper.

One reason for his reticence became apparent the next day when police found marijuana plants, the grave marker of a woman who died in 1900 and a dead opossum in the back yard.

He was already facing possession and cultivation charges in Haines City in neighboring Polk County. Authorities there found 29 marijuana plants in his back yard, a duffle bag with traces of pot, two bags of seeds, $3,375 in cash, and drug residue in a safe.

He was questioned for 2 ½ hours by Leesburg Police Chief Ralph Perry. Unfortunately, whatever was said has been lost to history. The session was almost over before the chief called Detective Jerry Chapel and assigned the case to him. Chapel's notes are confined to one page. He listed Ford as the "suspect."

The next day, police began putting together a timeline, and newspapers began cranking out stories. "Blood found at Haber home," the headline in the *Leesburg Commercial* reported on Aug.7. "The missing millionaire is still a mystery," read the headline on Aug. 19.

Police described Haber's $36,000 Mercedes-Benz as being gold or champagne-colored. Initially it was erroneously described as a "turbo." It was a high-powered diesel. A Mercedes spokesman said there were fewer than a dozen like it in a seven-state area. In a personal touch, Haber had the seats covered with sheepskin. It was fast but still got 30 miles per gallon and had 120 safety features. "It's a luxury car as durable as a Sherman tank" the salesman said (*Commercial*, Aug. 12, 1981).

As managing editor of the *Commercial,* the story was already consuming much of my time and energy when an advertising salesperson on Aug. 10 showed me a copy of a full-page ad for the next day's edition. "$5,000.00 REWARD

For Information leading to the discovery & Recovery of a 1981 gold Mercedes 300SD turbo diesel auto," the ad read.

The "$5,000" was in the largest type size I had ever seen. The ad included the Polk County license plate number and a front license tag number of some kind. It also listed an "any hour" phone number. "All Calls Confidential."

The ad was purchased by Pat Parent on behalf of Haber's wife, Flora Jo. Cops, who generally hate big rewards, obviously had few leads. The thing that struck me as particularly odd was that the ad offered a reward for the *car*, not Haber. However, the next day, the lead paragraph of the news story said the family was putting up the reward "in hopes of gleaning information about his whereabouts."

There were other developments, though legal and proper, that raised eyebrows. On Aug. 21, the *Commercial* reported that Flora Jo was granted guardianship of her husband's estate, including 18 businesses, worth over $1 million. Haber, the petition stated, "... has disappeared under circumstances including that he may have died, either naturally, accidentally or at the hands of another."

Among the things she was now authorized to do was to write a $2.8 million check to a developer.

Meanwhile, investigators were tracking Haber's last known appearances.

Haber's girlfriend, Susana Masters, told police she was with Haber all day on Friday, July 31, in Haines City until 10:30 p.m. When she called Haber's home the next day, Ford told her that he had never arrived.

One of the last people to see Haber was Ford's ex-wife, Roberta "Robin" Ford. She said Haber came to her north Haines City home between 10:30 and 11 p.m. She said the two talked until he left around 12:30 a.m. When he left, he was carrying ten $100 bills she had given him to repay a loan, she said.

Roberta Ford denied that there was anything but a friendly, paternal kind of relationship between the two. She said that she was separated from "Robby" in February 1980, and was left with "a small child, a bicycle, a baby seat, and a job at an elementary school, and [I] made less than $93 a week." The final straw came when she yanked marijuana plants up by the roots in their backyard and threatened to kick him out of the house. When he eventually left, he took their car. She didn't have any money, so she turned to Haber, who helped with her expenses, including getting a lawyer. He met with her frequently, provided an allowance, and showed her how to budget her funds, she said.

One night, things took an unexpected turn. She said she had packed a bag to spend the night at a girlfriend's house when Haber called to say he wanted to pay her bills, including medical expenses. The total came to about $500. "… so, we went back to his hotel room and took a piece of paper and listed out, you know, what bills I had and how much money and etc., when a knock comes to the door."

The investigator prompted her to continue. "You were inside the motel room?"

She replied, saying: "Inside the motel room, clothes on."

She said it was late, about 12:30 or 1 a.m. "… couldn't be anybody else but Robby. So, I asked Neil, 'Please don't open the door because I don't want to be here. I don't want to see him. Don't open the door.' So, we just sat there and waited until he quit knocking and went away."

She said Haber told her that Robby came back later, and they left and got something to eat.

In the interim, Robby had called his mother, Flora Jo, and said he thought Neil was having an affair with Robin. The next day, Flora Jo called Haber's apartment manager, June Wynn, to ask if it was true. June laughed and told her no. "So, Neil tells me this," Robin said. "OK, he told me not to worry unless they had pictures or tape recorders and stuff like this, all it was is hearsay and not to be worried about it, you know. So, now that was … also at this time, he was dating his girlfriend," she said.

"He [Robby] had hinted to me several times that he knew something about me that was just horrible, and he couldn't believe it," Robin said. "And after that little hotel scene I would just snicker about it. I would say, 'You can think what you want, and I don't care.'"

Robin said she knew something horrible about Robby but couldn't prove it. He had talked about burning their house down three days before their divorce was final.

He said it was the "best thing" to do, because they could pay lawyer fees and get a new house and furniture with insurance money. "A new beginning," is the way he described it.

He called her one day and asked if she was going to be in town. When she said she was going to be gone on March 1, 1981, the house caught on fire under suspicious circumstances. Robby still had a key to the house.

She said that although Haber promised to rebuild the house and replace appliances, "… he expressed fear of Robby hurting him or hurting the house or hurting the company and asked that nothing be done on the house until Robby was in jail [on the drug charges]."

***

The hot Florida sun does vile things to bodies stashed in car trunks. Veteran homicide cops smear vapor rub medicine under their noses to try and overpower the stench, but nothing could overcome the odor coming from Haber's car on Saturday, Aug. 22. A passerby spotted the car in an orange grove near Haines City. He would get the $5,000 reward, but no one would ever want to ride in the car again.

Haber had been shot in the right eye with a 9 mm. His pants pockets were turned inside out, and the ten $100 bills mentioned by Robin were missing. There was evidence of a bare footprint on the hood of the car and an unusual shoe print by the trunk. An impression was made of the left shoe print, which was 12-by-5 inches. The shoe had a "smooth sole median with a diagonal line across it," crime scene technicians noted. The impression did not match the passerby's shoe.

Technicians were able to lift 22 fingerprints from the car. Two matched Ford's, but he had access to the car before Haber disappeared.

The car was loaded with cassette tapes, papers, luggage, and a 19-inch Zenith color TV. The Polk County Sheriff's Office had been investigating a theft ring and said the TV had been stolen from a furniture store in Lake Wales. There were no fingerprints linking a theft suspect and the murder.

The car was towed to a nearby crime lab where the body was removed and identified with dental records.

Commercial reporter Peter Guinta and columnist Norma Hendricks reported the gruesome find and quoted police as saying that Ford had "changed his story several times."

He told one of the weirdest tales to Detective Chapel.

"He said he buried his father's watch and necklace in the backyard—but when I dug the location—and two others—they weren't there. He does not want his mother to know," Chapel noted in a report. Ford apparently indicated that he took the items off his stepfather's body.

He may have been telling the truth. Besides the antique grave marker, marijuana plants, and other items found in the backyard, police also found a shovel smeared with fresh dirt.

One item found in the car was a Borel wristwatch worn by Haber. Also in evidence was a Hamilton automatic wristwatch that Ford gave to his mother to be repaired. "The watch shows signs of stress on the watch strap buckle," crime technicians noted, suggesting that it had been snatched off someone's wrist.

Chapel wrote a note to the chief on Nov. 2, saying: "Pat Parent phoned Friday evening and asked if we could not return the watches to the family (see receipt). (I've already got back the lab report on them – negative)."

Flora Jo told the *Commercial* that she was resigned to the fact that her husband was dead. "The longer he was gone, with the amount of blood that was found, I just lost hope. He would have been injured and had to have had immediate medical attention," she said.

She said her immediate concern was settling the estate and managing the 20 businesses or so that the two of them had built up over the years. "I'm jumping in with both feet," she said, adding that she would be aided by Parent and managers of the companies.

A memorial service was held under the watchful eye of police, who took notes on the guests. Haber's body was interred in a family plot in New York.

But if the victim was buried, the investigation was not. Federal authorities got involved because Haber's business was building and managing federally subsidized housing complexes. Leesburg was already under a cloud in a project that had no connection to Haber. Managers in that project were arrested and charged with fraud.

Investigators were also getting tips about people who may have had some ties to Haber, including a banker who was supposedly kidnapped and shot, and a holding company executive who was convicted of using kickbacks for fundraising.

Investigators also took note of another body found in a nearby orange grove. Joni Sue Crocker, 24, was found partially nude more than a year earlier. She had been strangled with her bra.

Among the most promising leads was one that came from a cab driver in Leesburg. The 47-year-old woman told police that she picked up a fare at a restaurant in Leesburg at 3:30 a.m. on the morning of Haber's disappearance. It was the same person she had taken to the unemployment office a few days earlier, she said.

She dropped him off at a street near 9th Avenue but not before he asked her if she knew of a place to live. She identified Ford from a photograph. She speculated that a rolled-up bag he was carrying could have held a handgun.

The gun that killed Haber was 9 mm. Robby said that he had once owned such a handgun, but he sold it. That set off a mad scramble by Robby to track down the weapon, which he eventually did.

The FBI lab described the bullet as a jacketed hollow point. Because there was some distortion it was not possible to measure some of the rifling marks.

One year after Haber's disappearance, Leesburg police were no closer to solving the case. City officials were feeling the heat and getting pressure from the Sheriff's Office.

Taxpayers, meanwhile, were getting a whiff of what they believed to be a scandal. Investigators Chapel and Hal Reeves were seen wining and dining Flora Jo and Pat Parent. The *Commercial* wrote about the public's discontent and the lack of progress.

Parent and Flora Jo were incensed that their names were being bandied about. They wanted to know the source of the rumors and suspected a disgruntled project manager who was turned down for a job with Haber's company. They demanded that City Manager Rex Taylor apologize at a City Commission meeting.

Among the stories leaked to the *Commercial* was one stating that the city had considered hiring a private detective agency to investigate possible police misconduct.

Flora Jo, addressing a city commission meeting, said the story "smacks of *National Enquirer,* and said that city officials should have gone through proper channels. The seed is planted in the public mind. How do you strike something from their memory, especially when it's sensational?"

Parent said she wanted the city to hold a hearing to find out "who incorrectly reported the allegations."

Parent's husband, Jim, was more adamant. "Murder is an ugly word, but that is what we are dealing with here. Is the city of Leesburg more interested in playing word games than it is in solving a murder?"

Mayor Charles Strickland said: "This case is under investigation, and I don't think we should try it in the newspaper. This has been the problem in the past (*Commercial,* July 13, 1982)."

Included in the cardboard box archive is a record that Parent and Flora Jo kept of a meeting with Guinta and me at the *Commercial.* They were demanding to know the names of sources. Frankly, I don't remember it. Their notes said that I didn't budge, which sounds right, and I then excused myself so I could go to a meeting. The only reason to agree to such a meeting in the first place is to see if a story is in error or is somehow unfair. That was not the case. They claimed that Peter gave them a name, which is news to me.

***

On July 2, 1982, Chief Perry wrote a memo to his captain, Willard Dean, telling him the city was turning the case over to the sheriff.

"I expect each of you to conduct yourselves in a very professional manner during this transfer," he wrote. "Our goals and objectives are as they were – to clear this case at whatever the cost. We do not win friends and influence people without its costing us to do our jobs professionally."

***

Sheriff's Capt. Jim Brown liked to call himself "The "Screaming Eagle." It was a macho intimidation tactic.

Once, *Commercial* Editor Mike Archer and I met with State Attorney Gordon Oldham and Brown to demand that the sheriff release some public records.

Sheriff Noel E. Griffin Jr. was a hot-tempered, arrogant little king who once insisted that we fire a reporter who had the audacity to report on questionable things going on in his department rather than the crumbs he was tossing her way. We refused to play.

Brown jumped out of his seat to insist that the sheriff was above the public records law. Oldham, who could be an elder statesman, was also a tough old bird. "Sit down and shut up," he said. "Give these people what they want."

Perry defended his detectives. "These two investigators spent countless hours pursuing the case, sometimes at the expense of their personal lives, and made numerous contacts, at all hours of the day and night … sometimes volunteering to work on their days off, travel out of town (at a moment's notice), and incurring personal expenses for meals and phone calls," he said in a letter placed into the record.

He said the officers gave him updates and sought his advice "when confronted by outside professional political pressures, all generated by the complexity of the case."

He said he agreed with the officers that it was important "to win the friendship and respect of those witnesses through socializing with them." He told the officers to do whatever it takes as long as the methods were "legally and morally sound."

Perry said, "fellow police officers, through innuendo, gossip, and subterfuge, undermined the investigation by spreading unsubstantiated rumors outside the department." He said news reports implied that the two should be investigated, yet according to Perry, the two went to the city manager to ask for a query so their names could be cleared.

Brown, in an interview with the *Commercial* on July 31, 1982, criticized the police murder investigation. For one thing, officers never went to Maine to verify Flora Jo's alibi. He also said that police had incorrectly eliminated several possible suspects by using voice stress analysis only.

The technology was being touted by some as being more accurate than polygraph exams, yet like polygraph exams, stress analysis is not admissible in court. The sheriff's office was not eliminating anyone, he insisted.

Brown acknowledged that it was a complex case. There were several friends, family members, business associates, and competitors who could have profited by Haber's death. Plus, Haber had apparently engaged in numerous affairs.

Brown said the list of possible killers had been "narrowed to several suspects." He then boasted: "If I arrest someone, I'll have the case wrapped up so tight I won't need their cooperation."

It turned out to be a lot easier to bump Perry out of his job and become chief of police.

On Jan. 3, newly minted Chief Brown told Reeves and Chapel that they would be the subject of an internal investigation by a review board.

Norma Hendricks and I teamed up together to report on March 7 to report on a review board's finding that the officers made "one mistake after another."

Dean, for example, allowed Pat Parent to write Ford's statement because he was "too shook up" to do it himself. That gave Ford cover if he were to later claim that he was "too shook up" to understand his Constitutional right not to incriminate himself.

Dean did not make a record of the crime scene, and he allowed a small army of officers, family members, Pat Parent, and the family attorney access to the house. Parent and the attorney were allowed to help search for a weapon. When she found a handgun, she put it in her purse. It was not a 9 mm, however.

Ford was allowed to retrieve the bloody items from the trash bin and the container was not seized or searched for other items. The tarp was near the top. "What else was in the Dumpster?" the board wondered. Nor was there any search warrant or a record of Ford giving police permission to search the house.

After the body was located, the dental records were collected, not by a police officer but by Chapel's wife, who worked for the dentist. When she went to the office, she was surprised to see Jim Parent, who took the records from her. Jerry Chapel had to demand the records from Parent the next day, according to investigative records.

The whole process was "at best lax," the police review board noted. It was yet another breech of evidence custody, including another failure to get a search warrant.

Dean said he had no memory of telling Jim Parent to go and retrieve the dental records.

"Capt. Dean's credibility is in question ...." the board noted.

The detectives said they checked Flora Jo's alibi, but the board could find no evidence that they had ever checked on Pat Parent's whereabouts.

"It is apparent that the officers ... were somewhat intimidated by Mrs. Parent ...," the board noted. Not only that, "there is evidence throughout the statements given by all persons involved that Mrs. Parent at times far exceeded the role of a witness in this case, and from time to time, actually was allowed to investigate parts of the case."

Furthermore, they did not use all the "techniques available to them" to clear the 43-year-old woman as a suspect, the board said.

The detectives' answers about "social activities" also didn't go over well. The men claimed that they didn't talk about the case, except maybe once when they ran into the women accidentally at a service club. Sometimes the officers had their wives with them.

The board found it "very hard to believe" that the case was not being discussed with the wives present. If details were discussed, it was improper to discuss an open investigation with civilians present. The board also noted that "… adverse publicity could have been avoided to some extent if the officers had used some discretion in meeting with the Parents and Mrs. Haber.

In the end, Reeves was socked with two department counts each of conduct that reflected badly on the department, two counts of investigative failure, and one count each of associating with suspects and failure to remain impartial. Chapel was charged with the same noncriminal offenses except that he faced three counts of investigative failure, plus an additional charge of handling evidence improperly.

Dean was charged with communicating confidential information to an unauthorized person.

"There is no doubt in my mind what the multiple causation factors were that turned the Haber case into a classic illustration of impoverished management that lacked control, direction, coordination, and discipline, which in toto, was the catalyst for fiasco," Brown said.

***

One of the things that came to light was the relationship between Ford and Haber.

A friend of Robby's who worked for an ambulance service told investigators that Ford called to ask him if he had heard any news over emergency radio channels.

"He called me several times just saying, 'I can't find my daddy. They can't find my daddy," said Samuel Smilee. "His momma even called. Several times he was just in tears. I mean, sobbing."

Apartment manager June Wynn said Haber was always bailing Robby out of trouble. "All he did was use Neil," she told police.

"At one point Flora Jo hated him to the point she wouldn't let him in the house, but Neil would intervene," Wynn said.

Smilee said that if Ford asked for $200, Haber would give him $500, "that kind of stuff." He described him as "good old Pop," he said.

Robin Ford painted a dark picture, however, when a cop asked if she thought Robby was capable of murder if he thought she was having an affair with Haber.

"Yeah, I do. I believe that it was a thin line he was walking on anyway. Here, all of a sudden, he didn't have a family, didn't have a home life. He was in all kinds of trouble with the law, his dad...I mean him and his dad despised each other. I mean, Robby openly talked about it to me, about how much he hated his father. I think the most violent I ever saw him express that is when we were coming home from a marriage counselor right before we got separated and he just was blowing steam all the way down [U.S. Highway] 27 saying how his dad could have made him vice president and he would never forget it, you know, and he could have had so much if it wasn't for Neil ...."

He never said he wanted to kill his stepfather, but he did say what he thought he would gain if he died. "Like he would receive apartment buildings and he would be a very rich person when Neil died. Neil had told me that he disliked Robby so much that he wrote in the will that Robby only received $10,000 from his estate, and Flora Jo, Randy [his biological son], and [stepdaughter] Lynn, the properties and real estate would be split among them.

"I've seen him carry guns out of the house loaded on his drug deals. I've seen him carry and point a loaded gun from a stop sign toward a 7-Eleven [convenience store] at somebody who had supposedly ripped him off for some drugs, and I know, at one point, he flew up to Mexico and carried a gun then. He packed, carried a gun with him, on his drug deals most of the time."

She said one of the guns was a 9 mm. She wasn't sure about the other.

It was a "hate relationship," she said. She said Robby felt that Haber didn't offer enough opportunities, give him all the things he was supposed to have, that he had turned his mother against him, and "he owed him something."

She couldn't say that Haber was afraid of being harmed by Robby when he went home that night. "… it was his gut feeling that he did not particularly like the idea of going home and Robby was the only one there, Flora Jo wasn't home, and Randy wasn't home (he was in Atlanta)."

She said he was going to drop off a deposit, gather some clothes, and leave.

Trouble was brewing. Parent said that she had urged Haber to get rid of his mistress before the trip to Mexico. "It seemed suddenly that Susana was talking of marriage and becoming a business partner."

That would certainly have been a strong motive for Flora Jo. Flora Jo said she was unaware of the mistress.

Parent also speculated that the second car that pulled up to the garage that night could have been occupied by family attorney Charles Mayer and June Wynn. They could have driven Haber's car back to Haines City and dumped it in the orange grove to make it look like the crime occurred there, she said. Mayer said he and his son, who was also brought into question, both had alibis.

Mayer had a strong dislike for Parent. She had called him on that Sunday to say that Haber had not returned home on Saturday. He said he wanted to alert police immediately so they could put out a bulletin. She angrily refused.

Authorities wanted Mayer's fingerprints to eliminate him as a suspect. Fingerprints were found on the bloody plastic sheeting in the trash bin that could not be identified.

Mayer said he would do so only under court order. He claimed Parent had once brought a pocket watch and a vase to his office, "being very obvious that she was trying to obtain his fingerprints."

Investigators also noted "… he is unable to understand how a simple employee would suddenly become a business partner."

A separate investigative report also stated: "Mr. and Mrs. Wynn are very suspicious of Pat Parent due to the fact that she was only an 'errand boy' working for Neil Haber, and as soon as he became missing, she suddenly became 'business partner' with complete control."

June Wynn also talked to Parent that initial weekend when she could not reach Haber at home. Parent told her not to worry. "He's probably off on a fling with that Altamonte [Springs] woman," Parent said.

There is no indication of who that might be. His girlfriend, Masters, was attending the University of Florida in Gainesville. Altamonte Springs is in Seminole County outside Orlando.

***

Adding to the investigators' pile of leads was a call from a man who said he shared jail space with Ford in Polk County. The two men learned they both had longstanding disagreements with their fathers. "… out of the different conversations I had with him, he told me that his father was involved in organized crime through construction …."

David L. McKnight told investigators that "… he (Ford) figured some people from Fort Lauderdale that were involved in organized crime might have had his father knocked off."

He said his father had U.S. Treasury certificates in a safety deposit box. The certificates had a short maturity of three months to a year.

Neil Haber would raise money for construction, make a down payment on the job and then invest the rest in the certificates and make money off the interest. That was just part of it, however. He said, "… they were building these apartments at a low standard and ... money above what they were costing to build, they were all splitting it up. He was getting a percentage of it."

In telling this all this to McKnight, Ford said that before the homicide, there was $250,000 in certificates in the box and $180,000 cash. When the box was finally turned over to Flora Jo, the cash was missing.

Lake County investigators questioned Wynn about the safety deposit box on Aug. 4, 1982. She recalled that Pat Parent called her on that initial Sunday asking about money, papers, and a safety deposit key. Wynn denied any knowledge of it, "due to the fact that Neil had advised her that if anything happened that she should empty that safety deposit box ... and take it to Charles Mayer and that is what she did."

There were concerns raised about other money. A few hours before he left Haines City and headed for Leesburg, Mayer said Haber had stopped by his office and made out a deposit from a "liquid assets" account file. Mayer said he was not sure of the amount or if the deposit was mailed or if he took it with him. He said later three checks were missing from the file.

Haber's sister said she thought he was carrying four $1,000 negotiable municipal bonds.

A business associate said he expected Haber to bring him a $50,000 check on that coming Monday.

Investigative records are unclear as to what happened to any of these alleged funds.

In July of 1982, authorities arrested June Wynn on charges of grand theft, uttering a forged instrument, and forgery. The arrest report said that she had cashed a $39,600 check five days after Haber turned up missing. The check was to cover landscaping costs and was made out to a nursery owned by Wynn's husband.

There was a confusing series of events involving a stop payment when the check was found in Haber's car and another check was allegedly issued.

There was also an allegation that Wynn's husband had taken an $11,000 certificate of deposit out of a Haber safety deposit box and cashed it. He said he was owed the money for landscaping materials.

Wynn, who had worked for Haber for more than 18 years, was fired. There are no court records indicating what happened to the case. Charges may have been dropped or the case settled.

McKnight disclosed other conversations about his friend at the Polk County jail. Ford, for example, said he had a 9 mm stashed in Leesburg along with some marijuana, and said he might be willing to sell the gun.

McKnight said Ford also confessed to him that he torched the house.

As for the night of Haber's disappearance, Ford said he was "… out of my mind" after drinking and taking Quaaludes. He said he was sitting on the back steps and smoking marijuana when his stepfather pulled up. There were three other people in a "large, dark- colored, late-model car."

He said his view was blocked by a large wooden fence, but he thought one of the persons looked like Mayer. The fence had some knot holes, police noted. Ford said he fell asleep behind the fence at one point until about 4:30 a.m. or so (he had told police it was around 5:30).

***

Ford eventually went on to prison to serve his sentence on the drug charges. Records, however, contain a curious note from an investigator (unknown), who says he was approached by an attorney representing Ford.

He said Ford would come forward "and divulge his knowledge/participation in the crime…unless his client was the main principal or assassin …." He wanted total immunity on any accessory or conspiracy charge and wanted the state attorney to commute the remainder of his prison sentence (nine months).

The officer said Oldham would first have to know the extent of Ford's involvement. The attorney said he didn't know. The attorney was talking with Ford when the officer walked out.

***

If there was any doubt that Haber was disappointed with his stepson, the question was answered in his will, dated July 11, 1978. He said that when he married Flora Jo, she had two children under the age of 10. He said he regarded them as his biological children, just like his son, Randy.

"As the result of my experiences and knowledge of the said children, I am reluctantly forced to conclude that my stepson … is not as responsible with money as I would like him to be."

The will continued, saying that if Flora Jo died before he did, the estate should be divided into thirds among the children. However, in Ford's case, "this bequest shall not in any case exceed the sum of $10,000."

***

The Lake sheriff's office arrested Ford on Aug. 31, 1982 and charged him with murder. That started the legal clock ticking. A grand jury was called, and for three days, a parade of subpoenaed witnesses walked into the secret, closed door proceedings. Witnesses included Roberta, Susana, June Wynn, Ford's ambulance worker friend, the sheriff's investigator who took over the case from the city, the medical examiner, a crime scene technician, Haber's dentist, Pat Parent, investigators Reeves and Chapel, and the cab driver. Also testifying was an official from a bank in Polk County.

On Sept. 23, the grand jury announced: "There does not exist sufficient evidence that the defendant ... affected the death of Neil I. Haber ...."

Nor was it a "provable case," the panel said. The panel recommended that authorities continue to investigate.

"[Sheriff] Griffin is the one that messed that up," said a retired investigator for the State Attorney's Office.

"We begged him to wait," Dean confided to a friend.

The Leesburg Police review board had noted that problems in the investigation "are the result of a police department in transition ...."

It noted that the days of "casual policing" were over.

"This board also feels that there was no intent on the part of any of the persons interviewed to purposely violate department rules. In fact, the rank-and-file officers appear to be very concerned with professionalization and will, under proper supervision, become fine officers ...."

Chief Brown retired in April 1993.

Perry, who had once almost been killed when a car roared through a roadblock, died in 2006. He was an even-tempered, patient man, even with reporters. One night I tracked him down at the scene of an armed robbery where one of his officers had shot one of the suspects. As I approached his car in the alley illuminated only by headlights, he looked up and calmly said, "You're standing in my crime scene."

Flora Jo died in 2012. Her obit listed her as a businesswoman who loved photography and designing stained glass.

Pat Parent died in 1991 of cancer. She was 52. Her obituary in the *Sentinel* described her as an "energetic Leesburg businesswoman community leader." She formed her own property management company.

Ford was found dead in the shower of his apartment on Aug. 7, 1990. The death certificate listed his occupation as "concrete worker." Police figured it was an overdose, but there were no drugs in his system. The Medical Examiner's Office listed the cause of death as cardiac arrhythmia.

A lot of things can cause irregular heartbeat, including a congenital heart defect, but it can also be caused by a history of smoking and abuse of drugs and alcohol.

He had been arrested in 1987 for violation of probation when he failed a drug test. He was also charged with unauthorized use or possession of a driver's license, a third-degree felony, and he confessed to growing pot in a barn behind his house.

He was placed on a more controlled form of probation.

Like all criminal investigations, the murder probe came down to questions about means, opportunity, and motive.

Many people had motive. Flora Jo certainly did, especially if she thought she was going to lose her place in the business.

Mobsters, if any, would have been motivated by money.

June Wynn and Charles Mayer would have had motive if they looted the safety deposit box and took cash from Haber's body. There was no evidence to support this theory, however.

Robin Ford could have had a motive if she developed strong a romantic attachment to Haber. There was no evidence of that either. It seems unlikely that she would want to end a friendly line of credit.

Pat Parent might have had a motive if she could have used knowledge or her involvement to become a business partner.

As for means and opportunity, Mayer and Flora Jo provided alibis.

Ford had motives galore. He had a longstanding disagreeable history with his stepfather, thought he was entitled to a piece of the business, and blamed Haber for coming between him and his mother. He was also furious over what he perceived to be an affair between Robin and Haber.

He had the means and opportunity. A year after the shooting, he told a fellow prisoner that he had a 9 mm stashed in Leesburg – a different 9 mm than the one he sold and later produced for investigators.

Ford was also at home alone when Haber came home. The car and body were dumped in an orange grove several miles away, but when the cab driver identified him as a passenger in Leesburg at 3 a.m., it destroyed the timeline that he laid out for the police. He could have ditched the car, caught a ride back to Leesburg, and then caught a cab for a ride back to his neighborhood.

Prosecutors sometimes present "consciousness of guilt" evidence. Basically, it is guilty-looking behavior. Running away after a crime is committed is the most common example, but it can include such things as threatening witnesses or manipulating evidence.

The hiding of evidence and his decision not to call police seem to fall into this category. Did he have a guilty conscience? Was he afraid that the evidence would turn up later, so he figured that he might as well pretend to be helpful in retrieving it?

People who lie to police generally include some truthful tidbits, thinking that it will give their story more credibility. So, there could have been another car in the driveway, voices, and a "pop." The people in the other car, however, could have been one of his partners.

Robin told investigators that a "beat up," tough-talking character named "Jackie" came to her house one day claiming that Robby owed him $3,000. Could Robby have enlisted the aid of the man in the murder so he could pay off the loan? Haber was carrying a minimum of $1,000 cash.

Of course, Ford might not have committed the actual murder. He could have witnessed mobsters or business partners kill his stepdad. He might have been reluctant to call police because he didn't want the killers to come after him.

Pat Parent, for all her bull-in-a-china-shop personality, was right about one thing. She told investigators on July 20, 1982 that if Ford didn't do it, he knew who did.

Robin agreed. "I think if he did not kill him, he knows who did and he was right there," she told an investigator. "I don't think he would have sat in the back yard and heard a commotion and not look. I don't think he would have cleaned up the mess and sat in an empty house by himself for three days without telling anybody.

A former investigator with the State Attorney's Office interviewed for this book said it best.

"That boy got away with murder."

Chapter 6

Cases that keep cops awake at night

Where is Trenton Duckett? He was only 2 years old on Aug. 27, 2006, when his mother, Melinda, called 911 to report that someone had cut the screen on his bedroom window in Leesburg and snatched him from his bed. Today, he is no longer a toddler—if he is still alive.

Sadly, we will probably never know. His mother killed herself, creating a permanent roadblock to the investigation, igniting a media firestorm, and creating a lawsuit against TV crime show maven Nancy Grace. The former prosecutor's incessant questioning pushed the 21-year-old over the edge and caused her to kill herself, the lawsuit alleged.

Yet, it was Melinda's suspicious behavior that sparked a load of unanswered questions, starting with her call to the 911 operator.

"What is Trenton wearing, honey?" the operator asked (cbsnews.com, Aug. 31, 2007).

"I don't know. He was ready for bed," Melinda replied.

"You don't know what you dressed him in before he went to bed?"

Grace did grill Melinda in her trademark wood-chipper style of questioning on Sept. 8, but Melinda wouldn't give any details about how she spent the weekend with her son before she reported him missing Sunday evening

"Shopping," is all she would say. She refused to name any stores. "We didn't go anywhere specific." Grace kept asking but Melinda said, "I won't go into any specifics."

Grace persisted, wondering aloud why she wouldn't give details since she was the last one to see him before she reported him missing. The next day, Melinda went into the bedroom of her grandparents' home, took a shotgun out of its case, fired a test round into the ceiling, then walked into the closet and shot herself in the head—just before her taped interview aired on TV.

Her grandfather, Bill Eubank, was incensed and blamed police and news coverage.

"She was like a wild animal in a cage poked with a stick," he told me in an exclusive interview (*Star-Banner*, Sept. 10, 2006).

He said he questioned her himself.

"Honey, hold my hand," he recalled telling her the week before. "Raise your other hand and tell me, in the name of God, did you do anything to Trenton, or do you know where he is?"

"Papa, I don't know where Trenton is at," he quoted her as saying (*Star-Banner*, Sept. 10, 2006).

Leesburg police eventually named her as a suspect after her death. They then faced criticism for not arresting her right away and putting pressure on her in interrogations.

She had not been cooperative, police said. She refused, for example, to take a lie detector test, unlike her former husband, Joshua Duckett.

She was fearful of losing her hard-won custody of Trenton, Eubank said, though there was no apparent danger of that happening. A lawyer advised her not to take the polygraph exam, Eubank said. He did not name the lawyer.

The grandparents were crushed by the double blow.

"He's one of the most beautiful kids ever seen in this life," Eubank said. "He's smart, loving. He loves everybody."

Melinda, who had been adopted from South Korea, lived with her grandparents, coming to Florida to finish high school. That's where she met Joshua. They married in July of 2005 one month after Trenton was born. They divorced a year later in a bitter war that would eventually shed light on her twisted psyche.

She managed, for example, to gain custody of Trenton after claiming that Joshua had sent a threatening e-mail to her MySpace account. Experts later discovered that she had sent the message from her own computer. She had obtained his password to make it look like he was the culprit. It was a pattern, Joshua said, for her to do anything to keep him from getting Trenton.

She was involuntarily committed to a mental hospital in 2005 for 24 hours after Joshua said she threatened to harm the baby. He later recanted, which is not unheard of in these kinds of cases.

On Nov. 28, 2005, Melinda bit Joshua's mother, Carla Massero, on the arm after learning that she had given the baby a bath. She admitted to a sheriff's deputy that "she was mad because Trent was her son and she wanted to take care of him." The deputy also saw marks on Melinda's arms and body. She told the deputy they were "self-inflicted." Melinda admitted to having psychological problems and said she was adopted. She told the investigator that she "had thoughts she could not control" and "hated people (*Star-Banner*, Sept. 27, 2006)."

Massero did not press charges but made her agree to counseling. A year later she wrote an e-mail to the Okeechobee Sheriff's Office and Gov. Jeb Bush.

"The mother . . . not only has a history of self-mutilation, but also has made several threats on Trenton," she wrote.

She also accused Melinda of performing oral sex on two Bushnell police officers to get information.

"I am afraid for Trenton's life, and I don't want him to end up yet another story in the news," she wrote.

"I didn't have anything against her. I was just trying to get her some help," Massero told the *Star-Banner* in the Sept. 27, 2006 story.

Massero had already had more than her share of tragedy. In 1988, she was still married to 30-year-old James Duckett when he was convicted of murdering and raping 11-year-old Teresa Mae McAbee in Mascotte. Duckett was a rookie cop in the little south Lake County town and was the only officer on duty that night when he was arrested and charged. Teresa's fingerprints were found on the hood of his patrol car. Joshua was 2 at the time, about the same age as Trenton when he disappeared. Joshua's brother, Justin, was 5. Every evening after the trial she and the boys would stand on the sidewalk outside the jail and wave to Duckett. He denied killing the girl. He is still on death row.

As for Melinda, even the most sympathetic observer would have to admit that her state of mind was nothing short of a mess. There were conflicting reports that Melinda had been abused as a child.

The release of DCF records showed a controversial record of analysis, including noting that the young couple was immature and used the child as a "pawn" in fighting with each other. One report concluded that the parents did love the 2-year-old (*Star-Banner*, Sept. 30, 2006).

Records also disclosed that Melinda was in financial trouble and had applied for food stamps. Police also reportedly found a pornographic video of Melinda.

The couple had been forced to undergo psychological evaluations and take parenting classes following a Department of Children and Families report that cited neglect and inadequate supervision for Trenton.

Trenton was bounced between family members in the months of 2005 and 2006. Melinda, who had been diagnosed with obsessive compulsive personality disorder and depression, was awarded temporary custody of Trenton after claiming Joshua had sent her the threatening e-mails.

As the editor in charge of court and crime reporters, I pushed hard to make sure the *Star-Banner* covered every angle. The top editors were always conscious of staying within our primary circulation area, which was Marion County. Leesburg is in Lake County. But the Trenton story had major "legs" for our readers, starting with a massive search in the Ocala National Forest, which spans both counties. The case was also making national headlines.

The story gained even sharper focus (and sharper edges) when the Leesburg Police Department and Marion County Sheriff's Office grew apart in their views.

Reporters were initially told that Melinda had not left any suicide notes, but that was not true. She left three: one to her parents in New York (who had never seen Trenton), one to her grandparents, and one to the public.

"The main reason I'm doing this," she wrote in one letter, "is because even after my baby is found, I would not be a good mother with two jobs and full-time school (*Star-Banner*, Sept. 27, 2006)."

The note, with the phrase "after my baby is found," gave Marion County sheriff's investigators hope that Trenton was still alive. One year later they were speculating that she may have handed the child off to someone. One tipster reported seeing her meeting with a Hispanic or Asian couple south of town near a construction site, but that report led nowhere.

There were other clues, however. Investigators discovered her cell phone's signal on a tower near Ocala just hours before she reported him missing. Also, two employees at a Wendy's restaurant in Belleview reported seeing Trenton and his mother going through the drive-through. Belleview is a town between Leesburg and Ocala.

One of the witnesses thought she saw Melinda three times, however one of those times was also when Melinda's neighbor reported seeing her.

Sheriff's investigators also discovered that an Asian friend of Melinda's worked in Belleview near the restaurant. It was of no help, however. "The evidence doesn't suggest abduction. We continue to find no evidence of a handoff," said Leesburg Police Maj. Steve Rockefeller at a press conference (*Star-Banner*, Aug. 22, 2007). It left only one conclusion, but police weren't going to say it out loud.

Police released photos of some items in evidence, including items discarded after Trenton disappeared, including clothing, frozen foods, and vitamins.

Some people speculated that she was psychologically distancing herself from the child she would never see again. Rockefeller said Trenton had outgrown most of the clothing.

Melinda Duckett's grandparents told the *Star-Banner* the items were ruined by heavy fingerprint powder, but some things seemed like the kind of treasures that a mother would never part with, including a sonogram, a photo of Melinda and Trenton, a photo of Trenton as an infant, and a Mother's Day card that read, in part: "For You, Mommy, From Your Special Little Guy." There was also a freshly printed flier seeking information about his disappearance.

Melinda's grandparents believed her story of abduction. "I believe he's alive, and we pray for him every day," Bill Eubank said.

A one-year anniversary stretched to two, with candlelight vigils and pleas for information from Joshua, who set up a nonprofit center seeking tips.

Authorities meanwhile wondered why Melinda became a notary three weeks before Trenton's disappearance. Did she do it to stamp documents so she could slip him out of the country, perhaps to South Korea?

The lawsuit against Grace plodded along with motions, countermotions, and all the rest. In November 2010, both sides agreed to settle.

CNN established a $200,000 trust account to help find Trenton. Duckett's family issued an apology to CNN and absolved the network of any wrongdoing (*Star-Banner*, Nov. 19, 2010).

I can understand the shock and the hurt of the family, but I saw the interview on TV, and Grace did not do anything wrong. In fact, I have seen her act tougher. It would have been difficult to prove that Grace's questioning pushed Melinda over the edge. For one thing, there was no mention of the former prosecutor in any of the suicide notes. However, a jury trial is expensive and risky, and no one likes to take such an emotionally-charged tragic case to a jury, especially if the defendant is viewed as having deep pockets. As for show business, image is everything, and no one wants to come off looking insensitive.

None of this, of course, is any consolation for those who want to bring Trenton home. After seven years, does the family stop holding out hope?

"We trust God," Massero said. "It never leaves your mind. I get up at least three or four times a night to look out the window," she said in 2014.

"It was really devastating," Massero said. "What Melinda did was wrong but that was the last thing we wanted," she said of her suicide. She was the only one that knew what really happened to Trenton.

"I think she handed him off or sold him," Massero said.

It was also upsetting the way the Marion County Sheriff's Office and Leesburg Police were divided in their investigations. "It put us in the middle," she said.

The final straw, she said, was an individual's website that has spewed out hurtful lies.

"We don't even know this person," she said.

***

Georgia Crews slipped off a pair of cutoff shorts and put on a pair of jeans, but she didn't bother to put on any shoes. The tank top she was wearing was hand-sewn. If the 12-year-old, 80-pound blonde girl with a big smile had a care in the world, she didn't let on. It was a short walk to the convenience store where her mother worked in Montverde. The evening stroll wouldn't take long, and she didn't want to be late afterward for a visit to a neighbor's house where she planned to watch her favorite TV show.

She never made it to the store, never made it to the friend's house, and her name never made it into a detective's "Closed Case" file. It is one of several cases that keep detectives awake at night, staring at the ceiling and wondering "what did I miss?"

Montverde, on the shore of Lake Apopka in south Lake County, is still just a speck on a map. Its main feature is a topflight private school, Montverde Academy.

More than 100 people—almost everyone in town—searched for the missing girl on April 8, 1980. Sheriff Malcolm McCall's deputies were there, and so was the town marshal. The sheriff also asked the Orange County Sheriff's Office to lend its support with a helicopter.

Georgia's parents, Mike and Linda Crews, waited eight nerve-jangling days for the phone to ring with hopeful news. The phone finally rang on April 16, but it was the call they had been dreading. Her decomposing body had been found behind a Kmart 25 miles away in Fern Park in Seminole County.

She would be identified with dental records and a description of the colorful little top that her brother, Charles, saw her wearing when she walked out of the house for the last time.

She was also wearing a cross fashioned out of motorcycle parts. She did not own such a piece of jewelry, her mother said. Biker groups sometimes use a cross as a logo, police noted.

Linda Crews was devastated—and angry. She told the *Leesburg Commerial* more than a year later that she thought the new sheriff, Noel E. Griffin Jr., could have found her safe and sound had he been the sheriff at the time. Griffin reopened the investigation, but he had no luck.

In 1994, Ray Parker, the detective who worked the case for Seminole County, returned to Montverde hoping to get tips or clues. He and his partner, Herb Hartley, both retired, were lured back onto the trail with the report of a serial killer, but that didn't pan out. Like all conscientious cops with an unsolved case (Parker had two), he disliked unfinished business.

"Just the fact that it was a little girl that got murdered," Parker told *Orlando Sentinel* reporter Mary Murphy. "I think she deserves better than that. I *know* she deserves better than that (Oct. 8, 1994)."

He stood under an oak tree near Town Hall, smoked cigarettes, and talked to a few people. He received calls from others.

"We've come up with new things we'd never heard before," he told me (*Sentinel*, Oct. 21, 1994). None of the tidbits resulted in an arrest, however.

A key part of any investigation is eliminating suspects, no matter how disappointing. The biggest disappointment was eliminating a convicted killer in an Iowa prison, Albert Lara, who confessed to killing Georgia. The story didn't hold water.

In 2012, Seminole sheriff's investigators sighed, shook their heads, and plowed into the case again. There is nothing new in the case, said Detective Robert Jaynes. "There are a lot of holes in this thing that we're trying to patch. The cross is one of them."

There are no new tests that can be administered, he said. There is no evidence that she was sexually assaulted, so there is no DNA.

Her father identified footprints found in sandy soil as Georgia's. Nearby was a set of adult shoe prints, but hundreds of people searched for her. Did anybody stop the search and do forensics on all the prints? No, he said. The family lived on a dirt road, so footprints were not uncommon.

Jaynes understands Linda Crews' frustration with the Lake sheriff but adds, "I remember how things were done back then. I'm not saying it was right or wrong. It was just different."

"This is a very, very old case," Jaynes said, and noted that the case file is huge. One of the biggest problems is that at least three people were considered as possible suspects at one time and now they are dead.

Parker has also passed away but not the spirit that compelled him to leave his retirement easy chair in hopes of finding the monster that spilled innocent blood.

"I would love to solve this for the family," Jaynes said. "They've waited 32 years. "No 12-year-old deserves this."

***

Sometimes cases go unsolved because witnesses—150 or more, in one case—refuse to cooperate.

The comment, "I didn't see anything," was repeated over and over again after a street party in Leesburg was rudely interrupted by murder in September 1997. Yet, more than one person had to see something as three to six people were firing weapons when one stray bullet ripped into the chest of 20-year-old Tanza Bradley, causing her to fall face down onto the street littered with paper plates, broken bits of crack cocaine, bottles, and beer cans.

Many of the partygoers refused to even give their names because just being there would violate their probation. Others, including the shooters, took off before the cops could arrive. Adding to the investigator's collective headache was the fact that the area was a jurisdictional twilight zone that overlapped three different police department territories.

Police found two different kinds of shell casings—9 mm and .380-caliber—but some shooters may have fired revolvers, which do not eject shell casings. The other problem was that the shooting took place in front of the Blue Bird Café, a notorious illegal drug supermarket that had recently closed. Shell casings were not exactly a rare sight in the area bordered by woods, low-income housing complexes, and a few businesses.

The few who did report seeing a shooter were either lying or mistaken.

There was another reason for the crowd's reluctance to come forward. The people sponsoring the party were gang members known as "Da Front Boyz," police said. Flyers distributed all over town announced the bash. "Da Front Boyz Presents a Birthday Bash for Monkey Nutt, a.k.a. 'Ice Cream Man.'"

Police said a rival group of about three young men from nearby Wildwood crashed the party and started shooting.

Bradley, who worked at McDonald's and dreamed of becoming a nurse, started running but she couldn't outrun a bullet.

The first officer on the scene, from the town of Fruitland Park north of the shooting, found himself in the middle of an angry mob.

"She's dead! She's dead!" one woman yelled at the officer. "You haven't done anything for her!"

It was too late for Bradley, and with the refusal of people to come forward, it was too late for justice.

"It's a damn shame a beautiful young girl is killed like that, and people don't come forward because they're afraid of retaliation," Leesburg Police Chief Chuck Idell told me (*Sentinel,* May 24, 1998).

One man was arrested but prosecutors dropped the charges when one person admitted identifying him in hopes of getting out of jail. Another would-be witness could not identify him later in a police lineup.

Pointless, random, and lawless, the slaying angered Assistant State Attorney Bill Gross.

"An innocent girl's life has been taken. The murderer remains unpunished. It is such an incredibly stupid thing," he said.

***

Robert Wells, taking a break from his busy job as a grocery store meat cutter, decided to call home on March 15, 2000 to check on his wife and his 72-year-old mother-in-law, who were babysitting his niece and nephew.

He was surprised when his 4-year-old niece answered the telephone and told him that his wife, Esperanza, 42, was lying on the couch bleeding. Wells hung up and called 911.

Sheriff's deputies rushed to the old country house beneath big oaks, not knowing what to expect. Tarrytown, in south Sumter County, is in the middle of nowhere. The nearest town is Webster, home of a busy cattle auction site and a giant flea market that attracts thousands of tourists on Mondays.

What they found was horrifying. Both Esperanza Wells and her mother, Margarita Ruiz, 72, had been shot and stabbed. Fortunately, the 4- and 2-year-old children were unharmed. There was speculation that they may have hid under a bed during the slayings. "They may not have seen the whole thing, but they saw something," Sheriff's Lt. Gary Brannen said.

"They were a hard-working family. They lived a quiet, simple life," landlord and neighbor Dale Akins told the *Sentinel*, (March 16, 2000). Ruiz loved to care for her grandchildren, family members said.

There would be many more news stories written about the case. A year later, I wrote a one-word lead paragraph about the slayings: "Why?" (*Sentinel,* Feb. 12, 2001).

When I asked Brannen about the most likely scenario, he said: "There is no best theory."

The family had no enemies and had lived in the area for years. Nothing was taken. Could the killer have gone to the wrong house?

There was not much happening in the case despite a $25,000 reward being offered by the Sheriff's Office. Investigators tried everything, including searching the FBI data base for similar crimes.

Time moves on, even in a tiny town where time seems to be standing still. Eleven years passed before the sheriff's office got the break they had been hoping for.

The tip came from a frustrated, almost possessed prosecutor in Wisconsin, in the case of Bill P. Marquardt, who had had been ordered to spend 75 years in a mental institution following the slaying of his mother, Mary Jane. She had been shot with a 9 mm and stabbed.

Marquardt's father discovered his wife's body in the garage on March 13, 2000. Two days later, authorities obtained search warrant for a cabin in Eau Claire County, Wis.

At the cabin, officers found three dog carcasses and three dead rabbits. They also found bloodstains on carpeting, a quilt, and a tarp. Officers seized two rifles and a large knife with a sheath. Marquardt was charged in Eau Claire County with mistreatment of an animal resulting in the animal's death, and a warrant was issued for his arrest. On March 18, officers arrested Marquardt and found a folding knife and noticed blood spatters on Marquardt's shoes and jacket. Crime lab testing indicated that the DNA from blood on Marquardt's folding knife and on one of his shoes was a match for his mother's DNA, according to Wisconsin court records. The lab also discovered something else: DNA from two females who were related to one another.

There was a big legal hassle over technicalities in Wisconsin involving the search warrant, and whether Marquardt was mentally competent to stand trial. There were even issues over whether he could be forced to take drugs to make him competent. He wrote letters to a judge claiming to be Jesus, insisted that he had been mentioned by philosopher Nostradamus hundreds of years before he was born, and that he had discovered a cure for aging through the use of marijuana, rock music, and pornography.

Finally, a judge, following the district attorney's advice, sent him to the mental institution where he would be supervised for life (inhumane.org/data/BPMarquardt.htm).

Yet, this solution did not soothe the fighting spirit of the prosecutor, who wanted to take the case before a jury.

"I frankly believed I had a killer and a responsibility to keep him locked up," Jon Theisen said.

He decided that if he couldn't take Marquardt to trial, maybe someone else could. He knew that Marquardt fled the state after he killed his mother, eventually traveling to Florida. He began searching 400 newspaper websites looking for similar but unsolved murders. Finally, he clicked on the Florida Department of Law Enforcement's unsolved homicides page.

The blood, as it turned out, was a match for Wells and Ruiz.

Authorities believe he chose to unleash his madness at their house because it resembled his cottage getaway in Wisconsin.

"This prosecutor really made our day," Sumter County Sheriff Bill Farmer said at a news conference. "If he hadn't lost the one up there, we might never have solved two down here (*Sentinel*, June 14, 2006)."

Marquardt was convicted of two counts of first-degree murder and armed burglary in 2011. He has been sentenced to die by lethal injection on Florida's death row.

"Mr. Marquardt committed a crime in Florida, and he has now been subjected to the Floridian justice system," Theisen said. "I'm happy that he is not an issue for the Wisconsin courts ever again (*Sentinel* March 4, 2012)."

***

No parent should ever outlive their "baby."

That's what Alaphair Crosby called her 31-year-old daughter, Julia Croskey, so it was devastating when she found her dead in her home in Leesburg on Dec. 22, 1996. It was especially horrible because of the way the respiratory therapist died.

She had been shot in the back of the head. Her body was slumped over a bathtub, submerged in six inches of water.

She had been on the phone to her best friend when she said she had to hang up because someone was at the front door.

Police thought they had a rock-solid suspect. John Henry Jones, 29, was arrested and charged with forgery after cashing one of her checks for $650.

He denied killing her, saying he found the check outside her home. He knew her, but not that well, her friends said. He said she sometimes helped him out.

No one can put him inside the house at the time of the slaying, and police have no other evidence linking him to the crime.

Before he retired, Leesburg Police Capt. Jerry Gehlbach kept a stack of boxes in his office of the Croskey case and a few others that went unsolved during his many years as an investigator.

"They clutter up the office, but they are here for a reason. The purpose is to remind me every day of those cases.

"Sometimes at night you sit up and try to think if you've overlooked anything. If you're an investigator, you don't ever forget about these cases (*Sentinel*, Dec. 27, 1998)."

***

Brian Stephenson was a "happy-go-lucky" 21-year-old who still lived at home. He had a "fine mind," but was content with working the midnight shift at a convenience store, his dad said. A "night owl" by nature, he wasn't afraid of being hurt in a robbery because he would have helped carry the cash register for the thieves, Vernon Stephenson said (*Sentinel*, Feb.6, 1988).

So, it was a terrible shock to his family and friends that Brian was found shot to death behind the counter of the One Stop store on West Main Street in Leesburg in the early morning hours of July 24, 1987.

"At first I was bitter, but I'm not now. We just want justice to be done," Vernon said (*Sentinel*, Feb. 6, 1988). But it would be a long time coming—10 years—before he and wife, Jackie, would start seeing some justice.

It would come in the form of a jail tipster hoping for a get-out-of-jail-free moment. That's the kind of break that surprises normal law-abiding citizens but not police. The state of Florida has even printed up playing cards for prisoners with photos and unsolved crime information in hopes of getting tips. Prisoners with nothing to do but talk to each other hear all kinds of things.

Such a tip pointed to Lorenzo C. McCoy, who would have been 17 at the time of the robbery. Questioned in 1997, Lorenzo gave a statement to police and the State Attorney's Office. Defense Attorney Michael Graves said cops tricked him with a limited immunity offer. A judge ruled the statements were voluntary, however, and he prepared to go to trial.

He told police he was high on cocaine and eager for money to buy more when his companion, Namon McCoy, (no relation) convinced him that it would be easy to rob the store, which backed up to one of the worst neighborhoods in the city. He said the two walked to the back of the store where Namon handed him a pistol. He said he grabbed a soft drink out of the cooler and Namon grabbed some candy.

"So, I put the soda up and this kid said '66 cents.'

"I said, 'This is a robbery. It's a robbery.' And the gun was like so, the bare thing was like so raggedy and I'm pointin' it at this man, and he got his hands up, and he say [sic] 'Just get what you want.'"

He said bullets began falling out of the cylinder of the .22-caliber pistol. He said when he tried to move the cylinder up the gun went off.

He said the bullet struck Stephenson in the shoulder. He said when he reached across the counter with the gun it went off again.

"Namon just was grabbing the money. He didn't think of nothing. We started (inaudible) running. We ran and ran. We threw the gun in this water. In this lake that I had grew up around. And I was so scared. I wanted to go back and check on this man because I used to see him all the time. He was nice. And he say we couldn't. We couldn't go back. And all that high on cocaine. I couldn't even smoke no more. I was so, so, so, so, so scared ...."

It was the soft drink container that ultimately sealed the deal. His fingerprints were on it, but detectives were afraid that he might say he had touched the container long before the robbery but put it down and walked out of the store without committing any crime. At first, he denied buying or attempting to buy anything and said he was in the store earlier, but a cash register receipt showed that the soft drink was the last item that Stephenson rang up that morning before he died.

There was another problem, too. The jail tipster committed suicide. Fortunately, Lorenzo's genuine remorse led him to confess, prosecutors said.

"When you all came to me today, man, it was like I wanted to just to tell it all."

Lorenzo said he apologized to Stephenson but the clerk's last words haunted him.

"He looked in my eyes. He kept looking in my eyes and he just ... (inaudible) 'God. God loves you.'"

Medical examiners said such a conversation was not possible because of the kinds of injuries that Stephenson had sustained, which raises several questions. Was he lying? If so, why? Did he imagine it? Was he hallucinating, possibly because of the drugs? Or was it a supernatural occurrence? One thing is for sure. Unlike so many defendants, who claim they are genuinely remorseful, Lorenzo was truly guilt-stricken.

A year later, he pleaded guilty to avoid a death sentence in exchange for two life sentences.

"I'm sorry that his life ended this way," he said in court in a written letter to Stephenson's parents.

"Every night and day, I always pray that somehow you could except [sic] my apology. An [sic] if you could, it would mean the world to me. But if you [sic] not ready, I understand. But I hope you don't mind if I leave it in God's hand."

Namon McCoy, in prison in an unrelated case, at first denied any involvement but later broke down and admitted to being the lookout man.

It was a relief to the family. "We are very grateful, especially to Leesburg Capt. Jerry Gehlbach, who stayed with the case for years and kept us informed of what was going on," he told me in an interview. A lot of police departments would not have stayed with it (*Sentinel*, March 3, 1999)."

Chapter 7

Killer cop

Teresa Mae McAbee was 11 when she left her home to go to a convenience store to buy a pencil for her fifth-grade schoolwork. It was late—about 10 p.m. on May 11, 1987—but it was a quick errand and the store in the tiny south Lake County town was only about 400 yards away.

After buying the pencil she talked to a 16-year-old Mexican boy and the town's rookie police officer who happened to see them talking together. The cop told her she needed to be home by 10:30 p.m., because it was the curfew time for children.

What happened next will forever be draped in tragedy and embroiled in controversy, because Teresa never again burst through the front door of her home, hugged her mother, or laughed and played with other children on the school playground.

A fisherman discovered her body floating face down in a lake the next morning; her new pencil was snapped in two and tossed onto the ground nearby.

Her previously innocent body would give up terrible secrets to the medical examiner. She had been raped, choked, and drowned. Her panties were stained with blood and a single loose pubic hair was found on the fabric.

The 1,600 townspeople of Mascotte were heart-broken and sickened, and when investigators announced an arrest, they were shocked. The suspect was the cop.

James Duckett repeatedly denied harming the girl.

"I want to go home," he told *Sentinel* reporter Elizabeth Wasserman during a break in his trial a year later. "I got family at home. I didn't do what they said I did (May 6, 1988)."

He seemed to be the most unlikely suspect. Married with two young sons, Duckett had always wanted to be a police officer, but family obligations forced him to work at a phosphate plant in neighboring Polk County. But at the age of 29, when he was laid off during an economic downturn, he went for his dream job.

Friends and family were convinced that the easy-going "aw shucks" country guy was innocent, so they raised money for his household expenses and $50,000 to hire veteran defense attorney Jack Edmund.

"We're behind Jimmy a hundred percent," said Frances Jones, who watched Duckett grow up in the rural Sumter County community of Croom-a-Coochee (*Sentinel,* April 24, 1988).

"I've known him since he was 9," said Eva Mason. "My kids grew up with him. He's like my own son, and I just know the things they are saying about him are lies. They've got the wrong man. He's being used for a patsy, a scapegoat."

It was a circumstantial case but there were some disturbing clues, and when prosecutors added a handful of controversial witnesses it became explosive.

Mascotte Police Chief Mike Brady immediately called the Lake County Sheriff Office for assistance. His tiny police department did not have the manpower or the expertise to handle such a case.

Suspicion fell on Duckett almost immediately. Sheriff's Sgt. Chuck Johnson noted in his report that he had "a feeling" that Duckett was "somehow involved." Duckett seemed "somewhat nervous," was "not curious about the death" and told "a rehearsed-sounding story (*Sentinel*, April 24, 1988)."

Former sheriff's investigator Rocky Harris would later remark: "He was a rookie police officer, and for a rookie police officer, his lack of concern about a missing child was overwhelming (*Sentinel*, Dec. 18, 1997)."

Gut feelings are not enough for a conviction, but it added to the circumstantial evidence.

At about 11 p.m. that night, the girl's mother, Dorothy McAbee, walked to the store looking for Teresa. Then, for about the next hour, she and her sister drove around looking for the child. Finally, they drove to the nearby town of Groveland and went to the town's police station to report Teresa's disappearance. Groveland police officers called Mascotte and told her to go to the police station there. Once there, she waited 15 to 20 minutes for Duckett to show up.

She filed a missing person's report with Duckett, who told her that he had talked to her at the store. He went to the mother's house to get a picture and called his chief to say he was going to make flyers. He said he didn't need any help. His chief ordered him "to spend the rest of the night beating the streets looking for that girl. That's your priority (*Sentinel*, April 28, 1988)."

Duckett made flyers and went to the convenience store but then told the clerk not to post the flyer because it was not a good photo of the girl. He said he would return but never did, though he did post flyers at two other stores.

The clerk at one store said the officer usually came by the store every 45 minutes to an hour but on this night, he did not return until later when he came back with a flyer.

There was no activity on his patrol car radio from 10:50 p.m. to 12:10 a.m. At 1:15 a.m. he went to the Mexican boy's uncle's house to question him. At 3 a.m., he returned to the mother's house.

"By 5 a.m., he was out there again running radar and writing tickets," Assistant State Attorney Steve Hurm would later say in his statement to the jury. This, despite explicit orders to make the search his priority.

Even more damning was the fact that Teresa's fingerprints were found on the hood of the patrol car. She had apparently been sitting on the hood facing forward. Duckett's prints were comingled with hers. Duckett said she had not sat on the hood. The Mexican youth and his uncle said they saw Duckett put Teresa in the front seat of the car while still parked at the Circle K.

Another crucial bit of evidence came from a sheriff's evidence investigator. He noted what he said were unusual looking tire treads near the lake. Those treads seemed to match those of Duckett's patrol car. Sure enough, a local tire dealer would testify at the trial that the Goodyear Eagles were designed for Northern roads. He had received them accidentally and had sold just two sets in nine years—both to the Mascotte Police Department.

Duckett said he had not driven to the lake that night. However, evidence showed the tire impressions were made by driving into a mud hole. There was no evidence that Duckett had washed the car. Nor was any blood found on the car. His wife and a convenience store clerk also testified that his uniform was clean. A defense expert would testify that dragging the girl's body up a muddy embankment would have resulted in Duckett being disheveled.

Brady would later complain that the sheriff's technician had taken casts of the tires on a patrol car outside of the roped-off crime scene area where police cars were parked. Investigators would argue that it didn't matter. Duckett had keys to both cars.

The hair would spark a major controversy. It could not be tested for DNA because there was no root. However, FBI fiber expert Mike Malone would testify that the hair "had exactly the same characteristics" as 20 samples taken from Duckett (*Sentinel*, April 30, 1988)."

Investigators had first sent hair samples to the Florida Department of Law Enforcement. The state crime lab reported that 28 of 30 hairs were not consistent with Duckett's but two were similar. The state lab asked for more hair samples.

The sheriff's office then sent the 30 hairs to a privately-owned genetics testing facility, Lifecodes Corp. Because there was no root, the lab could not make a determination. All 30 hairs were destroyed in the tests.

Investigators then sent 40 to 50 new hair samples from Duckett to the Federal Bureau of Investigation, which prompted Edmund to claim that the state was shopping for an expert until they could get the results they wanted.

Malone's findings and the credibility of the FBI lab itself would later come under fire in an appeal when a U.S. Justice Department Inspector General's report in 1997 concluded that FBI analysts hyped evidence and jumped to conclusions to bolster the case against some defendants in major cases, including the Oklahoma City courthouse bombing.

"We found … significant instances of testimonial errors, substandard analytical work and deficient practices," the report said (*Dallas Morning News*, April 16, 1997).

An inspector general's report called out Malone in its report on the bribery trial of former federal Judge Alcee Hastings. Malone "testified falsely" and made "misleading" statements about a torn leather strap during that trial, the report claimed *(Sentinel*, Oct. 28, 1998).

A deputy assistant director of the FBI lab said Malone had never been disciplined and no questions had ever been raised about his work with hair. He was transferred to another office where he became a field officer. His work included famous cases like the Jeffrey MacDonald murders, in which a former Green Beret soldier was convicted of killing his wife and two children. The case was the subject of a best-seller and movie, *Fatal Vision*.

MacDonald's lawyers claimed the FBI withheld crucial information, but an appeal court upheld the conviction.

Seizing upon the report, Wells called Edmund to the stand at a hearing in October 1998, where he called Malone "a liar." Assistant State Attorney Donald Scaglione asked Edmund why he did not call his own hair expert. "If they had someone who could say it wasn't Duckett's hair, they would have presented them," the prosecutor noted (*Sentinel*, Oct. 28, 1998).

The Florida Supreme Court weighed in on the hair evidence in a 2005 ruling.

"The circuit court concluded that '[t]he attack upon Agent Malone of the FBI is unfounded and without merit.' The conclusion is supported by the record. At the evidentiary hearing it was established that Malone had received proficiency tests in the examination of hair and fiber, and no court has refused to recognize him as an expert. On direct appeal, we discussed Malone's credibility. 'Duckett's counsel extensively challenged Malone's credibility during the cross-examination of Malone and during the testimony of a Florida Department of Law Enforcement expert on hair analysis. It is not our responsibility to reweigh that evidence. The expert's credibility was resolved by the jury.'"

Wells continued her appeals, including complaining about the state's handling of the hair evidence. She ended up hiring an expert to review Malone's work in the Duckett case. Among the expert's concerns was Malone's testimony that there was "a very high degree of probability" that the hair was from Duckett. In a five-page report to Wells, the expert said Malone's statement overstated or exaggerated the accuracy of the test.

But in a ruling on Nov. 6, 2012, Circuit Judge William G. Law pointed out that Malone testified that the hair evidence was not as precise as a fingerprint, nor could he say that the hair might have come only from Duckett.

"Given what the jury heard, there is no need for an evidentiary hearing to determine whether forensic examiners in 1988 would describe hair analysis as being "probable, highly probable, or a very high degree of probability," Law wrote in his order.

Hair evidence aside, there was also damaging, controversial witness testimony.

Under Florida law, prosecutors may sometimes present evidence of a defendant's prior acts—if they are closely related. It is called the Williams Rule and judges are leery of it. It is the kind of thing that an appeal court might use to overturn a conviction. Defense attorneys hate it because they say all it does is prejudice the jury. They insist, and judges usually agree, that such information should be kept from juries.

However, Circuit Judge Jerry Lockett allowed prosecutors to present the testimony of three young women. They testified that Duckett tried to have sex with them in his patrol car.

One woman, described in Supreme Court records as "a petite 19-year-old," testified that she had an unwelcome encounter with him in his patrol car in February 1987. She said she was looking for her boyfriend. He said he was looking for the woman's boyfriend, too. She said he put his arm on her shoulder and tried to kiss her. She rebuffed the advance and got out of the car.

A second woman, described as "a petite 18-year-old," said he picked her up in his patrol car as she was walking along a road on May 1, 1987. She said he took her to a remote area in an orange grove, put his hand on her breast, and tried to kiss her. When she balked, he drove her to the place where she wanted to go and left.

The third woman, "a petite 17-year-old," said she voluntarily met him twice when he was on patrol, once in

March 1987 and again in either April or May and performed oral sex on him.

The Florida Supreme Court ruled that the testimony basically met the requirements of the Williams Rule. However, the third woman's testimony was different because she voluntarily participated in a sex act.

Duckett denied all three accounts by the women. Asked by the *Sentinel* if he thought they were lying, he said: "As far as I'm concerned, they did (May 6, 1988)."

The courts' rulings were questionable. Were the alleged encounters with the women really similar to rape and murder? Teresa was only 11 and a virgin. There's a huge difference between that 18, 19, and 17-year-olds. Nor were they raped. Testimony, in fact, indicated that he halted his advances on the two women immediately when they told him to stop.

But the strangest, most controversial, and in some ways most damaging testimony, came from a 16-year-old girl who claimed to have seen Duckett drive off from the store with a child in his patrol car.

Gwen Gurley testified that she went to the store with two other girls that night. She said she saw Duckett, a girl she later identified as Teresa, and some "Spanish boys." Duckett called them over and told them to go home because of the curfew. Instead of going home, however, Gurley said she said she hid on a path near the store. Duckett left about a "minute later," she said. She said she walked back to the store to use the phone. Teresa was in the store. Gwen said she saw the patrol car near the trash bin with its headlights off. Duckett called to Teresa and said, "Come here." Gwen said she hid in the bushes. She said she heard a car door shut. When she looked, she could not see Teresa. She said when the car backed away, she could see the heads of two people in the car. She said one was "a little person," according to court records.

During cross-examination, Edmund asked her why she waited until much later to come forward.

"I didn't realize it was the same girl until October," she said.

Duckett took the stand to tell his side of the story.

"I would not hurt that little girl (*Sentinel*, May 7, 1988)," he said.

He denied driving off with her in his patrol car.

"She walked down to the street, turned the corner, and that's the last I saw of her," he testified.

As for Teresa's fingerprints being on the hood of the car, he said: "It's my understanding from police work that you only have to touch something for a minute to make a print. If she jumped up there and the hood was hot, she must have jumped right down."

Gurley would later recant. In a sworn statement to Duckett's appeal team in 1992, she wrote: "I never saw a Mascotte patrol car or a police officer anywhere near the Circle K parking lot."

But by 1997 Gurley was under a lot of pressure, and she didn't like it. In opening remarks to Judge Lockett in a post-conviction relief hearing, Wells said: "Miss Gurley said to me, 'I will go to jail if I change my testimony (*Sentinel,* Oct. 30, 1997).'"

Wells said Gurley told her that prosecutor Scaglione threatened her with prison. She said Gurley had already changed her story "at least four times" in sworn statements. She said Gurley told her story originally to get favorable treatment in jail, where she was being held on grand theft charges.

In 1997, Florida had just passed a new law extending the statute of limitations for perjury in death cases. Wells asked Lockett to rule the new law unconstitutional.

In an unusual move, Lockett ordered the public defender's office to provide counsel for Gurley, and she invoked her right not to incriminate herself.

"So frustrating!" Wells exclaimed after the hearing (*Sentinel,* Oct. 31, 1997).

Scaglione told reporters he was surprised when she pleaded the Fifth. Wells, apparently, was not. Despite the setback, she presented a witness who was supposed to testify for the prosecution in the 1988 trial.

Kimberly Vargas said she saw Teresa walk around the corner of the store headed toward her home and saw Duckett ride off in his patrol car in a different direction.

Another witness, Richard Richards, said he was doing his laundry when he saw Teresa get into a blue car.

Gurley's friend, Vickie Davis, testified that they only went to the store once—not twice—like Gurley testified, but Gwen begged her to go along with her story. "Agree with what I say. Help me get out of prison."

Gurley's sister, Mary, testified that a sheriff's investigator gave Gwen a script to memorize. She said her sister told her that deputies would let her out of jail and cover her head with a jacket in the back of a patrol car so she could visit her mother and her boyfriend.

Prosecutors said Gurley was not coerced. Steve Hurm argued that her testimony was "material" but not critical (*Sentinel,* Dec. 18, 1997).

The Supreme Court in 2005 said new testimony by Gurley would not make any difference. It is doubtful she would say anything differently, if she said anything at all. The court also noted that recanted testimony is "exceedingly unreliable."

If nothing else, it gives lawyers a chance to ask their all-time favorite question in court: "Were you lying then, or are you lying now?"

Still, it is disconcerting to think that such a witness might play a role in a death penalty trial. What impact, if any, did her testimony have on the jury? What impact did the stories of the three women have on the jury? It really comes down to the individuals who served on the jury. Jurors, especially back then, tended to be conservative and lean toward believing law enforcement officers. They were registered voters and not just random holders of a driver's license like they are now. Gender also plays a role, of course.

I believe that courts and cops—at least the ones I covered in Central Florida—generally do a good job, but even I began to have some questions about this case.

Then, there was the FBI expert and the accusations surrounding the FBI lab.

But if Duckett had any credibility he may have lost it when he passed on a chance for experts to examine a semen stain on Teresa's jeans for traces of DNA.

Genetic evidence helps prosecutors convict defendants, but it also frees people who are wrongly accused. The Innocence Project, founded in 1992, has exonerated more than 200 people, some of whom were on death row.

The Florida Supreme Court on March 21, 2003, ordered the trial court to see if any DNA tests could be performed on any evidence. However, no test was performed on the semen sample because it would destroy the sample.

In 2004, Wells said Duckett no longer wanted the test to be performed.

"New methods of DNA testing are in the process of being developed that will provide a greater likelihood of success," she wrote in a memo to Judge Law. "The prudent course would be to wait until newer, more reliable methods of DNA testing become available."

Some legal observers immediately called it a ploy, a delaying tactic to keep Duckett alive.

"I am hard pressed to believe anyone would execute him with this issue hanging," said Lockett, who by this time was retired. "Remember how long it took him to ask for this. It is not news to James Duckett that the state of DNA testing is what it is. All of a sudden at the last minute he decides the state of the testing is not sufficient. I think this has been the plan from the start (*Sentinel,* Jan. 17, 2004)."

Wells said it was not a ploy. Duckett doesn't want to stay alive to live on death row, she said. He wants to be exonerated.

"Inconclusive is a win for the state, not a win for us," she said. "Conclusive is the only win for us."

Judge Law's order noted that a technician deduced that not only would the sample be destroyed but it would not produce a DNA profile. He ordered that the test not be performed but said the court was not going to allow Duckett "the right or privilege to pursue testing ... at a later date. That is a matter more appropriately addressed by the Florida Supreme Court (*Sentinel*, Feb. 7, 2004)."

Law had acknowledged earlier that it was a gamble on Duckett's part.

"This might have been their one chance to do this. Whether they will be able to resurrect that chance in the future is debatable."

It is not the only dark cloud hanging over Duckett. Some authorities in Polk County believe Duckett is a suspect in the slaying of a young girl there.

A former homicide investigator from Miami-Dade once championed Duckett's claim of innocence, but now believes he tried to fake an alibi in Teresa's slaying.

Duckett insists he is not guilty.

As for Teresa's mother, Dorothy McAbee, "I just want justice for my daughter. That's what I want. After 26 years I'm tired. I don't think I'll ever have closure 'cause he's not going to admit to it (CNN, *Death Row Stories*, March 31, 2014)."

Chapter 8

Mother Nature runs amok

"Everybody talks about the weather, but nobody does anything about it" – **Mark Twain (Quotationsbook.com)**

On Feb. 2, 2007, "Groundhog Day," I was still trying to shake the sleep cobwebs out of my head around 7 a.m. when my wife called for me to come see what was on TV.

The little town of Lady Lake and surrounding areas had been ripped apart by a deadly tornado. After a quick call to my boss at the *Ocala Star-Banner*, I was in and out of the shower in minutes, throwing on some clothes, and rushing to an area 10 miles away. I had stayed up late watching live TV coverage of a stormfront but I went to bed when nothing materialized. Afterward, around 3 a.m., the tornado struck.

In my rush to get to the scene, I hadn't noticed that the gas tank on my car was nearly empty. I found a gas station still standing but there was no power to run the pumps.

My little problems were nothing, however, compared to those of the shell-shocked residents, many of whom had lost their homes, suffered injuries, or were dead or missing. Twenty-one people died, ranging from the very young to the very old. Many were asleep in mobile homes and didn't realize they were in danger until it was too late.

The highway going into town was clogged with police, fire, and rescue vehicles from surrounding areas, so it took a few minutes to take in the full scope of the tragedy. Oak trees that had lined the road were down or had their tops chopped off like grass cut by a lawn mower with a dull blade. Across the highway, all that remained of the large Lady Lake Church of God was scattered pieces of metal and a concrete slab. Two women found the big pulpit Bible. A handful of men carried away the heavily damaged wooden cross.

The church had just finished a series of revivals. "I believe we made the devil mad," said church member Paula Countryman (*Star-Banner*, Feb. 3, 2007).

The Rev. Larry Lynn was praying and comforting the shaken people he encountered along the highway.

I had covered a twister that killed one person and seriously injured seven others in nearby Summerfield in 1995, but the scope of this disaster was overwhelming. Helicopters filled the sky, the wailing of sirens was never ending, and so was the sound of chain saws, cranes, trucks, and recovery teams shouting instructions.

The stuff of everyday life was scattered across the landscape. Bits of candy, clothing, Christmas decorations, and books were mixed with building debris.

Toppled trees crushed cars and rooftops. Big pine trees were snapped like match sticks.

Huge pieces of metal were hanging from tree limbs, as if placed there by a deranged Christmas tree-decorating giant. Power lines were down everywhere.

Some mobile homes had been blown off their foundations and rolled across the ground. Others were pinched in half by fallen trees, while some looked as if they had been smashed by a giant fist. A slab was all that was left of a shed, that, and an undamaged lawn tractor.

There was a strange smell in the air—a mixture of pine resin, garbage, mud, sewage, blood and death.

Chief Photographer Alan Youngblood found me trying to walk past a police roadblock (they were turning away cars). He picked me up in his vehicle. After going around the back way, we spotted a brick home that had been completely destroyed. The owner was sitting on a chair in the middle of the rubble.

His story was like so many others. The first thing he knew of the trouble was his wife shouting from another room. By this time, the roof was gone, rain was blowing in his face, and he was flying on his mattress. His wife was injured but he dug her out from beneath a pile of bricks.

In a pasture across the road, big pieces of wadded up metal strips from ruined mobile homes dotted the landscape like gum wrappers in a ballpark parking lot.

Linda Blickenstaff, 66, of Johnson City, Tenn., told a story that would be repeated by others.

"I was in the bed, and I heard terrible thunder and lightning. It woke me up. I could hear a roaring sound."

She said she called her dog, Little Bit, and they ran out of the bedroom just as the roof and walls of her mobile home blew out. She hit the living room floor behind the couch and stretched out across the dog to protect it.

She could have cried over losing her home. Instead, she said: "God was merciful (*Star-Banner*, Feb. 3, 2007)."

There was widespread damage in the nearby Villages retirement community—mostly to roofs—but no deaths or serious injuries. One man, who had set his garbage out for pick up, received a call from someone in DeLand, 40 miles away, saying his trash had been found in that town. Weather experts believe the winds reached speeds of 200 mph, damaging 1,500 homes, and cutting power to tens of thousands of homes and businesses.

Eight people died in Lady Lake and 13 others were killed in a forest area called Lake Mack. Like Lady Lake, tragedy sometimes mixed with heroism.

Becky Nolan was jerked out of a sound sleep when her husband began screaming and dragging her out of bed. William, 38, shouted for her to grab their 11-year-old son, Edwin.

"I heard him yell, 'I got [7-year-old] Jake.' That was the last thing he ever said to me."

The boy and his dad were found a long way from the trailer, both dead.

"He was being a man. He was taking care of his baby," she said, tears rolling down her cheeks (*Star-Banner*, Dec.30, 2007).

Back in Lady Lake, the only time it got quiet was when firefighters carried a shroud-covered body out from the rubble. The quiet seemed strange but appropriate. Unfortunately, there would be too many moments like it.

Two days after the storm destroyed his church, Rev. Lynn held a Sunday morning service in the shadow of piles of debris. There was a lot to be thankful for, he said. The twister could have struck while the church was full of people, killing and injuring the churchgoers.

Months later, he was among the recipients of the 2007 volunteer Points of Light Award, established by former Gov. Jeb Bush.

"We consider this whole thing an honor," he said while attending a reception held by then-Gov. Charlie Crist. "It comes in an awful package, but it was a gift. We've received help from people around the world. We've been able to minister to a lot of people that we wouldn't have been able to minister to otherwise (*Star-Banner*, Jan. 21, 2008)."

***

There's a great line in Bogie and Bacall's movie, *Key Largo*, describing hurricanes. "The wind blows so hard the ocean gets up on its hind legs and walks across the land."

It's true, even if it is in a movie. It's also true that Florida is asking for trouble, sticking out like the peninsula that it is, between the Atlantic and the Gulf of Mexico. It's bad enough that rising hot air off the land collides with cool sea breezes, making it the lightning capital of the country, but hurricanes ....

They're the stuff of legend—terrible legend. A Labor Day hurricane in 1935 smashed into the Florida Keys and then made its way up to South Florida killing 400 people.

That was the worst storm in state history until Hurricane Andrew blew down thousands of homes in 1992, causing $26 billion in damages and killing more than 60 people in South Florida.

Hurricanes don't just strike Florida, of course. In 1984, I was the news editor at the Wilmington, N.C., *Star-News* and bracing for Hurricane Diana. I sent my wife, three children, and a thoroughly miserable cat, to a motel in Charlotte several miles away.

Unfortunately, the storm waddled around offshore for days before finally blasting its way on shore as a Category 2 hurricane on Sept. 13.

We managed to put out every edition every day and we were updating a final when the storm made landfall and snuffed out electrical power.

The company had tested its emergency generator every day leading up to the time when we really needed it. Apparently, however, that testing consumed all of the fuel. Fortunately, I brought a camping lantern, sleeping bag, food, and other necessities. I had been to the rodeo before. My first hurricane was in 1968 in Jacksonville, Fla., but it turned out to be a lightweight and a silly excuse to party.

I had seen some more serious storms, including typhoons in Okinawa, Japan. High winds in the Pacific can pick up gritty volcanic ash and sandblast a car right down to the bare metal. I had dodged a potential killer, Hurricane Camille, in 1969, while stationed in the Air Force at Panama City, Fla.

The military's response was, "We've got to get these planes out of here. Stanfield, you stay here."

The storm was initially predicted to hit the Florida Panhandle. At the last moment, it curved toward the Mississippi Gulf Coast with winds of up to 190 mph. Before it was over, it claimed more than 250 lives, including people in the Caribbean, and caused more than $8 billion in damages. Had the murderous storm hit Panama City instead of Mississippi we might have been about six feet under water.

In Okinawa, the Air Force said, "We've got to get these planes out of here. Stanfield, you stay here." The squadron took off for South Korea.

I was beginning to get a complex. Later, when I was sent to Korea, I found myself in some danger of getting shot by our own jumpy guards while performing predawn preflight inspections. I was beginning to think the Air Force was out to get me.

Storms do strange things to people—like make them lose their minds. With Hurricane Diana howling at 115 mph outside the windowless, brick building, I was startled by two things. First, it sounded as if the roof was going to be peeled off like a can of sardines. At times the building creaked and groaned like a ship at sea. Then, the back door blew open.

"I was almost T-boned by a sign!" shouted the chief photographer as he and a reporter dragged an ice chest full of beer into the newsroom.

Great, I thought. Not only was there a smattering of *Star-News* employees in the newsroom that night, but there were reporters from other newspapers, too. Alcohol in the newsroom is never a good idea, especially in an emergency when you have to keep your wits, but I had to admire the initiative and the desire to keep everyone's spirits up.

"OK," I said, "but you make sure to tell Mr. *Miami Herald* over there that *no one* is actually drinking any beer in the newsroom. I had seen the look in the *Herald* reporter's eyes. He was bored and looking for a color story. There was no reason to worry, however. There wasn't enough beer to hurt anything. It would have taken a tanker truck full to alter the consciousness of even a small group of journalists. Of course, drinking and journalism is cliché. Some of us, however, stop imbibing when we realized that we can't afford to lose any more brain cells.

Visiting reporters from the *Charlotte Observer* were even sillier. When the regular office phones died, they braved crossing the street to use a pay phone, not realizing that we had a secure line to the Associated Press.

With nothing to do until the winds subsided, I slept on the floor by the copy desk. At daybreak, I was awakened by a phone call from the president of the New York Times Co.

"Are you all OK?" he asked.

I assured him that we were and that the building was still standing. I was impressed. He was first concerned about the people, not the property. For the record, no one said "Stanfield, you stay here." I volunteered for this one.

With the dawn came the reporters, photographers, and other editors. I went home for a while.

Proud of the work that we had done, especially in not missing any deadlines, I stopped by a convenience store and spotted a newspaper in a coin box. It was dated days earlier. The circulation people might just as well have tossed newspapers into the air from the loading dock. Depressed, I went home to an empty but undamaged house.

At least we had the story right. The BBC reported that the whole city was under water. It was not true, but there was flooding, especially in a neighboring county where the storm dumped 14 inches of water in a matter of a few hours.

***

The year 2004 brought four major hurricanes to Florida from the middle of August to late September.

We only covered three at the *Star-Banner,* and one of those only briefly. But by the time the last gust died down I was exhausted. You don't realize how tiring it is to stand up to hurricane winds until you sit down—or fall down. Hurricane winds are 74 mph and higher. By the time winds passed the coast and hit inland counties they had diminished to tropical storm wind force. Strong tropical winds start at 58 mph, but gusts can reach 100 mph or more.

Hurricanes are sneaky. Forecasters used to draw nice, neat little lines on maps, but that was misleading. Storm paths are unpredictable and clobber a wide area. Forecasters started drawing big blobs called "the cone of uncertainty," or as I jokingly liked to call them, "ice cream cones of death."

Hurricane Charley fooled the experts. At first, it looked as if it was heading toward the Tampa area, a massive disaster in the making for such a huge metropolitan area. Instead, it hit the less populated area of Punta Gorda to the southwest, but it intensified rapidly.

Photographer Cindy Skopp and I drove to south Lake County, several miles from the Ocala office, because it was supposed to be the point of the spear for Central Florida. It clipped just a corner of Lake County, however, and slammed into Orange County and the Orlando area, causing millions of dollars' worth of property damage.

Cindy raised her arms inside the SUV and went "*woo hoo,*" like she was on a roller coaster, as the wind rocked the heavy vehicle. A towering sign at a nearby a car dealership shattered, showering the highway with glass and shards of plastic.

The only business that was open was a drug store. The only people inside were the pharmacist and one customer, who crouched down behind a shelf and was babbling nonsense.

"Why didn't you interview him?" Cindy asked.

"Because he was crazy," I said.

Then again, who else but lunatics and journalists would be out in such a storm?

We did go to a school that had been turned into an emergency shelter and got everything we needed, including a well-intentioned effort by a volunteer who tried to keep us from going back out in the storm.

That was just a warmup, however.

Then there was Hurricane Frances and Hurricane Jeanne. We arranged to hunker down at Lake County's Emergency Operations Center for those two storms. Lake County now has a modern emergency center, with the latest communications gear, but at that time, officials were forced to gather in the county administration building. Built in the 1960s as a courthouse, it is round and modern looking, clashing dramatically with the historic courthouse next door, and the new courthouse, which looks like a modern hospital.

Before it was over, the open lobby of the round building would be evacuated because the dome was leaking, and it was feared that the wind might blow the lid off.

"I hope you're not the kind that doesn't want to go out into the storm," Cindy said. I assured her that I was as big a fool as anyone, though we tried to pick our spots and did our best not to be caught by darkness. It's harder to dodge tree limbs, flying signs, and sparking power lines when you can't see them. Besides, traffic lights were out, and homes and businesses were blacked out, too.

The storms pulverized some of the mobile homes nestled among cypress trees on the lakefront near the emergency center. It looked as if a giant had reached down and either flipped them on their sides or picked them up and smashed them into the other houses. Fortunately, no one was home. The same was true for a mobile home park in the southern end of the county, which was flooded.

But in one park, I caught sight of a golf cart zipping between mobile homes. A man doing reconnaissance for the other residents was making the rounds when we tracked him down.

Residents were wisely riding out the storm in the park's recreation hall, which was a sturdy concrete block building. There, we found people trying not to get on each other's nerves.

We were viewed as a novelty, welcomed as the drowned rats that we were, and graciously given hot coffee (we would have killed for some at this point). The wind, which had died down, began picking up again. People were putting on their best front, but they soon began staring out the window as the wind clawed the roof off a mobile home across the street. These were not wealthy people. They were retirees with small savings who had come to Florida to live out the dream that suddenly had become a nightmare.

Cindy's camera clicked frenetically in those days and the images are just as indelible in my mind. There was, for example, the man sitting in his flooded front yard, tethered to the inside of his home by a long, plastic oxygen hose. He was sick and weak but was doing what he could, using a stick to try and steer debris away from a storm drain to keep it from being clogged.

There was also the 80-something-year-old woman whose tiny wooden house was destroyed by a big tree that fell on the roof. Inside, branches and the tree trunk were sticking through the ceiling. She had lived in the house for more than 50 years and now had to leave it. Her family was there, gathering up all her meager possessions. Out front, she showed me the flowers she had planted. She was wearing her game face, saying it was good that she was moving to a better place. Maybe it was, but she would never water those flowers again, and the little rooms that housed so many memories of her late husband, her children and grandchildren, would soon become faded dreams and splinters.

It wasn't how she pictured her golden years.

One Sunday morning, we stumbled onto a small crowd at a church. Inside, the fellowship hall was teeming with energy as children played and Spanish-speaking people chatted with each other. The church had opened the building as a shelter. Soon, the group's pastor gathered everyone together for a service, a guitar was brought out and familiar hymns were sung in a beautiful but unfamiliar language to us.

Cindy was taking pictures in the darkened room when the pastor stopped and asked the group to pray for our safety in covering the storm. As he introduced us, everyone shined their flashlights on Cindy, who blushed at the attention. After the prayer, we went on our way, grateful for the blessing. It was then, I noticed, that for some reason, the script on my cell phone was now in Spanish.

We would see the group's prayers play out in a dramatic fashion. When the winds finally died down and we were making our final stop we went to another mobile home park to talk with residents huddled in their recreation hall. Cindy excused herself and went to the car to get some more gear when a giant tree limb gave way and crashed to the ground near where she was standing. A few feet closer and she would have been a goner.

Of course, we were not the only ones covering the story. The paper was filled with stories of millions of dollars' worth of damage, deaths, and injuries. One of the surprising, happy results was the look on grateful readers' faces as they learned about the availability of water and ice, relief tents, shelters, food, and other necessities—facts that they could not glean from TV, since they were without power.

News matters, and news can have a positive influence on a community. Long after the storm, people could read about how to make donations and how to help their neighbors in a community that was now filled with bright blue plastic tarps where roofs used to be.

Of course, that wasn't the end of the storms. Hurricane Ivan, later that year, blasted Gulf Shores, Ala., Louisiana, and Pensacola. It spawned more than 100 tornadoes and re-entered the Gulf twice, pouring millions of gallons of rainwater over wide swatches of land. The storm killed 92, including 25 in the United States, according to the National Hurricane Center.

With our storm-seasoned readership now interested in hurricanes, we decided to send a reporter-photographer team up the Gulf Coast as far as they could go to cover the effects of Hurricane Katrina when that terrible storm hit in 2005.

Whole towns along the Gulf were wiped off the map. Residents who had seen many a hurricane, including some killers, were stunned by the devastation. Katrina killed more than 1,800 people, including 14 in Florida where it first hit.

The coverage didn't stop when the team made its way back to Central Florida. Dozens of Gulf residents with nowhere to go came to Ocala. Stories were heart-breaking, so much so that many residents opened their homes to people who were suddenly homeless. Many never returned to their old homes.

This is when newspapers are at their best, telling stories of people who need help. Americans are the most generous people on the planet. It's a perfect combination.

***

Sinkholes strike fear into the hearts of property owners, but miraculously few people are injured each year. However, in 2013, a family was mourning the loss of a 37-year-old man who was swallowed up in a sinkhole in a small community near Tampa.

Jeff Bush, 37, was in his bedroom when the floor and the earth beneath it opened without warning, plunging him and everything else in the room into a sliding pit. His brother jumped in to try and save him, but it was no use.

A recovery-effort crane operator was able to lift the family Bible out of the rubble but little else.

"It means that God is still in control, and He knew we needed this [Bible] for closure, said Wanda Carter, a family member (Associated Press, Ocala.com, March 4, 2013).

The tragic story is a reminder that Floridians live on a thin crust of limestone and prehistoric seashells fused together to form a substance called karst. The material serves as a cover for underground caverns and water supplies, but it can open when there is too much or too little rain.

In 1994, a sinkhole swallowed up a chunk of busy U.S. Highway 27-441, not just once but five times over the span of a week.

"It eats anything we feed it," said Florida Department of Transportation spokesman Steve Homan. That led to the hole being nicknamed "Mikey," for the character in a TV cereal commercial about a kid who would eat anything (*Sentinel,* Dec. 23, 1994).

Workers poured in truckloads of sand, dirt, and concrete before the hole began to stabilize.

Six months earlier, Alfred Lindsey of Leesburg was looking out the window when he exclaimed, "My tree is gone! (*Sentinel*, June 11, 1994)"

The tree was a formerly puny wax myrtle that he had rescued and planted in his front yard. It ended up being swallowed by a sinkhole after the city was deluged with six inches of rain in a thunderstorm.

A basketball fan, he described the hole as wide enough to lay two Shaquille O'Neals head-to-head and deep enough for the 7-foot-1 giant.

"I'm just glad it didn't get my house," he said.

A sinkhole did get a family's house in Seminole County, and it was sickening sight. The family had left for church when the hole opened beneath the house in Sweetwater

Oaks, a nice subdivision in Seminole County. They were not able to retrieve very much. Every so often the hole would widen to the sound of breaking glass, snapping timbers, and tons of house sliding into the earth's recesses.

Neighbors watched in sympathy and in horror, worried that their homes might be next. No one was injured, fortunately.

The mother of all sinkholes was the 1983 monster that gulped down 250,000 cubic yards of soil in Winter Park, five Porsches from a foreign car repair shop, the deep end of an Olympic swimming pool, sections of two streets, and a three-bedroom home.

***

Florida has other dubious distinctions, including being called "the lightning capital of the world." That's what CNN called the "Sunshine State" on July 8, 1998, when it reported that three people were killed by lightning in one week—a schoolteacher standing under an avocado tree, and two men on a golf course in Central Florida. The report went on to say that 90 percent of recent wildfires had been sparked by lightning and 15,000 lightning strikes had caused 50 new fires.

In 2013, Florida was tied with Arizona for the dubious title. Each state recorded four fatalities (*Sentinel,* Oct. 9, 2013).

Lightning does strange and terrible things, like striking a fence, turning it into an electrical conductor and killing livestock way down the line. It ignites house and barn fires, too.

In 1994, I was sent to the Florida Citrus Bowl—not to do a review of the Billy Joel and Elton John concert, but to talk to the huddled masses of 56,000 fans under the bleachers who were hiding from rain and hundreds of bolts of lightning.

"Five dollars for this raincoat," shouted John Cochtostan, waving a large trash bag (*Sentinel,* Aug. 22, 1994).

"I think it's crazy," said Joe Susko 90 minutes after the 7:30 p.m. show was temporarily halted. "I'd go home, but when are you going to see two superstars like this together again?"

City officials said they tried to keep fans off the field.

The show eventually went on as the thunderstorm, in typical Florida fashion, passed quickly.

***

In 1998, whether it was lightning, a campfire, or a careless smoker, wildfires blackened thousands of acres of forest, destroying homes and shutting down major roads and spurring huge evacuations.

A headline in the *Orlando Sentinel* on July 2 said it all: "30,000 flee walls of flames, fires close I-95 up to Jacksonville."

Firefighters struggled for days to extinguish the blazes. Before it was over, 500,000 acres would be incinerated, and hundreds of homes destroyed.

Fires on "Black Friday," May 17, 1985, burned 150,000 acres to a crisp and destroyed 170 homes across 29 counties. Fire officials blamed the 13,000-acre blaze portion in the Ocala National Forest on lightning that caused "sleeper fires" in treetops two days before the fire spread to adjoining brush, according to a 20-year anniversary story by Joe Callahan of the *Star-Banner.*

The fire was made worse because a major freeze earlier had killed citrus and other vegetation, creating tinderbox conditions. And then, there was the wind at 40-50 mph. The inferno pushed flames 150 feet above the tops of trees.

Reporters were hot, tired, worried, and reeking of smoke. Editors were worried, too. Normally, a paved road acts as a fire break but fire produces its own windstorm, and it can jump fire breaks, including those carved out by bulldozers. When the wind switches, fires can kill professional firefighters, let alone journalists.

Wildfires also cause massive pileups on Florida's Interstate highways. In January 2012, 10 people were killed in a 20-vehicle pileup on fog and smoke-shrouded Interstate 75 near Gainesville. The Florida Highway Patrol was criticized for not closing the road, but the agency defended troopers, calling it a "judgment call."

One afternoon I was called to a report on a blaze that threatened a subdivision in Orange County. At first, all you could see was smoke. Then, as the smoke got closer you could see flames licking pine trees, turning them into torches. High-grass plains started smoldering, then caught fire. As the sun set, darkness was broken by the yellow and orange flames steadily making their way toward the community.

Residents, who had at first been looking at the fire excitedly, then clinically, grew silent. With fear etched on their faces, they turned their thoughts inward while wondering what to do. Some probably wondered why they had wasted so much time watching the fire when they should have been trying to evacuate and save a few precious items from their house. A few probably wondered if it would do any good to turn on water sprinklers or even try to fight the blaze themselves.

Fortunately for them, the wind changed direction, driving the fire away.

Florida also has more than its share of floods, freezes, and high winds that don't qualify as tornadoes, but tell that to the people who lose their homes and suffer major property damage. You haven't lived until you see backyard sheds blowing across the highway, or you end up thanking your lucky stars that the grapefruit-sized hail that fell from the skies in Seminole County one night didn't hit your car as it smashed windshields and pounded automobiles to a pulp.

The hail that fell on the downtown area of Orlando that night was "just" your average pea- to golf-ball-sized hail, but it thawed quickly and flooded streets. I thought my legs were going to turn blue when I took off my shoes and socks and rolled up my pants legs to push cars out of flooded streets.

Sunshine State indeed!

Chapter 9

Jane Doe, Bottomless Pit

To the hiker walking through the state wildlife preserve that day in 1991, something just didn't seem right. First, there was the Land Rover parked in the middle of the Rock Springs Run Reserve. The state park, miles from Sanford and Interstate 4, is in the middle of nowhere. Its primary features are the Wekiva River and tunnels built by the state that go under State Road 46 so deer, bears, and other wildlife can cross without becoming roadkill.

After spotting the abandoned vehicle, the hiker noticed drag marks in the sand. *Someone's poached a deer*, he thought. But his curiosity soon turned to horror when he saw a brush pile with a bare leg sticking out. "At first I thought it was a mannequin," Stephen Wilder told sheriff's deputies. He then noticed bear tracks. Walking closer, he could see that the leg belonged not to a store display model but to a dead woman. She had been so brutalized, that by the time he reached park rangers and sheriff's deputies, rumors were flying that she had been killed by a bear.

Forensic pathologist Dr. Manuel Leal immediately rejected that wild story. The killer, in a final, despicable act, had posed his victim by stretching the woman's index finger away from her otherwise-clenched fist to point to a broken bottle protruding from her vagina. He knew then, he said, that "no bear had committed the crime."

The killer was a human monster. She had been tortured ritualistically, had been bitten, raped, had her eyes jabbed with a stick, and had been strangled. It is not unheard of to find a "Jane Doe" discarded like yesterday's newspaper. Florida, with its swamps, woods, and waters, has always been a favorite dumping ground for crime victims. But this case would make headlines because the sleuth that would find this killer was not some violin-playing, pipe-smoking, Sherlock Holmes, but a computer that was analyzing previously unknown scientific secrets.

In 1995, four years after the grisly discovery of the still-unnamed victim, an analyst with the Florida Department of Law Enforcement in Orlando was filing records of DNA evidence. "When I fed the information into the computer, the guy in Tallahassee yelled," David Baer told me in an interview (*Sentinel*, Feb. 4, 1996). DNA found on Jane Doe was a statistical match to Joseph A. Rolle, Jr., 29, a convicted rapist. There were about 10,000 samples in the computer in 1995. Florida's DNA database is now one of the largest in country and continues to grow.

In 1995, however, genetic evidence was still a fairly new thing in trials, though it was first used in an Orlando courtroom to convict a rapist in 1987. Deoxyribonucleic acid, or DNA, is the chemical basis for molecules in the body. No two individuals' genetic makeup is alike, except for identical twins. Excited prosecutors started referring to DNA as "genetic fingerprints," but defense lawyers went back to school to learn how to confuse jurors. Defense lawyers in O.J. Simpson's murder trial in 1995 convinced Los Angeles jurors that blood evidence had been contaminated after being allegedly mishandled by technicians and laboratory experts. They also accused cops and crime scene technicians of planting evidence. One defense lawyer was downright "intellectually dishonest," Assistant District Attorney Marcia Clark said in her book, *Without a Doubt*.

The Lake County Public Defender's Office in the Rolle case called on a locally respected private defense attorney, Jerri Blair, to question the way FDLE examined semen and to argue against the use of astronomical statistics. "It's not unusual to say that a sample is one out of several hundred million," Baer said. In Rolle's case, it was 400 billion-to-1.

Blair didn't win her argument, but the defense did score a crucial victory when the judge agreed to ban the testimony of women who had been attacked by Rolle in the past. A 62-year-old woman testified in a pretrial hearing about going to the home of a friend in 1992. Her friend wasn't home but her friend's boyfriend, Rolle, was. After offering her a beer and waiting 30 minutes, he said: "You don't get to leave until you give me a kiss." He then dragged her upstairs and assaulted her for four hours. "There was all kinds of madness," she said, including Rolle choking her until she lost consciousness.

She eventually managed to escape. She later noticed crescent-shaped marks on her legs she believed were bite marks, which were apparently inflicted when she was unconscious.

Also testifying in the December 1996 pretrial hearing was a convicted prostitute. She also testified that Rolle choked her until she passed out. She reported suffering several bruises which may have been bite marks. Rolle's former girlfriend also testified, saying that he bit her on her face during two different arguments. Defense attorney John Spivey, citing the broken bottle, argued that the cases were dissimilar. Trial judge G. Richard Singeltary agreed and ruled against the state.

The trial, set for April 1997, was supposed to be a case about DNA and staggering statistics, but Assistant State Attorney Bill Gross, aware that jurors sometimes get lost in the maze of complicated details, had an appointment with a dentist that would end up being pleasant, not painful.

Dr. Richard Souviron, 60, turned out to be a nice man for someone who spent his professional life poking around inside people's mouths. He had a private practice in Coral Gables, but he also headed the forensic dentistry department at the Dade County Medical Examiner's Office. Among his duties was helping to identify 110 passengers and crew members of a ValuJet who died when their plane plunged into the Everglades. Police sharpshooters floated along in airboats to keep alligators away from divers.

Souviron once repaired a tiger's tooth that was broken during a fatal attack on a zookeeper.

His proudest accomplishment was using his expertise as a bite-mark expert to help send serial killer Ted Bundy to the electric chair. He did that by matching Bundy's teeth impressions to bite marks on one of the young women killed in a sorority house at Florida State University.

Bundy attended the odontologist's pretrial deposition. "How does this work?" he asked, picking up a model of his teeth and holding it up in front of a photo of the bite marks on the victim. "It was a perfect match," Souviron said.

"Wait a minute," Bundy said as he put the display back on the table.

"You had it right the first time, Mr. Bundy," Souviron said.

When the hearing was over and Bundy was taken back to jail, prosecutor Larry Simpson turned to the dentist and said, "This is the first time Ted Bundy's ever been scared (*Sentinel* April 2, 1997)."

Rolle's defense team was lining up its own fascinating expert. Dr. John R. Feegle had been the former associate chief medical examiner of Atlanta, director of the pathology residency program at Emory University, and former chief medical examiner in Tampa. He was teaching at the University of South Florida when called to testify in Rolle's trial. Besides being a doctor, he was also a lawyer. At one time, he studied to become a Jesuit priest, but then he fell in love and married a nurse.

Like Souviron, he also had a claim to fame in putting away a notorious serial killer, Wayne Williams. Forensics experts found carpet fibers on the young boys slain and dumped along roadways in the Atlanta area in the late 1970s. Feegle performed nine of the 28 autopsies. Authorities, desperate for leads, let it be known that the fibers were being found on the bodies. That led Williams to try and dump one of the bodies in a river from a bridge. He was spotted by a police officer and arrested.

"We literally tricked him," Feegle said (*Sentinel* May 7, 1997).

Feegle wouldn't be testifying about bite marks. That would be another defense expert. Feegle's role, as one who had performed more than 10,000 autopsies, was to cast doubt on the way crime scene technicians collected evidence, including thinking that the woman had been killed by a bear.

"If someone had said that to me, I'd have said they should have their head examined," said Feegle, who at 64 resembled Santa Claus in *Miracle on 34th Street*. "It should have been treated as a homicide until proven otherwise (*Sentinel* April 12, 1997)." He ripped the sheriff's technicians for not putting every tree limb into a bag and taking them to a crime lab, for brushing dirt into her wounds, for not wearing protective shoe coverings, and for removing the bottle from the woman's body at the crime scene. They should have wrapped her body in a clean white sheet or body bag so they could look for evidence indoors. It was getting dark at the time. "You never know where a clue is going to come from," he said.

FDLE's Baer testified about the DNA evidence. Jurors tried to stay with it, but nit-picking defense questions and the mind-numbing details were making their eyes glaze over.

Souviron saved the day for prosecutors. A natural-born teacher, the engaging dentist testified for three hours, using models, photographs, and plastic overlays. Somehow, he made the technical testimony interesting—so interesting, jurors wanted to ask questions. Assistant Public Defender Mark Nacke objected to that. He couldn't stop him from making a joke, however. When Gross asked if lawyers had bigger teeth, Souviron quipped: "They certainly have bigger mouths."

Nacke also wanted to bar any talk of the Bundy case, fearing that would wow the jurors even more, but the judge allowed it as part of his testimony about his expertise.

The big moment came when Gross asked: "Doctor, bottom line. Who bit that lady?"

"Mr. Rolle," he replied.

The defense presented opposing testimony from its own expert, Atlanta dentist, Dr. Tom David, but jurors seemed to be sold on Souviron's opinion.

There was other evidence. Two hairs from an African-American person were found in her socks. She was Caucasian. They were too short to test for DNA. Another unidentified hair, this one from a white person, was found on her sweatshirt.

The defense also relied on an old standby: Cast doubt on someone else—anyone else. In this case, it was the owner of the 1989 Land Rover. On the surface, the man looked like a good candidate to be a patsy. He was a big, swarthy man with deep, dark eye sockets, uneven big white teeth, and a strange accent. A bar owner, he had been an Iranian pilot before revolutionaries toppled the Shah. Even worse, he seemed to laugh at inappropriate times when asked pointed questions.

The Land Rover had been stolen, he testified, but defense attorneys also put a former employee—a bouncer— on the stand. The bouncer admitted telling his wife that he helped his boss by pretending to steal the Land Rover so he could collect insurance money. The worker said when the car turned up near the murder scene, he told his wife he would have to leave for a while. That was just a ruse, however, the employee testified. He said he made up the story so he could be with another woman.

Defense attorney Michael McDermott pressed the bar owner as hard as he could, including bringing up what he said was an arrest by vice officers for trying to solicit a prostitute. The man denied it and said he "settled" the case with authorities. That may have placed some doubt in juror's minds, not only about him, but about the character of the victim, without directly calling her a prostitute. Of course, Lake County sheriff's investigators had already considered the possibility. Before the computer fingered Rolle, they noticed the dead woman's muscular legs and also wondered if she might have also been a waitress or a dancer. Detectives visited every topless bar in Orange and Seminole counties showing her picture and asking if anyone could identify her.

"What did Jane Doe do to you?" McDermott asked the bar owner.

"I do not know any woman, Jane Doe, in 1991," he replied in his fractured English.

The next day, in closing arguments, Gross took to the podium to tell the jurors to pay no attention to the bar owner theory, saying the bouncer and his ex-wife admitted lying. Gross also cited the "illogic" of killing a woman and leaving her near his Land Rover, which was reported stolen four months before Jane Doe's body was discovered.

"It's hard to tell who the defense will turn into a scapegoat," Gross said.

Nacke told the nine-woman and three-man jury that prosecutors "can't span the gap. They want you to do it for them," he said, standing in front of a cartoon of a bridge that did not span a large gorge.

"There is not one shred of evidence by anyone when, where, or how that sperm got... [on that woman]," Nacke told the 12-member jury. In other words, there was no proof that she didn't have consensual sex with Rolle, and that someone else came along later and killed her.

It was a desperate tactic. The defense team was asking 12 people to overlook the strong circumstantial case, though it helped that the jurors did not know anything about Rolle's earlier offenses.

After deliberating for an entire day, the jury reached its decision: not guilty of first- degree murder but guilty of one count of rape. If Rolle was expecting a lesser sentence, however, he would be disappointed. He was sentenced to life in prison without the possibility of ever getting out of prison.

Sadly, the story still has no end. No one identified Jane Doe from artist sketches or from clues found on her body. A sister, a daughter, a wife maybe, she had given birth to at least one child. Early on, her teeth were carefully taken care of by an orthodontist but in later years they showed signs of decay. She had cocaine in her system, which may explain why her teeth were no longer so important to her. She was white, 25 to 35 years old, 5-foot-4, 124 pounds with hazel eyes. Authorities said she had a razor cut design on the sides of her hair. The back of her brown hair was shoulder length and had blonde tinting.

Because no one claimed her body, she was buried by the county. A simple piece of metal marks her grave, but prosecutors did save her jawbone in hopes of one day being able to identify her through dental records.

There was one positive note. Detectives sent her fingerprints to 230 cities that had computerized fingerprint searches at that time. About 240 agencies responded with details about missing persons in their jurisdiction. An investigator with the Florida Department of Law Enforcement met with police agencies, and by process of elimination, authorities were able to solve four unsolved homicides.

Prosecutors did find one woman who may have met Jane Doe. The woman owned a hair salon in the small community of Sorrento where Rolle, of all things, once worked as a pressman at a *Sentinel* printing plant. Six years after the fact, Sherie Mitchell thought she recognized an unusual hearts and stars earring found in the woman's hair. Nine months after Jane Doe's death, she was able to help police artists complete a rendering.

Mitchell described her as having an olive complexion, "very, very dark hair" and an "Indian look." She said she was wearing a white T-shirt with lace "and something with pink on it." Gross said that could have been a good description of Jane Doe's clothing. Though she was found naked from the waist down, she was wearing a red sweatshirt and a white blouse underneath that.

"She was beautiful," Mitchell said.

***

Robert Craig, racked with guilt, and in an unfamiliar very bad place in his life, was about to spill his guts to the Lake County sheriff. He had been reminded of what alligators do to human bodies dumped into a watery grave. Plus, the 20-year-old, who had never been in trouble, couldn't get over the fact that his greed and that of a fellow ranch hand led to cattle rustling and the murder of his rancher boss and foreman. So, he cried and confessed, and led investigators to the bodies, which were weighted down with concrete blocks 60 feet below the surface of a murky, isolated lake created by a sink hole. Wall Sink, a legendary "bottomless pit," had been used by criminals for generations to the hide evidence.

Even with Craig's help, it took divers a long time to find the bodies of John Eubanks, 32, and Bobby Farmer,

29. Recovery was a relief to their families who were eager to give their loved ones a decent Christian burial. Without Craig's help, authorities may have never found the bodies. During the search, authorities also found a stolen Dussenberg automobile used in a 1920s bank heist.

The 1981 murder case would turn out to be a long, hard-fought legal battle, lasting for years. Craig would claim that he had been unjustly sentenced to die in the electric chair and that his partner, Robert Schmidt, was the real bad guy, and yet he received a lighter sentence of second-degree murder. Before it was over, the reputations of a sheriff, a prosecutor, a court stenographer, and the judicial system would be questioned, and the murder victims' families would be outraged.

The crime itself, aside from being despicable and senseless, started out being a relatively simple case, even with both men telling somewhat different stories.

Eubanks owned an agricultural investment company in a nearby county. Craig and Schmidt handled the daily chores. One day Eubanks remarked that cattle seemed to be missing. The two cow hands were stealing eight to nine cattle at a time and selling them at area markets. Craig said that Schmidt, 23, told him they would have to kill Eubanks or risk going to prison. Craig said he didn't take the remark seriously because Schmidt was always saying that one day he would "have to kill someone." Tensions soon reached a boiling point, however, when Eubanks later showed up with Farmer to help look for cows. Eubanks planned to hire Farmer as foreman.

Craig testified that Schmidt told him: "Farmer knows too much, and we have to kill him, too."

Craig testified that he was nervous when they got to an oak hammock near a lake, but he still didn't think Schmidt would open fire. He said he and Farmer heard two shots and the two men started running toward the sound. When they entered a clearing they found Schmidt, who was pointing a gun at them. Schmidt told Craig to shoot Farmer or he would shoot him, too. Craig said he fell to his knees, covered his eyes, and fired. When Farmer fell, Schmidt came over and fired a round into the cattleman's head to finish him off.

Sheriff's investigators, responding to a missing persons call, found blood and eventually discovered Farmer's Jeep parked 20 miles away. The trail eventually led to the two ranch hands.

The legal complications started the moment Craig began confessing. Craig's attorney called the sheriff's office to demand that all questioning of his client stop immediately. The deputy who answered the call put the attorney on hold and went directly to his boss, Sheriff Noel E. "Evvie" Griffin, Jr. Griffin told the deputy to say he didn't know where Craig was. When he was later challenged on his story, the sheriff denied hiding Craig and violating his right against self-incrimination. Unfortunately for the sheriff, the lawyer had called in on a recorded line.

A disgusted judge told Griffin he could not be believed and tossed the confession. Suddenly, prosecutors had a problem. Their solution was to offer codefendant Schmidt a plea deal. He would testify that Craig was the main bad guy. Later, however, defense attorneys learned that after taking the plea offer Schmidt allegedly laughed and said, "I shot both of them."

Fifteen years later, Craig's appeal lawyer, Jerri Blair, was filing motions asking that Craig be released from prison so he could seek a new trial or sentence. "... Craig has lived 16 years on death row, either because of a prosecutor's mistakes, personality problems, or politics when he did not receive a fair trial, and that demonstrates that he could have easily been found not guilty of first-degree murder. His culpability depends entirely upon Schmidt's testimony. Schmidt's testimony coincides with the evidence on points where he and Craig did not disagree. However, at the crucial points where there is disagreement, Schmidt's testimony is not consistent with the evidence or even consistent in and of itself," she wrote in a writ of *habeas corpus* in August 1997.

Because the victims were members of prominent families there was a lot of pressure for prosecutors to win— no matter what, she said. Farmer's brother, Travis, was a longtime Sumter County sheriff's deputy. By 1996, he was furious at the thought of a new trial and the chance for a get-out-of-death-row-free-card. "It's getting to the point where there is no justice anymore," he said (*Sentinel,* Nov. 10, 1996).

One of Craig's two first-degree murder sentences had already been reduced to life in prison in an earlier proceeding, when justices decided that prosecutors should have told jurors that Schmidt got a better deal. In 1996, the Florida Supreme Court vacated the death sentence and ordered that Craig be resentenced by another judge and jury. Blair and her defense team were busy gearing up for the new trial.

"This is the case that proportionality is based on," defense attorney Michael Graves argued in claiming that Craig's sentence was woefully unfair.

One of Blair's witnesses was former *Sentinel* reporter Jim Runnels, who alleged that the court reporter/stenographer drank during lunch breaks, fell asleep, and sometimes didn't talk into his recording mask. Because the stenographer was dead by 1997, there was no cross-examining him. Runnels also alleged that former Assistant State Attorney Jimmy Brown pointed a gun to his head and collapsed on the floor during an over-the-top re-enactment. Brown denied the charges. "I don't trust guns that much," he said.

Runnels also claimed that Brown plied Craig's ex-wife, Jane, and his sister-in-law, Cathy Lewis, with booze to glean information.

"Were you intoxicated?" Blair asked Lewis.

"Probably."

"I felt like he needed to hear the other side. He seemed very compassionate," she testified. "I didn't know I was not supposed to talk to him."

Brown said he didn't learn anything new.

A State Attorney paralegal had a hard time believing the story about Brown. She testified that relations with the family were anything but friendly. Craig's family screamed and made threats outside the courthouse in Tampa.

Blair also said prosecutors never told her client about Schmidt's statement about shooting both men.

Schmidt took the stand. He said it was Craig who suggested stealing the cattle and Craig who fired the first shot—at Farmer. "I pulled my pistol and shot Mr. Eubanks," Schmidt said.

He said Craig shouted to him: "I can't tell if he's dead. Shoot him!"

Blair told jurors in her opening remarks: "This is about credibility and culpability." Schmidt grew up with guns and once went to juvenile court on a knifing charge, she noted. She presented the testimony of a prison guard who said Craig was such a nice guy he wouldn't mind having him as a neighbor.

"It's a very, very complicated case," countered Assistant State Attorney Jim Phillips during jury selection. As for negotiating a plea bargain, he said it was like "making a deal with the devil to find out what's going on in hell (*Sentinel*, May 5, 1998)."

Graves seized the moment, asking one prospective juror: "If you ask the devil a question, will he tell you the truth?"

"He is the father of all lies," she replied.

But it would be Craig himself who turned out to be his best witness. He wept the day before jurors began deliberations. "I want to live," he said.

"I never had any intention of hurting anyone." He admitted that the cattle thefts were "a betrayal."

He blamed Schmidt for the shootings, saying he twice rejected the idea. "I can't do that," he said.

He said he was shocked when he heard Schmidt fire two shots. He said Farmer began to run.

"I heard running behind me," Craig said, then the sound of a bullet flying past his ear.

"Shoot him, shoot him!" Schmidt said.

Craig said he closed his eyes and fired. Afterward, he said his instinct was to go and try to help Farmer, but he never got the chance. Schmidt went over to Farmer and fired a round into the back of his head with his .357 Magnum pistol.

"I got pulled into this," Craig said, adding that he didn't know where to turn for help.

Phillips countered that he had several chances to stop it or report it afterward.

"I should have stopped Schmidt," Craig said.

"Why didn't you shoot Mr. Schmidt instead of a man you just met?" Phillips asked.

Blair, too, was choked with emotion. She asked jurors to consider the fact that until the slayings, "His whole life he spent as a kind person." As a child, he ran away from home when his father killed animals on the family farm, and he once stopped an angry Schmidt from shooting a horse. His ex-wife and others testified that he had shown true remorse and Christian faith since the crime.

"I don't know why I did it," he said.

The next day, jurors deliberated into the late evening hours before voting to commute his death sentence to life in prison. Chief Circuit Judge William Swigert gave Craig two consecutive life sentences without the possibility of parole for 25 years. That was the legal definition of a life sentence when Craig originally went to trial. Today, life means life. He will not be eligible for parole until the year 2030.

Farmer's family was outraged. The great thing about living in the community you cover as a reporter is that you face the people you write about. It makes you a better reporter. So, it was not surprising that a trip to the grocery store would result in an angry confrontation with an unhappy family member who apparently thought I was writing favorably about the killers.

"How would you like to have this happen to your family?" she asked.

The truth is, I found myself reporting the way I always do, as objectively as possible, even though I tend to relate more to the victims' families.

I also know that a bullet doesn't just travel through a victim, but through the victim's family and the family of the shooter. I have seen parents, siblings, and friends of killers sob with grief, even guilt, though the killer is the one who needs to take responsibility. What the grieving family member at the grocery store did not realize, is that there is always another day and another side of the story.

Toby Farmer, 20, spoke eloquently about the dad he only remembered in "flashes" like lightning. "It's getting extremely hard for my family to deal with this," said the soft-spoken college student and part-time meat-cutter.

He was speaking not only about Craig's resentencing but also appearing before a parole board that was set to meet on Schmidt's future. Schmidt had already caught some lucky breaks. Four years earlier, prison officials slashed years off his projected release in 2007. He was placed in a work release program where he installed carpets in people's homes, and he was released on weekends to sleep with his girlfriend.

Toby Farmer, his cousin Sumter County Sheriff Bill Farmer, and others appeared before the parole board the following month.

"I can't tell you how it is to grow up and know that someone can take a life, especially your father's, and do so in cold blood, like shooting a bird or something," Toby said (*Sentinel,* May 21, 1998).

"We firmly believe this was a heinous crime ... that should not go unpunished," Sheriff Farmer added.

A priest argued on Schmidt's behalf. "I believe in redemption. I believe a person can change," the Rev. Ralph DiPasquale said.

The parole commission wasn't so sure. They denied Schmidt's plea.

Craig got off death row, but it wasn't much of a bargain.

"You are surrounded by constant noise, isolated from the outside world, from love and affection .... The only escape is when you are asleep, and even then, the nightmares of reality seem to find their way through the cracks of your heart and mind," he wrote in a letter to his attorney.

Chapter 10

Kayla

A helicopter buzzed around the apartment complex while dozens of volunteers and police officers beat the bushes—literally—in hopes of finding the missing 6-year-old girl. Police radios crackled as bloodhounds, their saggy faces practically dragging the ground, snorted, and sniffed, trying to pick up the scent.

Kayla McKean's dad met officers outside with his dog. He said Kayla went to the playground outside their Clermont apartment at 9:30 a.m. An hour later, when she had not returned, he went looking for her. He finally called 911 around noon.

It was Thanksgiving Day, Nov. 26, 1998. Dozens of neighbors and strangers who heard the news on TV immediately quit thinking about turkey and football and came running to help.

Over the next three days, hundreds of civilians would join the search, handing out flyers, walking through woods and fields, and trying to lift the spirits of the little girl's mother, Elizabeth McKean, who wept, paced, and clutched a teddy bear.

"You know, I went to a convenience store last night and I heard people saying they weren't going to find her," McKean told the *Sentinel* (Nov. 29, 1998). "They are going to find her. This teddy is my daughter's … and I'm going to give it to her."

Kayla's dad, Richard Adams, had custody. Elizabeth, who had been fighting with Adams, had not seen Kayla since Halloween. Elizabeth and Richard never married. Their two-month long romance in high school resulted in the birth of Kayla. Adams didn't even know he had a daughter for the first four years of her life. He found out when Elizabeth applied for welfare while staying at a domestic violence shelter and caseworkers tracked him down for child support. A judge ordered him to pay $118 per month. A month later, he quit paying. He was later jailed as a deadbeat dad after falling behind by $7,414. He was ordered to pay $40 a week to catch up.

McKean, facing severe money problems, staying with friends and boyfriends, and now the mother of another little girl, turned Kayla over to Adams' family.

During the search, Adams mostly stayed inside with his wife, Marcie, and their infant son, Lee. He said very little to reporters. McKean said of him, "He's a good father. He's never done anything to Kayla that would make me think otherwise."

Cops weren't so sure. Adams, 24, who claimed to be a karate expert, had a violent past, including assault and burglary. The aluminum-porch installer claimed to be lot of things, including a philosopher and a mystic capable of astral projection.

McKean agreed to a lie-detector test. Adams, on the other hand, stopped talking during one interview at the police station and ran to the bathroom, claiming to be sick. He would not submit to another test until Monday, four days later.

The FBI was persistent and masterful, however. Kayla was dead, law enforcement officers believed. They decided to work on Adams' conscience, suggesting he didn't mean to do it, whatever "it" was, and using Marcie as leverage.

"Can you promise me my wife won't have to go through this?" Adams asked one detective.

"I can't promise ...."

"Don't have to do no time?"

"There's a good chance that she won't have to, but it depends on what you tell me, OK?"

In fact, investigators had already talked to Marcie and confirmed their worst fears. Now, they wanted to hear it from Adams.

Adams admitted that he had difficulty dealing with Kayla.

"She's independent, and Lord knows she wouldn't listen to a thing I said to her," he said. He recalled one time when she jumped off his knee when he tried to spank her with the paddle. He said he tied her wrists together with rope.

"I was worked up to a T. I was about to blow," he admitted.

Kayla knew it, too. She kept calling for Marcie to intervene.

"I don't like feeling out of control," Adams said.

The last moments of Kayla's life began, Adams said, with her soiling her pants. Then he said: "I don't remember what happened. All I know is she didn't cry; she didn't ask me to stop. I kept bearing down on her."

He said, "I lost all control." He said he spanked her twice with a paddle, which was crudely crafted from a heavy 2-by-4 piece of lumber. He also admitted hitting her on top of the head with the board.

A: "Just the spankin'... the two spankings didn't go through and she ...

Q: "And you just lost ...."

A: "No, I just ... no, no, no."

Q: "OK. Was that when she got quiet?"

A: "No. It was … I started hitting her. I started hitting her in her stomach. I started smelling something nasty. She pooped her pants. I put her in the bathtub, told her to wash off. And she wasn't doing nothing, she looked like a vegetable."

Q: "So you took her out of the tub?"

A: "I pulled her out of the tub real quick, I threw her against the wall. Nothing happened to the wall. She still just looked like she was just ignoring me. She was standing … she was standing, and her body was limp. I hit her."

Q: "With your hands?"

A: "And feet. I don't know how much power I got."

He said he tried to revive her with cold water and laid her down on the bed. When Marcie came home from the grocery store, he asked her to look at Kayla to see if she was dead.

He said he then put her body in the trunk of the car and drove to a mall so he could get some tobacco. The family then drove several miles to DeLeon Springs, a remote place in Volusia County where friends lived. They eventually ended up burying Kayla in a shallow grave in the Ocala National Forest.

Back at the command post, sheriff's deputies ushered Elizabeth into the RV operations center and broke the news to her. After a few minutes, deputies told the crowd of volunteers outside that Adams had confessed to killing Kayla.

"Oh no!" they groaned. There was silence, and then there was anger.

"I just can't believe he killed the baby," one woman said, sobbing. "All these people out here for days, searching and looking and praying (*Sentinel,* Dec. 1, 1998)."

Marcie, who was charged with improper disposal of a body, a misdemeanor, led authorities to the grave. It was described by friends as Kayla's "favorite spot." It was near a creek with a rope swing dangling over the water near Alexander Springs.

After confessing, police walked Adams outside in handcuffs for a "perp (perpetrator) walk" and into the glare of news camera lights where he said, "Accidents happen."

Then he said: "I asked for help. I asked for help with my anger management problems."

Suddenly, with just a couple of off-the-cuff remarks, Adams managed to light the fuse on an explosive case of terrible publicity for Florida's Department of Children & Families, and he created a shock wave that would rock the child safety-net system to its core.

"I think we made some bad decisions," said Pamela Paulik, the district DCF administrator said on Dec. 2. She said she didn't see any "major malfeasance or any of that kind of thing, (*Sentinel*, Dec. 3, 1998)."

That could change, she conceded, and it did. DCF, as it turned out, was well acquainted with Kayla and her family, and the agency had failed her repeatedly.

In April of 1997, investigators responding to a report found unexplained bruises under her left ear while living with her mother in Seminole County. They also noticed circular dark marks around her eyes, which were blamed on a spider bite. Caseworkers referred the family to the local health department.

When Kayla was four months old, she was treated for red marks and oozing bumps from flea bites. At age 5, she watched in horror as her 3-year-old half-sister fell backwards three stories from an open apartment window. Fortunately, she landed safely in shrubs.

Things went from bad to worse under Adams' care.

On May 25, Adams took Kayla to a hospital emergency room. She had two black eyes, a fractured nose, and a fractured wrist. She fell off a bike, he said, and Kayla backed up her dad's story. The doctor wrote that he could not find any signs of physical abuse, but there was possibly medical neglect. She was placed in a shelter overnight. A judge convened a shelter hearing and he returned Kayla to her father after a state caseworker classified the risk as "low" and a DCF lawyer indicated she would be fine.

On June 23, Kayla was in front of a doctor again, this time after being referred by the Lake County Boys Ranch, which had contracted with DCF through its Bridges program for protective services.

There were scratches and bruises on her back, chest, abdomen, and trunk. She also had a black eye and a mark on her temple.

After Adams admitted beating her with a paddle, the doctor decided she was in "imminent danger," but she was returned to her home anyway.

On Oct. 28, she had a knot on her head, two black eyes, and was walking with a limp. Adams told investigators she got the bump on her head when she fell in the tub. The black eyes were the same injuries she received five months earlier, they just had not healed, he said. The injuries were made worse when the dog walked on her face while she was sleeping. As for the limp, she fell down some steps while trying to take the retriever out for a walk, Adams said. Kayla supported her dad's story but disclosed that Adams tied her wrists together with rope. Adams admitted doing that but said he did it for only a minute so he could force her to bend over and get a spanking for misbehaving at school.

The next day, Elizabeth McKean was told of the injuries. Despite what she said to reporters later about Adams being "a good father," she told investigators in October that she was afraid of Adams' temper, and she wanted Kayla removed from his home. Kayla was not removed, however. Less than a month later she was dead.

The day after the district DCF administrator made her bland statement about "bad decisions," the department announced that caseworkers would be disciplined.

"No child should suffer like this child suffered," said Director Ed Feaver. "We had some clues, and we could have saved this child's life. I hope this isn't happening in other cases."

He promised changes, including providing an entire case file to a judge who had to decide if a child should be returned home.

"If I had known one-tenth of what I know today I would not have sent her home," Circuit Judge Jerry Lockett said of his ruling on May 26, a day after Adams took Kayla to the hospital emergency room.

Two days after a doctor said on June 23 that Kayla was in "imminent danger" after Adams admitted beating Kayla with a paddle, Bridges caseworkers urged the DCF attorney to review the case file to see if Kayla should be removed from the home. He refused.

"By God, if this case had gone before the judge, Kayla probably would still be alive," said Tom Manning, director of the Boys Ranch.

The tragedy was having a ripple effect in state government. Gov. Jeb Bush endorsed the idea of making changes in the system but said the state agency was not entirely to blame.

"To think that a father could kill his own flesh and blood reflects a hollowness of the heart that goes way beyond whether a government responded properly," he said. "Our greatest challenge is to organize ourselves into a society where children are our highest priority (*Sentinel*, Dec. 4, 1998)."

Officials called for more training, more awareness, and more accountability. Kayla did have some people looking out for her, including officials at her school. Two teachers and two counselors at Minneola Elementary School made dozens of calls to DCF after seeing bumps and bruises. She even showed up for class wearing makeup in an effort by someone to hide her black eyes. She was taken out of school for two sick days in late October. When she came back, she was limping.

Caseworkers assured the school that the case would be reported up the line, but because of bureaucratic bungling and a lack of understanding, the case was "pencil-whipped" by caseworkers and supervisors alike.

In December, a Lake County grand jury indicted Adams on first-degree murder charges. It praised the school workers for being vigilant, "especially in light of the inexplicable lack of vigilance and perseverance of the Department of Children and Families."

Meanwhile, a judge placed baby Lee with Marcie's mother. By late December, Marcie was allowed to have supervised visits. Marcie's mother was protective of her daughter, blaming Ricky and saying Marcie had been coerced. Marcie's attorney, Michael Graves, had said earlier that Adams threatened to harm her and the 13-month-old child if she did not go along with a cover-up.

By January, the Legislature, prodded by editorials, columnists, and intense news coverage, was demanding changes in the state that had seen 350 child homicides over the past five years. A Senate committee called witnesses and heard about the causes of Kayla's death, including, confusion and a lack of coordination between state and private agencies; no follow-up by DCF with Kayla's school; and no individual oversight. Her case was shuffled from one caseworker to another.

Witnesses testified about low pay, high turnover, lack of funding, and a myriad of other concerns within the child safety welfare system.

Before it was over, several caseworkers and supervisors would be fired, demoted, or forced to resign. Private contractors hired by the state would be disbanded. The Lake County Boys Ranch, a longtime fixture and a decent organization that had sheltered kids for years, would go out of business. Other private agencies would pop up and pop out. Today, much of the system is managed by regional, private, nonprofit companies.

Pressed not to overlook any child again, DCF began putting kids in shelters en masse. Foster parents were pressured to take on more kids than they were licensed to care for. Kids who were not supposed to stay more than the mandated 30 days ended up staying for months. Because there were not enough foster homes, children were forced to sleep on the floor in DCF offices and in motels. Bewildered, angry parents claimed the agency was overreacting in removing children from their homes.

One DCF caseworker said she had put 30 children into foster care in a month's time— more than she had placed into protective custody in 18 months in nearby Seminole County. Cases included a 14-year-old girl who became pregnant when assaulted by her mother's boyfriend, a 12-year-old girl who was sexually assaulted by her stepfather and forced to live with her siblings in a filthy house, and five children beaten with a belt by their father.

She had a caseload of 40. The recommended caseload was 12 but it was lighter than what previous caseworkers had, including those who were fired after Kayla's death.

Annette Murphy said things were looking up, however. The agency's focus seemed to have shifted from "family-centered to child-centered," she said (*Sentinel*, April 29, 1999). The emphasis is still on trying to keep the family together through training classes, counseling, and supervision until a family can adequately cope with all the challenges.

The overall number of children in protective care in Lake County shot up from 180 to 400 in one year.

Hearings, a death review panel, and meeting after meeting was held to unravel the tangled threads in Kayla's case. One report said workers ignored too many signs. Kayla also was not interviewed properly. Adams answered questions for her. Not surprisingly, the quiet little girl didn't dispute her father's stories.

State investigators began looking into case files and noting discrepancies, including notations when there were no meetings.

A video surfaced in the court file of Kayla at a birthday party, sitting alone, looking haggard and bearing two large black eyes.

Among those who tried to help Kayla was the couple who lived in DeLeon Springs that Adams went to see the night she died.

"We loved her," Kathie Stooksbury said.

It was Lonnie and Kathie who insisted that Adams take Kayla to the emergency room. Lonnie initially thought she was wearing some type of Halloween mask. Her face was so swollen and battered you could hardly see the tip of her nose, and her wrist was severely swollen.

"You could just see purple dots where her knuckles should have been," he told me in an exclusive interview for the *Sentinel* (Jan. 17, 1999).

When he asked her what happened, she said, "I don't know, I don't know."

Adams told Lonnie the bike accident story, and said it happened five days before. Stooksbury was aghast that he had not taken her to a doctor.

"Ricky acted like nothing was wrong. Right then, he wasn't my friend anymore."

At the hospital, Adams lost his temper when questioned by hospital workers and began yelling and slamming his hand against the wall.

The DCF caseworker said, "If you're acting like this in front of me, I can't give you your child back." She also warned him that she was taking notes. After spending one night in a shelter, she was returned to Adams, but Adams told his friend that he didn't want her.

"He told me she was evil," Lonnie said.

The couple took her in. She had blisters on her feet because Adams forced her to do jumping jacks as punishment. She said she liked the new experience of taking baths with warm water and having a bed to sleep in (the baby had a bed; she slept on the floor). Sometimes she "freaked out," especially at night, screaming and going into uncontrollable crying jags.

School records from Orange County, where she attended school before coming to live with her dad, said she had "a communication disorder" which hindered her from understanding what people wanted her to do. She also had a speech impediment and some behavior and impulsivity problems. Her new teachers reported that she was making good progress and "is a sweet little girl."

Adams gave the impression that he was going to get papers giving the Stooksburys custody, but after a few weeks he showed up and took her back.

"If he didn't want her, why didn't he let us keep her?" Lonnie asked.

In late April 1999, the Legislature sent the Kayla McKean Child Protection Act to Gov. Jeb Bush. It provided for several changes, including tougher penalties for people who did not report abuse and a mandatory call to law enforcement so cops could work with caseworkers. The bill was sponsored by Sen. Anna Cowin, R-Leesburg, who wept at a Senate committee meeting.

"The story of what happened to Kayla tore the heart out of our community. Something had to be done to protect the children of Florida," Cowin said (*Sentinel*, May 14, 1999).

Not included in the legislation was a mandatory filling of open positions at DCF. She vowed to come back next year with another bill.

Like everything else in the Kayla story, the new law became controversial immediately. A measure that required abuse hotline operators to take down more information jammed phone lines for up to 30 minutes, causing frustrated callers to hang up.

It jammed every aspect of the system, as it turns out. Sheriffs grumbled that it tied up too much of their deputies' time, and the law required a full medical examination for every child reported as a possible abuse victim.

A year later a new law was passed, restoring some discretion to caseworkers, and relaxing some law enforcement requirements.

Kayla's maternal grandfather, Joseph McKean, a member of a parents-rights group, asked that Kayla's name be removed from the legislation because of controversial aspects.

By October, Marcie Adams was able to reach a plea deal. She was placed on five years' probation with judgment withheld. She pleaded guilty to charges of tampering with evidence and obstruction of justice and no-contest to medical neglect. Prosecutors had been waiting for the results of a polygraph test in which she said she had been abused by Adams.

She said she did intervene when Adams tied Kayla's wrists. "I told him to untie her. He threw me up against the wall, but he untied her."

"I don't want anyone to think that I did anything to protect him [Adams]," she told me in an interview for the *Sentinel* (Oct. 13, 1999).

She claimed she tried to get DCF's contractor, Bridges, to provide services for Ricky and Kayla "but they didn't call back." She said she also told a caseworker about the ropes but to no avail.

By late 1999, the wheels of justice began creaking their way forward for Adams. Defense attorneys argued for a change of venue, citing an incredible amount of publicity. They also argued against showing jurors Adams' videotaped confession. Circuit Judge T. Michael Johnson eventually approved the prosecutor's bid to air the videotape.

The trial was moved from January to May. In April, defense psychologists filed a motion saying that Adams was "under the influence of a mental or emotional disturbance" when he killed Kayla. He "could not appreciate the criminality" of his actions, they claimed.

The defense team also argued that jurors should not hear about Adams' alleged abuse of Marcie. They also wanted to keep secret the fact that Adams lied to police for three days and buried Kayla in the forest several miles away, insisting that it would be "highly prejudicial and inflammatory."

Prosecutor Bill Gross argued that the "campaign of lies" was inextricably intertwined with the murder and showed that Adams had a guilty conscience.

There was a lot at stake. The state was seeking the death penalty. Defense attorney Candace Hawthorne said Adams was a man "with poor parenting skills" who had a child with several behavioral problems.

Prosecutors were fighting to keep some things in and some things out of the earshot of jurors. The panel should not be allowed to hear that Adams had asked for help, they said.

Adams had been referred to a Bridges program by the hospital emergency room. There was a scheduling mix-up, however, and the case was closed before Adams could see anyone.

Prosecutors argued that it was not the kind of case where someone else could have prevented the crime if they had stepped in.

The judge ruled that jurors could hear testimony about Adams' lies and the burial of Kayla, but he ruled for the defense that jurors would not be able to hear about earlier abuse, including the emergency room visit. In another win for the defense, Judge T. Michael Johnson ruled that jurors would not hear about Adams' drug abuse or about him abusing Marcie.

He sided with the prosecutors about excluding Adams' comments to the press about asking for help.

Days before the trial, it became apparent that Marcie's testimony would be key. In a dramatic disclosure about the day Kayla died, Marcie told authorities that one minute Adams was crying, the next he was saying he wasn't going to call police.

"Do you know what they would do to people like me in jail? And she wasn't worth it," she recalled him saying.

She said in her deposition that when she found Kayla unresponsive, she cried, screamed, and tried to wake Kayla up. He asked her what she was upset about. He then told her she would never see their son again if she told anyone what happened.

In his opening remarks, prosecutor Bill Gross told jurors that Kayla died after receiving "malicious punishment." He said Kayla's body gave up her secrets to the medical examiner while her innocent little classmates were having a party at school.

Jurors winced as he described the injuries, including a blow to the right side of her head so severe it caused a whiplash which fractured the other side of her skull.

She suffered from fractured ribs, a liver torn into three pieces, a dislocated hip, and bruises so severe that they bled through the skin.

Her right thigh was swollen to twice the size of the left. "It appears to be bowed outward," according to the autopsy report.

She died of internal bleeding, Gross said. He had the medical examiner, Dr. Susan Rendon, hold the thick paddle in her hands while she described the cause of death as "massive blunt force trauma." In other words, she suffered the same kind of injuries as a person hit by a car. She also said that besides throwing her up against the wall, Adams may have stomped her.

Hawthorne told jurors: "He didn't realize he hurt her so severely."

Jeffery Pfister, the primary defense attorney, tried to mediate some of the damning testimony in case jurors were thinking that it was prolonged torture.

"It didn't appear to be planned," Rendon said in response to his questions.

On the day before Thanksgiving, Kayla was kept home from school as punishment for staying outside on the playground too long. Adams was not feeling well, he had a toothache, Hawthorne said.

When Kayla came to him and said she had soiled her pants, he told her to clean herself up. He thought she was disobeying him when she didn't respond right away, Hawthorne said.

He pulled out the paddle to scare her into doing what he told her to do, then "lashed out," she said.

Prosecutor Ric Ridgway called it premeditation or aggravated child abuse, which made it a first-degree murder case. Hawthorne called it manslaughter. If jurors sided with the state, it was life in prison or execution. If it was manslaughter, he could face up to 30 years in prison.

Once the opening statements were finished, jurors began hearing from witnesses, including a pale, thin Elizabeth McKean, who tried to choke back tears.

Adams had come to her house on Thanksgiving Day and accused her of taking Kayla, she said.

Prosecutors played a tape of the 911 call so jurors could hear Adams calmly report Kayla missing.

Crime lab technicians identified bloody clothing belonging to Kayla, saying the chance it matched someone else was 1-in-1.1 million.

Clermont Police Officer Norman Fails testified that Adams told him she might have "a couple of bruises" on her. Fails, who was the first officer on the scene, was crestfallen.

He had seen Kayla before on the playground in the past and tried to wave to her, but she was too shy to respond.

Clermont Police Chief Randy Story testified about being led to the secret grave by Marcie.

Hawthorne told jurors all the falsehoods were "mistakes by young parents."

The next day the defense called a dentist to bolster its claim that Adams was somehow driven to the brink by pain. The dentist testified that he pulled eight teeth for Adams in the jail between February and May. But he had to admit that he did not know if Adams was suffering from pain when he killed Kayla.

Marcie testified that Adams had teeth problems before that awful day. She also repeated the damning statements about Adams not wanting to go to prison because she wasn't "worth it."

Hawthorne grilled her, bringing up the fact that she had opportunity after opportunity to tell someone what really happened. She also hid the soiled underwear, Hawthorne pointed out.

Gross asked her why she lied and what Adams had said to her.

"If I didn't do what he told me to do, I would never see my son again."

The judge stopped Gross from questioning her about being abused by Adams.

"I'm not going to have this man convicted of murder because he's a wife beater," Johnson said when the jury was out of the room.

Marcie was given the chance to say one more thing to the jury, however, about the threat of violence. "I saw what he did to Kayla (*Sentinel*, May 6, 2000)."

Adams wept when conferring with his attorneys when they asked if he wanted to take the stand in his own defense. He said no. Jurors always want to hear from the defendant, but prosecutors lick their chops at the thought of tough cross-examination.

Prosecutors decided not to play the taped confession for the guilt phase of the trial. So much for the image of a stressed-out man telling authorities he tried to be a good dad and how he didn't like it when he lost control—if he could have gotten any sympathy out of that.

The trial recessed for the weekend. On Monday, jurors heard closing arguments.

Gross pointed to Adams and said: "This man right here used his fists, his feet, and this paddle to kill a little girl." He held up a pair of bloody jean shorts behind Adams' head and said, "He killed a little girl who wore these pants."

Police had found the bloody clothing in Adams' house the day after he reported her missing, making him the prime suspect. As bad as they wanted to call off the search by hundreds of volunteers, they felt they needed proof, including her body.

Pfister attacked Marcie's testimony, calling it "the new and improved truth-telling by the State Attorney's Office." He also disclosed that the day before the trial, she was allowed to see her son, Lee, without supervision. The implication was that her testimony had been bought and paid for.

Two hours after they began deliberating, the jury returned with the verdict: guilty of first-degree murder and aggravated child abuse.

Adams' mother, Sandy, wept and so did other family members.

After a break of a few days the jurors returned for the sentencing phase.

Adams took the stand, wept, and said he didn't deserve mercy.

"I didn't even get to show that to my own daughter," he said.

Jurors now heard, for the first time, the videotaped confession, including changing his story four times.

Ridgway picked up the 2-by-4 paddle and approached Adams on the stand.

"I just wanted to give her a 'knuckle head,' Adams said. "When I tapped her on the head it was too hard. It was way too hard," he said, beginning to cry.

The testimony was emotional, but jurors had not heard anything yet. Kathie Stooksbury, who was sitting in the spectator section of the courtroom, began sobbing loudly when Adams said he considered burying the little girl the couple loved on their land. By the time she was escorted out of the courtroom she was screaming.

Lonnie, who heard the screaming outside, rushed past deputies at the courthouse's front door and crashed into the heavy, locked wooden doors of the courtroom. He beat on the doors until four deputies were finally able to bring the big man down, handcuff him, and arrest him.

The defense went to the only strategy it could with the notion that Adams pleaded for help and didn't get it.

Social workers disputed the claim.

"At no time did he say, "I need help," said Kelly Mahoney, who was at the hospital emergency room for the "bike accident."

Another DCF caseworker had the same recollection after the June 23 incident.

Adams' defense expert, psychologist Elizabeth McMahon, talked about the counseling session that he never got. Anyone could have seen that the dad-daughter custody arrangement "was the worst possible combination."

Every time Kayla did not act according to his wishes Adams considered it to be an act of defiance.

Adams' sister, Tammy Shank, testified about being physically abused by her mother but could not recall a time when Sandy Adams "lashed out" at Ricky.

Adams' father, Richard, said he had no idea things were so bad. He told the *Sentinel* a year-and-a half earlier that he and Sandy loved Kayla but a rift between them and Ricky kept them from seeing much of her.

"She was a wonderful little child," he said. She liked to hunt for bugs in the yard. He also said, "I love my son, but I am clearly ashamed of what he did (Dec. 4, 1998)."

At trial, he said of his son: "He was turning his life around and doing well. There was no reason Kayla shouldn't be with her father."

When he finished testifying, he walked toward the door of the courtroom, turned, looked at his son, shook his head, and walked out.

In closing arguments, Pfister insisted the death would not have happened if the eight to 10 social workers had done their jobs. Even prosecutors admitted the workers were "grossly negligent," he said.

There was no premeditation, he said. Adams simply lost it with a child he didn't know existed for the first four years of her life.

After deliberating for 3 ½ hours, the jury voted 8-4 in a recommendation for a life sentence.

"It was like bringing two storms together to form a tornado," juror Herb Todd told me after the recommendation was announced.

"He did ask for help. He didn't get it," said Keith Canada, another juror said (*Sentinel,* May 16, 2000).

Judge Johnson immediately imposed a life sentence. "I don't think anybody can fathom the terror and horror your daughter experienced. It is my intent, Mr. Adams, that you never walk the streets a free man again."

Less than a month later, Adams was back in court to ask for a new trial. The request was denied but my request for an exclusive interview at the jail was granted.

"I was standing there by myself. My arms were crossed in front of me. I couldn't help her," he said, his eyes filling with tears (*Sentinel* June 6, 2000). "I can't talk about this."

He said he was not upset about not getting a new trial. He was being punished in greater terms than that, he said.

"Nothing is tougher than reliving it. I've lost a piece of me. I'll never get it back," not surprisingly sounding like he was feeling sorrier for himself than for Kayla.

He also dumped some of the blame on the child welfare system.

"If one person had stepped in and said, 'Hey, this isn't going to work,' this wouldn't have happened. They're the experts," he said.

"The major responsibility is mine because I was the father. But the system failed Kayla, and there was no excuse for that," he said.

He denied hurting her before the fatal Thanksgiving weekend—despite the fact that by now the public knew about the horrific injuries he inflicted on her in May and June of that year.

He said he was shocked to hear how extensive her fatal injuries were.

"The only time I cried during the trial was when I heard about Kayla's injuries. I never thought it could escalate into something like this. There was no abuse in my house."

He said there were some "good times," like when Kayla played with her baby brother.

He claimed to have found religion with the help of jail ministry, and he didn't care if he lived or died.

"I just want to go home to Kayla," he said.

***

It would be great to end this chapter by saying that child abuse stopped, or that it was at least curtailed by lessons learned in the Kayla case. Unfortunately, that did not happen.

In 2002, DCF's Miami district announced that 5-year-old Rilya Wilson had been missing for 15 months while supposedly under the watchful eye of caseworkers. Kathleen Kearney, who had been appointed secretary of DCF after the Kayla debacle, resigned.

Kearney had cleaned house in the five-county district that included Lake County. She ordered a review of 3,000 cases and told a grand jury about new training and changes to help abused kids.

She tried to defend her agency after a report came out saying DCF failed to meet new requirements passed by the Legislature. *The Orlando Sentinel* also reported that children as young as 5 were being locked up for months in a mental health crisis unit in Orlando because DCF could not find placements for them.

In another Miami case, a caseworker was charged with falsifying home visitation records for a 2-year-old boy on the same day he was beaten to death.

Rilya, whose body was never found, became the new poster child for a system in chaos. In 2003, the new DCF secretary, Jerry Reiger, issued a report saying Miami caseworkers were so busy running from one emergency to another they had little time to focus on the welfare of the children. The study said that supervisors provided "insufficient oversight" for abuse investigators and said there was no system to track medical and education needs (*The New York Times*, April 27, 2003).

Prosecutors said Rilya's caretaker, Geralyn Graham, 67, caged the child and smothered her with a pillowcase in abuse that was filled with "lies, deceit and cover-up, (*Miami Herald*, Jan. 23, 2013)." She was sentenced to 55 years in prison.

The truth is, there is no foolproof system. Government is rarely capable of doing things right, other than growing, taxing, and spending. Who can forget Hurricane Katrina, for example, with images of parked, flooded school buses, while people were packed in the Superdome, or on bridges and roof tops?

In July of 2013, Miami-Dade Circuit Judge Cindy Lederman was sick and tired of DCF's failures after five children died in two months. She called for the agency to transfer its investigative responsibilities to law enforcement or community care organizations.

"They need to get out of the child-protection investigation business," she said. "Anybody but DCF (News Service of Florida, *Sentinel*, July 24, 2013)."

Some court officials are not only frustrated with the number of tragedies, but the way jurors look at cases. The average person has a very limited understanding of human depravity because they are decent themselves. Jurors often can't bring themselves to believe that a parent could kill their child on purpose.

Adams blamed the state child welfare system, though he is the one who landed the blows. He was partially correct. The system has failed Kayla, Rilya, and countless other children. They were trapped by birth or circumstance to end up in the care of people who shouldn't have been allowed to have a dog, let alone a child. In fact, Adams' dog was treated far more humanely.

Chapter 11

Gators and other monsters

Cold-blooded monsters lurk beneath the gloom of murky water; silent, remorseless killers who either drown or crush their victims with a ferocious chomp. One minute the water's surface is as smooth as glass, the next, it is ripped apart with a splash and gashing teeth.

Alligators are mean, green, killing machines. Built for speed on both water and land, the descendants of dinosaurs continue to thrive—even in Florida where bulldozers threaten to replace them as the new icon of the rapidly developing state.

But it's not just alligators that can harm or kill you in Florida. There are bears, panthers, coyotes, snakes, sharks, barracudas, and crocodiles, not to mention bobcats, flying fish, monkeys, rabid animals, boars, and packs of half-wild dogs that could hold their own in any Jack London book. Yet, gators are the monsters that cause the most ruckus and wide-awake nightmares.

Sometimes their victims don't know what hit them. In 1993, a 70-year-old woman, either heavily medicated, confused by dementia, or both, wandered from her home in a golf community and fell into the jaws of several alligators in ironically named Lake Serenity. Trappers looking for the guilty culprits killed several alligators, including a 9 ½-footer. What they found surprised them. Alligators eat all kinds of things, from fish to deer, but times were hard for these predators. Their stomach contents revealed sticks, rocks, and other non-edible materials.

Deadly attacks have included the heartbreaking deaths of young children, including a 4-year-old girl who was playing with her brother and a puppy, and in 1997, 3-year-old Adam Binford, who walked away from a roped-off swimming area in a quiet Volusia County park so he could play with lily pads. Suddenly, there was a "big splash," and he was gone. His killer was an 11-foot alligator. In 2016, an alligator killed 2-year-old Lane Graves at a Disney resort.

Sometimes there is a common theme. One woman was killed swimming in a lake at dusk—prime feeding time. Often, the gators are attracted to dogs, but their masters sometimes pay the price. Such was the case of an 82-year-old man who was dragged off a path while taking his terrier for a walk. He lost his leg to a 10-foot-9-inch alligator.

In late 2012, one man successfully snatched his "best friend" dog from the jaws of a 7-foot gator, while a woman lost her arm in a separate attack. Dog owner Steve Gustafson, who lives in the massive Villages retirement community, told *The Orlando Sentinel*: "For whatever reason, I don't know, I just yelled, 'You're not going to get her,' and just leaped on the gator... just like you do some belly flop in a pool. The only difference was I landed on top of a gator." Gustafson and his West Highland Terrier, Bounce, survived and had only a few stitches to show their friends (Sept. 19, 2012).

"I would do the same thing if it was my dog," said Florida Wildlife Commission biologist Lindsey Hord. Like a lot of heroic acts, fighting with an alligator is not something you think about in advance. In fact, the less thinking the better.

A few days after Gustafson saved Bounce, there was another attack reminiscent of the 1993 incident. A seven-footer attacked an 84-year-old woman who somehow ended up in a canal behind her home. When her 68-year-old neighbor, Delmas Zickefoose, saw what was going on, he jumped in to save her.

"I held her," he told the *Sentinel*. "I just held her, telling her everything would be all right, that rescue was on the way (Sept. 27, 2012)." He said he didn't think the alligator would attack him.

Licensed trappers caught the 7-foot-5 bull gator. They didn't find her arm, but the alligator's stomach contents revealed a hamburger patty, indicating that someone had been feeding him. Alligators and wild animals in general are most dangerous when they lose their fear of man.

Earlier in the year, in July, a 17-year-old had to pull his arm free from a 10-footer in the Caloosahatchee River, severing his arm just below his elbow.

A 12-year-old boy swimming with friends in the Dead River in 2003 in Lake County wasn't that "lucky." The other boys had climbed out of the water when they noticed the alligator was heading toward their friend. "Get out!" they screamed, but it was too late (*Star-Banner*, June 20, 2003).

The boy, described in loving terms by his teachers as fearless, didn't have a chance. Like the gator who attacked the 84-year-old woman in the canal, the naturally fearful alligator had also apparently been fed by humans.

Sometimes it's a matter of being in the wrong place at the right time for an alligator. One couple in Orlando thought it would be a good idea to go skinny-dipping in cool lake water until an alligator clamped down on the woman, ripping her leg open to the tune of 70 stitches. You don't even have to be in the water to wind up on the wrong end of a gator. One man, who wondered why his indoor dog was going berserk, stepped out onto his darkened porch and into an alligator's snapping jaws. Both master and dog survived.

A young artist from Tennessee who returned to the Ocala area where she once lived did not survive her encounter with an alligator. Annmarie Campbell, 23, was staying at a cabin in the Ocala National Forest when she went snorkeling with friends in Sweetwater Springs. She became separated somehow, and when her friends found her, she was in the mouth of a 7-foot-9 alligator. Thinking she might still have a chance, her friends fought to pull her from the gator's jaws, poking the beast in the eye and suffering bites themselves before finally getting the monster to let her go. She was dead, of course, expertly drowned, which is what alligators do to large prey.

"You just don't think of your daughter dying from an alligator," said Campbell's mother, Dawn Marie Yankeelov (Ocala.com, May 15, 2006).

Trappers baited massive steel hooks with beef lungs and waited for Campbell's killer. Four days later he made the fatal mistake of taking the bait. It took four men to carry the 400-pound, 11-foot-5 gator up an embankment. The gator's carcass was sent to the Medical Examiner's office so forensic experts could match teeth marks in the young woman's body.

One of the men who freed Campbell from the gator's jaws also went to the M.E.'s office to identify the animal.

"It was horrible," he said of the attack.

Alligators are fascinating and so are the people who try to either protect or kill them.

After 3-year-old Adam was killed, *Sentinel* photographer Joanne Vitelli and I teamed with a state biologist to film an episode for a *Sentinel* cable TV show in Lake County.

Lake Griffin is a part of a chain of lakes in Central Florida that looks indistinguishable from other lakes, but at the time it was one of the most gator-infested places imaginable. Several years ago, during a planned water drawdown, an aerial photograph showed thousands of the confused reptiles lined up like cars in a traffic jam. Before we could leave the dock or raise a camera lens on this day, a 12-footer using its powerful tail pushed off from the bank where it had been sunning itself.

While filming, a three-footer swam up to the boat and the wildlife officer grabbed it and held it while I asked questions. It made a kind of squealing noise, which I interpreted as a cry for mama. Females guard their nests ferociously for a year after laying their eggs, protecting their young against snakes, birds, and any other creature desperate enough to come near, including people.

Vitelli and I had a close encounter with a mama gator once before. We were with another game biologist and standing near a spring. We heard a weird croaking noise, but we didn't see anything. "Get in the truck," the biologist whispered. Like the true gentleman and hero that I am, I tried not to knock Joanne down as I scampered into the truck.

Alligator mating season is another dangerous time, with males cruising one water hole after another, sometimes ending up in people's swimming pools. Note to self: Turn on pool lights at night before jumping in.

After a lengthy interview aboard the airboat, the biologist noticed that the wind had pushed our craft into the middle of the lake.

"We can't let him out here," he said. "He'd be food for another gator." So, he taped the gator's snout shut and handed him to me, much to the amusement of Vitelli.

Gator jaws are incredibly powerful when they are snapping shut, but the muscles that open the jaws are so weak a man can hold the snout shut with one hand, hence the duct tape on our curious friend. Still, the little guy was wiggly and eager to get out of the boat. I let the biologist remove the tape. I didn't want the biologist to think I was trying to do his job, you know.

Amazingly, despite having a mouthful of big teeth, the reptiles cannot chew, so if they cannot swallow their prey whole, they stash it on a sandbar or at some hiding place until it begins to rot. They come back, clamp down and do what the experts call the "death roll." Using their powerful tail, gators flip and sling their heads until parts of the carcass come apart.

Once listed as an endangered species, the animals have made a comeback. The state receives about 16,000 complaints of threatening alligators each year and hires licensed trappers to either relocate or kill pesky alligators. In 2010, the state received 13,047 nuisance complaints and 5,856 gators were dispatched to the big swamp in the sky.

For all the primal fear the cold-blooded killers invoke, relatively few actually harm people, wildlife officials say.

"The actual risk is slight," said biologist Hord. Officials keep records of provoked and unprovoked incidents. A provoked attack happens when someone is handling or feeding an alligator. Since 1948, there has been an average of five unprovoked attacks per year. Twenty-two of the attacks resulted in deaths. Sometimes it's a matter of not using common sense.

"There are 1.3 million alligators in Florida," Hord said. "Sometimes you say, 'Wow, what was that person swimming there for?' You put yourself at risk."

Take the case of an airboat captain, for example, who liked to entertain tourists by feeding alligators. One day the gator got a little extra in his lunch—the captain's hand.

Gators are most active between dusk and dawn, so don't go swimming at night, the commission warns. Alligators are most active in warmer months.

Years ago, two friends of mine running crab lines near the beach decided they would wrestle a curious 6-foot alligator. It seemed like a good idea at the time, one friend told me later, especially after consuming a few six-packs of beer. They were able to grab the tail and even the toothy end before they realized they had a problem they summed up in two words: "Now what?" Somehow, they managed to let go without losing any of their appendages.

Sometimes the primal urge to hunt is not fueled by alcohol. Florida issues annual hunting permits to the public.

The state issued 5,000 permits in 2012, allowing just two alligators per hunter each year. The number harvested by hunters increased from 2,552 in 2000 to 8,103 in the year 2011. The prize, besides the thrill of the hunt, is the sale of the meat in the tail and the hides.

For many, the challenge is irresistible if not foolhardy. Hunters on shallow-draft boats shine flashlight beams across the dark water, sometimes spooking themselves, when they see the reflection of red eyeballs staring back.

The hunters sometimes thrust high-caliber "bang stick" guns between gators' eyes, but that's just the start of the fun. Using ropes, muscles, luck and prayer, the hunters bring their prey alongside, trying to avoid the sweeping tail, snapping jaws, and ugly disposition. Sometimes "dead" gators come to in the boats and try to take a bite out of their captors.

Even an experienced hunter like Robert "Tres" Ammerman does not realize just how big his prey is at first. He found out on the last day of hunting season in 2010.

Ammerman, his Orlando area neighbor Sam White, and his nephew, T.J. Schauf, an Afghanistan war veteran, were searching through the waters of Lake Washington, an area of the St. Johns River in Brevard County, just after midnight. Fittingly, it was Halloween when they set out in his 14-foot johnboat with an 8-horsepower motor.

"We slid up on him face-on—it's real hard to tell their size from that angle," Ammerman said. "As we got to within about 3 feet of him, I could tell he was big, and just as he dipped into the water, I threw my harpoon and hit him where the neck and head come together."

The gator took off like a furious Moby Dick, but the harpoon was attached to a float and 50 feet of line.

"The line was spinning off my buoy," Ammerman said. "He pulled us around the lake for about 45 minutes before we tried to work him up to the side of the boat."

Despite pulling the boat for 45 minutes, the alligator still had plenty of fight in him when the men finally brought him alongside.

"He death-rolled and knocked my boat around; it got pretty exciting," he said (myfwc.com, Nov. 8, 2010).

The gator, at 14-feet, 3 ½ inches long and 654 pounds, broke a 13-year record for length. The heaviest was a 1,043-pound monster killed in 1989.

"That was the second luckiest day of my life; the first was when I married my wife, Janette," the nursing center licensed practical nurse told game officials.

***

Alligators aren't the only creatures descended from prehistoric monsters. If ever there was a natural killing machine (besides man) that evolved to the highest level it would have to be the shark.

The water was warm and frothy off Gulf Island National Seashore Park on July 6, 2001, when it was suddenly split by a fin, a flash of gray, and mammoth jaws gashing an 8-year-old boy swimming 15 yards offshore. In split seconds, the 6 ½-foot, 200-pound bull shark's teeth tore through the thigh and right arm of Jessie Arbogast, spilling precious blood into the surf. His uncle, Vance Flosenzier, in a fit of bravery, madness, and love, dragged the shark to the beach, which was still clinging to the boy by his arm. A park ranger shot the shark three times and first responders, using forceps, recovered the severed arm so it could be reattached in a tense 12-hour surgical battle.

His aunt administered cardiopulmonary resuscitation until he could be airlifted to a hospital.

Jessie survived, though because he lost so much blood, he is confined to a wheelchair. The family said in a 2009 interview that he was a happy teen who attended special education classes in high school. He doesn't remember the attack, family members said (sharkattacksurvivors.com).

It was this incident and others that led a national news magazine to ring alarm bells in 2001 with the headline: "Year of the Shark."

There wasn't much else going on that summer, said George Burgess, director of the Florida Program for Shark Research at the Florida Museum of Natural History at the University of Florida.

That doesn't mean that this kind of story has become a thing of the past. Every year Burgess shows up in news stories after a fatal attack citing the latest annual report from the university's International Shark Attack file.

Local news organizations stir interest with headlines like "Volusia County, Shark Bite Capital of the World." Volusia is across the state, on the Atlantic, from where Jessie was attacked.

The Shark Attack file's 2013 report again listed Florida having the most unprovoked attacked attacks at 23. The number the year before was 21. Volusia County had eight, the most within Florida.

Volusia County, home to Daytona and New Smyrna beaches on the Atlantic, is also home to Ponce Inlet, a favorite of fishermen and surfers. It is also "a smorgasbord for sharks," Burgess said.

Jetties, which help form exciting waves for surfers, also create underwater sandbars. There is also an influx of cold water, the nearby warm Gulf Stream, algae blooms, and a nutrient-rich environment for plankton, which attracts fish. "It's a good place for a shark to make a living," he said, although turbulent water can reduce visibility.

Burgess is not the only one studying sharks, of course. Stephen Kajiura of Florida Atlantic University videotapes some of the thousands of black fin sharks that make their annual migration from North Carolina to South Florida.

In one section, from Boca Raton to Jupiter Inlet, about two football field lengths out, he has counted 15,000 sharks in a single trip.

"That's a huge number of sharks," he told the *Orlando Sentinel* in its Jan. 20, 2013, edition. "They are very close to shore. They're sometimes 30 feet from shore…If you're sitting in the water, you have an average of one shark within 60 feet of you."

The good news is that black tips rarely attack people, and when they do, they usually just nip a foot or hand in murky water, thinking it is a fish.

Surfing itself is "provocative," Burgess said, with its extra bubbles, splashing, and dangling arms and legs. Now, thanks to new technology, there's even more reasons for people to hit the beach, thanks to wave runners, sail and paddle boarding, and diving. Divers near mangroves in the Keys also face the threat of barracudas. Fishing is another draw for both tourists and sharks. "We used to fly over north Tampa Bay in a helicopter, look down and see guys fishing waist deep surrounded by sharks," said former Tampa Police Officer Chester Wood.

For all the fanfare and all the opportunities for a shark attack, Florida only averages a fatal attack about once every 10 years (recently, there were two in a 10-year span). As for attacks, there are attacks, and then there are *attacks*. Most of the bites in the New Smyrna area, for example, are hit and run, bite and release strikes. Stitches, sometimes a lot of stitches, are required. Injuries are worse if ligaments are torn. "Most people want to get back in the water," he said.

Jessie's attacker was different. "A bull shark is more aggressive. It's more of the *Jaws* type of attack. That's why they call them bull sharks," he said, noting that bull sharks will come back again and again.

Burgess and other experts who crunch the numbers of sharks crunching people are now taking special note of the predators becoming prey.

"Shark attacks sell newspapers and magazines, but the real story is Man Bites Shark," he said, conjuring up a headline. Fisheries are killing 40 million to 70 million sharks each year. Many fishermen cut off their fins, which are considered a delicacy in some parts of the world and throw the defenseless creature back in the sea.

"Who's killing who?" Burgess said.

All things considered, the sea is pretty "benign," Burgess said. Numbers don't lie. "Maybe it's the psyche," he said. Or maybe there's the chilling realization that there's a creature out there with a mouthful of teeth swimming around in a murky water "smorgasbord."

***

Of course, everyone knows that if you're going to dive into a smorgasbord you might end up as part of the main course, but if you're in a boat shouldn't you feel safe from the possibility of a fish jumping out of the water and smacking you in the head? April Miller Baker thought so while cruising down the Suwannee River in 2011, but a leaping Gulf sturgeon crushed bones around her right eye, forcing a surgeon to install three titanium plates in her face to protect her eyesight, according to the *Gainesville Sun*.

Like sharks and alligators, the present-day sturgeon is a survivor from prehistoric times, though you might not know it by their suicidal behavior. About 11 jumped into boats in 2011 with six injuring boaters.

A subspecies of the Atlantic sturgeon, they can grow up to 8 feet long and weigh 200 pounds. They spend the winter feeding in the Gulf of Mexico and return to the Suwannee River for spawning and refuge.

Baker's mother was so angry she complained to state officials, saying the fish should be taken off the threatened species list and that people should be allowed to fish for the bouncing bozos to thin the herd. The state said no, suggesting instead that boaters slow down. That also keeps boaters from turning manatees into speed bumps.

Manatees are fascinating, harmless creatures with their own colorful history. In the early days of Florida exploration, sailors sometimes mistook the giant mammals for mermaids. That itself, is probably the strongest argument of all time for giving sailors more shore leave and eye exams.

***

Alligators and sharks are not the only animals that wreak havoc on Floridians. Snakes slither into living nightmares, too. The state has 44 kinds of native species, including six poisonous creepy crawlies. Sometimes they show up in unexpected places, including potted plants in the garden section of department stores.

A pressman at the *Leesburg Commercial* where I worked in the early '80s was surprised to learn that the "baby snake" that had bitten him in the hand while he was goofing off outside the building one day was in fact a pygmy rattler. The silly stunt of picking the snake up with his bare hand, with the resulting painful swelling and illness, made him a company legend until he was outdone by a fellow worker who cut his thumb off with a chainsaw while working in his yard on his day off.

The *Commercial*, a small local newspaper, indulged its readers in those days with pictures of locally picked vegetables that looked like Richard Nixon, and other curiosities, so it was not surprising when a man pulled up in a full-sized pickup truck one day to show off a dead diamondback rattlesnake so huge that it filled the truck bed. It had stretched all the way across the road and was about 3 or 4 inches in diameter when the driver added tire tread marks to the diamond pattern.

Snakes are everywhere in Florida. A neighbor of mine was working in his yard one day when a water moccasin slipped up behind him and bit him. He was in the hospital for days.

In another incident, an acquaintance regaled a group of us with a story about trying to be romantic with his wife on his boat until a huge water moccasin dropped down into the boat from an overhead branch. "That was the end of that," he said, her screams still echoing in his head.

Personally, I've been known to make noises like a little girl while making a herculean effort to set the world's high jump record. I almost stepped on one in the Everglades one time while rushing down a path trying to get away from a hungry swarm of mosquitoes.

It's not enough, of course, that Florida has its own snakes. Pet owners have dumped thousands of non-native exotic pythons and boa constrictors into the great outdoors. In 2005, state officials said that 144,000 Burmese pythons alone had been imported to the U.S. Often, when they outgrow their cage and their "cuteness," (really?) they are dumped outside. Fluffy beware, not to mention rare and endangered animals like Key deer.

Sounding like the kind of science fiction movies that they used to make in Central Florida, like *Creature from the Black Lagoon,* Everglades National Park officials reported finding a 6-foot alligator that had been swallowed by a 13-foot Burmese python. Too big and too tough for the python to handle, the gator struggled mightily, causing the snake to explode. It would be nice to say that it all ended up resembling a nice handbag and shoe display, but it was more like someone tried to stuff a telephone pole into a pair of panty hose— sideways.

***

Black bears on the other hand, if not engaged in titanic battles with other animals, are certainly bigger crowd pleasers as the beasts wander into neighborhoods, including some near downtown Orlando. In Ocala, one resident complained that she could not use her gazebo or her hot tub for days because a bear showed up there every night like Northern kinfolk in town to visit Disney World.

Young male bears are pushed out of their normal habitat each year by older, stronger bears who are staking their claims to the females—sort of like upperclassmen in high school. Spooked by people or barking dogs, they often scamper up trees, where they are watched by big crowds of people. Often, the bears are attracted to the neighborhoods by backyard trash cans. Bears in the national forest are drawn to backyard cans, too, but when they can't find garbage they will attack pet goats, pot-bellied pigs, and whatever else they can find.

Famed writer Marjorie Kinnan Rawlings, who lived in the Ocala National Forest, captured the horror of such an encounter vividly in her classic 1938 novel, *The Yearling*. Hunting dogs Julia and Rip flew into the livestock-killing bear named Slewfoot: "The dogs had him at bay. He swayed sideways on his thick, short legs, growling, and baring his teeth. His ears were laid flat in his fury. When he turned his back for further retreat, Julia nipped at his flanks and Rip rounded him to spring for his shaggy throat. He slashed at them with great curved claws. He backed away. Rip swung behind him and sunk his teeth in a leg. Slewfoot squealed shrilly. He wheeled with the swiftness of a hawk and raked the bulldog to him. He caught him up in his fore-paws [sic]. Rip yelped in pain, then fought gamely to keep the jaws above him from closing on his backbone. The two heads tossed back and forth, snarling, and snapping, each trying for the other's throat while protecting his own (*The Yearling*, page 350)."

When bears are treed, police and wildlife officers urge people to back off and leave them alone. Eventually the animals do climb down and skedaddle but sometimes they come back. It is then that they are shot with a tranquilizer gun, tagged, and relocated to a safer place.

The Florida Fish and Wildlife Commission offers what is, no doubt, good advice on what to do if you encounter a bear, including "remain standing upright, back up slowly, and speak to the bear in a calm, assertive voice." It also advises making sure the bear has a clear escape path, then make a noise or bang pots and pans to scare him away. Don't run, don't climb a tree, or play dead, officials warn. Bears can run at speeds up to 35 mph and climb 100-foot trees in 30 seconds.

The Commission's website also states: "**Avoid direct eye contact** (Commission's emphasis). Bears and many other animals may view this as aggressive behavior."

The problem is, if you come face to face with a bear, how do you *not* look directly at the bear? You're not only going to look, but you're going to hyper focus.

Ask a holdup victim what they focus on when a robber sticks a gun in their face. It happened to a friend of mine several years ago. He was a knowledgeable gun enthusiast. "What kind of a gun was it?" I asked. "Big," he said. Not only was it "big," but the muzzle looked big enough to drive a truck through, he added.

As for the "calm, assertive voice," one has to wonder what the reaction would be if the voice suddenly became weak and squeaky. As for a loud noise, how about the sound of peeing in your pants?

Then, there is the issue of making sudden movements. How about when you turn and run out of your shoes?

They can also pose a danger on roadways at night. Recently, while driving through the forest, a friend and I passed a dozen deer standing placidly along the side of the road. However, a young bear took it upon himself to make a mad dash across the two-lane highway, just barely making safe passage. His black fur made him virtually invisible until he was picked up by the headlights.

In 1998, a 51-year-old motorcyclist was killed when a bear darted into her path and that of her husband. Stanley Elkins suffered injuries, including several broken bones. In 2000, he sued the state of Florida saying it "allowed a dangerous condition to exist upon the roadway; specifically, they allowed Florida black bears to exist upon the roadway."

People should be warned, the suit maintained. A judge dismissed the case in 2001.

Despite few people being harmed, a 54-year-old Longwood woman suffered serious face and head injuries in December 2013 while walking her dogs in her subdivision.

Wildlife officials baited traps and caught three bears. Two were destroyed and the third was spared because she was too young and small to have carried out the attack.

Four months later, a 44-year-old woman was mauled by a 200-pound black bear, also in Seminole County, a bedroom community for Orlando area.

The bear, which had broken into garbage cans in her garage, inflicted wounds on her scalp, right arm, abdomen, and right leg.

Officers with the Florida Fish & Wildlife Conservation Commission reluctantly killed seven bears in her subdivision.

"We don't want to kill bears. We just don't have a choice," an officer told the *Sentinel* (April 18, 2014). Several of the slain bears walked right up to officers standing in the road, which proves that they had lost their fear of man.

Critics of the killings lashed out at people who were feeding the bears either deliberately or by not securing their trash.

Humans are frequently the problem.

One man, for example, ran afoul of his neighbors in a suburb of Orlando with garbage pails packed with pungent pig poop. The Altamonte Springs sanitation department said it had a problem with the sheer volume. The man's pet porkers were filling 12 to 14 32-gallon garbage cans with animal waste, weighing 80 to 100 pounds each.

The man defended his pot-bellied pigs, Beauregard and Penelope, saying they were "fastidious," were always licking themselves clean and used litter boxes. He met me outside his house. There was a stench, but he said it was the smell of fertilizer spread on his lawn. I suspected there were more than two pigs inside the garage.

To further his case, he made a visit to the *Sentinel's* bureau office in nearby Casselberry, bringing one of the pigs with him. Like Arnold the pig on the '60s TV sitcom, *Green Acres,* Beauregard liked to watch TV. His favorite show was *Bonanza.*

After the *Sentinel* photographer took the pig's picture, porker and pal left the office, leaving a chagrined bureau chief with her nose out of joint, for more reasons than one.

Beauregard's case was more humorous than threatening, but sometimes stupidity can be deadly.

Who, for example, would think of using a quilt as a lid for a 100-gallon aquarium tank housing an 8 ½-pound Burmese python when you have a 2-year-old sleeping in a crib in the next room?

Shaianna Hare was strangled to death in 2009 by "Gypsy," who had been purchased by the child's mother, Jaren Hare, for $200 at a flea market. He was described as "real gentle," by Charles "Jason" Darnell, Jaren's boyfriend, during questioning by a Sumter County sheriff's detective.

The toddler's grandmother saw the danger, especially when her daughter said they didn't have enough money to properly feed the grossly underweight snake. It weighed 13 ½ pounds a month after the attack. A healthy snake of the same age should have weighed 150 pounds, a snake expert would later testify in court. After strangling the child, the snake tried to eat her.

The couple didn't own one just snake. They also had a Columbian red-tail boa, but because that snake was more "finicky," it got a real cover and latch for its cage. Darnell admitted that Gypsy had escaped its pen several times in the days leading up to the attack.

"They were at worst guilty of making a stupid decision and having a stupid pet," their defense attorney J. Rhiannon Arnold argued (Ocala.com, July 14, 2011).

Assistant State Attorney Pete Magrino disagreed, calling it "needless, senseless, careless," and arguing that the child died while the couple was committing child neglect.

He also cited the case of the snake versus alligator in the Everglades.

"It doesn't take a rocket scientist. If that kind of snake will take down an alligator, it will eat something else, even a small 2-year-old girl."

The jury agreed. Hare, 21, and Darnell, who had a baby together, were convicted of manslaughter, third-degree murder, and child neglect. They were sentenced to 12 years each in prison and five years' probation.

Unfortunately, people tend to forget earlier incidents that could serve as dramatic, sensible warnings. In 1999, an 18-month-old toddler was bitten in the face by a 13-foot pet Burmese python. The strike tore the tot's lower and upper eyelids from his face. The bite also penetrated the boy's skull. The boy suffered through two hours of surgery, but doctors were able to reattach the eye lids and stitch up his scalp.

***

Sometimes even man's best friend becomes the worst enemy.

Alice Broom, 81, grew up poor and largely stayed that way in her rural community of Citra in Marion County. But the kind, generous woman who loved to dance and go to church could never have imagined that she would be killed in 2003 while being torn to pieces by pack of mixed Pit Bull dogs owned by her friend and neighbor.

When Robert Freeman, 67, pointed out Broom's body to a paramedic, the rescue worker didn't know what he was looking at.

"He pointed to what I had assumed was a pile of garbage," Steve Martian said. "I thought it was a rolled-up carpet. She was really dirty. I suppose she was rolled all over the dirt" (*Ocala Star-Banner*, Nov. 17, 2007)."

In fact, she was "rolled all over" while being shredded while still breathing, and eventually mauled to death.

Like the deadly python case, there had been warning signs leading up to the death of the helpless elderly woman. Freeman's dogs had attacked a small dog and had bitten neighbors. His answer to the problem was to try to keep them inside his dilapidated mobile home, but the dogs would barge through the broken door, windows or through holes in the floor. On the day Broom was attacked, he latched the door shut with electrical cord.

Freeman loved his dogs, his attorneys said, and he was full of remorse. But he was found guilty of manslaughter and sentenced to 12 ½ years in prison.

"Robert, I love you. I forgive you because God forgave me," said Broom's daughter, Helen Hector. "But Bobby, you loved your dogs more than you loved my momma .... You knew those dogs were mean and you didn't do nothing about it (Ocala.com, June 9, 2006)."

Chapter 12

Cops

If the hackles stood up on the back of anyone's neck when the domestic violence call came in over the police radio, nobody mentioned it. Every call is potentially deadly but cops steel themselves when lovers' spats turn into World War III.

Sara Heckerman told the Lake County sheriff's dispatcher on Feb. 9, 2005, that her 29-year-old boyfriend, Jason Wheeler, had "hog-tied" her the day before, sexually assaulted her, and threatened to kill her if she called police.

"I need an officer to come—well, not my house, down the street from my house, because my old man's lost it and he's promised me that if a cop pulls in my driveway it's going to be a gun battle …. He's very violent, so I'm telling you this because I'm worried about everybody. He is asleep. But he's as big as this house (*Star-Banner*, Feb.10, 2005)."

She said she was calling from a friend's home and gave directions.

"He's sleeping, so if they come out with sirens he's going to go off. He's literally lost it. They'll see when they see me," she said, explaining that she would be on foot.

"My truck's broke. He broke it. He's a big boy; you may want to send more than one [deputy]. He almost killed me yesterday."

She had not called the day before, she said, because she had not yet moved her children to safety. She spent the night at a motel in DeLand.

The dispatcher sent three deputies to the house in Lake Kathryn Heights in the Ocala National Forest.

Deputies Wayne Koester, 33, Bill Crotty, 39, and Thomas McKane, 26, each arrived in their own patrol cars.

Crotty met with Heckerman at the corner, while deputies Koester and McKane, 26, checked out a travel trailer on the property.

McKane and Koester found the main house, a large mobile home, which had been wrecked by a series of hurricanes the year before. Wheeler had been trying to fix the house, which was surrounded by debris, abandoned vehicles, and trash.

After looking around, the deputies began roping off the area with crime scene tape. That's when all hell broke loose.

"I could hear something behind me sounding like a shotgun racking, and there was some commotion and then there was a blast from behind me," McKane said in a sworn statement. "I turned around just in time to see the dust and debris coming out the end of the shotgun in my direction (*Star-Banner*, May 24, 2006)."

McKane and Koester began running. McKane took cover. Koester, who lost his gun in the battle, began running down the long dirt driveway toward the parked patrol cars. Crotty and Heckerman heard the shots as they arrived.

"I saw Deputy Koester running up the driveway,'" Crotty said in his statement. "Deputy Koester had a gunshot [wound] to the face. It looked like a bird shot. His face was bleeding. He tripped coming up the driveway. I thought he was going to fall."

Wheeler shot Koester three times in the back as he ran down the driveway, but all three wounds were non-fatal.

"I saw Jason raise the shotgun and try to shoot Wayne in the back .... I pointed my firearm at him to let him know that I was going to shoot him, but I couldn't get a shot off because Deputy Koester was in my line of fire," Crotty said.

Koester made it to his car where he grabbed a shotgun, but Wheeler shot him in the head, killing him.

Crotty fired and Wheeler ran into the woods. Crotty and Heckerman scampered to take cover behind another police car. Wheeler then ambushed Crotty, chasing him around the patrol car, shooting at him and riddling the automobile with shotgun pellets.

"I yelled at him," Crotty said. "I said: 'Jason, what the hell are you doing?' He said, 'I'm going to [expletive] kill you, man.'"

Heckerman crawled under the patrol car. Crotty, who was shot in the leg, tried to shoot under the car to hit Wheeler's legs.

McKane ran out into the open on a parallel dirt driveway and began shooting at Wheeler as he retreated.

McKane ran to Koester, who was lying face down near his car. McKane grabbed Koester's shotgun and Wheeler ran out of the woods again, shooting and hitting McKane in the leg.

The dispatcher listening to the chaos over the radio heard the words: "I've been shot!'"

Wheeler retreated on a yellow dirt bike as McKane fired his weapon in his direction. The gun battle, which must have seemed like it had lasted for hours, was over in seven minutes.

Florida Department of Law Enforcement crime scene technicians later covered the ground with numbered, yellow evidence markers and tiny blue flags to mark spent shell casings in an open, sandy area near the mobile home. Investigators recovered about a dozen shotgun casings from that area—one of three spots where shooting took place. An additional 12 to 15 shell casings may have come from the deputies' weapons. More spent shells were found in the yard and the front gate.

Between 500 and 600 law enforcement officers were soon swarming the piney woods and swamps, and no telling how many reporters and photographers.

I was at home when I heard the news and I jumped up and started scrambling for something to wear. As the night city editor for the *Star-Banner,* I wasn't scheduled to go in for hours. *Star-Banner* police reporter Austin Miller headed for the woods, and I tore off to the hospital in Eustis where all three deputies were taken.

I wrote: "The faces told the story outside Florida Hospital Waterman Wednesday—tearful, pained, shocked, relieved, and saddened—as the friends and families of two injured and one slain Lake County sheriff's deputies gathered to cling to hope, or have those hopes dashed (*Star-Banner*, Feb. 10, 2005)."

Rich Crotty, the powerful Orange County mayor in nearby Orlando, said he had a bad feeling when his pager went off that morning but was glad his brother's injuries were not life-threatening.

His brother wanted to be a police officer "ever since he was a little boy," he said. "My guess is he can't wait to get out of bed and get back on the job."

Deputy Crotty's wife was relieved, too. A registered nurse at the hospital, she greeted him in the emergency room.

McKane was surrounded by familiar faces, too. He had two sisters working in the hospital, one of whom once worked as a cop in Umatilla.

McKane was hit in the face, shoulder, and leg with shotgun pellets but "was doing fine," said a family member. McKane was a fourth-generation law enforcement officer, and his wife, Andrea, was a student at the police academy. It had been a terrifying experience for her. She was a dispatcher that day and had talked to Crotty and her husband.

It was a devastating time for Koester's family, including Victor Koester, who described his brother as "an awesome law enforcement officer."

He had only been a deputy since June, but before that he had been a well-respected sergeant with the Umatilla Police Department.

"This is what he wanted to do. This is what he wanted to be," Koester said as he thanked the community for its support and acknowledged that it was going to be tough. "We're just getting by .... He's going to be missed."

He said his brother was married with two children, a 9-year-old son and 13-year-old daughter.

The sheriff's chaplain, the Rev. Bob Whitworth, was on hand to comfort the families.

Asked how they were doing, he said: "Two out of three are doing great. What can you say?"

Meanwhile, the hunt continued for Wheeler, a man described as an avid hunter and a deeply troubled man.

Friends and family said the stress of trying to fix the storm-damaged mobile home and growing domestic battles with Heckerman had taken its toll. The home was a shambles and he was taking methamphetamine to try and stay awake at night so he could fix it. The couple was forced to live in a jammed travel trailer with their children.

Among a series of domestic violence calls from the house was one in which Heckerman was charged with allegedly trying to stab Wheeler with a butcher knife. Charges were dropped in that case. Wheeler pulled her hair and pointed guns at her while threatening to kill her, according to court records.

David Dugan, who lived with the couple for about a month before the gun battle, said in a deposition: "I seen [sic] Jason tear her clothes off one time. I seen the both of them slap each other around (May 24, 2006)."

Heckerman threatened to leave him and take their children to Ohio.

On the weekend of Feb 5, Dugan and his fiancé went to Daytona Beach with Heckerman and Wheeler.

On Feb. 8, Wheeler dragged Heckerman by her hair.

"He hog-tied her. Threw her on her stomach and stuffed mulch in her mouth, and tried to wrap her head with duct tape," another Wheeler friend, John Tilghman, said in a sworn statement.

"And the kids are screaming, 'My mommy, my mommy!' And they're pissing all over themselves. I am freaking out at this point .... All I could think about was taking these kids away from here," Tilghman said. "I am screaming. I said, 'Man, I am going to take these kids to the park. Man .... call me when you are all done beating the hell out of each other.'"

That night, Heckerman and the children stayed in a motel room in DeLand with Dugan and his fiancée. Heckerman asked Dugan to go see Wheeler and tell him that she needed money to return to Ohio. She mentioned the idea of calling the police to get "help" for him.

Wheeler handed Dugan almost $600. He was under the impression that if he gave Heckerman money she wouldn't call law enforcement officers, Dugan said.

Sheriff Chris Daniels' staff set up a command post at a nearby elementary school as hundreds of officers from dozens of agencies looked for Wheeler. At around 5:30 p.m., officers spotted Wheeler on an island in nearby Blue Lake.

"He was adamantly screaming to us, 'Shoot me! Shoot me,'" Sheriff's Cpl. Joseph Schlabach would later testify (*Star-Banner*, May 18, 2006).

"He had his hands up and he made . . . in a quick motion, grabbed a weapon, what I thought was a weapon. I was in fear for my life," Schlabach said. "I shot him. I was told I got five shots at him. I thought it was six. He fell with his head pointing to me."

Wheeler had been hit in the abdomen, one shot went through both legs, and one shot struck him in the left buttock, according to a deputy at the scene.

Wheeler was taken to Orlando Regional Medical Center. Later, while watching news coverage of Koester's funeral from his hospital bed, Wheeler told a corrections officer he had wanted to go "out in a blaze of glory (*Star-Banner*, Aug. 19, 2005)."

Instead, he will go out in a wheelchair, paralyzed from the waist down and hauled off in a hearse, either from a dose of poison in a lethal injection execution or from the effects of rotting away in a prison cell.

He said the only reason he went to the house that day was to kill Heckerman, but when deputies arrived, he "was worried because deputies had guns and he was in trouble."

That's when he decided to shoot the deputies.

"It's been a tough day," Sheriff Daniels told reporters after Wheeler's capture. Later, he praised the professionalism of his law enforcement officers, including the three who were shot (Feb. 10, 2005). They did nothing wrong, he pointed out.

"The one thing you can't protect yourself from is an ambush," Daniels said (*Star-Banner*, Feb. 11, 2005).

Nor could law enforcement and the community they served protect themselves from grief.

"Umatilla is a two-square-mile town," said Jill Cook, an administrative assistant with the town's police department. "Everybody knew everybody. Everybody knew 'Officer Wayne' in Umatilla. He was requested on a lot of calls. It's a major shockwave."

Koester's sister, Paula Cassella, said he always wanted to be a police officer and when he got the chance he worked hard and took every class he could to become a well-rounded officer.

The sheriff's office praised his work, saying he got high marks in his performance reviews.

Besides two children from his first marriage, he was stepdad to wife Ashley's 12-and 7-year-old daughters. He and Ashley would have celebrated their second wedding anniversary the following month.

Hundreds attended the funeral, including cops from as far away as Canada, along with firefighters and rescue workers.

"Wayne fell last week, but he fell into the arms of God," said Koester's uncle, the Rev. Kevin Van Duser, the youth pastor at a Baptist church in Naples.

Also speaking was an emotional Daniels. Like others that day, he quoted John 15:13. "Greater love hath no man than this: to lay one's life for one's friends."

The newly elected sheriff reminded the crowd about the "thin blue line" that separates law-abiding citizens from lawlessness. "Last Wednesday there was an attempt to breach that line. The line held but at a terrible cost."

Daniels, 46, would be dead himself in a year-and-a-half in a freak accident while driving an old school bus on a racetrack at a charity event.

Prosecutors announced they were seeking the death penalty for Wheeler, which was no surprise. Another given was that the trial would be an excruciating experience for those who knew and loved the playful yet dedicated lawman.

Assistant Public Defender William Grossenbacher described Wheeler as a hard-working man who worked day and night to get "his family's home back into shape (*Star-Banner,* May 18, 2006)."

He also said in his opening statement: "My client is not guilty of premeditated murder. I urge you to listen carefully to the evidence."

The incident happened because of "rage brought on" by what the deputies were doing, he said.

The deputies' family members, forced to remain mum in the courtroom, fought a losing battle with tears, however. Ashley Koester covered her face and wept quietly but her body was racked with tears as a tape of the dispatch calls was played. Other family members stared angrily at Wheeler. Andrea McKane also cried.

Bill Crotty broke down in tears when he testified about Koester running down the driveway and the shotgun wound to his face. "He was running toward the patrol car. At first, I saw him trip …. He had a frightened look on his face (*Star-Banner*, May 19, 2006)."

Tears poured when the guilty verdict came back, too. He was found guilty of first-degree murder of a law enforcement officer with a firearm, two counts of attempted murder of a law enforcement officer with a firearm, and two counts of aggravated battery of a law enforcement officer with a firearm.

For some, the grief was still too raw, the loss too hard to comprehend. Such was the case for Koester's biological children, said his ex-wife, Virginia Bevirt.

"They knew their father was shot but they didn't know the specifics," she said. "It's hard for the kids to put into perspective that their father was running with fear in his eyes, that Wayne fell to his knees, that he was blue (*Star-Banner*, May 20, 2006)."

"Wayne will never be back. There will never be no more football games. No more coaching. No daddy to walk my daughter down the aisle," she said, with tears coming into her eyes.

The penalty phase of the trial was also gut-wrenching.

Grossenbacher argued that his client was under extreme emotional stress. State Attorney Brad King cited the law's definition of aggravating circumstances that allows for death penalty sentencing, calling the crime cold and calculated.

"He charged Wayne Koester 131 feet down this driveway. At any point, he could have turned away or surrendered," King said. "But he continued to load his shotgun until Wayne Koester was dead."

The jury voted 10-2 to recommend that the judge impose a death sentence.

Wheeler wrote a five-page letter to Circuit Judge T. Michael Johnson, calling himself "a broken man" and apologized to Koester's family (*Star-Banner*, July 8, 2006).

"I swear I would give you my life if it would bring him back, but it won't and I'm sorry," he wrote.

"Satan was on a mission from hell to destroy me" he said. "I was so caught up in drugs and sin. I didn't see it that way. I thought it was just a streak of bad luck. I look back now and say to myself, I would give anything to go back and change that day. Well, once again, I would be wrong because that day wasn't what needed changing." He said it was his behavior that needed changing.

God had made him a new man, Wheeler wrote. "Every day I wake up and go to bed feeling blessed rather than cursed."

His letter included a reference to Bible verse Romans 6:23, which he quoted as ". . . the price for sin is death." The New International Version on Biblegateway.com has it as: "For the wages of sin is death, but the gift of God is eternal life in Christ Jesus our Lord."

Wheeler also wrote: "When you think I would be feeling sorry for myself, I'm not. What I'm worried most about now is other people falling into the trap of sin I fell in."

Wheeler's mother testified for her son in the penalty phase, but no one from his family showed up to beg for his life at a presentencing hearing. Certainly, no one from Koester's family wanted his life to be spared.

"You took one of my soul mates," said Koester's sister, Paula. "You do not deserve any mercy …. You showed Wayne no compassion. So, you deserve none. This court owes you no mercy and I owe you no forgiveness (*Star-Banner*, Sept. 16, 2006)."

By October, Wheeler sat in his wheelchair and faced Judge Johnson, a man who spent most of his life as a public defender trying to keep men and women off death row.

"This court regretfully sentences you to death in the manner provided by law," he said. He also sentenced Wheeler to four life sentences.

Wheeler looked straight ahead, not showing much emotion. The tears flowed again for Koester's family members, however, as they cried softly and held onto one another.

"We're just trying to finish this. I'm glad it's over, but it's a false sense of security because we don't know how his appeals will turn out or how long they'll take," Cassella said outside the courtroom.

Among the hundreds of law enforcement officers searching for Wheeler in the woods were some sheriff's deputies from neighboring Marion County. They needed no extra motivation to hunt for a cop killer, nor did they need to be reminded that one of their own had been mowed down almost exactly a year to the day.

***

Marion County Sheriff's K-9 Deputy Brian Litz was doing a good deed. He was performing a well-being check on a 74-year-old mentally ill man who lived alone when the man gunned him down.

Forty-five minutes later, gunman Ivan K. Gotham was dead, too.

The State Attorney's Office cleared Marion County deputies in the death of Gotham, but the shooting sparked a controversy over the way people treated—or failed to treat—Gotham's mental illness.

"The way I see it is that once Brian Litz was shot, they lost their emotions," Ivan Gotham's son, Gary, told the *Star-Banner* in a telephone interview from his home in Virginia.

"They acted as the jury, a judge, and the executioner when they killed my dad (Feb. 27, 2004)."

The Marion County Sheriff's Office said that Litz, 36, was shot in the neck and collapsed on the porch. Gotham hid and then ran inside the house, refusing to obey deputies' commands to surrender while they tried to rescue Litz.

Several minutes went by before Gotham—apparently unarmed at this point—grabbed the barrel of a deputy's shotgun, which discharged, killing him.

Gary Gotham, who had called the sheriff's office to ask for a well-being check on his dad, warned deputies his father had a gun. He was sure the deputies could have handled the situation differently. They did not use tear gas to get him out of the house, for instance. Nor did they use a crisis-negotiator.

At one point, a nearby deputy signaled to others that Litz was dead, therefore it was a recovery and not a rescue operation, he argued. Sheriff's spokesman Lenny Uptagraft, however, said no one could be sure. "If there is a shred of hope that someone's life can be saved, the members of this agency are going to do whatever they can to save that person's life, even at great risk of their own."

The shooting was not the only controversial aspect. The elder Gotham had been involuntarily committed to a mental hospital a month earlier after he wandered around a nearby neighborhood without pants and rattled the locked door of a man's house. He was hospitalized for six days.

His family said he didn't need to be hospitalized.

A month later, Gotham took his case to a Senate hearing in Washington. John Breaux of Louisiana, the ranking Democrat on the Senate Aging Committee, was trying to get support for bills to include mental illness coverage in seniors' health care and to expand research into elder abuse.

Gotham said his father's primary care doctor failed to diagnose dementia. He also testified that no one notified the family after his father was involuntarily committed.

"I had spent the last two years fighting the global war on terrorism," said Gotham, a Navy officer, "and returned to America only to learn that terrorism had struck my dad in Florida (*Star-Banner*, March 23, 2004)."

Lawsuits were filed. Cherie Litz, the deputy's widow, sued the mental hospital and one of the psychiatrists there, claiming malpractice. She also sued the Gotham's estate and the family's insurance company.

The Gotham family notified the sheriff's office that they might face a lawsuit. The sheriff's office said such a suit would have no merit.

"If there wouldn't have been a gun, none of this would have happened," sheriff's Capt. Dennis Strow said (*Star-Banner*, June 14, 2005). The family should have removed the gun from the house, he said.

Litz, 36, who was shot just above his bulletproof vest, was always preaching and teaching safety, deputies said. He even made sure his K-9, "Justice," wore a vest.

He was also a "merciless self-critiquer," said one deputy (*Star-Banner*, Feb. 12, 1994). "I can just about hear him now, reaming himself over what happened and not allowing that this was a mindless, senseless, awful moment that cannot be changed, something no amount of training or experience could have prevented."

On the day of the funeral, with hundreds of law enforcement officers in attendance, no one could take their eyes off one deputy who seemed especially lost. "Justice" had lost his partner, his master, and his best friend.

"I just about lost it when I saw that dog walk down that aisle," a veteran reporter told me.

In an act of sterling kindness, the sheriff let the dog retire and move in with Cherie and Brian, 5.

The issues surrounding the Gotham case have dissipated, at least publicly. They are still unresolved, however. Mental illness is like a plague in this country, and the older the population becomes, the bigger the problem becomes. One family is mourning the loss of a father of four while another family and the community is sorely missing a lawman of character, service, and honor.

***

Police officers are watched like a hawk, treated like a dog, and loved like the plague while making split-second decisions and keeping their emotions in check in a pressure-cooker.

Suspects often run, lead officers on dangerous car chases, refuse to obey simple commands designed to ensure their safety, or assault officers, including police dogs.

A suspect taking off on foot is not uncommon. Listen to a police scanner and you can hear police officers huffing and puffing as they try to run down kids who could qualify for the Olympics. That's when police dogs are released to catch the suspect. Personally, I would rather be shot than be bitten by a German shepherd.

I almost feel sorry for the bad guys who suddenly end up with a face full of fangs and fur—almost.

Sometimes suspects want to argue instead of immediately obeying commands. Other times, they reach into their pockets to pull out a cell phone or grab the waistband of their trousers, apparently to keep their baggy pants from falling.

People are unpredictable and potentially lethal in almost every situation.

One Leesburg officer tried to stop and question a pedestrian after he was almost hit by a car, but the man kept walking, finally walking off the roadway on soft ground toward an apartment complex. No longer able to follow in his patrol car, the officer got out on foot.

"I could see that he was wearing a shoulder holster for a handgun," Officer Joseph Iozzi wrote in his report on Dec.

31, 1999. "I could see there wasn't a gun in the holster, so I continued to approach him on foot."

He said he kept telling the man to stop but he kept walking.

"I finally got up to him and started to grab his left arm when he quickly turned around with a knife in his right hand. He swung the knife around at me in a slashing motion."

The officer drew his sidearm and the man eventually dropped the knife but kept walking. The officer called for backup, and when he reached the apartment complex, he used pepper spray to subdue the man.

***

Sumter County Sheriff Jamie Adams summed it up nicely when he retired in 1996 after four terms in office.

"The angels were looking out for us," he told me in an interview (*Sentinel*, Dec. 26, 1996).

In the early 1980s, the former game warden scared himself and everybody else within the sound of the blast coming from his own rifle.

The sheriff's office had received a report about a suspicious engine noise deep in the woods. "I thought we were dealing with an airplane taking off with drugs. "I loaded a carbine with tracers. I didn't want that airplane to get away."

Adams and his deputies didn't find an airplane, but they did find a suspicious mobile home that was being powered by a generator. Adams removed the tracers from the rifle and replaced them with conventional rounds.

"I kicked in the door and three people inside scattered."

As he stepped forward, he slipped on the floor. He fired three shots in the air to make the Colombians stop running. They froze in their tracks—not because they were afraid of being shot, but because they were afraid of being blown to smithereens. Adams and his men had stumbled onto a high-tech cocaine processing plant, complete with heat lamps and open containers of volatile pure ether.

"If I hadn't changed bullets ...," he said, shaking his head.

***

In 1996, Eustis police were trying to save the life of a man who had been threatened the day before by his crack cocaine drug dealer.

The man said the dealer threatened him with a tire iron over a $60 debt. Cops searched but could not find the dealer.

The dealer showed up at the customer's house the next day, however, and began banging on the door with the tire iron. The customer ran out the back door and practically into the arms of a police officer responding to the man's call for help, but not before hearing the dealer's .380-caliber handgun being fired.

On the other side of the house was an officer who had pinned on his badge just four months earlier. The officer had told the dealer to place his hands on the patrol car. Instead, the man reached down the front of his pants and shouted: "I have a gun."

The two men began wrestling for control of the weapon. The gun went off but neither man was hurt. Finally, the man dropped the gun and took off running. Other officers arrested him in a nearby field. Police learned that after the gun went off, the next round jammed in the weapon.

***

Clifford Matthews, a corrections training officer at the Lake County jail, had just left the Leesburg airport where he was acting as the spotter for the sheriff's helicopter pilot. The two men were looking for a career criminal who escaped from a work release program in Gainesville.

On his way home, at 5:45 a.m., he saw the man raping a convenience store clerk, who had stepped outside to check gas tank levels.

"Don't make me kill you," David Mitchell, 26, told his victim, while beating her savagely (*Sentinel*, June 23, 1998).

Matthews chased the man to a nearby auto repair shop and held him until police arrived.

"Cliff's conduct was exemplary of what you'd expect from a law enforcement officer," said then-sheriff's Capt. Chris Daniels. "This shows that there is no such thing as off duty."

***

When Clermont bystanders and rescue workers looked inside a car crushed in a five-car pileup they were horrified to see a toddler trapped inside with his hair on fire.

"My baby! My baby!" screamed Claudia Delpino, as witnesses dragged her away from the burning wreckage (*Sentinel*, Feb. 6, 2001).

Lake County Sheriff's Deputy Rob Parker emptied a fire extinguisher on the burning car and grabbed a special protective blanket covered in fire retardant gel and crawled through the flames to 18-month-old Cody.

Passers-by pulled off their shirts, soaked them in water, and began beating out the flames.

"Everybody came running with fire extinguishers, hoses, whatever they had," said motorist Jeff Taylor.

Paramedic Russell "Rusty" Robinson, who was driving by, stopped, climbed into the other side of the car, and helped the deputy shield the tot from the flames.

"I had to borrow a knife to cut away the headrest so he could breathe. I was just hoping they would hurry and get the fire out," Robinson said.

Firefighters arrived and put out the flames, then began cutting the roof off the car to free everyone inside.

Cody, Parker, and Robinson suffered first-degree burns. Parker was also treated for smoke inhalation.

Five other people were taken to a nearby hospital, but their injuries did not seem to be serious.

"It's all part of the job," Robinson said, but it sure seemed like a lot more than that to the child's mother.

***

A rookie cop on the Fruitland Park police force received a call from an off-duty officer working security at Wal-Mart on April 15, 1999, that a video camera supposedly picked up a 15-year-old boy and a man, later identified as Jerome Richardson, stuffing cigars into their pockets. The security officer searched the juvenile but found no cigars. When the two left the store at about 2:30 a.m., the off-duty officer called Fruitland Park police to say the two had been "acting suspicious."

When they left the store, the 15-year-old driver struck a shopping cart, ran a stop sign and then led the patrol officer on a car chase down several streets. When the car finally stopped, the teen jumped out and ran.

The incident was typical foolishness—not even worth a brief under crime news—but what happened next was seared with controversy.

"Richardson was either seated in the passenger seat of the subject vehicle, was in the process of standing with his hands in the air, or was standing with his hands in his pockets," according to a civil rights lawsuit filed against the officer and the city.

The officer said he told Richardson to take his hands out of his pockets "four or five times," and when he finally did, the officer, thinking Richardson had a weapon, fired his .45-caliber semi-automatic handgun. The bullet struck Richardson in the torso. There was no weapon or cigars in his pockets (*Sentinel*, April 30, 1999).

The officer left the department. Two years after the shooting, the city's insurance company settled the lawsuit for $70,000.

＊＊

Sometimes the victims of crimes are injured in police shootings.

Carjacking victim Bob Whittaker, 76, was injured when a bullet fragment went through a 15-year-old suspect and struck him in the arm.

The Leesburg officer who did the shooting said he had to fire his weapon because the elderly man's Mercury Grand Marquis accelerated toward him.

"He was looking right at me," the officer said of the teen. "I had my firearm drawn and I said, 'Police. Stop. Police. Stop.' Over, and over again (*Sentinel,* Feb. 10, 2001)."

Officer Michael Cassidy told investigating Lake sheriff's deputies that the teen had "every limb, from his feet to his hands, inside the car and he began snatching on the driver."

Whittaker told the *Orlando Sentinel* that the car never moved forward. On Jan. 14, however, said: "The vehicle did accelerate, but I don't believe that I did that." He said he didn't see the officer either.

On Feb. 10 he said, "I still don't know what happened. I was kind of busy."

Fortunately, the bullet fragment went through the fleshy part of Whittaker's arm. His wife suffered minor injuries from flying glass.

The teen survived his injuries and was charged as an adult with attempted carjacking. His 24-year-old partner ended up climbing a tree, but he was arrested and charged with grand theft auto.

Authorities ruled it a justified shooting, not only because the officer feared for his life but because he was trying to stop a dangerous felony.

Fortunately, "collateral damage," as the military calls it when civilians get hurt, is rare. It can be fatal, however.

In 2012, Lake County Sheriff's deputies went to the Blueberry Hill apartment complex, knocked on a door, and shot the man who opened it because he was armed. Unfortunately, it was the wrong apartment and the wrong man.

Deputies were looking for a suspect who had beaten a man in Leesburg. The problem was that they didn't identify themselves as law enforcement officers when they knocked on the door.

Friends of the deliveryman were outraged. People who didn't even know the man were angry.

The sheriff's department said the deputies did not have to identify themselves. In fact, they made the decision not to because they felt it would be safer.

Sheriff Gary Borders said the deputy was in fear for his life. "The door flung open—and that's the deputy's words—and there was a gun pointed in his face (*Sentinel,* July 20, 2012)."

On May 15, 2013, the *Orlando Sentinel* ran a front-page story by staff writer Amy Pavuk headlined: "7 shootings by law enforcers concern community, FDLE."

All of the fatal shootings had occurred in Central Florida within the past month.

"We're seeing more violence against police officers when they're trying to effect arrests," said Danny Banks of the Florida Department of Law Enforcement. FDLE investigates cop shootings. "And I think there's a mental-health issue that's causing people to want to confront and get in violent confrontations with authority."

Cases like the Blueberry Hill shooting, however, can incense and alarm residents. A lawsuit was filed against the Lake County Sheriff's Office, but the lawmen prevailed.

On July 24, 2013, the *Sentinel* reported that the Orange County Sheriff's Office settled a civil rights lawsuit filed by the estate of a man who was struck by 20 of 130 shots fired at an apartment complex while he sat in his SUV.

Deputies said he rammed their cars as they tried to arrest him in a car theft investigation. Terrified neighbors said bullets from the officers' guns were flying everywhere and feared their families would be killed. The dead man's family claimed deputies used excessive force. Authorities and a grand jury cleared the 10 deputies, but a federal judge compared it to an "execution."

One of the things that concern some people is that both cops and robbers now have more firepower. After long complaining that they are being outgunned by drug dealers and career criminals carrying AK-47s and other automatic weapons, some police departments are stockpiling M-16s, armored cars, and other military equipment.

On the same day the *Sentinel* carried the Orange County lawsuit story, editors also published a photo of more than a dozen weapons seized in the arrest of 20 people in a drug ring—including assault weapons.

On July 27, 2013, Constitutional lawyer and author John Whitehead appeared on *The Mike Huckabee Show* to promote his book, *A Government of Wolves: The Emerging American Police State.*

He was decrying what his press release described as "the final stages of transformation into a police state, complete with surveillance cameras, drug-sniffing dogs, SWAT team raids, roadside strip searches, blood draws at DUI checkpoints, mosquito drones, Tasers, privatized prisons, GPS tracking devices, zero tolerance policies, overcriminalization, and free speech zones."

Ironically, his appearance was upstaged during a news break on the Fox channel with reports that an armed man had killed seven people and was holding two hostages in Hialeah, Fla. Police wearing military gear could be seen running down the streets. Eventually, talks with a crisis negotiator broke down and police had to break in and shoot him before he could harm hostages.

It was unclear if he was one of the many gunmen who decide they want to commit "suicide by cop."

In one story that I wrote, I quoted a police report saying that an officer had gone to a man's house "to make sure he was OK after someone called questioning his safety." Like Gotham in the Brian Litz shooting, the man was mentally unstable, in this case, because he had stopped taking his medication to control wild mood swings.

He threatened the officer with a tire iron.

"Shoot me. Go ahead and shoot me!" the man shouted (*Sentinel*, Sept. 9, 1997).

Finally, he put down the tire iron, but then kicked the gun out of the officer's hand. After a struggle, the officer was able to subdue him.

All of these incidents, of course, predated the murder of George Floyd by a Minneapolis police officer in 2020. The murder sparked massive protests and a call for police reform. Among the new ideas is having social workers show up on certain calls instead of police officers.

Over the years, officers have used non-lethal weapons like pepper spray and Tasers or stun guns. Unfortunately, some people have died after being shocked with those devices, sometimes because the suspect is on drugs or because of unknown medical conditions.

Deciding when to use a Taser is the key. In one case, an officer used a Taser on a suspect handcuffed to a hospital gurney when he refused to cooperate and give a urine sample. It might have brought some satisfaction to the officer, who had probably been putting up with a lot of verbal abuse, and probably won some supportive laughter in the squad room, but it was clearly inappropriate.

Law enforcement agencies started using them on their own officers in training sessions to demonstrate what it felt like and to show how effective and safe they are. One of the public information officers in Marion County decided to be the guinea pig for a demonstration video. The stun gun fired two electric probes attached to wires. The device did the job all right, but it was because one of the probes hit him in the one place you *never* want to be injured, especially if you ever want to have children.

"Yeah, he took one for the team that day," a female public information officer would later laugh—off the record, of course.

* * *

Felons endanger the lives of cops and innocent bystanders in high-speed car chases.

Officers in Casselberry, Fla., were warned to clear an intersection on a major road in their city because a stolen car was headed their way. It was early, dark, and foggy. They had gone to the site in the first place because a truck had spilled its load. They got out of the way, but a tow truck driver who did not get the word showed up just as the speeding car approached.

Lt. Steve Bengelsdorf walked over and ordered the tow truck driver to move the vehicle. The next thing he knew, he could hear bawling tires, crunching metal, and found himself looking up at the tow truck's tires.

The stolen car had swerved, missing the tow truck but it slammed into a parked car. The officer, in a hurry to get out of the way, ran into the side of the tow truck. He was OK, and so was the driver of the stolen car, but the thief faced five charges, including being a habitual drunk driver (*Sentinel*, Feb. 12, 1993).

In the 1980s and early '90s, police took a big step back from high-speed chases after a series of tragic accidents.

In 1989, an officer in Longwood, Fla., gave chase to a 15-year-old through five cities after the teen failed to dim his high-beam headlights to oncoming cars. The kid lost control of the car and crashed, killing a 13-year-old passenger and a 20-year-old woman after hitting her car head-on. Sometimes police crash their patrol cars during car chases, injuring innocent bystanders.

Naturally, lawsuits follow. It was during this period that Leesburg Police came out with a policy stating that officers were not to go 20 mph over the speed limit in pursuits.

"Every second that a high-speed chase continues will increase the chances for death, injury or property damage," read the city's policy manual.

But on Nov. 2, 1991, a rookie patrol officer spotted a motorcyclist parked in what he described as a "rough neighborhood" and pulled his car around to see if he could "assist" the man. He said he thought his bike may have broken down.

The biker took off before the patrol car could reach him, running stop signs and streaking down a main thoroughfare at speeds estimated to be 85 mph.

The rookie estimated his speed at about 75 mph in the area posted at 40 and 35 mph, but he said he wasn't trying to stop the motorcycle, just keep an eye on him.

"He's not going to stop for me," the officer told the dispatcher. Less than a minute and half later the motorcyclist crashed into a stone and concrete sign.

Robert Whitton's parents were devastated by the death of their 21-year-old son. His sister said her family "will never be what it could have been (*Sentinel*, Dec. 8, 1995)."

A family friend said the crash "took the life out of his family. They were not the same people after the accident (*Sentinel*, Dec. 7, 1995)."

The family sued the city police department, claiming negligence. Like so many other individuals caught up in the legal system, they were determined to either get their pound of flesh, make sense of the senseless, or both.

Police Chief Chuck Idell, who had been a lieutenant and the watch commander that night, testified that the officer "was in a follow mode, not a chasing mode or a pushing mode."

It would prove to be a turning point in the trial for the five-man, one-woman jury.

Also crucial was the testimony of a newspaper carrier. He estimated that the motorcycle was going about 85 mph. He was a motorcyclist himself but not an expert in estimating the speed of passing vehicles, the plaintiff's attorneys noted.

Even more controversial was the pathologist who testified that Whitton's blood-alcohol level was 0.07. The legal limit at that time was 0.10. It is now 0.08, yet the doctor testified that it could have affected Whitton's judgment.

The alcohol level was "irrelevant, immaterial and unfairly prejudicial," the Whittons' attorney argued (*Sentinel,* Feb. 27, 1996).

The jury found for the police department. The judge rejected the family's request for a new trial.

The lawyer also thought it was irrelevant that Whitton's driver's license had been suspended and that he did not have a motorcycle endorsement on his license.

Circuit Judge Jerry Lockett wasn't one-sided in his rulings. He did not allow the trial jury to hear Whitton's mother's comment when a priest and an officer went to her home to deliver the bad news.

"I told him that motorcycle was going to get him killed," she cried out (*Sentinel,* Dec. 7, 1995).

***

Car chases are irresistible fare on TV. Can you really take your eyes off those pursuits with a news helicopter videotaping from above? They go on forever but you're afraid to walk out of the room because you might miss the inevitable foot race or the driver losing control and flipping the car.

They are even more irresistible when the chase goes right by your newsroom.

That was the case one day as we all sat listening to the police scanner while a car led a parade of police cars on a slow-moving pursuit from another county. The fool had driven over the "stop sticks" that punctured the tires on the little Japanese car. By the time he reached us in Tavares he was driving on the rims—slowly—and spreading a shower of sparks as he went along.

A couple of us jumped into our cars to watch the chase unfold—not a good idea, as it turns out. I was almost hit head-on by an unmarked sheriff's pickup truck making a U-turn to join the pursuit. The idiot felon made it all the way into Leesburg, 10 miles away, before losing it and crashing into a row of new cars at a Chrysler dealership.

***

Sometimes the chase is the least of it.

There used to be an infamous hole-in-the-wall called the Blue Bird lounge on the west side of Leesburg. To call it a lounge was a joke. It was more like a concrete block box with a trash-filled, dirt parking lot and a giant oak tree that shaded an outdoor crack cocaine flea market.

A Lake County sheriff's deputy was doing a booming business posing as an undercover drug dealer on May 5, 1995 and watching his law enforcement brothers take down buyers.

One man driving a blue Ford Thunderbird reportedly said he wanted "a 30," slang for $30 worth of crack. "I pulled out a $10 bag and a $20 bag," the officer testified. He said he then pulled off his hat and said "later," which was the signal for officers to move in.

Deputies jumped out from behind bushes and two others drove vehicles into the parking lot to block the exit.

The man then stomped on the gas pedal, causing the car to fishtail in the soft sand. The rear of the car struck the undercover officer, knocking him into the air. The car then struck an unmarked deputy's car as the driver took off on a brief, speedy chase.

It would have made interesting video and it might have even helped the prosecutor's case. As it was, however, the jury found the man not guilty of battery on a law enforcement officer and resisting arrest with violence.

He didn't know he was running from police. "He thinks he's going to be killed," defense attorney Candace Hawthorne argued.

The defendant took the stand. He said he had stopped to ask for the phone number of a man named "Doc." He owed the man money for car repairs, he said.

Assistant State Attorney Larry Houston practically laughed in his face, especially when he could not remember Doc's last name. The deputies who jumped out of the bushes were wearing black vests with the words "sheriff's deputies" written across the front in big, white letters, he pointed out.

The state had some big problems with its case, however. A tape of the transaction showed that it was the officer—not the defendant—who used the term "30." That made it entrapment, Hawthorne argued.

The state did score something of a victory, however. The jury found him guilty of driving with a license that had been suspended for three years.

Mistakes are going to happen sometimes. Some are funny later, much later. I remember two officers who tried to bust through a steel door with a battering ram. Inside, a Haitian drug dealer who spoke no English was cowering behind furniture thinking that rival crooks were trying to kill him. At least *he* was thinking. The cops failed to notice that in addition to being made of steel, the door opened outward. There was no way in the world the two men would be able to beat the door in. Unfortunately for the cops, the frightened man also had a gun, and while the battering ram couldn't get in, a bullet did manage to get out, right into the shin of one of the officers.

Sometimes officers are gullible, even veteran cops.

A retired Marion County sheriff's deputy was transporting three prisoners through Lake County in the back of his patrol car in 1996 when one of the men began screaming.

"Demons are after me! Let me out. Let me out (*Sentinel*, May 22, 1996)!"

The deputy stopped and unlocked the back door to check on the man when he bolted.

The man, who had been charged with violating house arrest rules in a case of aggravated assault with a weapon, was later arrested at a bus station in Tallahassee, several miles away.

***

Sloppy work by law enforcement officers can result in an acquittal.

When state troopers rolled up on an accident scene in Sorrento, they found a car driven by a 70-year-old woman that had collided with a vehicle driven by a 32-year-old man.

The woman was making a left turn when the landscaper's 1988 Honda Prelude slammed into the woman's 1989 Oldsmobile, the impact pushing more than two feet of the Honda inside the Olds, and knocking both cars 10 feet down the road.

The woman died shortly after the crash. The man was charged with DUI manslaughter. Three years later, the case went to trial.

Defense attorney Terrence Kehoe pounced on the state's witnesses. The trooper on the scene testified that he didn't know the woman was going to die. He didn't talk to her or the other driver. He admitted that he did not take measurements or photographs, did not get written statements of witnesses, did not inventory either vehicle, and he failed to place a hold on the vehicles or order blood-alcohol tests. He figured the woman was at fault for making a left turn while being overtaken by the other car. It wasn't until eight days later when a homicide investigator took over the case that the pieces began to fall into place.

"Speed is one factor," said the investigator. "His decision to pass was another. A reasonable, prudent person might think someone might be turning (*Sentinel,* Nov. 14, 1996)."

The man was injured in the crash and was taken to a hospital in Orlando. The hospital did a blood draw and concluded that his alcohol level was 0.223 – more than double the 0.10 limit at the time.

There was confusing testimony by a tow truck driver, who said he and a trooper found a liquor bottle in the man's car. He later changed his testimony to say that the man's family retrieved a liquor bottle from the car, and that he told troopers what he had learned.

"We've got people changing their stories all over the place," Kehoe said.

The lawyer also cast doubt on testimony regarding the blood alcohol report, which had to be subpoenaed from the hospital.

"He's assuming the blood was drawn correctly," he said.

The jury, either confused, leery, or both, deliberated for six grueling hours, twice sending questions to the judge. Once, they asked for a trial transcript. A second time they asked if the medical report on the blood alcohol level should be treated as a "hard fact."

Circuit Judge Don Briggs said blood evidence should be weighed like the rest of the evidence.

In the end, the panel found the landscaper to be not guilty.

Assistant State Attorney Jim Fuerenstein was fuming but prosecutors resist the temptation to criticize cops—their natural allies—in public.

"Justice delayed is justice denied," he said of the case that took three years to make its way to court.

Doctors move on, people's memories fade, and witnesses become harder to find, he said.

***

Cops are sharp, stupid, careful, careless, good people, thugs, perverts, loving husbands and wives, careful, careless, good stewards, or thieves. Unfortunately, when the rare bad apple falls it smudges every officer's reputation.

More than one officer has been arrested for driving under the influence. Not all of them, however, file a false-arrest lawsuit against the agency that arrested them.

Lake Sheriff George Knupp fired one of his deputies in 1992 when he was stopped for a suspected DUI by a Leesburg Police officer. The clincher was that the man refused to take a field sobriety test. That resulted in an automatic suspension of his driver's license for a year. No license, no ability to work, the sheriff said.

When the DUI case went to trial, the ex-deputy was acquitted. Emboldened by that decision he decided to sue Leesburg, saying he was arrested "without probable cause, warrant or other legal authority (*Sentinel*, July 29, 1997)."

Because of the arrest, he said he "suffered damage to his reputation and community standing, humiliation, mental suffering, physical discomfort, lost wages and other employment-related benefits..."

The jury disagreed. In addition to losing the lawsuit the former deputy was ordered to pay the city's legal costs.

Sometimes the alleged trouble gives crazy a bad name.

Take the case of a Leesburg police dispatcher who was accused of ordering her two elementary school-aged children to shoot their father with BB guns.

The wife and husband had reportedly gotten into a pushing and shoving match when the mom ordered the 6- and 8-year-old kids to open fire.

Police found the man in the emergency room with seven BB gun wounds.

The man's sister told the *Sentinel* the woman was an abuser. She said she even tried to find a spouse abuse shelter to help her brother, but they refused.

"The system is geared toward women who are abused by men. They don't know how to help my brother (Aug. 13, 1997)."

Even more worrisome, the sister said, was the possibility that child welfare workers might come in and take the children. "… he hasn't done anything wrong," she said.

Leesburg police said they would do an internal investigation to see if the three-year employee should be disciplined. The family lived in Groveland in the southern part of the county.

Sometimes the cases are just sad.

A 38-year-old Mount Dora police sergeant with a good record overall had to resign when she was arrested and charged with fraudulently obtaining prescription pain killers by "doctor shopping." Investigators said she went to eight different doctors to get the highly addictive drugs.

She suffered from fibromyalgia, her husband said, but doctors interviewed by the *Sentinel* said none of the painkillers prescribed would "cure" the pain (Sept. 18, 1997).

The police chief said her performance had been slipping.

In another case, a sheriff's deputy was fired for filing a false insurance claim for $3,700 worth of stolen property at his house that wasn't really stolen.

Other officers, including corrections officers, have been arrested and charged with fondling or raping prisoners, including women stopped for speeding.

One Lake County corrections officer was arrested and charged with raping a friend's former wife. The arrest report said the man had been dating the woman for about a month when he invited her to come to his house for "a possible romantic encounter (*Sentinel,* March 8, 1996)."

But when he became abusive and she started to cry, he threatened to have her arrested and charged with trespassing. And when she rejected his advances he bent her arm behind her, put his hand over her mouth, forced her onto the bed and raped her, she said.

***

The biggest fall from grace, of course, comes when the "high sheriff" himself is caught with his hand in the taxpayer's purse.

Few cases compare with the shock felt by Marion County residents when Sheriff Ken Ergle was caught stealing more than $170,000 from a fund set up to pay informants in undercover drug investigations.

Ergle began working for the sheriff's office in 1972 at age 19 as a dispatcher. He climbed the ladder in the fast-growing county, eventually becoming the sheriff's right-hand man. In 1992, he defeated his former boss in his first election win. He was re-elected in 1996.

During that time, the department grew dramatically to 700 employees, with a huge budget for helicopters and other high-tech gear.

Ever the politician, he made news by banning junk food, coffee, and cable TV at the jail. He also set out to make prisoners pay for their own medical care.

When the Legislature passed a tough sexual predator law, he became the first sheriff to walk the streets posting warning fliers about specific offenders moving into communities.

But the 45-year-old lawman was leading a double life. He drove a $30,000 Jaguar. He would later claim to have spent $9,000 for vehicle repairs, $4,000 for a boat, $7,900 for two vehicles, $6,000 for Christmas gifts and $16,000 for a family vacation.

He also said he spent $23,400 to help care for an invalid brother and $6,000 for his own medical bills. Despite this accounting, he still could not say where all the money went. He said he did not keep receipts. About $66,000 went toward a mortgage he took out on some property he purchased.

Meanwhile, he was helping himself to thousands of dollars from the department's drug investigation slush fund. Eventually, people within the department became suspicious.

He cried when he was confronted and said he was afraid he would go to prison where he would be an easy target for criminals.

"I took the money," Chief Deputy Dan Henry quoted Ergle as saying (*Sentinel,* April 23, 1999). When Ergle couldn't say exactly how much money he had taken, Henry was even more shocked.

"You mean you can't account for this money?" he said. "It struck me, and it struck Ken what he'd done."

Ergle wrote a letter to Gov. Lawton Chiles, admitting that he had "committed a sinful, wrong, and criminal act while sheriff *(Sentinel,* Oct.18, 1998)."

He pleaded guilty to grand theft and official misconduct.

A local judge took himself off the case and a retired judge from the Tampa circuit was assigned the case.

It was a repentant ex-sheriff who apologized to the court.

"It will haunt me forever," Ergle said (*Sentinel,* April 23, 1999).

His former deputies offered no excuses for their former boss.

"This one goes right to the heart of being a law enforcement officer," Sheriff's Maj. Tawles Bigelow testified.

He got a crucial boost from a defense psychologist who said he suffered from deep depression and post-traumatic stress syndrome. She said he had repressed memories of drowning victims, shootings, and children's bodies for years. The theft was a compulsive behavior stemming from those traumatic conditions, she testified.

"You've dug a big hole for yourself, Mr. Ergle," Senior Judge Robert W. Rawlins Jr. said the next day at sentencing.

Even after listing the illegal expenditures, investigators said $90,000 could not be accounted for.

"There's two questions I have, Mr. Ergle. Why? And where is the rest of the money?" the judge said.

State Attorney Brad King described Ergle's actions as "a betrayal."

Many people had written supportive letters to the judge, including a local congressman, but King said Ergle should be judged for his crime, not his position or that he was "a good man" for much of his life.

The prosecutor had already said he wasn't going to ask for the maximum sentence—up to 35 years in prison—or the minimum sentencing guideline, which called for 2 ½ years to 36 months behind bars. That would be up to the judge, he said.

The judge told Ergle that whatever the sentence, he would suffer personally, including the possible loss of $76,000 per year in his law enforcement pension.

"You've brought shame and disgrace to yourself, your family, and the law enforcement community," Rawlins said.

He chided Ergle for not being able to say no. "You tried to be all things to all people, and that's impossible," Rawlins said.

In the end, the judge handed down a surprisingly lenient sentence: two years of house arrest followed by

18 years of probation. He ordered Ergle to pay $200 per month restitution, including $36,000 investigative costs of the Florida Department of Law Enforcement. He was also ordered to perform 240 hours of community service and undergo counseling.

His wife, Susan, wept. She would later file for divorce.

Outside the courtroom, Ergle said: "Like I told the FDLE, the only thing wrong with the Sheriff's Office was me."

He also said: "I can't apologize enough to the citizens of Marion County."

When Ergle took department money for his own use, he was being stupid and greedy, but he was no more sophisticated or dishonest than the chairmen of the youth soccer team stealing from the uniform fund. When you hear of such embezzlement cases you always ask yourself, "How could they not know that they will be caught eventually?" They have to be deceiving themselves as much as they deceive their victims.

There are a couple of key elements to sheriffs breaking the law to feather their own nests. One is greed, simple everyday covetousness. The other is a sense of entitlement as big as all outdoors. *I've worked hard, I deserve it, and I am entitled to it.* It's another form of self-deception.

***

Lake County's Property Appraiser Ed Havill was acting a little unusual on Feb. 25, 2004, even for a guy famous for his sometimes flamboyant, no-holds-barred stands on low taxes and penny-pinching government spending. One of his most famous protests was when the county spent vast sums of money for new furniture at the county administration building during a renovation. He himself vowed to keep using the worn furniture in his shabby office.

One red-faced county commissioner said that if he had known it was going to be that big of a deal "I would have sat on an orange crate."

In 2004, Havill was flailing the hide off a fellow Republican powerhouse, Sheriff George Knupp. The 64-year-old long-time elected official was practically doing a jig outside the jail as he waved copies of a letter he had written to the governor urging him to fire the sheriff.

Knupp, 63, had just been indicted and then arrested on two counts of lying to a grand jury about questionable car deals. Sheriff's officials promised that their man would walk out the front door the jail after being arrested and released on his own recognizance, when he suddenly slipped out a side door.

"Sneaking out the back door is what criminals do!" Havill shouted to the reporters, almost jumping in the air. "If he was an honest person, he would go back to work (*Star-Banner*, Feb. 26, 2004)."

One of the things the grand jury was looking into was the sheriff personally purchasing two cars that his department had traded to a dealership.

"The indictment states that when he gave information on how those arrangements were made, he misrepresented material facts," said Chief Assistant State Attorney Ric Ridgway.

The buying and trading of cars wasn't the issue, the grand jury decided. In fact, the transactions were so convoluted it was impossible to tell exactly what transpired. But lying to the panel was another thing, a thing that resulted in a third-degree felony charge.

It was impossible to tell from the records just who had negotiated the transactions, the dates, or the value of the cars.

One of the transactions involved a 1993 Ford van. The sheriff testified that a car dealer called him about the van, which he purchased for his wife. He claimed he didn't realize it had once belonged to his department until he went down to the dealership. The Sheriff's Office had spent more than $2,200 on the vehicle to install a new engine and air conditioner compressor. Knupp bought the van for $500.

"It was agreed that the vehicle would be 'washed' by transferring the title through a third party to disguise the fact that the sheriff was buying the department van," the grand jury report said.

The sheriff later traded the van for another vehicle. It is not clear how much the sheriff got on the trade-in, but the dealer sold it to someone else for $2,400.

The sheriff testified that the engine smoked. The new owner testified that there was nothing wrong with the van.

The sheriff, using the same used-car salesman, bought a 1995 Ford Thunderbird. The title to that vehicle was also "washed" by transferring the title through a third party, the grand jury said.

"While we have been instructed that no law would be violated by such action, we agree such a purchase creates an appearance of impropriety," the grand jury wrote. "The sheriff's actions...were at least poor judgment, if not an abuse of his office. The sheriff's attempt to disguise the true nature of the transactions only compounds such appearance. We find that the sheriff's motive in testifying falsely before us was to attempt to prevent this grand jury from arriving at the truth of these transactions."

Havill said that even if the car deals were not criminal it was a waste of taxpayers' money. He said the former Democrat was "an embarrassment" to the Republican Party.

Before leaving the jail, Knupp met with his captains and majors. He told his staff that he disagreed with the grand jury's findings. Maj. Chris Daniels quoted Knupp as saying, "We have 232,000 residents and 600 employees. We have a service to perform and a job to do. Let's keep doing it."

Knupp did not respond to a request for an interview with the *Star-Banner*.

Gov. Jeb Bush suspended Knupp and named a temporary replacement.

The next day, in the spirit of dogged determination, or plain old denial, the four-term incumbent and 44-year veteran lawman said he wasn't ready to quit.

"If I have the support of the community, which I do, I've had thousands of calls and there have been calls to the sheriff's office, I would run again. It depends on how all of this turns out and how long it takes. It could run past the qualifying period (*Star-Banner*, Feb. 27, 2004)."

He said that since he had been suspended, he would be looking for another job in the meantime.

By April, however, he and his attorney, Michael Graves, were wriggling their way toward a pretrial intervention, starting with a letter of resignation to the County Commission. He admitted his answers to the grand jury "were not totally accurate and did not represent complete and thorough answers (*Star-Banner*, April 30, 2004)."

He could have faced up to five years in prison and a $5,000 fine. Under the terms of the agreement, Knupp got to keep his pension—a one-time payment of almost $320,848 and monthly payments of $6,236.77—starting in February 2005.

A lawman's badge is supposed to be shiny, not tarnished, and once the shield loses its sheen it can't be restored.

Judge Rawlins recognized that fact after sentencing Sheriff Ergle. He quoted from Shakespeare's *The Tragedy of Julius Caesar*: "The evil that men do lives after them; the good is oft interred with their bones."

Chapter 13

Accidental mayhem

The rescue helicopter blades chopped through the storm-darkened sky enroute to the 19-year-old man ensnared in the industrial steel monster.

Somehow, Tyme F. Dowding had fallen into a giant corkscrew-like grain auger, which was being used to unload grain from train cars.

Rescue crews had been frantically trying to free him since receiving the call at 4:44 p.m. on July 15, 1993. They had requested special ladders from the fire department, compressors, hydraulic cutters and spreaders, wrenches, and torches in an effort to free the feed company worker from the 12-inch auger that had swallowed him up to his waist.

Nothing worked. Now, his only chance for survival was in the hands of two passengers on the helicopter: a surgeon and his assistant, who would amputate one of his legs to free him from his deadly workplace trap. His other leg was already severed.

Bringing a doctor to an accident scene is practically unheard of, but when the call went out for a volunteer physician at what is now Advent Health Waterman in nearby Tavares, Dr. David Wooldridge said he would hop aboard the Orlando helicopter.

A crowd gathered outside a tall chain-link fence surrounding the feed mill in little Sorrento, drawn like moths to the sight of manic flashing red lights bouncing off the farm company's now silent equipment. I sat inside the perimeter beneath giant steel towers just a few feet away from Dowding, who was moaning. Nobody challenged me. I had a hand-held police radio receiver. Rescue workers thought I was a cop. Thanks to fate, chance, or a lead foot on the accelerator, I had a front row seat to horror. Emergency crews had nothing to worry about. I wasn't about to get in the way of any rescue attempt.

Dowding remained conscious, pleading, cursing, and answering questions while rescue workers hooked up IVs and poured pints of blood into him. He didn't pass out until they finally freed him, and his blood pressure hit bottom.

As he was being loaded onto the helicopter, Dowding's mother collapsed into her husband's arms in a heart-wrenching scene captured on film by *Sentinel* photographer Phelan M. Ebenhack.

Two hours later, Dowding was dead.

"We still don't know how it happened. Anything we say at this point is speculation," the plant manager said 10 days later.

One theory that wasn't mentioned publicly was that Dowding had taken a protective cover off the auger to kick free a blockage and then fell in. It was never proven.

A lawsuit was filed against a manufacturer of parts for the auger, but a judge dismissed it. Also dismissed were suits against the plant owner, operator, and manager. The company that serviced the machine reached a settlement with the family for $80,000.

Federal safety inspectors levied $9,600 in fines against the farm company. Had there been willful violations, fines could have been as high as $50,000.

When funeral plans were announced, the family urged people to donate to The Haven, a shelter for women and children fleeing abuse. Dowding's mother worked at the home and Dowding liked to help by playing with the kids.

"He was exceptional with the children," said Pam Terry, the director (*Sentinel*, July 18, 1993).

***

Sometimes a parent accidentally injures their child.

In 1994, a preschooler was burned everywhere but the top of her head and the bottoms of her feet when her father accidentally set his little girl ablaze.

"He knew he wasn't supposed to be lighting a fire with gasoline, but he had done it thousands of times," his wife said.

He was putting a bowl of gasoline-soaked wood chips under a barbecue grill when fumes drifted to a nearby flame and ignited the chips. He tossed the bowl over his head, realizing too late that it was headed right for his daughter.

He tore the burning clothing from her body and rolled her on the ground. He suffered burns, too.

She was sent to the Shriners Burn Institute in Cincinnati.

Her mother wanted to stay by her daughter's side for what doctors said would be a series of extensive skin grafts but living expenses and loss of income would be a severe problem. She had just opened a pet grooming shop and feared she would lose the business, the family's only source of income since her farm worker husband was out of work because of his injuries.

A benefit fund was set up to help with expenses.

"The thought that he would somehow hurt one of his children has always been his worst nightmare (*Sentinel*, Sept. 29, 1994)," the child's mother said.

***

In one case, it was the testimony of a young boy that helped send his father to prison for causing an accident that killed his mother.

Darrell Higdon testified in his trial he had stopped and had just driven back onto the road when he looked over and realized that his wife, Jennifer Kemp, had fallen from the pickup truck.

Higdon tried to resuscitate her while 8-year-old Dakota ran to a nearby house saying that his mother was dead and that "she needed help (*Sentinel,* Dec. 17, 2001)."

Higdon said the truck was barely moving. The medical examiner, who had done autopsies on several motorcyclists, estimated the truck was going as fast as 35 mph.

The boy was 9 when he had to testify, adding to the unbelievable trauma in his young life.

He said his parents were driving back from a wedding reception and were arguing about the radio. He said his dad was using "bad words" and cranked up the volume on the radio.

Kemp had been driving but eventually let Higdon drive. At one point, Kemp demanded that Higdon stop, and she got out with Dakota.

He drove back and Kemp and the child got back into the pickup truck. She told Dakota to close the door.

"I didn't close it all the way," Dakota said (*Sentinel,* Dec.21, 2001).

Dakota said he begged his father to slow down.

He said his dad started using "bad words" again and hit his mother several times with his forearm. Higdon claimed he just slapped her hand away from the radio.

Kemp put Dakota behind her to shield him from the blows and told the child to open the door. When he did, she tumbled out onto the road.

Blood alcohol tests revealed that Higdon had incredibly high alcohol readings of .252 and .246 one hour after the accident.

Higdon said his son was mistaken in his view of the way things unfolded. It was a despicable but understandable attempt to put spin on the story. He could have been charged with second-degree murder with a possible life sentence.

Defense attorney Michael Graves argued that Higdon was only guilty of driving under the influence. It was not his fault that his wife fell out of the vehicle, he said.

The jury didn't see it that way. He was charged with DUI manslaughter.

He appeared to be on the verge of tears as the clerk read the verdict: Guilty, DUI manslaughter. Higdon held it in but relatives who packed the courtroom could not. They wept and wept some more.

The judge sentenced him to 10 years in prison.

***

If you fly over the Sunshine State, you can look out through the plane's window and see a mass of glittering turquoise dots. Those dots are swimming pools—inviting, cool, fun, and dangerous.

Every year I would cringe as the summer months approached because I knew what was coming. Florida leads the nation in the rate of drowning deaths for children younger than 5—6.29 per 100,000 between 2017 and 2019, according to the Florida Department of Health.

One of the most heart-breaking drownings occurred in the city of Altamonte Springs in Seminole County.

Neighbors, alerted by a frantic family, joined a hurried search for a 2-year-old boy at 10:15 a.m. on March 30, 1993. It wasn't until 45 minutes later that he was found beneath the surface of an algae-choked pool in the back yard. Searchers had walked past the pool three times, but the water was so murky no one could see the bottom. It wasn't until the boy's dad and another man jumped in that the little boy's lifeless body was found.

"He was playing on the screened-in porch where he keeps his toys," his father told me at the hospital.

"I called to him, and he didn't answer, so I started looking outside. He has a little puppy. He must have fallen in while following the puppy," he said.

Back at the family's home I found a shocked, angry neighbor.

"I'm mad," said the man whose house was directly behind the boy's home. He said he had complained the week before to the city's code enforcement officer about the green, swampy pool and about a privacy fence that had been knocked down during a recent storm. He said he was worried about the safety of children in the neighborhood.

As I was leaving, I looked back at the house. There, on the front steps, was the puppy looking for his young master.

***

Boats are another big draw in Florida. The standard joke is: "You're never so happy in your life as the day you buy your boat and the day you sell it."

Unfortunately, many people are hurt or killed on the water. Seventy-nine people died in boating accidents in Florida in 2020, an increase of 14 from the year before, according to the Florida Fish and Wildlife Conservation Commission. There were 836 accidents, 113 more than in 2019, a 16 percent increase.

An accident in 1993 was a case in point, when the 36-year-old dad was severely injured and his two daughters, ages 5 and 2, were seriously hurt when they fell overboard and were struck by the boat's propeller. Boats without a pilot often circle back around and strike the defenseless castaways.

It can happen quicker than you think. Once, while doing a fishing story, I was almost tossed overboard when the speedy bass boat struck a wave broadside on the St.

Johns River. The river is very wide in some places and the normally peaceful waterway can turn mean when the wind suddenly picks up. The captain was also tossed up in the air, but he was tethered to an automatic motor kill switch. Had we landed in the drink, at least the boat wouldn't come back to kill us.

While I was at the *Leesburg Commercial,* a family disappeared while boating on one of the county's largest lakes. Day after day relatives went out on a law enforcement craft, hoping against hope that family members had managed to swim to shore, were stranded on an island, or were somehow still clinging to life vests or some other buoyant item. Hope faded every day until finally the search turned into a grim recovery.

Sometimes boaters survive under incredible circumstances.

Donny James was fishing with two other men and a 14-year-old boy in 2000 when he noticed water in the bottom of the boat and heard a noise that sounded like a faucet running. That was alarming. There was no faucet on board, and he wasn't fishing in a lake but in the Gulf of Mexico 18 miles from shore.

Boat owner Jim Richardson started the bilge pump, but it soon failed. Before he knew it, water in the 25-foot Wellcraft had swamped the batteries and was about to flood the engine. Soon, the water was two feet deep in the boat.

One of the men used their cell phone to call the bait and tackle shop where they launched. The shop quickly called the Coast Guard and urged Richardson to drop anchor, but that brought the bow up and the boat began to swamp faster as 5- to 7-foot swells poured over the stern.

Teen Jeremy Stokes grabbed a life vest. One man grabbed a 4-foot ice chest. Richardson, who had been in the bow when it went vertical, tried swimming for the ice chest and the others, but they were all drifting away.

"I wasn't getting anywhere," he said. "After a while, I couldn't swim. My muscles were getting all cramped up. The water was 65 degrees.

"I went down a couple of times. I thought, 'This is it. I'm going to die.'"

He said he began praying and told the others he was going to drown.

Jeremy's father, Mike, gave his son's life vest to Richardson. Then, all four held on to the ice chest, which still held ice and fish. Soon, however, it began sinking.

"The biggest thing going through my mind was keeping my boy with me," Mike said.

Soon, Richardson's prayers would be answered.

A boat trolling for grouper snagged Richardson's boat, which was pointing bow up from 21 feet below the surface of the water.

"He turned around to see what he had snagged. That's when he saw us."

Soon, a charter boat arrived. That boat's skipper heard the distress call and raced 11 miles to find the sinking boat. Then, the Coast Guard arrived.

Only 45 minutes had elapsed, but it was long enough to put the boaters in danger.

"Hypothermia can set in if the water is a 1-degree temperature difference of your body," said Mike Manning, a Coast Guard petty officer who received the distress call in Yankeetown.

For Richardson, it was the second time he had been on a sinking boat in the Gulf. The first time he was able to get a tow.

"There won't be a third time," he said (*Sentinel,* March 6, 2000).

***

Most accidents are so common they rarely get more than a passing notice as a brief in newspapers. But they are uncommonly traumatic to the victims and their families, and a river of tears have been shed in courtrooms over so many reckless, preventable crimes, especially hit-and-run and fatal drunk driving accidents. For years, the illegal blood alcohol content limit was 0.10, but in recent years Florida reduced it to .08.

For Carroll and David Stewart, the death of their 15-year-old son Christopher in 1995 was so devastating it was hard to comprehend. He was walking home from a nearby church with a Bible under one arm and a basketball under the other when he was mowed down by a hit-and-run driver. A few days after the accident they set out to select a burial plot. Along the way, they found the missing vehicle.

Witnesses had described the pickup truck leaving the scene of the accident. Acting on a tip from Christopher's friends in nearby Lady Lake, the couple went looking for the truck.

"I was about to give up," Stewart said. "My husband decided to turn down one more road. He got out and looked at the truck and it was damaged (April 1, 1995, *Sentinel)*."

They found Lake Sheriff's Deputy Kelly Cromwell, who was searching for the vehicle.

By matching paint chips from the accident scene, authorities were able to determine that the truck belonged to a 40-year-old carpet installer with a long history of traffic law violations. Michael Schwind, who claimed that a man named "Jimbo" may have borrowed his truck, had been driving with a suspended license, a license that had been yanked for drunk driving. He also had an earlier DUI and other infractions over the years, including driving with an open container of alcohol, running a stop sign, and driving too fast for conditions.

"With the mother finding the vehicle … I'd call that the guiding hand of God. He led her right to it," Cromwell said.

There is justice in the courts and there is divine justice, but there is also grief and anger over a man's callous disregard for life and leaving the scene of an accident with injuries.

"This is homicide," said Mary Dempsey, the wife of Christopher's grandfather. "How can you live with doing this to a child? It takes no conscience."

Carroll Stewart could have crumbled. It would have been completely understandable. Instead, she turned her anger into meaningful action and formed a local Mothers Against Drunk Driving chapter.

She still worried about the future.

Because Schwind would possibly qualify for early release "gain time" under prison rules if he behaved in prison, she feared that he would be freed in as few as two years.

"How will we react when we see him in the grocery store buying liquor, if that is what he chooses to do?"

She answered her own question while speaking to other grieving families at a victim's rights ceremony when she advised: "Find your support group (May 1, 1999, *Sentinel*)."

Schwind didn't get off as easily as he hoped. He pleaded no contest to DUI manslaughter, driving with a suspended license, leaving the scene of an accident with injury, and not having a proper tag. He was sentenced to 10 years in prison.

Schwind, a man familiar with the system, appealed in 1998 claiming incompetent counsel. He said his trial attorney should have told him to enter the plea before a new state law banished gain time. He wanted to withdraw his plea and go to trial.

His attorney at trial, Michael Graves, testified that he told Schwind that he might serve up to 25 years if convicted by a jury. He had two prior DUIs and was on probation for one of them.

"There was a lot of negative reaction in the media," he told the judge.

The judge said Graves did nothing wrong and dismissed the claim.

The legal jousting didn't impress Stewart or change her opinion of Schwind.

"He's still a murderer (*Sentinel,* June 12, 1998)."

***

Few things are worse than the death of a young person, but in one case, a tragedy was compounded over and over. It was the only case out of thousands that caused me to have nightmares.

Michael Cermak Jr., his former girlfriend Heather Steverson, her best friend Sherri Blundell, and another teen were having a good time on June 13, 1987. Blundell was president of her graduating class and the homecoming queen. Steverson was class vice president. Both played softball and both had earned scholarships to the University of Central Florida. Cermak, 19, was the son of a Tavares city councilwoman. The Cermaks owned a chain of popular sandwich shops.

The teens had just left a wedding reception for Cermak's sister. Cermak was driving. Heather and Sherri were in the back seat. They were traveling down a scenic lakeside drive at 11:25 p.m., when he lost control of the 1978 Buick. It left the curved road, slammed into a pine tree, spun sideways, and crashed into another tree.

One of the popular blonde girls died at the scene. The other was taken to a hospital in Orlando in a coma. She died six days later. The third girl and Cermak both sustained minor injuries.

The accident stunned the community, especially those at Tavares High, where everyone knows one another. More than 700 people attended the funeral for Sherri at Tavares Baptist Church.

"Her life made a dramatic impact on hundreds of people," the Rev. Sanford Colley said in his eulogy. "Her influence may never be totally known (*Sentinel,* June 24, 1987)."

The girls, best friends in life, were buried side by side beneath a huge, spreading oak tree.

Four hours after the service, Cermak was arrested and charged with two counts of DUI manslaughter. His blood alcohol level was 0.15. The legal limit at that time was 0.10.

He appeared before a judge dressed in the same blue striped suit he had worn to the funeral. Bail, originally set for $20,500, was reduced to $1,000. Both families had sent word to the judge and State Attorney's Office that they were OK with no bail being set. The judge ordered Cermak not to drive.

I was as shocked as anyone else by the next development. When I went to work as the assistant county editor on a gray September morning a few weeks later I found police reporter Wesley Loy standing by my desk.

"You're not going to believe this," he said. "They think they buried the girls in the wrong graves."

He had been at the cemetery that morning where authorities had quietly exhumed one of the bodies. It would be just a matter of hours before the truth came out.

The Blundell family had been sitting at Heather's bedside, who was in a coma, for six days thinking that they were with their daughter.

"The state of mind that they were in …. They told them that this was their daughter, and she wasn't going to live. I doubt if I'd have noticed the difference," said Heather's father, Herman, who owned the funeral home that handled both services.

The Steversons would later say that individually they both experienced "something" urging them to go to the hospital, but they disregarded the feeling and did not share their misgivings with each other. They didn't want to bother the Blundells, and they didn't want to even consider the possibility that it was their daughter in the hospital and not Sherri.

Yet, Herman had not been able to shake the feeling that something was wrong, that somehow everyone had mistaken the girls' identities, even though their faces were injured in the crash.

Both girls were remarkably similar. Both had athletic builds, with only six pounds difference between them. They even had similar hair styles. At a distance, they had been hard to identify. Even their eyes were similar.

At the funeral home, Herman thought that the girl in coffin had thinner arms and darker hair than Heather's.

Dianne Steverson thought Heather's fingers and fingernails should have been longer. The girl had a veil over her face in the coffin.

"It's the lighting," Herman thought.

"After my wife first clued me in, I tried to convince myself it was emotions she was talking about," he said. "But she knew *(Sentinel*, Sept. 29, 1987)."

The jewelry returned by the Eustis Police Department wasn't right either. He just assumed that the envelopes had been mixed up. Police had not positively identified the bodies, but they knew who was in the car and came up with a seating chart during their investigation.

As the injured girl was airlifted to an Orlando hospital, police located a relative of Sherri's and directed her to go to the hospital to see if it was Sherri. The relative identified the girl as Sherri. After the girl died at the hospital, another relative identified the girl as Sherri. By this time, her hair had been shaved to allow for medical procedures and she had two abrasions on her face.

There were other clues, however. Steverson's funeral home received paperwork with the body believed to be Sherri's. Records indicated that she had contacted a dangerous strain of Hepatitis B. Steverson thought that was odd. He knew his daughter had it. Could Sherri have possibly gotten it from his daughter?

He paid a visit to associate medical examiner Dr. Thomas Techman, who showed him photos of the body believed to be Heather's.

"I said, 'Dr. Techman, I'm about 90 percent sure that's Sherri and not Heather."

The body that turned out to be Sherri's did not have any trace of hepatitis.

Finally, he persuaded authorities to exhume the bodies and take fingerprints. Heather had been fingerprinted in 1984 at the mall by a sheriff's deputy as a part of a missing children's prevention program. Sure enough, the girl he had buried as his daughter was really Sherri.

Steverson was at the cemetery during the exhumation but did not look inside the coffin.

"I couldn't handle it. I knew it wasn't going to be my daughter."

Sherri was reburied nearby in a different plot so she could be near her family.

It was another stunning, sorrowful blow.

The Blundells sued the Cermaks on Sept. 17, claiming they "willfully and unlawfully" allowed their son to drink and "failed to exercise parental control."

The Cermaks said they followed Eustis city rules and had a Eustis police officer at the reception. The judge, citing a 1987 Florida Supreme Court case, said hosts were not legally responsible for the acts of a drunken guest. He also said parents were no longer responsible for the actions of their sons and daughters when they turned 18.

Art Blundell, a private detective, was upset.

"The ruling by [Circuit Judge Earle] Peterson indicates that, by law, parents aren't responsible for the actions of their children after they have given them alcohol, and that is wrong," he said (*Sentinel,* July 2, 1988).

There was movement in the criminal case, however.

Eight months after the accident, Cermak, 20, abandoned by his friends and tortured with remorse, entered a plea agreement to two counts of DUI manslaughter. His attorney said Cermak wanted to "spare the community and the families the agony of going through with what would have been a public re-creation of the accident."

Blundell asked the court not to go below sentencing guidelines. The Steversons said a harsh penalty would do more harm than good. Both families sat on opposite sides of the courtroom. Each family got what they asked for.

The state temporarily severed a third charge—having a fake driver's license showing he was 21 years old—because having a third charge would have boosted the prison time to seven years. The fake license had nothing to do with the DUIs, both the defense and prosecutors agreed.

Circuit Judge Jerry Lockett sentenced Cermak to three years in prison. He was placed in a youthful offender "boot camp," which meant he would get out early. He was also sentenced to 10 years of probation and 500 hours of community service.

Dianne Steverson walked out of the courtroom with her arm around the shoulder of Cermak's mother, Elaine. Michael had spent many weekends at the Steversons home.

"I'm sorry I put their families through all this," Cermak said while leaving the courthouse, with tears welling up in his eyes. "I miss those girls just as much as they do (*Sentinel*, Feb. 4, 1988)."

There was one final set of legal T's and I's that needed to be crossed and dotted before the system could close the books on the tragic story.

In May of 1988, prosecutors charged Michael Cermak Sr. with four misdemeanor charges of serving alcohol to minors. One of the teens reportedly shown in an evidentiary video holding an alcoholic beverage that night was the 17-year-old girl who was slightly injured in the car. Another was young Cermak. A pretrial intervention plan was drawn up and the state dropped the charges when conditions were met. One of those conditions was that they go with their son when he talked to students at schools so they could discuss their role in the tragedy.

Instead of paying a fine they were allowed to donate $500 to the Heather Steverson-Sherri Blundell Scholarship Fund.

"The agreement was something that made the point for everyone," said State Attorney Ray Gill. "I told my assistants from the beginning that we were not out for blood in this situation (*Sentinel,* May 19, 1988)."

As for Steverson, he said getting the girls buried in the right graves was "a load off our minds but we wasted six days of life with our daughter. "My wife and I really regret those six days (*Sentinel,* Sept. 29, 1987)."

***

Justice can seem fickle, especially if the defense in a DUI manslaughter case is strange. But few claims could ever be more bizarre than that of a businessman, whose F-250 Ford pickup truck collided with a Ford Tempo killing a mother and daughter on their way to their jobs at a hospital as licensed practical nurses.

Billy Nichols, Jr. was driving on the day after Thanksgiving 2004. His blood alcohol levels two hours after the crash were 0.103 and 0.104. The legal limit is .08.

Those were the facts, but his legal team's experts testified that intoxication was not the cause of the accident because he wasn't drunk until *after* the crash.

Sleep, combined with a heavy amount of food from the night before and an inability of his body to absorb six shots of whiskey, caused him to be sober at the time of the crash and drunk afterward, his experts said. The alcohol and food overload caused the pyloric valve in his stomach to close and not allow food to enter the small intestine for absorption.

The state's toxicology expert testified that the idea was ridiculous.

"I've never seen any piece of data that suggests...fluid sitting in the stomach and magically starts getting absorbed." Dr. Mark Montgomery also added: "You can't fool Mother Nature or the brain when it comes to alcohol (*Star-Banner*, Oct. 19, 2007)."

But apparently you can dazzle a jury with such a theory, because Nichols was acquitted.

"I get to start my life over," he told a friend on a cell phone after hugging his lawyer and leaving the courthouse (*Star-Banner*, Oct. 27, 2007).

There was no reset button for Adrian "Stretch" Cummings, however, who lost both his wife and his daughter in the accident.

"He [God] sent me Nancy to show me what love and compassion was all about and removing the hate in my heart after coming back from Vietnam," he wrote of his wife in a letter to the editor thanking his lawyers and others who helped him get through the trial.

"And Holly. The parent is supposed to inspire the child. In my case it was the child inspiring the parent, especially the work you did for the veterans from the time you were 4 years old until just before you were taken from us. Your compassion for others influenced me. You also reminded me to always be proud of being a Vietnam veteran," he wrote (*Star-Banner*, Nov. 8, 2007).

He suffered yet another jarring blow, however, when *Star-Banner* reporter Mabel Perez discovered that the jury foreman failed to mention during juror questioning that he had been convicted of DUI—not once as he said, but twice. He said it would not alter his ability to render a fair verdict. He said he copped a plea to reckless driving the first time. Court records stated otherwise.

The judge noted that the state had six chances to dismiss a prospective juror but only used five.

"It's a little different in retrospect than it was at the time, naturally, but I really can't go into my thought process," the prosecutor said. "I think we made a mistake keeping him on the jury."

It was too late for the criminal trial, but Cummings would get a sliver of justice in his lawsuit against Nichols.

The judge in the civil case ordered Nichols to get an independent medical examination and to produce his medical records. Cummings' attorney had told the judge that he wanted to check for any tendency by Nichols for delayed gastric emptying, or gastroparesis, and see "whether he had something particular going on with his pyloric valve, unlike other people (*Star-Banner*, Sept. 19, 2008)."

By January 2010, as his civil trial was about to begin, Nichols waived his right to a jury and admitted liability in a legal move that would end all questions except for the amount of the damages.

He was not admitting he was drunk at the time of the crash, his attorney said.

"It's been Billy's position all along he bore some responsibility for this accident," Mike Donsky said, adding: "He was absolutely not impaired (*Star-Banner*, Jan. 20, 2010)."

The judge ordered Nichols to pay $3 million to Cummings, who had received only $500,000 from an insurance claim at the time Nichols declared bankruptcy. A federal judge, however, refused to wipe out the $3 million judgment debt.

Cummings' lawyers had to prove in federal bankruptcy court that Nichols was driving drunk. The case was reheard in federal court in November 2011. A ruling in the rehearing allowed for a less stringent burden of proof. The court found Nichols was negligent because he was drunk.

"He was drunk when he killed my wife and daughter, and it took seven and a half years for that truth to come out," Cummings said when the rulings were announced.

His lawyers warned the disabled veteran that it might take 20 years to get the money. At age 64, he said he would probably never see it.

"In the end I win, but I also lose, too (*Star-Banner*, March 26, 2012)."

***

You have to figure that if your nickname is "Rooster" you should do everything you can to stay out of a courtroom. Your friends, after all, might have a sense of humor about your nickname, but judges do not. Steven J. "Rooster" McMennamy, however, had a penchant for making trouble for himself and causing horrific pain for others.

Marcia Beitl had just pulled into her driveway on March 30, 1998 when McMennamy lost control of his 1974 Pontiac, ran off the road onto the shoulder, slid sideways, and slammed into her pickup truck, injuring her and killing her 14-year-old son, Konrad.

McMennamy was charged with DUI manslaughter, leaving the scene of a death, leaving the scene with injuries and DUI causing great bodily harm.

A late-in-life child for Marcia, Konrad was born prematurely on Mother's Day. Though he had dyslexia, he was doing well in school. He was sweet-natured, helped elderly neighbors with chores and was the love of his single mother's life.

Marcia, who was still suffering from her physical injuries, told the court she relived the nightmare every day: "I was not even allowed to hug him or touch him," she said of Konrad's final moments.

McMennamy, 19, apologized through his lawyer and said it would never happen again. The judge sentenced him to six years in prison. He was supposed to be sentenced to 15 years, but the sentence was reduced after a negotiated plea. Neither Marcia nor the judge was convinced he would live up to the strict terms of probation, which included giving up his driver's license forever.

Less than three months after the fatal accident McMennamy was arrested again on charges of reckless driving, fleeing and eluding a police officer, possession of less than 20 grams of marijuana, and two counts of having drug paraphernalia. When Highway Patrol troopers arrested him, he tried to kick out the windows of the patrol car.

"That hardened me," she said of the second incident. "I am angry (*Sentinel*, July 15, 1999)."

Circuit Judge G. Richard Singeltary said he hated to send a young man to prison.

"It's a terrible place. Terrible consequences, the result of your conduct," he said.

But McMennamy would get out of that "terrible place" only to go back. In 2012, he was sentenced to five years in prison after pleading guilty to burglary. He was also sentenced to five years on a charge of driving with a permanently suspended license.

The apparent strong urge to self-destruct and take others with you is unfortunately not unique to McMennamy.

Terry Eddie Jenkins, 30, once called a "vehicular terrorist" by a judge, was arrested a year after serving nine months in jail for violating probation on a new drunk driving charge. It was his second DUI offense. The first time he killed a man. Altogether, he had racked up more than 30 traffic convictions by January 1997. So, when he was arrested for driving with a suspended license and then escaping from the patrol car by kicking out a plexiglass divider, the sister of the man he killed was outraged.

"I can't believe the light bulb hasn't gone off in his head," said Ginger Bonnay. "I was dumbfounded. I just couldn't believe it. He really can't be driving again (*Sentinel,* Jan. 23, 1997)."

Jenkins was driving with a suspended license at the time of the fatal accident, too.

The family sued and was awarded $159,000.

By March, he was asking a judge to reduce his bond from $81,500 to $26,000. Besides damaging the patrol car to escape, he also gave a false name and date of birth.

"My mission is to stop him," Bonnay vowed. "He has no respect for the law (*Sentinel*, March 14, 1997)."

He was sentenced to 18 months in prison.

***

How much is a life worth? Does it have more value than a few dollars' worth of gasoline stolen from a convenience store?

At about 2 a.m. one morning in 1993, a motorist pumped $14 worth of gas from a convenience store pump, jumped in his car without paying, and took off down a long, sometimes winding two-lane road in Leesburg. The store clerk hopped in his own car and followed, trying to get a license plate number so he could call police.

As the thief approached a bridge over a narrow lake inlet, he lost control of the 1978 Ford, which hooked a guardrail, snapped two concrete posts, and plunged into 10 feet of murky water.

It took eight hours for Lake County sheriff's divers to find the submerged body of the 33-year-old man.

No one could tell how fast he had been driving but the man's body ended up 60 feet from the car.

"We couldn't find any skid marks," the state trooper said (*Sentinel,* Dec. 3, 1993).

It took two hours for a tow truck to haul the vehicle out of the lake, but that was not the end of the story. After motorists were allowed back on the road, I heard another call on the police scanner.

Divers had found another car.

Sure enough, another tow truck was soon hauling a second vehicle out of the lake, but it was obvious this one had been in the water for some time. It was a rusted, silver 1964 Chevy, its top missing. Water rushed out of the back doors as it was hauled onto shore up a steep embankment. How that car ended up in the lake and whatever happened to the driver remains a mystery.

***

Sometimes drunken drivers do not harm anyone else. Toll booth workers at the entrance ramp to Florida's Turnpike were surprised in 2000 when a car drove up and a woman passenger got out and took off on foot. They were even more surprised when the driver parked in a toll booth headed in the wrong direction. He then turned the car around blocking traffic in both directions.

Troopers said he was disheveled, reeked of alcohol, and could barely walk. But the clincher was the man's driving record. Russell L. Bishop had at least 15 prior DUI convictions, dating back to 1965.

He was sentenced to 30 months in prison. The maximum would have been five years, the minimum 25 months.

Carroll Stewart, who was still grieving over the death of her son, Christopher, to a drunk driver five years earlier, was not happy with state laws that allowed someone to reoffend that many times without tougher penalties.

"I don't understand. Why do they want to wait until they kill somebody before they do something (*Sentinel*, Jan. 6, 2000)?"

***

Drunks are responsible for so much heartache, but there are other forms of reckless behavior that are just as deadly.

One accident in December 2001 had all the markings of a Greek tragedy.

Dwight Samples, 21, was tearing down State Road 19 near the small town of Umatilla in Lake County at 6:30

p.m., in the new Mustang that his mother had bought him for Christmas. He was racing the car beside him and going about 100 mph when he slammed into the back of a car in front of him. The other car was being driven by his mother, who had a 72-year-old passenger by her side. The driver of the other speeding car kept going.

"Never mind about me," he frantically told paramedics. "Save my mom." But it was too late. Diane Samples and her passenger, Vivian Green, were dead.

The reckless racing, with its unfathomable consequences, stunned everyone when they learned of the accident. Everyone wondered what kind of punishment he should he face when he was already facing a lifetime of guilt.

"I'm sorry for everything I've done," he said two years later, his voice breaking with emotion as he turned to look at a member of Green's family sitting in the courtroom.

Samples' family members who showed up to whisper words of encouragement fell silent as the judge imposed the sentence: Four years in a youthful offender prison, two years of house arrest, and three years suspension of his driver's license. He was sentenced to 15 years' probation on the second count of vehicular manslaughter.

"You're a young man, and I hope the youthful-offender program teaches you something, and that probation teaches you something," Circuit Court Judge Don Briggs said. "I hope you and everyone else can get through this tragedy and get on with their lives."

His father, Elliott, disagreed with the sentence.

"I don't feel prison is the answer for this. I believe in punishment, but this is not the answer," he said.

"He is mentally distraught," he said. "Wouldn't you be if you had killed your mother?"

Sample's brother, Doug Crane, 30, said Dwight was already rehabilitated.

"He will have to explain to a wife one day where those scars came from," Crane said. "He will have to explain to his children why they only have one grandma. Our justice system does not have the power to issue the kind of punishment this man has endured. The punishment never ends."

The family was given a great deal of consideration, said prosecutor supervisor Willard Pope. He could have been sentenced to 30 years in prison, with a recommended minimum of 18.

"He got four," Pope said. "I understand that they are angry with the system, but we can't let that control what happens (*Sentinel*, April 8, 2003)."

* * *

Truck drivers used to be known as "knights of the road." Not only were they top notch professionals but courteous, too. Today, because truck drivers are in such demand, their ranks are filled with at least some who don't have a clue about what the previous generation was like. They speed, run red lights, overload trailers, pop pills to stay awake, fake mandatory rest logs, and they don't think twice about cutting off a car to get to where they are going.

Phyllis Oechslin, 71, ran into such a driver—or more correctly—the truck driver ran into her at a busy intersection in 1999. She was on her way home from the grocery store. She and her husband, a retired Navy captain and jet fighter pilot, had celebrated their 50th wedding anniversary six months earlier.

Calvin Morgan, 47, of Tampa, was driving his truck down U.S. Highway 27 in Leesburg to avoid paying tolls on Florida's Turnpike. That fact did not set well with the jury, especially after hearing from an expert say that Morgan should have known he had to slow down and be prepared to stop more than 1,000 feet from the intersection after the yellow light flashed on the traffic signal. Morgan swore it never changed to red.

One man escaped the crash when he saw the truck barreling down on him from behind. He cranked the wheel to the right and hit the gas, but that left Oechslin's car exposed to a crushing blow by the truck on her driver's side door. After the crash, she sat up and talked briefly, but the collision, at 58 mph, was too much. She died of her injuries.

Witnesses at the trial spoke of bawling, smoking tires and an overwhelming feeling of helplessness. "I watched in horror," one man said.

Another man said, "There seemed to be an explosion in front of my car. I thought a bomb went off or something."

Morgan's lawyer pleaded with jurors to find him guilty of a lesser charge, if anything, but they found him guilty of vehicular homicide and the judge sentenced him to 10 years in prison.

***

The words pain, grief, and anger don't even begin to describe the feelings of a parent who loses a child in an accident.

It is understandable then, that Norma Eubanks' emotions were still raw five years after her son, Jonathan, was hit and killed by a pickup truck at a dark, unlighted school bus stop.

"People tell you, 'You need to get on with your life and forget it.' That doesn't happen," she testified in her family's lawsuit against Lake County schools on March 21, 2000 (*Sentinel*).

It wasn't just Norma and her husband, Bob, who recognized the 15-year-old as a special person. After the accident, one of his teachers at Leesburg High wrote: "… sometimes, like a glittering star on a quiet winter's night, a certain, special child will appear, to let you know that all the work, all the disappointment is all very worthwhile …. Your son has been that glittering star."

No one doubted it. Even the defense attorney became teary in his closing arguments, but the question was, where did the blame really lie?

The Eubanks blamed the county for operating a dark, unsafe bus stop, and accused school officials of "deliberate indifference." They were seeking $2.5 million each. Their attorney cited three other accidents at various bus stops.

The county blamed the driver of the pickup truck who turned too sharply at the corner. The piece of evidence that ultimately swayed the jurors was a photo of the pickup truck's fogged up windows and windshield on that misty morning.

The couple was devastated by the verdict.

"The people of Lake County need to know there is no such thing as a safe bus stop," Robert Eubanks said after the trial. He said from the beginning that the lawsuit was not about the money but was about trying to force school officials to provide safe bus stops.

"They're not going to change anything," he said bitterly. "There's no policy to keep kids safe. It's just wrong."

***

It is never a good thing if school buses are in the news. There have been instances of fighting, enraged parents entering buses to confront bullies, lewd acts among students, and wild behavior that threatens the safety of everyone on board.

A Polk County school bus driver was socked with various charges after allegedly taking a busload of children miles out of the way to her house so two feuding girls could get off and fight. A sheriff's report quoted her as telling the 13- and 16-year-old that she would "give them Vaseline or baby oil to put on their faces so their faces wouldn't get scratched during the fight. (*Sentinel*, May 10, 2013)." After the fight, she loaded everyone back on the bus and took off, then stopped when the girls went at it again. When they finished, she started driving again after telling everyone: "What happens on the bus, stays on the bus."

Apparently, she forgot about all the students who carry cell phones. Several videotaped the fight.

Most school bus drivers are good, but even the best can't stop others from slamming into their buses. That was the case in September 2008.

The Marion County school bus had stopped on U.S. Highway 301 in the tiny community of Citra to let three or four students disembark, when a semi slammed into the rear of bus. About 20 middle and high school students were knocked around or thrown to the floor as the vehicles pitched forward and burst into flames.

"It just hit. It happened too fast," said Jamar Williams, 14. "It was just so smoky it was hard to see (*Star-Banner*, Sept. 23, 2008).

Despite the shock and confusion, kids began helping each other get out of the bus, including Williams, who picked up a fallen cousin and stopped to help the bus driver get out of her seat belt.

A passing truck driver going the opposite direction stopped to help get kids off the bus, as did three other bystanders.

Within five minutes a series of explosions ripped through the wreckage.

Despite all of the heroic efforts, one child, Frances Margay Schee, 13, died in the accident. She had been in an earlier news story by the *Star-Banner*, in a plea for a heart donor for her father.

Fifteen people were injured, including the bus and semi drivers. Two were listed in critical condition.

Truck driver Reinaldo Andujar Gonzalez, 30, of Orlando, told a witness that he never saw the school bus, its flashing lights, or extended stop sign. He would later tell investigators that he had been on the phone, "put the phone in the cup holder and looked up" just before the crash.

He was convicted of reckless driving and vehicular homicide and sentenced to three years in prison.

The Highway Patrol concluded that fatigue and use of the cell phone contributed to the crash.

Not content to just grieve and go away, Frances' mother, Elissa Schee, launched a fight to outlaw drivers talking on cell phones.

In 2012, she told *the Star-Banner* that she was frustrated by a lack of legislation by lawmakers in Tallahassee and Washington, D.C.

She said there have been legislative proposals to make cell phone use while driving a secondary citation but said, "We need consequences and enforcement," she said.

In 2013, the Legislature did pass what the *Sentinel* called a "watered down" law against texting and driving.

It bans texting while driving, but it is OK if a driver is stopped in traffic or at a traffic light. It is "secondary" offense, which means that an officer can't stop a driver and issue a ticket for texting unless he is also stopping them for some other infraction like reckless driving.

She said she fights to "keep anyone from walking in my shoes for even a minute." The pain "never goes away," she said.

"We already have the solution to cell phone-free driving: the off button. These cell phone-related accidents are 100 percent preventable (Sept. 2012)."

Chapter 14

Ruthless

"RUTHLESS, adj. having or showing no pity or mercy" -- **Encarta World English Dictionary.**

Fred Anderson Jr., his smooth tenor voice in perfect form, sang the gospel song about mercy so beautifully.

"Come, ye disconsolate, where'er ye languish,
Come to the mercy seat, fervently kneel;
Here bring your wounded hearts, here tell your anguish;
Earth has no sorrow that heav'n cannot heal."

Anderson wasn't in church when he sang this song. He was singing from the witness stand, and his audience was the jury in his murder trial.

Anderson's eyes were misty. Three jurors wept.

Anderson had made a lot of mistakes in his life, including writing bad checks, and stealing money from a college where he worked. Singing a song about mercy was probably another, especially when he showed no mercy to two tellers in a bank robbery.

"Please don't shoot! Don't hurt me!" one of the tellers screamed.

He had a short reply: "Which one of you guys want to die first?"

It was on a Saturday morning, on March 20, 1999.

"Thank goodness I don't have to work today," I said as I sprawled out on the floor in front of the TV. I wasn't feeling well—some kind of bug. It wasn't that bad, but I didn't feel like getting up off the floor, let alone answer the clanging phone.

It was my editor, of course.

"There's some kind of shooting in Mount Dora," she said. "Maybe three people dead in a store …."

I got up, got dressed, and it was the last time I thought about not feeling well for the next 12 hours.

Within minutes, the editor called back. She had learned that it was a bank that had been robbed. One person was dead, another was hanging on.

The strip shopping center on U.S. Highway 441 was swarming with cops and rescue vehicles. An air rescue helicopter was taking off from the parking lot.

As I approached the United Southern Bank branch next to the Publix grocery store, I could see relatives getting the bad news, their hands reaching toward their heads in shock and disbelief, their faces blotted in a sea of tears.

"No, no, no!" shouted one man. Another man cried and shouted as family members tried to comfort him (*Sentinel*, March 21, 1999).

"She was just trying to make a living!" he screamed.

Heather Young, 39, was dead. The other teller, Marishia Scott, 25, was critically wounded and on her way to Orlando Regional Medical Center, which has a level one trauma center.

My job, of course, was to gather all the facts I could as quickly as I could, and then get to the bureau and write up the story.

Anderson, 30, had pulled out two guns and ordered the tellers to go into the vault and load up a trash can with cash.

Sherry Howard, who worked at the bank's branch in Eustis, entered the Mount Dora bank shortly before noon with her children. The first thing she noticed was that there was no one in the lobby. It was then that she noticed a man she described as a medium to heavy-built black man wearing a white or red T-shirt and a white or red cap standing in the vault room. She said his arms were extended out from his shoulders. His back was turned toward her, so he did not see her. She later apologized to police for the conflicting descriptions. She didn't want to stick around long enough to be another victim. He was, in fact, 5-feet-11 and weighed 276 pounds.

"I heard screaming and [someone] saying,' Please, no, no!" Howard said.

She said she thought it was Scott who was speaking. She had worked with Scott in Eustis.

Howard pushed her children out the door and they all ran toward the Publix grocery store next door. The door had barely closed behind her when she heard a shot.

She found a grocery store clerk and ran toward the customer service counter to ask someone to call 911. The clerk had heard a shot, too.

Instead of immediately fleeing in a borrowed car, Anderson stuck around to try and get the cassette tape out of the security camera recorder. He had the recorder in his hands when police burst into the bank with guns drawn and arrested him.

On the floor beside Anderson was a .22-caliber pistol and a trash can filled with thousands of dollars. Another weapon, a chrome-plated handgun, was in the trash can.

"There was enough money to choke a horse," said arresting Mount Dora officer Cpl. Steven Cantwell.

Anderson had been in the bank for about 40 minutes. He began the robbery shortly before 11:50 a.m.

He took no money from the front cash drawer and warned the tellers not to give him any "bait" money or touch any alarm buttons before ordering them into the vault. Bait money might be a stack of $20 bills, for example, with a GPS tracking device tucked inside.

Scott was fighting for her life as she was loaded onto the Orange County Sheriff's "Chase One" helicopter.

"Please don't let me die," she begged paramedics, mouthing the words. "Please tell my boyfriend I love him. Please tell my mom I love her."

One of the paramedics told her that police had arrested a suspect.

"Thank you, God," she said. "Did they get the other one?"

There was another black man in the bank shortly before the robbery, leading police to think that Anderson had an accomplice. In fact, there was no second robber.

Customers told police that they had gotten "a bad vibe" from Anderson and the other man. One of the witnesses said she was making a deposit around 11 a.m. and that Anderson especially made her "very nervous."

"It was a gut feeling. I don't know. I just watched him and did not directly look at him. He...just felt very uncomfortable. The fact that he let two people go ahead of him and then when I left, you know, he had his hands in his pockets, standing in the corner of the bank. It just did not feel comfortable with me."

She later picked him out of a lineup.

Scott also asked, "How is my friend Heather?"

The paramedic said he didn't know.

With Scott still on the way to the hospital, I grabbed the highest-ranking officer at the scene. He was walking away from the shopping center with his head down. I had already learned Young was dead.

"How is the other one?" I asked.

"She didn't make it," he said, shaking his head.

With deadline looming for the Lake County edition, I drove to the office just a few miles away. I wrote that both tellers had been killed and attributed the information to police. I was hurrying to try and get back to the scene when the phone rang.

"Scott is not dead," the editor said.

I don't remember what I said, but it was probably something like, "But, but …."

After making some more calls, and with the help of reporter Rich McKay in Orlando, I learned that Scott was indeed still hanging onto life, and we were able to change the story in time.

I wasn't the only one who had received wrong information.

Scott's fiancé, Clint Brighurst, recalled being met at the police station by a cop. "… he turned around and kind of put his hands around behind him, and [said]: 'Well, there ain't no easy way to say this, but Marishia's dead.'

"And I just fell apart. And we sit there and cried about an hour. I mean, I just fell down, you know. 'What do I do?' But a paramedic walked over and said it was Heather that had expired, and that Marishia was in the hospital, airlifted," Brighurst testified in a deposition.

Back at the bank, family, friends, and people who didn't even know the women were filling up the sidewalk with flowers.

At police headquarters, FBI agents and local cops were firing questions at Anderson.

Lake Sheriff's Deputy Jeff Taylor asked why he shot the women. He said he didn't know. He indicated that he did not even remember what happened.

He then asked Anderson if he was on drugs.

"No," he replied.

Sheriff's detective Linda Green wrote in her report: "He stated that the victims had given him money and they had obeyed his every order, he did not know why he shot them. He stated he guessed he just panicked because the shooting was unprovoked."

"I'm sorry," he said.

They asked why he tried to remove the tape from the recorder.

"Because of my face," he said, indicating that he did not wear a mask during the robbery.

"Both were shot to cover his tracks," Sheriff's Detective L.P. Brown told the *Sentinel* (March 22, 1999).

Anderson told Officer Bruce Clark that the robbery was not planned. He just "decided to rob it."

That was a lie. He had been in the bank the day before the robbery. On that day he pretended to be a college student writing a paper on the banking industry.

"He came into my office and asked questions concerning banking services, customer and employee relations," branch manager Allen Seabrook said in an affidavit. He said he gave him brochures about various accounts.

"As we talked, any time I lost eye contact with him when I returned my eyes to his they were on my video equipment that is located on the left side of my desk."

Anderson was already familiar with the thriving, locally-owned chain of banks.

As a young man he had worked at the branch in Umatilla where he lived. He also knew some of the employees.

Police knew him as a con man who liked to forge signatures and write bad checks.

In 1995, it resulted in a $1,100 loss for the bank, but because the bank knew Fred's mother they treated it as a loan, using his mother's house as collateral. But when the loan was not repaid, the bank moved to foreclose on the house.

In January 1997, Anderson tried to cash a check at the Publix grocery store in Mount Dora. The store clerks called police and two officers walked up behind him.

"Oh no, not you two guys," said Anderson, who knew them from previous arrests.

"… which is why, I think, at the bank, why he wanted the video, because he knew as soon as we saw the video, we would know who it was. But he likes that bank. They probably treat him nice at that bank, so he went back," one of the officers later reflected.

He didn't like Scott, however.

Two days before the robbery he went to a Colonial bank in an effort to pull the same student scam. He ran into someone at that bank that he had worked with at the bank in Umatilla. He complained that Scott had been "rude."

A sweet person by nature, it seems extremely unlikely that Scott had been rude. She may, however, have been suspicious.

Anderson needed money. He was about to be picked up and forced to work at a probation restitution center to pay back $4,594.30 to Bethune-Cookman College where he had stolen admission funds. There was to be a 4 percent collection fee and a surcharge of $244.63. A judge also ordered that he be placed on stricter community control probation for more than 500 days. He was also facing new worthless check charges.

"I sent him a violation," state probation officer Kathryne Carter said in a deposition. "He knew because I had told him repeatedly that he needed to make a good faith effort, weekly, monthly, or whatever, to show that he was paying something, which he didn't do. He didn't listen to me."

With an arrest date looming, he called probation officials on March 19.

"Hey, I've got the money," he said. "Now I won't have to go to the half-way house (*Sentinel*, Sept. 24, 2000)."

What he didn't say was that the money was going to be coming from a bank robbery in less than 24 hours.

Authorities grilled Anderson for eight hours after the robbery while I sat outside with a small cluster of reporters in the police station carport.

Finally, they brought him out. He was wearing a white jump suit because they had confiscated his clothes and sent them to the crime lab. Big and fat, he shuffled toward a patrol car so officers could take him to jail. Officers had to gently fold him down to stuff him into the back seat.

Investigators were also fanning out across the county interviewing everyone they could think of to help fill in all the blanks in the investigation.

One of those questioned was his cousin, the owner of what was supposed to be his getaway car, a Ford LTD.

"She just couldn't believe that of him; that he could have done it by himself, because he has never had to work [hard]. They [his family] worked hard to put him through school and college so he wouldn't have to work in the crops," an officer noted in his deposition.

Sheriff's Detective Brown couldn't believe it either. He had known Anderson and his mother from his days as a patrol deputy in Umatilla and considered him to be intelligent and polite.

"We're all surprised that he would do something like this," Brown said.

He had worked as a nurses' aide in a crippled children's hospital and later worked at a Boy Scout camp serving food. He also sang in a church choir.

It was Scott who would be crippled now. One of the many .22-caliber bullets that struck her hit her spinal cord.

"Because the spine is severed and liquefied, there is no chance of [full] recovery. Zero," said Dr. Richard A. Douglas (*Sentinel*, March 25, 1999).

She would never again be able to help her fiancé on their farm, walk, or even feed herself. She would be a paraplegic for the rest of her life.

She couldn't even hug her fiancé or her dad, who took the news very hard.

"If any of you out there have a daughter, see if you can have her hug you tonight. I won't ever get that again," Carl Scott said at a press conference with his wife, Sandy.

The slaying of Heather Young cut the heart out of David Curbow.

"She was my partner—we kept our love between us, and all our free time was spent together," he told the *Sentinel* (March 23, 1999).

The two opened a pizza shop together after she had managed pizza restaurants in the area for some time. They sold the shop, and she was working at the bank when Anderson shot her.

The couple loved the outdoors, visiting islands in the Caribbean, and parasailing in Key West.

"Just to understand how happy she was, you'd only have to look at her face," he said. They were together for 15 years.

The pastor who conducted her funeral service comforted the 250 mourners who came to the service.

"She's not dead. She's living in heaven. If you could talk to Heather, she would say, 'I am having fun,'" said the Rev. Stan Hannan of the First Baptist Church of Eustis.

Police and prosecutors, meanwhile, were working on the case against Anderson. Scott identified Anderson from a photo lineup in a dramatic moment captured on videotape just three days after the shooting.

Unable to speak because she was on a ventilator, Mount Dora Police Sgt. James Jicha asked, "You want to look at some pictures for me?"

He asked if she needed anything or if she wanted her mother by her side, then he said: "One wink for yes, two for no (*Sentinel,* July 9, 2000)."

Her eyes widened when the saw the card with six mug shots.

'Did you see him in there? Relax now, you're doing fine."

She shook her head no each time when shown a photo until she got to the fifth image. She nodded her head yes. Jicha turned the lineup sheet to the camera and pointed to number five. It was Anderson. He went to the sixth and she shook her head no. When he showed her number five again, she nodded yes, made a sniffling noise, and fought back tears.

Scott was sent to the Shepherd Center in Atlanta, one of the top spinal rehabilitation centers in the nation, for treatment.

"I've made it this far, and I'm not giving up," she said at a big welcome-back celebration. "I'm just happy to be home (*Sentinel*, Aug. 2, 1999)."

Investigators and prosecutors stayed busy. One of the things they learned was that Anderson had stolen one of the two .22-caliber pistols used in the robbery from a friend's shed.

Defense attorneys were busy, too. Assistant Public Defender Clint Doud noted the life-and-death aspect of the case in a motion, noting "… upon conviction, the state would like to legally murder him by electrocution or lethal injection."

The defense team unsuccessfully challenged the state's request to do DNA testing on his blood. They also tried to challenge Anderson's confession and expressed concern that "sensational" pretrial publicity would make it hard to pick a jury (*Sentinel*, Sept. 19, 2000).

After an extensive selection process, however, a jury was selected in Lake County.

Sherry Howard, the woman who entered the bank as the robbery was taking place, was one of the first witnesses.

Tears welled up in her eyes as she recalled hearing Scott's voice.

One of the arresting officers also testified about rushing in to find Anderson trying to destroy the security video.

Anderson identified himself as a janitor. Nice work if you can get it. He had cleaned out the vault to the tune of $72,500 cash dumped into the trash can.

Jurors also heard the gripping testimony of paramedic Lt. Mark O'Keefe who worked feverishly to save Scott, including pulling out a scalpel and performing an emergency tracheostomy so she could breathe.

She quit breathing on the helicopter, too. Her lungs had collapsed, so he had to again pull out a scalpel, this time to puncture her chest so he could insert a tube. She was breathing again within about 30 seconds.

"It seemed like hours," he testified. "The experience will stay with me for the rest of my life (*Sentinel,* Sept. 29, 2000)."

She kept mouthing words, including "Don't let me die."

Jurors saw some physical evidence, including four spent bullets and three teeth that had either been knocked out with a blow or blasted out by gunfire.

They also saw the baseball cap Anderson was wearing that day, which was emblazoned with the words, "DON'T BUG ME."

Medical Examiner Dr. Susan Rendon also testified that the women had been struck over the head with a blunt instrument and shot.

Young was shot seven times with most striking her in the chest and abdomen. One bullet, however, was fired into her right temple from just eight inches away.

Would it have knocked her unconscious? Chief Assistant Public Defender Bill Stone asked, in what would be a successful blocking of the state's possible use of the heinous, atrocious, and cruel "aggravator" for the death penalty.

"Probably," Rendon said, "but I couldn't say if she was not feeling any pain."

The following day jurors got to see a portion of the walls, a door, and countertop removed from the vault. Jurors listened for hours as lawyers battled with a crime scene analyst over his interpretation of highly technical blood spatter evidence.

The court adjourned for the weekend. Monday, however, featured the most compelling witness possible.

The packed courtroom was hushed as Scott maneuvered her motorized wheelchair down the aisle.

She struggled but managed to keep her composure as she recalled the words she said as she pleaded for mercy that day.

"Please don't shoot! Don't hurt me! (*Sentinel,* Oct. 3, 2000)."

Anderson took the stand to try to ease the growing landslide of evidence against him, including gunshot residue on his hands and DNA blood evidence. His clothing had been spattered with Scott's blood.

He said he drove around the shopping center parking lot for 20 minutes trying to decide if he was going to go through with the robbery. "I had not made a final decision," he said.

He left and came back. His greatest concern, he said, was what would happen to his disabled mother while he was at the halfway house.

He claimed he had no plans to hurt Young and Scott.

"I was going to take the VCR," he said.

The biggest tale of all, however, was that one of the guns went off accidentally.

"In the course of telling her [Young] to shut up, I remember hearing a gun fire," he said.

Assistant State Attorney Bill Gross, who has a flair for being able to set up vivid visual images in jurors' minds, handed the smaller, unloaded revolver to Anderson and had him point the gun at him.

He reminded Anderson of a gun expert's testimony who said the weapon had an unusually heavy trigger pull of 17 pounds.

"So, you're telling this jury that this gun, which is like picking up three 5-pound bags of sugar with your finger, went off by itself?"

He continued ripping into Anderson's story of only hearing three shots and not recalling any of the rounds being fired by the other handgun. One of the guns had to be cocked manually each time before it could be fired.

Anderson also denied hitting the women, though Scott testified that she had been struck by some kind of black, heavy object.

The Florida Supreme Court noted in its ruling: "At trial, the State offered the theory that after shooting the two victims, Anderson went to retrieve the VCR, and while he was doing so, he heard voices coming from the vault ... upon returning to the vault and discovering that the victims were still alive, Anderson hit the victims in the head with the VCR or some other blunt object. In addition to the pathologist's testimony regarding blunt force trauma, Scott testified that she remembered a "black object" coming at her forehead after being shot. The State speculated that this object was the VCR. There was testimony that the VCR was dented, but it was not clear at trial how this damage occurred. Anderson testified he returned to the vault with the VCR, was surprised to see blood coming from Scott's neck, and dropped the VCR."

Gross looked at his foe and said: "You will do anything to save your life, won't you, Mr. Anderson?"

"No sir, I'm telling the truth to save my life."

Gross countered by asking what possible reason Scott would have to lie.

He then pulled out court records showing that Anderson had been convicted of worthless check charges 16 times.

Normally, prosecutors cannot bring up past convictions, but things like check charges are allowed during cross-examination because they show a history of dishonesty, which has a bearing on the veracity of their testimony.

"The only way you figured you could get away with it was by not leaving any witnesses, right?" Gross asked.

Anderson did not answer.

It took the 12-member jury only three hours to decide that Anderson was guilty.

Defense attorney Bill Stone had tried to soften the blow, arguing that Anderson was unsophisticated and had not planned the robbery; he just needed money.

"This was stupid, absolutely stupid. He was unsophisticated to violent crime. He was scared and he was desperate," Stone said (*Sentinel,* Oct. 4, 2000).

He ripped some of the testimony of the medical examiner and crime scene evidence, including the notion that the women were beaten and whether the shots were fired point blank. He also criticized the blood-spatter evidence on the disassembled bank vault room.

Gross countered in his final argument that Anderson was trying to put on a "dumb crime defense," yet he had attended college, was intelligent, and had a good memory. "But he doesn't remember the embarrassing things," he said, including Scott's pleas for mercy.

He also reminded jurors of Anderson's question to the women: "Which one of you guys wants to die first?"

Marishia's mother, Sandra Scott, said she felt sorry for Anderson's mother, but she was bitter about Anderson's merciless question about which one of the tellers wanted to die first.

"She (Marishia) didn't get a chance to pick," she said.

Certainly, the robbery was planned, Gross said. Why else would he bring two guns? Why shoot the tellers and try to get the videotape? It was because he did not wear a mask, he said.

"If I was going to do a bank, I'd get a mask and a gun. It wouldn't even matter if the gun had any bullets in it. They're going to give me the money," he said.

When the trial moved into the penalty phase, witnesses tried to paint a picture of a softer, religious side of Anderson. Anderson capped it by singing the song about mercy.

Scott's and Young's family members stormed out of the courtroom in disgust.

Robert Young II said the singing by his sister's killer "made me sick."

Gross seized on the chilling question that Anderson posed to the terrorized tellers that day. He repeatedly squeezed the trigger on the unloaded guns and imagined what Anderson was saying to himself as he blazed away with the weapons.

"I'm not going to stop until you are dead. I don't really care who's going to die first, but you are both going to die."

Assistant Public Defender Doud argued that his client's life should be spared. "If you kill a man, you kill the bad, but you also kill the good."

But the jury voted 12-0 in its recommendation that the state should kill all of Anderson.

Young said he would attend Anderson's execution. "I'll buy the popcorn."

Lawyers appealed Anderson's death sentence. "By his own account, he had no intention of hurting anyone, Assistant Public Defender George D.E. Burden wrote in his motion. Of course, "by his own account" is not a compelling argument for a known con man and thief, but his attorneys were trying to counter the court's finding for statutory aggravating factors for the death penalty, including the one dubbed CCP, or cold, calculated, and premeditated. The others involved pecuniary gain and contemporaneous conviction of attempted murder of the second person.

It was not a crime of emotional frenzy or panic, the Florida Supreme Court noted in upholding the death sentence.

Under the law, premeditation can be as quick as a few seconds, but Anderson had plenty of time. He left the bank, saying he was going to get a business card from his car. Instead, he came back with two handguns as the bank was getting ready to close, the high court noted.

The trial judge allowed several defense "mitigators," including "strong religious faith." Courts can allow just about anything as a mitigating circumstance. Judges then assign weight to the mitigators. But that argument, which did not carry much weight with the judge, had to be especially galling to any faithful Christian who could point to the Ten Commandments' ban on murder, stealing, lying, and coveting, not to mention honoring your father and mother.

Anderson is still awaiting his fate on death row.

Scott filed a lawsuit against the company that provided the bank alarms.

The suit claimed the company should have provided panic-button alarms at the teller stations and that the placement of the VCR was a security risk.

Among other things, the suit demanded money for 24-hour nursing care, lost wages, and pain and suffering.

The suffering, she told me, was indescribable. "You can't put a dollar amount on it (*Sentinel*, Feb. 7, 2002)."

But the jury came up with a figure—$27 million—and a judge upheld it.

The victory would be short-lived, however. An appeal court ordered a new trial, which was set to begin in May 2005. In January, Scott agreed to a negotiated settlement.

The financial amount was confidential but Bryan Crews, one of her attorneys, said Scott "will be taken care of for the rest of her life (*Sentinel*, Jan. 29, 2005)."

She had been forced to live on workers' compensation, about 66 percent of the salary she was earning as a bank teller nearly six years earlier. The money only paid for minimal health care. She was dependent upon assistance from her fiancé and her family.

"She has been living at the poverty level," said Scott's lawyer, Don Van Dingenen.

The settlement allowed her to receive around-the-clock care and for her to move from a manufactured home to a farmhouse with a tin roof and a wraparound porch so she can view the countryside from her wheelchair, he said.

"And if anything happens to her fiancé, this money will be available to her on a monthly basis for the rest of her life," Crews said. "That was one of the motivating reasons behind our recommendation that she accept the settlement."

It was some relief, at least, and a small measure of justice in a case of merciless murder and mayhem at the hands of a man too lazy and too self-centered to face up to the normal responsibilities in life.

Scott died in 2015. She was only 39 years old.

***

Ricky Martin sat outside the Barnett Bank in his blue pickup truck shortly before 9:35 a.m. It was Aug. 9, 1994, a Tuesday. A creature of habit, he was preparing to make a bank deposit from the Checkers fast food restaurant in Leesburg where he was a manager.

It was hot that day, as usual. A retiree was out for his routine morning stroll. But what happened next was anything but routine.

A schoolteacher opening a new account inside the bank jumped when she heard gunshots and the sound of shattered glass.

She looked out the window in time to see a man dressed in loose-fitting dark clothing with a cap and a bandana reach inside the pickup, grab a white bag, and walk away rapidly, leaving five other bags filled with cash inside the truck.

"I ran to the truck to tell him he was going to be OK, that help was on the way," she said, but all the help in the world couldn't have saved him (*Sentinel*, Sept. 7, 1995). Four of the five rounds from a .380-caliber semiautomatic handgun had found their mark and killed the 35-year-old father of two.

Within minutes police had stopped a white 1984 Ford Tempo headed north on U.S. Highway 441/27 and arrested three young men inside: Jereme Ware, 18, Jamous Walker, 20, and Devin Jarrett, 16.

Officers found $821 folded up under the front passenger seat where Ware was sitting.

Jarrett, who had worked at the restaurant until two days earlier, was mouthy. "That son of a bitch fired me," he said of Martin.

The case seemed fairly neat and tidy, but Bill Gross and others would have to work for the convictions.

For one thing, police could never find the gun. Leesburg Police Capt. Jerry Gehlbach testified that officers searched for three days, even draining swampy areas and using metal detectors.

By January of the following year, the State Attorney's Office was able to get a conviction on Jarrett in an emotionally charged trial for both the Martin and Jarrett families.

"He begged me not to bring him down here," said his mother, Robin Jarrett, who moved to Lake County two years earlier to escape the legendary violence of Detroit (*Sentinel,* Jan. 14, 1995).

Jarrett's attorney, the locally well-known, well-versed, and feisty defense lawyer, Ron Fox, blasted the guilty verdict and the life sentence.

"I've never had anyone convicted for sitting in the back of a car," he fumed (*Sentinel,* Jan. 14, 1995). In fact, Jarrett was convicted of felony murder. In other words, he was an active participant in an armed robbery in which a murder was committed by someone else.

There was more to it than that, of course. Prosecutors pointed out that he was the inside man, the one who knew Martin's deposit routine and the layout of the restaurant, plus he was angry at Martin.

Walker was also convicted and sentenced to life. Prosecutors clearly had their sights set on Ware, however, the suspected gunman. They announced they were seeking the death penalty and hoped to get his codefendants to testify. Both balked, however.

Martin's father, Ken, wrote an emotional letter to Walker on June 5, 1995, begging him to testify against Ware.

"We sat through the trial and heard the defense attorney tell how you came from a caring family. How you played the organ in the church and that your grandmother is a pastor. If all this is true, then you know that you have a responsibility to God to testify … so that he will never be able to hurt or kill another innocent person again."

"Father's Day is this month. I will not have the joy of sharing it with my son. We used to go to church together. Also, he sang in the choir. We use[d] to love to play golf together. He use[d] to help me do many of the things I am unable to do because of my Parkinson Disease and heart problems. He will never be able to do that again, nor will he be able to spend time with his two children and be a daddy to them.

"I will close in saying that our family, by the grace of God, prays for your salvation because hell is eternal. It is so sad to see all of these young people that were or are members of this gang wasting their lives in acts of crime and violence and how someone could have called Ricky Martin and warned him of these plans and saved his life."

He ended the letter by writing: "Remember, you do have to live with this for the rest of your life."

Walker did not change his mind, but Gross had built a strong circumstantial case in the face of some daunting challenges mounted by the defense. Because the gun was never found, for example, prosecutors had to find another way to put the gun in his hand.

Ware's defense attorneys pointed the finger at Jarrett. Even before he was fired, "Every time Martin gave Jarrett an order, he said harsh words under his breath," said John Spivey (Sept. 7, 1995).

The defense team had its work cut out for it, too. Among other things, they tried to keep quiet the fact that Ware was a leader of the local Folk Nation gang.

Among the first to testify was the retiree out for his morning stroll. He recalled seeing the car backed into a parking spot near the Leesburg bank.

"It bothered me very much. I almost went back to look at the tag. I thought maybe the bank was about to be robbed," he said.

He could see a black man in the car but only from the eyes up. After walking about 100 yards away, he heard gunshots.

The schoolteacher who had been inside the bank opening a new account conceded that she was not good at estimating height. At first, she thought the gunman was about 5-foot-8. Later, she thought he was about 6 feet tall. Ware is 5-foot-7.

The prosecutor's ace-in-the-hole was a 15-year-old friend of Ware's, Alex Negron. Ware told his friend he needed two things: a gun and a car. Negron replied that he told Ware that he knew of a "phat" (highly desirable) gun that belonged to a friend's stepfather in the city of Winter Garden (*Sentinel*, Sept. 8, 1995).

Ware later stole the gun and a box of bullets and told Negron it was the "first tool" he needed to rob the restaurant.

The next "tool" he needed was a car. One night, while riding home from a party, he made a friend, Jeff Hoyle, "swear on a "pitchfork," the gang's symbol, that he would not tell anybody about his plans to rob Checkers.

"I'm not going to kill anybody," Ware said, according to Negron's testimony. "I'm going to try not to shoot anybody."

He also disclosed that he was getting inside information from Jarrett, including the fact that it was Checkers' policy not to resist during a robbery.

He said his plan was to hide out at a nearby motel when Martin arrived for work at 7 a.m. He would then put on a mask, rob the manager at gunpoint, and lock him in a rest room. He would then go back to the motel and wait for things to "cool off" before making his escape.

Hoyle testified that he wanted nothing to do with it.

"You'll get caught," he told Ware.

Negron said he was supposed to later go to a party with Ware, but he never showed up. The next thing Negron heard about his friend was that he had been arrested.

"Maybe if I had said something, he wouldn't be in the trouble he's in now," he speculated.

Prosecutors presented some physical evidence to bolster their case, including a crime lab expert who testified that there were minute bits of glass found on Ware's clothing, glass that was consistent with the type used in a windshield. An FBI expert testified that the spent bullets and the unused bullets in the box were from the same manufacturer.

Investigators also learned that Ware was his own worst enemy when it came to keeping his story straight. He told detectives that the money found under his seat was from the sale of fancy rims from his BMW. He said he had sold them to a man named Josh. He gave investigators the name of a former girlfriend and said she could verify it. But when police contacted her in Orlando, she said she had not seen Ware for months and had never heard of the man that supposedly bought the rims.

Ware also told police he had spent the night at a Leesburg motel with a man named "Chris" the evening before the shooting because his parents had locked him out of his house as punishment for breaking curfew.

That story was blown out of the water, however, by a surprising witness: Jamous Walker's mother. Ware had spent the night at her home, she said.

The defense fought back. They presented Negron's friend, who testified that it was Negron, not Ware, who stole the gun. Negron stashed the gun and bullets at her house, she testified.

The attorneys also presented Checkers' employees who quoted Jarrett as saying, "I'm going to get Rick (*Sentinel*, Sept.9, 1995)."

During closing arguments, Assistant State Attorney Scot Roti compared Ware to a "deadly spider" that spins a "web of lies."

When jurors ended their six hours of deliberations, Martin's family held hands and waited for the clerk to read the verdict. It was guilty.

"Great, one more day," Ken Martin said.

The "day" was the penalty phase. It would be a day of testimony from defense witnesses trying to save Ware's life. Ware had "mild to moderate mental illness," a psychologist testified, citing test results. His condition may have worsened when he suffered a head injury trying to break up a fight in Tampa, he said.

As a 4-year-old, he sometimes thought he was hearing bells or his name being called and thought people were outside, according to friends and family members interviewed by the psychologist.

The jury recommended that Circuit Judge Mark Hill not sentence Ware to death. Hill sentenced him to two life terms with no chance of parole.

"You were given a light sentence," said Martin's sister when the family was given permission to speak.

"I hope you think about it every second for the rest of your life," said Barbette Strohschein as Ware hung his head (*Sentinel*, Sept. 15, 1995).

"You were brought up in a loving home," said Martin's mother, Judy. "You knew right from wrong. One day, you will stand before God, and unless you change your ways, you won't have a defense attorney to plead your case."

There were earthly appeals, of course.

Two years later, Ware was back in court complaining that the sentence was unfair. Hill had sentenced him to life on the murder charge, and then he went beyond the sentencing guidelines and sentenced him to life on the armed robbery charge. Sentencing guidelines at the time called for a sentence of eight to 13 years in prison.

The robbery sentence was legal, Gross argued, because it was imposed in conjunction with a capital offense.

The news got worse for Ware. The clerk had made an error in the paperwork when he was sent off to prison. She had written that the two sentences were to be concurrent. However, when the case came up on appeal, the clerk's office noticed the mistake and corrected it to match the judge's intent: two consecutive life sentences.

"He majorly messed up," a fellow prosecutor noted when the court was adjourned.

The Martin family knew, even before the trial, that there would be appeals.

"As long as there are appeals, there can be no closure," Judy Martin said (*Sentinel,* Aug. 10, 1999).

Shortly before the trial, the restaurant posted on their big road sign: "In Memory of Rick Martin."

The family came to express their appreciation and posed outside the restaurant.

"I think it's great that they're doing this," Judy said, but the photo, taken on a rainy day, clearly shows the family members with drooping shoulders, joyless expressions, and pain seared into their souls.

"We pray for these three young men," she said. "We think they should say in prison, but we pray for them and for their families."

The family also spoke plainly about the empty seat at the table, the loss of a father to Martin's 9-year-old son, and the missed golf games.

"You always think it's going to happen to someone else," she said.

"In some ways, it seems like yesterday, but it has been a long time since we had the chance to hug him," she said (Aug. 10, 1999).

***

Fast cars, "stash houses" filled with marijuana and cocaine, thick wads of money, hired guns, and bullet-riddled bodies were the hallmarks of one merciless drug gang in the '90s.

The gang was reportedly doing a brisk business—shipping 20,000 pounds of marijuana and 600 pounds of cocaine from 1992 to 1996—before arrests, indictments, and informants began dismantling the little empire. The gang paid Texas airport security guards $100 per pound of marijuana to look the other way when pot was packed in bags from Mexico. The drugs, first sent to Central Florida, were eventually shipped to Puerto Rico and the Eastern Seaboard. Cocaine was shipped from Puerto Rico.

One of the biggest blows to the operation came on Nov. 2, 1994, when deputies lifted a 6-inch-thick slab of concrete off the secret grave of a drug dealer. The site had been disguised as a dog pen.

The parents of an 18-year-old man were hoping it was the body of their missing son—and praying that it wasn't. Timothy Lassiter was "not a street-smart kid," Ann Brogan told me in an interview (*Sentinel*, April 26, 2000). "We're not saying he was perfect," said Mark Brogan. What they were saying was that he may have been blinded by wads of cash and the gang's flashy lifestyle. He had been missing since July 1993.

It was not Lassiter, however, who had been entombed for more than a year behind a mobile home on a rutted, sandy road in the woods. It was a 22-year-old dealer named Eloy Benavides.

The murder trail led to Ron Ridgeway, a 515-pound tattooed "do boy" and bodyguard who ran errands for gang leader Juan Miguel Diez. He wasn't the trigger man who put a bullet through the logo on Benavides' Marlins baseball cap, but he would be the first of many gang members to go on trial in the complex case.

The trail led to the 21-year-old Ridgeway because he started running his mouth about the murder seven months after the slaying. He started talking about how he and his "baby brother," 450-pound Geoff Ridgway, tricked Benavides into coming to the stash house that was rented under his name.

The two brothers were known as "The Fat Boys" in drug circles.

Ron Ridgeway said he "could still see his [Benavides'] face" when he fell, his friend, Jessica Jones Lilly, testified (*Sentinel,* Nov. 10, 1995).

He said he started talking about it because it bothered him. Other witnesses, however, said Ridgeway and others would joke about it, pointing to Marlins baseball caps in stores and saying, "Pow!"

After being convicted of murder, Ridgeway would later testify against the shooter, Daniel Wert. Ridgeway said he thought his brother Geoff was going to do the shooting.

"He [Geoff] told me to stay in the car and cover him, but before he could get out of the car, I heard a loud bang (*Sentinel*, May 22, 1999)."

Benavides was shot, witnesses testified, because gang boss Diez didn't want to pay him the more than $200,000 that he owed him for 250 pounds of marijuana.

Ridgeway also told others about how he doused the body with acid to speed up decomposition, something he learned in college. But he also used lime, so the acid and the base canceled each other out.

The result was a macabre mess that once was a handsome face. Photos of the gruesome discovery would later be fixed in the minds of jurors. Forensic anthropologists showed jurors gruesome images from the makeshift grave but with a twist. Their video combined time-lapse images of Benavides when he was alive—as if putting flesh back on the bones—to show that the corpse was indeed Benavides.

Diez didn't want to be around when the shooting took place, Ridgeway would testify five years later as a witness against his former boss. The gang leader went to Disney World on an overnight trip. When he returned, he wanted to see "proof" that Benavides was dead. Wert showed him the grave behind the house. Diez urinated on the site and laughed, Ridgeway testified.

The concrete slab was unique in more ways than one. Because it was six inches thick, gang members had to buy 3,000 pounds of ready-mix concrete to do the job. That fact was not lost on a hardware clerk who later testified about the sale. Second, there was a long pipe that ran vertically through the slab. The pipe was built into the slab so that Diez could run a steel rod downward and poke the body. That was the ultimate proof that would satisfy Diez.

A deputy who helped dig up the body also noticed that there was a small plastic air freshener hanging in the dog pen, an air freshener that looked like a king's crown. The implication was the air freshener had come from Benavides' Corvette.

Benavides wasn't the gang's only murder victim. Authorities said Diez was also responsible for the death of his partner, Angel Medina, 20.

There was a bitter disagreement between the two men. Medina wanted to pay Benavides for the drugs he had supplied; Diez did not. Sniper Danny Wert was following orders from his boss, Diez, when he climbed atop the stash house and ambushed Benavides with a .22-caliber rifle.

"He [Diez] was out to reduce the overhead, to increase the profit margin by killing a creditor," Assistant State Attorney Bill Gross told jurors during Wert's murder trial (*Sentinel*, May 29, 1999).

Gross was always focused on Diez. The assistant state attorney scored murder convictions against the Ridgeway brothers and Wert. Federal prosecutors had already obtained racketeering convictions against several gang members by 1999. But Gross wanted a murder conviction against the drug kingpin, too.

I asked Gross why he bothered. After all, Diez was going away for the rest of his life on racketeering charges. I even used some courthouse gallows humor, hinting that there were no "real" murder victims. "These people were killing drug dealers. They should get a medal," I joked.

Defense attorneys have their own version of this kind of joke. There is a crime in Florida called shooting into an occupied vehicle. Attorneys defending clients for shooting unsavory people derisively call it "shooting into occupied clothing."

Not only was Gross determined to get a murder conviction for Diez in state court in the Medina slaying, but by April 2000 he was also seeking the death penalty.

There was motive galore, Gross told jurors. Diez had been" disrespected" by Medina three times: Medina was having an affair with Diez's fiancée, he went behind his partner's back to sell five kilos of cocaine to dealers in New York for $100,000, and he lied to his business partner when he claimed that cops had confiscated $100,000 in cash, Gross said.

Stephanie Diez-Bell testified that in 1993 Diez found a love letter addressed to her from Medina. Diez picked up a handgun that belonged to her and confronted Medina.

"Get out of my house," he said (*Sentinel*, April 5, 2000).

The two men eventually made up. At a New Year's Eve party at a nightclub, Diez sent a bottle of champagne to Medina's table with a message: "Don't let this happen again."

"He loved him like a brother," Bell told defense attorney Michael Graves on cross-examination.

Gross soon found himself in troubled waters. He had granted immunity to Diez's lieutenant, Cesar Farrait, if he would testify against his former boss. But once that immunity was granted, Farrait admitted that he helped plan the murder, came up with the weapons, and hired his friend, Joel Rivera, to be the hit man.

Defense attorney John Spivey called the prosecutor's deal "dirty business."

"He was the man who would be king," Spivey said of Farrait. "He was the man who had the most to gain and the man who lost the least." Farrait moved up in the gang following Medina's death.

Hit man Rivera testified in the Diez trial.

Rivera was a piece of work. At a pretrial hearing, he had pleaded no contest to first-degree murder in the slaying of Medina—without a plea deal—in hopes of avoiding the death penalty. The move was so stunning and so spontaneous no one was sure at first if the court reporter had captured the moment on her steno machine. Graves subpoenaed my notes. It turns out, however, that the court reporter had recorded Rivera's statement.

"You had it exactly correct," Graves told me.

"What did you expect?" I said, happy for the opportunity to tease him.

Rivera testified that he searched Puerto Rico for a hit man known as *El Gato,* or "The Cat," but he wanted $100,000 for the job.

Rivera told Farrait that he would pull the trigger himself for $10,000 and 10 pounds of pot.

He said Diez instructed him to make Medina get on his knees, deliver a very personal message, and shoot him two times with a .45-caliber handgun.

"He told me he wanted me to tell Angel that it was payback for what he did with Stephanie and all the money he stole from him (*Sentinel,* April 2, 2000)."

Instead, Rivera shot him in the back of the head while Medina was driving his pickup truck in the Ocala National Forest. Rivera, nicknamed *Gordo,* or "Fat," had squeezed his 290-pound frame into the back seat. Geoff Ridgeway was in the front seat. After the deafening gun blast, the truck slammed into a pine tree. Neither Rivera nor Ridgeway was hurt in the crash.

Farrait's half-brother, Ernesto, also testified against Diez. He said he had worked closely with Medina and said he was shocked when he learned Medina had been slain.

Like others in the federal trials, Ernesto had received a reduced sentence for testifying against others.

"You're a professional snitch," Graves shouted at him during his cross-examination (*Sentinel,* April 6, 2000).

It would become a common theme, with Graves contemptuously calling the parade of seedy convicted felons "snitch world." That statement and a cartoon propped up on an easel during closing arguments would make a lasting impression on jurors. The cartoon showed rats lining up to get out of federal prison.

Not only would Gross not end up getting a death penalty recommendation from the jury, he wouldn't even get a murder conviction. It was a rare loss for Lake County's homicide prosecutor, who retired in December 2013 with more than 100 convictions. Later, however, Diez agreed to plead no-contest to racketeering and being an accessory in the slaying of Benavides, just days before he was scheduled to go to trial on murder charges in that case. Circuit Judge G. Richard Singeltary sentenced Diez to 12 years on the state racketeering charge and five for being an accessory after the fact for murder.

It was a symbolic gesture, however. The sentences would run consecutively with Diez's federal life sentence for racketeering.

The biggest letdown of all, however, was felt by Timothy Lassiter's parents.

In 1996, two years after Benavides' body was found, a construction worker found bones in Osceola County several hundred yards from the spot a tipster said they would find

Lassiter's remains. The long wait, through empty-chair holidays, family gatherings, and cold lonely nights was over.

"That's the day we turned off the porch light," Lassiter's mother said.

She found temporary solace in 1997 when Diez was convicted in federal court of racketeering.

"Judgment day!" she shouted as he was led from the courtroom in handcuffs, sentenced to life in prison. "Judgment day! Judgment day!"

"It's been seven years now," said Ann Brogan after Diez was sentenced on the state charges.

"Their family members can visit them, they can talk to them and touch them," she said. "We can't."

At one time, investigators speculated that as many as five homicides had been committed by gang members. To date, no one has been arrested and charged with Lassiter's death.

Chapter 15

Wacky

Some of the funniest people in the world are in jail. It's not that they intended to be funny, but rather they said or pulled off some of the dumbest things to wind up there.

Take, for example, the cop who rolled up on a naked guy walking down the middle of the road one night.

"It's not as bad as it looks!" the man shouted.

"No … from where I'm sitting it looks pretty bad," the cop said. "Get in the back seat."

Former longtime Public Defender Howard "Skip" Babb Jr. got the naked truth out of a job candidate one time by asking a question he had never asked before: "Do you have any skeletons in your closet?"

The woman thought for a moment, then asked what he meant.

A few months earlier, Babb explained, an assistant state attorney was caught riding around drunk and naked in Tampa with a court bailiff.

"That was me!" she exclaimed.

She got kudos for telling the truth, but she didn't get the job.

Being caught with your pants down is never a good idea. One 59-year-old man was on his way to work one morning when someone flagged him down to say that the tail lights on his car were burned out. He did a U-turn and headed back home. When he got there, he saw a pickup truck parked in his driveway, and once inside saw his wife walking out of the bedroom nude.

"Where's Sam?" he shouted.

"I don't know," she replied.

When he looked in the closet, Sam was standing there, also nude.

"What are you doing here?" the enraged husband asked.

Sam, apparently struck by the dumb question and obvious answer, laughed. It was a bad move. Soon, he was struck with bullets ("three or four times," the husband figured in his statement to police).

Sam survived. Instead of laughing he probably should have come up with a credible answer, like: "It's not as bad as it looks *(Sentinel,* Oct. 26, 1999)."

The pilot of a private plane and his passengers couldn't come up with a good answer when they were caught flying naked over Leesburg one night. Neighbors were complaining about the 3 a.m. flight—not because the folks inside were naked (they couldn't see that from the ground)—but because the plane seemed to be buzzing houses to the point of almost crashing downtown.

The pilot, who owned a body shop (a car body repair shop, that is) smelled of alcohol, police said. He claimed he had merely taken his shirt off. Police said he was pulling up his pants. He said his three passengers—two women and a man—were skydiving friends. Flying naked seemed like a good idea after drinking several beers, apparently.

The passengers were embarrassed. One woman reportedly covered herself with a map, presumably unfolded. The other two passengers doubled over in an effort to present the smallest exposed areas to the curious cops.

But the funniest thing was the pilot's cop-like "nothing to see here" routine. Everyone was just looking out the windows, he said (*Sentinel,* Oct. 18, 1993).

***

Sometimes you don't have to get naked to get into trouble.

Ricky Adams may have been a detestable scum bag for beating, kicking, and stomping his little 6-year-old girl to death, but that didn't seem to deter his defense attorney's paralegal from falling in love with him. He had no future except life behind bars. Nor did it give her pause that she was panting for a child killer, and that she had a 7-year-old son and a teenage daughter.

At some point, while going over depositions and other paperwork, she fell in love and began holding hands beneath a thick acrylic window at the jail. She also smuggled in a marijuana cigarette, chewing tobacco, lighters, love notes, and even a signed glamour portrait of herself, according to arrest reports. She was charged with possessing felony jail contraband and smuggling.

The portrait was signed: "To Ricky Lee Adams with all my love, Your Butterfly. She drew a little heart beside the inscription. She called him "Cupcake."

One of the notes read: "I love you, steadfast and never wavering, no matter what the cost."

It could have cost her five years in prison and the loss of her family. Instead, she got two years' probation and a weekend in jail.

Sondra London, a writer, was for a time the post-arrest fiancée of Danny Rolling, the "Gainesville Ripper," who butchered five college students in 1990. She broke up with him but not until he courted her in court, singing to her during one pretrial session.

London, who showed up as a spectator in the Vampire Cult murder case in Lake County, tried to explain the attraction to me in an interview for a story I wrote about lockup love.

"I as a woman look at a lot of men who are either gay, married, fat, or a wimp," she said. Men in prison have a lean and mean look. "It's an illusion," she concluded. "What's love got to do with it (*Sentinel,* Sept. 30, 2000)?"

She's not the only one. Prisons are flooded with letters from would-be lovers, mostly women. People can let their fantasies run wild and write ridiculous romance-novel love letters without having to deal with the real-life drudgery of having to live together and pay bills, get old, fat and sick, argue about the kids, and what to watch on TV. Many times, women think they can "fix" a man and turn his life around.

The head prison chaplain had his own theories.

"Mystery," said the Rev. Alex Taylor. "There's also the element of the forbidden fruit. Loneliness is a big factor."

Another explanation, he said, is that "he's safe. He's behind bars (Sept. 30, 2000)."

T. Michael Johnson witnessed the madness firsthand when he was chief assistant public defender. One day he caught his paralegal kissing serial killer-rapist Billy Mansfield.

"What do you think you're doing?" he asked. "They found four skeletons in his back yard!"

Sometimes men log-on to pen pal sites for women inmates. You might see a glamour shot of a woman who says she likes to take long walks on the beach in the moonlight, but she might forget to mention that she chopped her husband into 100 pieces and flushed him down the toilet.

Some end up getting married behind bars in a brief ceremony in a dreary visitation area. There are no conjugal visits in Florida prisons.

Serial killer Ted Bundy probably received more letters than anyone. Handsome and charming, he killed dozens of women, yet one agreed to marry him in court during one of his murder trials. The judge and jail director refused to permit it but the two worked out a plan.

"Do you want to marry me?" he asked her in an Orlando courtroom.

"Yes."

"I do hereby marry you."

It was witnessed by a notary who was sitting in the courtroom, so it was legal.

Not so legal was the trick they pulled when they allegedly conspired to make love in a visitation area of death row and conceived a child, a daughter.

Carole Boone divorced him before he was executed in the late 1980s.

***

Sometimes crooks make crazy demands, like the one who held up a convenience store and told the clerk to hit the floor and "count to a million." When she started counting, he shouted: "You're counting too fast (*Sentinel*, April 4, 2000)."

Guns make clerks nervous. Panicked by one gunman, a clerk at Home Depot did just the opposite of what she had been ordered to do.

"Oh my God, I shut the drawer," she thought (*Sentinel*, Oct. 13, 1999).

She wasn't the only crime victim who freaked out.

One woman had just filled her minivan with gas when she noticed a man standing by the pump. When she went in the store to get a snack, he was gone. As she drove off, she noticed a warning light indicating the side door was open. She continued munching but looked in her rear- view mirror just in time to see the man standing over her trying to put a rag over her face.

"Don't panic," he growled.

It was too late. First, she blurted out words that you can't print in a family newspaper, then she jerked the wheel, causing the van to swerve all over the road.

"You don't want to do this, lady!"

"Honestly, I was so scared, to tell you the truth, and mad that he was in my van to begin with, all I wanted to do was get out," she said in a sworn pretrial statement.

So, she did, but by this time the van had reached 45 mph. She landed on her backside and her head struck her purse. The impact bent the purse but saved her life. Apparently, it was one of those purses that could double as a suitcase and she had enough tissue, powder puffs, and Juicy Fruit in it to cushion the blow.

The van crashed and the crook was arrested.

"So far in Florida, I've been here three years," she said. "Our Camaro has been stolen, and I've been carjacked. You know, welcome to Florida, (*Sentinel,* June 8, 1998)."

***

Police officers may be a lot of things: brave, conscientious, and long suffering, but a lot of them can't spell cat if you spot them the first two letters. One officer described a person's religion in a report as "Israel Lite." Another described a pair of trousers as military "camel flies." The section marked for distinguishing marks on one report didn't list scars or tattoos, but it stated that the suspect had "a Yankee accent," Babb noted.

Sometimes tattoo artists are the poor spellers. One man had a "tat" that read: "Born to loose."

"That says it all," the officer noted in his report.

***

Courtrooms, which are famous for life and death seriousness, have their share of unintentional humor. Police arrested a drunken motorcyclist who had led them on a 100-mph chase. They really became concerned when he began ranting about President Bill Clinton.

"The president had better watch out because God is going to take care of him." It was especially noteworthy, officers said, because he was referring to himself as God.

In court, the assistant public defender, thinking he might have Democrats in the jury box, told the jurors to disregard his client's political views. "That's not evidence of a crime (*Sentinel*, Feb. 2, 1996)."

A man charged with burglary and grand theft asked a judge if he could get probation or house arrest. His girlfriend was pregnant, he said. "She is struggling to pay the bills because she can't work that much, and she needs me to help her."

The judge noted that he had a prior grand theft conviction and a violation of probation on that charge. The man's two codefendants were sentenced to three-year terms.

"She had plans for a future, but you were doing burglaries," Circuit Judge Mark Hill said.

He had two options, the judge said. He was looking at up to 20 years if convicted in a trial or 22 months if he pleaded guilty in a plea deal.

"To quote Clint Eastwood [in *Dirty Harry*], do you feel lucky today? Well, do you?"

The man agreed to 22 months.

"Maybe you can get your act together, come out and be a real father," Hill said.

The man thanked him as he was being led off to prison (*Sentinel* Nov. 22, 2000).

One prisoner wasn't so thankful in his comments to a judge, however.

"I'll see you in your coffin," said Craig S. Floyd, 40.

The judge wasn't worried. In fact, Circuit Judge Jerry Lockett, who once was threatened by a defendant who hired a hit man, chuckled and mentioned his upcoming retirement.

"I'll be living down a long straight road, and I'll have a rifle with a scope on it (*Sentinel,* Sept. 23, 1999)."

Floyd was sentenced to life in prison with no chance of parole.

Floyd never did help his case. One day during his trial, he refused to come out of his cell.

He had a rap sheet so long the Leesburg police chief decided to unfurl it for a *Sentinel* photograph (Aug. 4, 1999). Despite holding it over his head and doubling it waist high, the printout still hit the floor and rolled out of the picture.

Floyd was caught walking down the street with a laundry bag filled with a stolen microwave and other items. His defense attorney argued that Floyd was too big to fit through the broken window of the business. The jury, however, agreed with prosecutor Cori Phelan. "He was literally holding the bag."

Sometimes you can go straight to jail after entering the courthouse door. Everyone empties their pockets before walking through a metal detector. People take out their keys and other metal objects, but one man also took out a small packet of marijuana.

It was a "do not pass go, do not collect $200" moment for the 35-year-old man, though he didn't have a monopoly on stupidity. Others have been caught with guns and knives.

By 1999, judges started complaining privately about the quality of jurors after the state changed the requirement from being a registered voter to simply having a Florida driver's license.

In the old days, men on juries wore coats and ties and women wore dresses. Suddenly, people began showing up in tank tops, and some were convicted felons, who had to be excused. Once there, many begin trying to weasel out of their civic responsibility by claiming that they could not be impartial.

"I don't like men," one woman said. "And it's not just defendants," she explained. She didn't like her husband, either (*Sentinel*, Sept. 11, 1999).

Divorce court can be especially nasty. Several years ago, one couple demanded an emergency hearing over University of Florida season tickets. They couldn't care less about tickets to the Kentucky game, but those Tennessee Vols ....

Sometimes couples fight just to keep the other ex-partner from getting something, even if they don't really want it themselves. At other times, real money is involved.

Attorney Jerri Blair told the *Sentinel* (May 4, 2002) that one woman wanted a share of her husband's cocaine sales territory.

"I told her she needed to get her head straight. 'You've got children.'"

Sometimes too much money too suddenly is a bad thing. I interviewed a couple who won a $5.4 million lottery fortune. The couple said "we" are going to do this, and "we" are going to do that.... But soon they were on the outs and headed for divorce court.

It was all very baffling to her, she said in 1997, as their divorce case headed to court, especially when he claimed that he bought the lottery ticket with *his* money. First, he said he bought the ticket from dollars "segregated in his pocket" from a check he had cashed from his mother's estate. Later, he said the money came from the sale of scuba equipment he sold to a friend. The equipment belonged to him before his marriage to his third and soon to be ex-wife.

The two reached a settlement before Judge Hill granted their request for divorce. They split the profits from the sale of a new $275,000 house and she received 38 percent of the lottery winnings.

"Winning was not so lucky after all," said Suzanne Savall. "It was a blessing gone bad (*Sentinel*, Oct. 24, 1997)."

Two years earlier I had written about another couple who won a share totaling more than $9 million. They set up a family trust fund and had plans to buy a new Oldsmobile.

Another winner, however, shut down his restaurant and issued a trespass warning against an employee who said he was just trying to collect a day's pay that was owed him.

"It's not just the pay, it's the courtesy of it," said the man who made $2.13 per hour plus tips (*Sentinel* July 19, 1995).

Courtesy had nothing to do with one lawsuit, according to the man who filed it in 1997.

It was a sexual harassment case with a twist: he said he was the victim of name-calling, lewd comments, grabbing, touching, and teasing by other heterosexual males until he was forced to leave his job and get counseling.

He estimated he had been touched 6,000 times, so he sued his employer for $6 million— $1,000 per touch. A jury was not convinced, however.

***

It is not known if the plaintiff in the sexual harassment case was embarrassed after supposedly "baring" his soul in a losing effort. But imagine how a prisoner at the Lake County jail felt when corrections officers learned that "she" was really a man.

"Jocie," who worked for a lawyer as a secretary in Tavares, was arrested when she was picked up on a warrant from Texas. The lawyer hadn't bothered to run a background check on her when she hired her more than six months earlier. She said she didn't have to. She had known her for years, and the two often chatted for hours while getting their nails done. But when Jocie was ordered into the shower at the jail there was no mistake about her/his true identity.

"I'm sure the female corrections officer was quite surprised," said Sheriff's Maj. Gary Borders (*Sentinel,* July 15, 1997).

Lake County jailers were embarrassed about an escape at their new, $23.5 million jail in 1993. It was too easy. Two prisoners found the one window that was not barred and shatter-proof. It was the third escape in a year.

They stole clothes off a clothesline. They had to. They had shucked their striped jail trousers in the parking lot.

"We were kind of hoping they'd fall in the septic tank," the homeowner's son said. "The tank lid was open for repairs just inches from the clothesline (*Sentinel,* Aug. 6, 1993).

A month earlier, an escapee led officers on a confusing foot race until a warrant deputy, Allen "Tracker" McPherson, got his man by looking under a house a block away.

The resident heard a bump in the floor but said, "I wasn't scared. Cats go up under there sometimes," she said (*Sentinel*, July 10, 1993).

Most of the people who end up in jail want to get out, of course, including a band of 1960s-style hippies known as the "Rainbow Family."

The loose-knit group has driven Ocala National Forest rangers to the brink of insanity for years with their trespassing, pot-smoking, skinny dipping, munchy-craving, shoplifting ways. Small store owners dread the annual invasion. Sugary treats like Mallomars were always in danger of being lifted, but bars of soap were safe. It was the only group that could leave a ring around a lake once they shucked their clothes and jumped in.

The courthouse always reeked when they were in town, including the time a sweet-faced, 18-year-old Canadian girl was arrested on charges of scuffling with a ranger at a roadblock. When she was released on bond, her friends were at the jail to greet her in a giant hug fest, including a wincing reporter from a rival newspaper caught in the squeeze. He looked like he was about to pass out.

Sometimes prisoners "outsmart" themselves, like the one who was accused of giving a false name to jailers.

"I didn't give any false name," the man said at first appearance.

"Oh, so your name is Osama bin Laden?" the judge asked.

"Oh! I must have been drunk," the man conceded.

The jail has two mail systems: One is for confidential attorney-client correspondence. The other is for regular notes and mail, and these are read by corrections officers for obvious security reasons. Sometimes prisoners get it mixed up.

"I've thought it over and I want to go with story number two," one man wrote, thinking that he was addressing his attorney.

"Will I be allowed to keep the six pack of beer that I stole during the robbery?" another wrote.

Sometimes prisoners upset their lawyers with their comments before they even get to the jail. *Star-Banner* reporter Austin Miller asked one suspect how he was doing while awaiting transport to lockup.

"Chillin' like a villain," he said, looking into the lens of Austin's video camera.

***

Not everybody ends up behind bars. Three 14-year-olds were surprised to see a 5-year-old carrying a shotgun down the street. Asked what he wanted with the shotgun, the little boy said he wanted "to shoot a bird."

The 12-gauge shotgun had four live rounds in the tube but none in the chamber.

The gun's owner said he had left the house to pick up his children from day care. "It has happened before," the man said of the young burglar taking arms out of his house.

In one case, a burglar was glad to see the cops show up. Police receiving a call about a burglary in progress found the thief beaten and bloody outside of an apartment in Leesburg. A group of men said he tried to break into one of their pickup trucks. One man said the suspect had been making suggestive telephone calls to a 15-year-old girl across the street. Sure enough, when police grabbed his cell phone, there was a record of the calls.

One burglary case in 1999 had some people wondering if the long arm of the law can reach out and nab a burglar from the grave. One 20-year-old man had the audacity to steal a double-barreled shotgun from the son of the late Sheriff Willis McCall, who ruled as the iron-fisted "high sheriff" of Lake County from 1945 to 1972.

The man not only stole the antique firearm, engraved with McCall's name, but a badge and some gold-plated elk's teeth. There was no explanation in the report about the teeth.

The genius thief left a trail of pawn tickets with his name and driver's license number. They also found drugs and a box of baseball cards with the owner's phone number scrawled on the side. That might have brought a smile, at least, to the lawman.

***

One man had to face Circuit Judge Don Briggs on a drunken driving charge after hitting Sheriff George Knupp's mailbox.

"You must have the worst luck of anyone in the United States," Briggs said. "There must be 250,000 mailboxes in the county, and you run over the sheriff's (*Sentinel*, Feb. 11, 2002)?"

At least one driver had good fortune—ultimately. He was driving down U.S. Highway 441 and eating a hamburger when a chunk of meat went down the wrong way and got stuck in his windpipe. He lost control of the car, which struck a utility pole. The impact of the crash, however, dislodged the hamburger, he said. Sure enough, there on the floorboard of his car was the chunk of burger that nearly choked him to death. Call it a miracle or call it Heimlich maneuver by power pole, it worked. I can only imagine the look on the insurance agent's face when he read the accident report.

One man tried to make a break for it in a very slow-speed chase—on a pontoon boat. Fish and game officials tried to make the man pull over because he was creating a wake in a no-wake zone in a crowded area on Memorial Day weekend. Instead of stopping, he began weaving in and out of heavy holiday boat traffic.

"You don't know who I am," he shouted at the officers, then jumped overboard and swam to the swampy shore. Officers managed to stop the boat and began asking the men, women, and children aboard for the name of the rental boat's captain (*Sentinel*, Feb. 28, 1996).

When they threatened the mum crew with obstruction of justice charges, a woman spoke up and identified the mystery swimmer as her husband. He jumped overboard, she said, because he was afraid of being charged with operating a boat under the influence of alcohol.

Officers found the man and were prepared to hang him out to dry with several charges, including a felony fleeing and eluding, but the prosecutor decided to drop that charge. You can't go that fast on a pontoon boat, he said.

Another pontoon captain wasn't so lucky. Then again, he had a more sinister plan in mind. When his wife tried to answer the call of nature in the middle of a large lake in Central Florida, she made her way out to the tip of one of the pontoons, pulled down her pants, and began to relieve herself. That's when her husband picked up an emergency paddle and nudged her off the edge and into the water.

If that wasn't bad enough, he took off, making wider and wider circles away from her as she cried for help. He claimed he just couldn't turn the boat around in a tight circle to rescue her. Fortunately for her, someone else came by and hauled her out of the water.

If not unlucky, some are just plain dumb.

One man on probation robbed a bank while wearing a global positioning ankle bracelet.

Others are just as hapless.

Lady Lake Police Chief Ed Nathanson was investigating an armed robbery when a woman rushed in and said, "Where's the man who was inside? I was supposed to be the getaway driver."

Another time he walked up to a burglar who got away. But about that time, he heard a man's voice coming from the window.

"I'm going to pass the TV out the window," the man said. Then he said, "Catch me, I'm coming through the window."

The chief was only too happy to oblige.

One defense lawyer was startled to find his entire retail theft case blow up in his face. At issue was the identity of the thief caught on a security camera stealing a dress. When the jury members looked over, they realized the woman was wearing the dress.

"My attorney told me to wear my best dress," she later explained.

When Johnson wasn't reprimanding a paralegal for making out with a serial killer, he sometimes got a good laugh over the schemes his clients cooked up. Police were able to track one riding-lawn mower thief to his shed by following the trail of freshly cut grass.

Another was caught red-handed with bolt cutters and broken chains that had been attached to boat motors.

"I bought these motors from some guy," he told police.

"I was rolling on the floor," Johnson said. "I can't wait to argue this one in court."

***

Sometimes a story comes along that is just so bizarre headline writers and reporters can't resist having some fun.

Such was the case when a developer came up with the idea of building a 50-story high pyramid to hold the remains of 1.3 million people.

"Pyramid raises a grave point," said the *Sentinel* headline on my story on Sept. 3, 1994.

"Pyramids' biblical size wins few converts, many skeptics," noted another headline (*Sentinel*, Oct 2, 1994). Plans called for two pyramids, the biggest having a base of 777 feet per side and cover 14 of the development's 600 acres. In the Bible, 7 is the perfect number.

When the top executive of a national funeral home chain heard about the proposal, he exclaimed: "Holy Moses!"

Some of the people who had adjoining property in rural Sumter County were thinking: "Let my people go."

"Tacky, tacky," is how Robert McMorris described it.

It would be 19 stories higher than the biggest building in Orlando at that time—the 31-story Sun Bank Tower.

McMorris said the structure would block the sun on his property, including land he used for pasture. It would take more than 90 vertical cows, head-to-tail, to reach the summit.

It would be 14 feet taller than The Great Pyramid in Egypt.

Plans also called for a smaller pyramid at 171 feet tall, which would hold the remains of 30,000 people.

Pyramids Unlimited, meanwhile, was putting out breathless press releases.

"Not since the great pyramids of Egypt were first designed some 4,500 years ago have architects had an opportunity like this one—the chance to fashion the equivalent of a 50-story pyramid-shaped mausoleum for Americans, not Pharaohs."

But why Sumter County, where only 416 residents had died the year before?

The answer, developers said, was that it would be visible from Interstate 75. Tourists would be drawn to the site, not only by the pyramids but a 25,000-square-foot visitors' center, "a magnificent, covered walkway; parking with a grand entryway; and splendid Garden and Meditation areas."

Would "dead world" billboards compete with signs for Disney World, Sea World, and other attractions?

The development, which would include a crematorium, would bring jobs, taxes, and "clean industry" to the area, the company spokesmen said. But cow chips were hitting the fan.

Unconvinced residents, including some from a neighboring, modest, African-American community, said it would bring traffic, crime, and weirdness. "I don't want that thing looking down on me," one woman said. Besides, there wasn't even an exit off the Interstate at that spot, critics pointed out.

Because the proposal would require a zoning height exemption (the maximum allowed was three stories), and it would have to meet state cemetery requirements, the proposal was heading for a showdown with county officials.

By Oct. 12, the hieroglyphics were on the wall. "Tut, tut, tut: Pyramid plan bites the dust," the headline said.

"The pyramids are history ...," I wrote in the lead paragraph.

Chapter 16

Jessica

Agony, heart-pounding terror, and shock. They are all good, descriptive words, but they can't begin to characterize the explosion of emotions that swept over Mark Lunsford when he came home on Thursday, Feb. 24, 2005, to discover that his 9-year-old daughter, Jessica, was missing from her room.

"She basically vanished from her house," said Ronda Henninger-Evan, the spokeswoman for the Citrus County Sheriff's Office (*Ocala Star-Banner*, Feb. 25, 2005).

She told reporters that the child's disappearance from her west-Central Florida home in Homosassa was "being treated as a missing child [case] under extremely suspicious circumstances."

Authorities released a photo of "Jessie," as she was called by her family. A pretty girl, she was wearing a pink, soft fuzzy hat in the photo and was smiling as only a child can smile, with wide-eyed innocence. It was an image that would forever be etched in the minds of people across the nation.

A flyer that was sent out nationwide described her as white, 4-foot-10, 70 pounds, with light brown shoulder-length hair and brown eyes. She was last seen wearing a pink silk nightgown and white silk shorts.

"If you have any information, contact the Citrus County Sheriff's Office ..." the flyer said.

Lunsford said he last saw her at 10 p.m. Wednesday night when she went to sleep. He spent the night with his girlfriend, leaving her with his parents in the home they all shared. When he came home at about 5:45 a.m., he said he could hear the alarm clock going off in her room, but when he went in to check on her, she was gone. The clothes that had been laid out for her the night before had not been touched.

Lunsford's story checked out, investigators said, but added that there was no sign of forced entry into the house.

About 75 to 100 law enforcement officers, including some from the Florida Department of Law Enforcement and the Federal Bureau of Investigation began searching the area.

"We wouldn't have this type of manpower out if the child had left the home before," Henninger-Evan said. "We are just simply exhausting any and all leads that we have."

Thursday dragged into Friday as the search continued with volunteers, helicopters, and dogs.

"I want my daughter home," Mark Lunsford said through his tears to unblinking news cameras. "If there is anything anybody knows ... help me find my daughter and bring her home (Associated Press/Ocala.com, Feb. 25, 2005)."

Authorities checked a computer in her room. Technicians found no evidence of stalking.

She had recently taken a class in cyber safety.

The FBI interviewed the girl's mother, Angela Bryant, 31, in Morrow, Ohio. "I don't know where she is," said Bryant, adding that she hadn't seen her daughter for four years. "Her dad didn't let me see her."

Ruth Lunsford described her granddaughter as an obedient child "who doesn't roam. She's a friendly child. She's very smart, very well-mannered, and she's a beautiful child. When God made Jessie, he made an angel. We have always called her 'Princess.' If somebody's got her, she needs to be with her family."

But the family's pleas went unanswered. Days stretched into weeks. The search was curtailed but not ended. Footprints, even impressions in the sand where she might have sat down, were examined fruitlessly.

Finally, on Friday, March 18, the sheriff's office made the announcement that jerked the rug out from beneath everyone's feet. A registered sex offender, who was living within "a stone's throw" of the home had abducted and killed Jessica.

An adult cousin felt her knees give way as she dropped to a squatting position against a patrol car, her eyes closed in a vain attempt to shut out the pain.

A man who did not know the family, but who had driven several miles to see if he could somehow lend moral support, said: "I have a 9-year-old daughter and I can't imagine what they're going through."

A neighbor said, "I hope it's one big lie."

It wasn't.

"John Couey was polygraphed today," Sheriff Jeffrey Dawsy said, "and at the end of the polygraph he said: 'You don't need to tell me the results. I already know what they are. Could I have the investigators come back in?' And the investigators came back in. He apologized to the investigators for wasting their time (*Star-Banner*, March 19, 2005)."

The sheriff began choking up when he added: "John Couey admitted to abducting Jessica and subsequently taking her life."

Couey also admitted to raping the third grader.

Couey, who was only 46 but looked 20 years older, began talking to detectives the day before, after being picked up by police in Augusta, Ga., on a Citrus County warrant for violating his probation.

Couey told investigators where they could find Jessica's body.

The sheriff said he had a good, solid case against Couey, who had spent a lifetime on the wrong side of the law. "I've got my man."

Firefighters and paramedics joined in the recovery effort. Big lights were brought in to pierce the growing darkness as evidence technicians prepared for the final, grisly discovery.

The focus was outside of the mobile home where he had been staying.

He was staying in his half-sister's mobile home within view of the Lunsford home, a mere 200 yards away, yet it was not the home he had registered with authorities as a convicted sex offender. His long criminal record included fondling a child under 16 and grabbing another girl during a break-in.

Couey told his family that police were looking for him, so he left town for Savannah, Ga., with a bus ticket under an assumed name.

He was questioned by police there, but he was released when they decided they didn't have probable cause to hold him.

He went on to Augusta. He was walking down a street when a person in a homeless shelter recognized him from a wanted bulletin and notified police.

Couey was a nobody, a loser, and a pathetic excuse for a human being.

In his confession he said: "I got high, and I was drunk. I went over there and took her out of her house. I'm a sick person. I didn't mean to do what I did to the child (*Star-Banner*, Feb.11, 2007)."

He said he was high on crack cocaine and angry with his sister, Dorothy Dixon, because she was sharing their drugs with others. He told investigators he felt alone and needed "someone close to him."

He also said he felt a compulsion to exert control. "I wanted that power," he said. "I wanted to be in control. I don't know why (*Star-Banner*, June 24, 2005)."

He said he entered the unlocked home at about 3 a.m. (Archie and Ruth Lunsford insisted they locked the doors). He said he went into the bedroom of the "very polite" girl and ordered her to come with him. She asked if she could bring a purple, stuffed dolphin toy that her father had won for her at the state fair the weekend before (Feb. 11, 2007).

Couey said they got into his bedroom through the window, and then he raped her.

"I was going to let her go ... And then I got scared 'cause everyone showed up, and I panicked," Couey said, referring to officers.

He told rambling, conflicting stories, including one about keeping her captive for days.

"I went out there one night and dug a hole and put her in it. I buried her alive," he said.

He forced her to get into a garbage bag. She was kneeling, apparently in prayer, her hands were wrapped around her dolphin.

"I knew she liked it," he said, referring to the toy. "I thought it would make her feel more better."

The horrific story unleashed a torrent of emotion.

A female adult relative told sheriff's deputies that Couey had touched her inappropriately when she was younger.

She was upset with herself, the deputy noted, because "she had never confronted him about incidents that allegedly occurred with her and her sister (*Star-Banner*, April 22, 2005)."

She said Dixon "always protected John Couey in his actions."

The deputy noted, however, that she was "obviously intoxicated" when she gave the statement. When he talked to Dixon, she was also drunk, he said in his report. She reportedly knew about past allegations but allowed him to stay in her home, "because he's my brother."

The accuser claimed she had told Dixon about Couey touching a child within the past year.

A woman who was not a relative told deputies that Couey had exposed himself to her when she was 13 or 14 years old.

Couey's confession was eventually thrown out by a judge because Couey repeatedly asked in vain for an attorney, as was his Constitutional right.

That foul-up sparked criticism of the sheriff's office. But the State Attorney's Office made a decision that incurred the wrath of Fox News commentator Bill O'Reilly.

Soon after Couey's confession, Dixon and two other people who were in the mobile home were arrested and charged with obstructing an officer. They did not tell officers that Couey had been living in the house after she disappeared, authorities said.

State Attorney Brad King dropped the charges, however. He said there was no evidence they knew that Couey had abducted Jessica, therefore they had not broken the law.

O'Reilly said the prosecutor was "off-the-chart misguided (Star-*Banner*, May 11, 2005)."

Much of the controversy stemmed from Couey's confusing, conflicting statements about the timeline. He told detectives that he kept Jessica alive in his bedroom closet from two to six days.

Prosecutors weren't buying it, however.

"It just doesn't make any sense that he would try to keep her alive," said Chief Assistant State Attorney Ric Ridgway (*Star-Banner,* June 24, 2005).

Couey also claimed that he gave her food, but autopsy results showed no food in her stomach.

Had Couey actually kept her alive in the mobile home for days, it is likely that someone would have seen Jessica, which would have made his housemates guilty of covering up the abduction.

He probably buried her on the same day he abducted her, Ridgway said.

"(I) just covered a bunch of leaves over it where I dug the hole at and then went back in the house and went to bed," Couey said in his confession.

He said that happened at about 2 a.m. However, he said he broke into the Lunsford house around 3 a.m.

On June 27, 2005, O'Reilly criticized the investigators who botched the confession, King's decision to drop charges against the half-sister and her roommates, and *The St. Petersburg Times*.

"Over the weekend, the *St. Pete Times* ran an op-ed by King saying Couey lied about keeping Jessica captive in his trailer for days. King doesn't believe that happened. King may be right. But what definitely did happen, is the two people in the trailer who lived there with him helped Couey escape to Georgia … (FoxNews.com, June 28, 2005)."

O'Reilly was also angry in an earlier show, pointing out that someone in the house purchased Couey's bus ticket (Couey's niece, Maddie Secord, bought the ticket in her name. Dixon furnished the money for the ticket, according to reports).

"This guy King should come out and say, 'We're investigating these people….' Instead, he's hiding under his desk," O'Reilly said.

King would not be budged. "I am not going to charge somebody because Mr. O'Reilly thinks he can threaten me into something inappropriate (*Star-Banner*, April 14, 2005)." He also said: "While we may believe what they did was wrong, legally it's not a crime. To charge somebody just to make the public feel better, I'm not going to do that."

Nor would King and his chief assistant, Ridgway, accept an invitation to go on O'Reilly's show, *The O'Reilly Factor*. "Going on Mr. O'Reilly's show is like wrestling a pig," Ridgway said. "All that happens is that you get dirty, and the pig has fun."

Prosecutors said it was Dixon who gave authorities a big break in the case.

On March 14, 2005, just days before they questioned Couey in Georgia, Dixon gave written permission for investigators to search her home. She said Couey didn't live there anymore and that he had gone to Savannah.

Police collected DNA evidence from Couey's mattress. It would take a while for the results to come in, but Jessica's blood was found on the mattress, in addition to Couey's semen.

"At that point, John Couey again was just a [registered] sex offender, lived in that area and was gone. There was not anything to tie him to the murder but that. So, I don't believe at that point that they had probable cause for a search warrant," Ridgway said (*Star-Banner*, Feb. 11, 2007).

Timing was everything, Ridgway explained. Without Dixon's consent, police would have gathered the physical evidence after Couey's unconstitutionally obtained confession.

Defense attorneys argued that none of the physical evidence, including Jessica's body, should be allowed to come in against their client. Circuit Judge Richard Howard ruled that with the genetic evidence collected at the home (with permission), police would have inevitably gotten a search warrant and Jessica's body would have eventually been found.

"If she [Dixon] had said no, they would not have searched the room until they had a search warrant after his confession. But the search warrant from his confession gets tossed out and then we would have probably lost the DNA, the body, the confession, and we would've been left with nothing," Ridgway said. "So, say what you want about Dorothy Dixon ... but the fact that she consented may have been the turning point in this entire case."

***

Sheriff Dawsy, who spoke at Jessica's funeral, said Jessica's murder stripped away the community's innocence and forced him to review his own life's purpose (*Star-Banner*, March 27, 2005).

"It really shattered everything. It took into question everything I thought was right," he said, his voice cracking.

"I now feel like she's part of my family. Jessica's face was compelling," Dawsy said. "We got to know Jessica very well, even though we never got to meet her."

He even apologized to her grandparents, who were interrogated relentlessly.

"We beat them up .... But my job was to work for Jessica," he said, and he apologized for not bringing Jessica back to her family alive. Mark Lunsford said no apology was necessary. Everyone was doing their best, including volunteer searchers.

Lunsford would not always feel so generous. He would later sue Dawsy, claiming he had not done enough, but he then dropped the suit.

"Children. They are all we have," Lunsford said at the public service. "They are our next senators. They are our next sheriffs. They are our next truck drivers."

Days earlier, Lunsford, a truck driver who liked to wear a baseball cap over his long hair and earring, had stood outside his home and talked about the finality of authorities finding her body.

"Everyone heard me say, time and time again, that she would be back home. She's home now. And it's over. And now we have a new struggle (*Star-Banner*, March 20, 2005)."

He had a message for parents: "Make sure you get that hug and kiss before you leave each day," Lunsford said. "I did."

About 1,000 people came to pay their respects at the church service, including Karen Wade of Lakeland.

"I can't imagine what that grandmother's going through," she said. "I have eight grandchildren of my own. I'm here for reasons I'm not totally sure of. I just know things have to be changed."

Others were very sure about what needed to be changed. Many were determined to sign petitions calling for tougher punishment for sex offenders who committed crimes against children.

Dawsy and others went to Tallahassee to lend their support to that idea.

On May 2, 2005, Gov. Jeb Bush, with Mark Lunsford and the mother and aunt of another child who was murdered in a separate case, signed the Jessica Lunsford Act into law.

The law set a mandatory sentence of 25 years to life in prison for people convicted of certain sex crimes against children aged 11 and younger, with lifetime tracking by global positioning satellite after they are released from prison.

Lunsford thanked the governor.

"I'm still lost, I haven't really dealt with it yet," he admitted after the ceremony (*Star-Banner*/Associated Press, May 3, 2005).

Bush said the state's sex offender laws were already strict. "This bill will make our laws even tougher. I think it is right and just."

***

There was more controversy ahead for the upcoming trial, however.

Because Citrus County is small, and because pretrial publicity was so prevalent, Judge Howard decided he would try to find a jury in neighboring Lake County. Lake County, however, also abuts Marion County, where the *Star-Banner* covered every detail of the crime, and Orange County, where Orlando TV and the *Orlando Sentinel* had covered the case.

He finally gave up and moved the trial to Miami in February of 2007. The Tampa Bay area was out because of the intense media coverage in that area. Cases are supposed to be moved, if necessary, to a similar community. Homosassa and Miami are not remotely alike. Many of the prospective jurors were still excused, however, because they said they knew too much about the case to be impartial.

Moving the trial resulted in another huge delay and a lot of expense, especially when the judge announced that the jury would be sequestered. That brought out a lot of hardship arguments by prospective jurors.

Some of the excuses were ridiculous. One man said the trial would interfere with his observation of Rosh Hashana, but the Jewish holiday is in September.

He was eventually excused when he said he thought Couey was guilty.

One woman was excused when she said she had no one to take care of her pet ferret.

The trial was also a challenge for the *Star-Banner* and its modest budget. The paper had to rent a condo for a reporter and a blogger. Photos were shot by a pool of news organizations and Court TV carried the trial live.

Before the trial could begin, there was another thorny issue for the court. Corrections officers came forward just weeks before the trial was set to begin with stories of Couey making a confession to them.

For the most part, that confession matched the one he made to detectives. However, Couey told the jailers that Dixon and her then-boyfriend, Matthew Dittrich, knew Jessica was being held in the mobile home.

Couey told them he hit Jessica in the head with a shovel when she tried to get up and wiggle out of the shallow grave.

"He said that she was in the bag in the hole, and she started wiggling around trying to get out, and he started hitting her over the head," Nathelia Windham testified (*Star-Banner*, Feb. 25, 2007).

There was no indication of head trauma in the autopsy report, however.

Defense attorneys questioned the motives of the corrections officers and argued that the statements were "coerced (*Star-Banner*, Feb. 14, 2007)." They even suggested the situation was comparable to the Abu Ghraib prison in Iraq where Army guards abused prisoners.

Jailers conceded Couey was isolated from other prisoners for his own protection. Ridgway, however, argued that Couey wasn't deprived. He had access to the law library and other facilities.

The guards denied allegations that they were trying to extract a confession from Couey.

Couey is a "dead man walking," Windham said. "If he's released on the street, he won't live 30 minutes. If he is put in population in a prison, he won't live an hour. If he is put on death row in a cell somebody's going to get to him. He's a dead man walking. I have stress in my personal life. I do not need the stress of John Couey. Couey done it to himself when Couey confessed," she testified in her sworn statement.

Guards are not supposed to discuss inmates' cases with them and their decision to come forward late in the game was "very suspect," said Richard Sharpstein, a prominent Miami defense attorney interviewed for his perspective by Mabel Perez of the *Star-Banner*.

The guards, who worked for a private corrections company, said they talked about Jesus, let Couey watch his favorite TV show, *Dr. Phil*, and occasionally slipped him extra food or a Coke.

"It's a fine line," Sharpstein said. "They befriend him, and they help him because they're going to say that's their job; and that they are just humane people who want to reach out to someone who otherwise doesn't have any other freedom. He's not their friend but ... there's two ways to look at it. Their motive was either to go in there to get a statement to help the government, or Couey just voluntarily made it to the people he's in custody with, his captors, who have now befriended him and who are now playing cards...."

The judge ruled the jail confessions could stand.

The jailhouse confessions were problematic for prosecutors however, because of his claim that Dixon and her boyfriend were aware of Jessica's presence in the mobile home.

He said a lot of things to a lot of people.

In Georgia, he not only denied that he had done anything wrong but insisted that he was incapable of hurting anyone. "I just think that ... I don't have violence in me ... I don't even like to be around violence. I ain't a violent person (*Star-Banner*, Oct. 12, 2005)."

"I mean, I made one mistake in my lifetime and ... I mean, because I was raped in my lifetime when I was a kid by ... my dad, my teachers," Couey said to Savannah police. "I got raped and stupid me never reported it. And you know ... I seen my dad rape .... My dad raped my own sister ...," he said.

"And I just committed one little crime and ... I only got five years for that 'cause nothing happened. You know what I'm sayin? I mean ... I didn't ... nothing happened ... I just .... Like I did ..., bugs me because every time something happens everybody wants to grab me."

There was another confession controversy. Two detectives from the Orlando Police Department, who had come to question Couey about an unsolved 1985 case, said Couey also made a confession to them about Jessica.

Like the confession to Citrus County detectives, the judge also threw out that confession.

"The Orlando officers appropriately 'Mirandized' Mr. Couey prior to their interview and specifically told him that they did not want to know anything about his current case," Judge Howard wrote, referring to the fact that he had the right to an attorney (*Star-Banner*, Jan. 9, 2007).

"On the other hand, the Orlando officers did not ask if Mr. Couey was represented by an attorney, even though they testified that they understood the normal procedure was that after first appearance, a defendant was usually represented by an attorney."

The Orlando detectives said Couey confessed to killing Jessica during their interview.

The judge also questioned why the detectives never told the Citrus County Sheriff's Office about the confession. The detectives did not come forward until Couey's confession in Georgia was ruled inadmissible.

There were other issues, motions, and preparations, including an effort by prosecutors to let jurors know about the 1978 case in which Couey broke into a house and touched a child. The judge said the case was too old and the cases too dissimilar. It would simply be prejudicial, he said.

Eventually, the jury was picked, and the trial began.

Family friend, Sharon Armstrong, testified that she dropped Jessica off on that fateful Wednesday evening.

"She turned back and signed 'I love you.' And she went inside," Armstrong testified with tears in her eyes. "She was an easy little girl to love (*Star-Banner*, March 1, 2007)."

Lunsford, sitting on the front row of the spectator section, cried.

Defense attorneys knew their work was cut out for them. Jurors blanched when prosecutor Ridgway told them: "She had not been shot, strangled, stabbed, or beaten. ... She had been smothered to death in the black, plastic, garbage bag."

The next day, prosecutors asked Dixon when Couey lived with her.

It was defense attorney Daniel Lewan who brought up her drug use and cast doubt on her claim that she didn't know Jessica was in her home. "You don't remember anything funny going on (*Star-Banner*, March 2, 2007)?"

Mark Lunsford testified and remained unemotional until he was asked to identify the stuffed purple dolphin in a photograph.

The emotional roller coaster continued the next day as detectives identified photos of Jessica's hands tied together with speaker wire. A bailiff passed a tissue box around to jurors. Lunsford bent forward, his body trembling.

As the trial resumed after the weekend, an expert identified the genetic evidence on the mattress as Couey's and Jessica's. Another identified Jessica's fingerprints in his bedroom.

One of the witnesses was Matthew Dittrich, Dixon's boyfriend at the time.

Couey had told corrections officers that at one point, Dittrich was in the bedroom while Jessica was in the closet. Dittrich said he was never alone in the bedroom.

Another witness was Gene Secord, the second husband of Couey's niece, Maddie. She also lived in the mobile home. Secord said he was in jail when Couey was arrested. He and Couey talked a lot about religion, he said.

"I asked him if he believed in religion so much, how could he have done something like he did (*Star-Banner,* March 6, 2007)."

The final day of the state's case was devastating.

Jessica was fighting to stay alive when she was suffocated, pathologist Dr. Stephen Cogswell testified while explaining a hole in the bag and the condition of her body.

"Those two fingers were poking at the bag to push through. ... She is poking her fingers out of the bag (*Star-Banner,* March 6, 2007)."

Jurors wept some more.

Jailer Windham testified about the reason Couey gave for killing Jessica. "He was afraid that they would find her and that he had to get rid of her. He told her to get in a plastic bag 'cause he didn't want people to see her crossing the street."

It took the jury just four hours to find Couey guilty of murder, kidnapping, sexual battery, and burglary.

Couey, looking shaken, lifted his head back and stared at the ceiling as if looking to God for mercy. It was too late, and he certainly didn't deserve it.

Jessica's mother, Angela Bryant, had stifled the impulse to react audibly when she heard the verdict.

"I wanted to cry out, but we were told we weren't supposed to," she said, with tears rolling down her cheeks. "It made me feel a little better on the inside. He finally got what he deserved (*Star-Banner*, March 8, 2007)."

Dawsy felt vindicated. He blasted what he said was the "poisonous" criticism of the "entertainment media," for his department's mishandling of the confession, mentioning Bill O'Reilly by name.

Lunsford, who had never taken his eyes off Couey, said: "He ain't dead. It's not over yet. This is only the first part. We still got the second part," he said, referring to the penalty phase, where the state was seeking the death sentence.

Defense attorneys, who claimed their client was mentally ill, called upon relatives and mental health experts in an effort to try and come up with some mitigating circumstances. Robert Berland, a psychologist, said Couey had a "broken brain" from physical head trauma, emotional abuse, and heavy drug use (*Star-Banner*, March 13, 2007).

Testimony also claimed that he was born prematurely at seven months and had developmental problems.

Psychologist, Richard Carpenter, testified that Couey's IQ was somewhere between 61 and 69. That's considered mentally retarded.

A psychiatrist, Dr. Joseph Wu, testified that positron emission tomography scans indicated that Couey did not have a normal brain. He was prone to hyper-sexual tendencies and poor impulse control.

Relatives testified that Couey's father tied him to the bed post for wetting the bed. Once, when his father came home and found that his mother had freed him, he put Couey's head between the jamb and the door and repeatedly slammed the door on his head.

Ridgway dismissed the story, calling it a "family legend story."

There was also testimony about how children in the little community of Homosassa were affected by the tragedy.

"Several students living in the neighborhood began sleeping on parents' bedroom floors or in their beds, were afraid of the dark, too scared to ride the bus, or play in their neighborhood," a teary-eyed Debbie Harmon testified while reading a victim impact letter. Harmon was a guidance counselor at Jessica's school.

"With details too gruesome to comprehend, this created more disturbances to everyone, and especially affected the innocence of our children's lives. Our children no longer felt protected. Many questioned their mortality," she said.

Dr. Cogswell with the Medical Examiner's Office again testified about Jessica's last moments on earth as she tried to claw her way out of the bag. She had only 1 to 5 minutes of breathing time, he said.

One of the jurors glared at Couey.

One person who was not allowed to testify was Mark Lunsford.

"It sucks .... I wanted to testify. But that's not what they wanted. They were concerned with my emotions and appeals," he said.

"We have to decide whether we can get his case past the Florida Supreme Court," King said.

As it turned out, it was a relatively easy decision for the jury. The six-man, six-woman panel deliberated for only an hour and 15 minutes before voting 10-2 to recommend the death penalty.

"There was a lot of evidence," said juror Thais Prado, afterward. "A lot of scientific facts (*Star-Banner,* March 15, 2007)."

The "scientific facts" included the DNA found on the mattress.

Afterward, she hugged Mark Lunsford on the courthouse steps.

"It was very emotional to see a father that experienced such a great loss. [There was] such an outpouring of emotion, tears in his eyes, the gratitude," Prado said of the jury's recommendation.

She was joined by another juror and an alternate in consoling Lunsford.

"This is justice for Jessie, but not just Jessie. I'm sure there's other victims out there," Lunsford told reporters. "If you crossed paths with Couey and he hurt you, you also got justice today."

Justice or not, it couldn't make up for the loss. "We imposed the death penalty but it … does not compare to the misery they [murderers] cause to their victims," he said.

King, whose eyes welled up with tears, was relieved. "This has been a very long road, two years, and we have always had our eye on one goal and that's to see that a jury recommended a death sentence for John Couey."

Now, it was up to the judge. First, there was the issue of whether Couey was mentally retarded.

"The actions of the defendant in this case are far from simple acts," he said in a hearing one month later. "A person who is mentally retarded simply could not have planned such a sophisticated crime and escape (*Star-Banner*, Aug. 9, 2007)."

The judge cited various aspects of the crime to bolster his argument, including Couey breaking into the Lunsford home and kidnapping her without waking up the rest of the family.

"He brought her to his sister's home and successfully hid her … When police were searching for Jessica, he planned her murder and carried it out," Howard wrote.

He got his niece to buy him a bus ticket, "because he had no photo identification," the judge noted.

"A person who is mentally retarded simply could not have planned such a sophisticated crime and escape."

The judge also pointed to IQ test scores ranging from 64 to 89. He cited one score of 78 as the most accurate.

The defense team was not finished. They were still bound to try to save the life of their client, even a miserable, evil excuse for a human being.

They didn't have much to work with, so they claimed that Jessica didn't suffer long before she died.

"There was no evidence of defense wounds, no bruising of her wrists indicating she struggled, or other evidence to indicate that the defendant did anything other than asphyxiate her in a way similar to the way that Dr. [Jack] Kevorkian assisted his patients when they were committing suicide," wrote Assistant Public Defender Alan Fanter. "Jessica's murder was not "heinous, atrocious, or cruel (*Star-Banner*, Aug. 22, 2007)."

"To my recollection Dr. Kevorkian didn't bury his patients alive," prosecutor Ridgway told the *Star-Banner*. "To compare what she went through to someone who committed suicide by inhaling carbon monoxide … is not a fair comparison."

Finally, it was judgment day.

It was an emotional day for Judge Howard who that ruled that the murder was "heinous, atrocious, or cruel," and "cold, calculated, and premeditated," and he sentenced Couey to die by lethal injection.

"Her last thoughts as she felt the soil enveloping her body, clutching her favorite stuffed toy, with her wrists securely wired by the defendant, can never be fathomed," Howard said, reading from his sentencing order. "Simply stated, civilized society recoils in horror at the image of the abject fear and terror that Jessica experienced in her final conscious minutes of life. Her only source of comfort during this horrific experience was her purple dolphin (*Star-Banner*, Aug. 25, 2007)."

Couey, who was dressed in a red jail jumpsuit, looked around the courtroom, moved about in his chair and looked up at the ceiling.

"This was a determined, albeit savage manner of a planned murder with absolutely no pretense of any moral or legal justification," Howard said. He added that Couey made "crude, vulgar, and repulsive comments about his sexual experience with a 9-year-old."

"John Couey is an animal," Dawsy said in a news conference. "He is the worst of all kinds that is made in this country or in this world ... Worse than a savage, he's an animal."

Jessica's Sunday school teacher, Sharon Armstrong, trembled with anger during the hearing. She had kept newspaper clippings but had not read all of them.

"I can't read it. I have not allowed myself to listen to all that stuff," she said, her mascara washed away with tears.

"I didn't want to hear all that stuff he had done to her," Armstrong said. "Today, I had to hear it all."

She was surprised when she looked at Couey in hopes of gaining some insight to his emotional core.

"There's nothing there. He's like looking at a blank wall."

Mark Lunsford smiled, but there was no joy.

"I'm grateful at the outcome, he said. "But it's not going to bring my daughter back. Justice was served for this little girl, but what about the rest of them? The ones that live. Who's got it worse? The child who dies or the child who lives and never gets justice?"

It was painful to hear all of the details, he said, painful every time, but he would do it again if his goal of tougher punishment for sex offenders was achieved.

"I'll break my own heart 100 times if it saves one more child," he said.

He continued his mission. In 2008, he traveled to Utah to lend support to a proposed "Jessica Law" in that state.

***

Couey, who began the slow process of rotting on death row, would never see the death chamber.

He died on Sept. 30, 2009, at a hospital in Jacksonville where he had been a patient since Aug. 12. Prison officials declined to discuss his cause of death.

"I knew he was diagnosed [with cancer] and in the hospital in serious condition," Ridgway said (*Star-Banner*, Oct. 1, 2009).

It was a relief to Jessica's grandmother, Ruth.

"Thank you, Lord," she said. "I wanted to live long enough to see him die. It's done; it's finished. I'm glad we didn't have to wait too long for him to get the needle."

It was a letdown for the sheriff.

"I was a little disappointed. I really wanted the state of Florida to put John Couey to death. I wanted to look into his eyes when they injected him with the serum," Dawsy said.

Mark Lunsford was strangely quiet, and he made no public comment.

In April, he had revealed in an interview that he was a father again. His girlfriend gave birth to a baby boy in 2007—12 years to the day of Jessica's birth.

Calling the child's birth a "miracle," Lunsford said the fact that the baby was born on Jessica's birthday was a clear signal to him that God had given him a second chance at being a father (*Star-Banner*, April 11, 2009).

"I don't think it's a reward or anything. But it's like God was saying, 'OK, Mark, I hear you complain about how much you miss Jessie every day. So, here's another one. Take care of him.'"

He said he kept the birth a secret so the child would not be in the spotlight. He refused to make public the name of the child.

In February of 2009, fire destroyed the vacant mobile home where Couey had lived.

"It was an intentionally set fire," said a spokesman for the fire marshal's office.

The only other vandalism that had taken place at the home had occurred shortly after the murder, when someone threw a concrete block through a window.

Dawsy, reflecting on Jessica's death, said: "It was traumatizing to [the community]." He then said something jarring but undeniably true: "This type of crime will always be with us."

Her simple headstone at a cemetery in Homosassa says: "Daughter. Jessica Marie Lunsford. Oct. 6, 1995. Feb. 24, 2005."

There is also an engraving of an angel on the stone—a comfort to all who knew her and those who never got the chance. It is also a reminder that angels carry us home, to a place where evil cannot follow.

Chapter 17

Crazy

Diane Evers was doing a normal thing on Jan. 1, 1980, a thing that all mothers do. She was bathing her twin 4-year-old daughters, Sherrie and Carrie, and her 2-year-old daughter, Mandy, at her parents' home in Leesburg. Her family thought everything was OK but within minutes they were horrified when they realized that Evers, claiming to be the Virgin Mary, had drowned all three of her children in the bathtub.

It was one of the most disturbing, tragic child homicide cases in the history of a county already stained by the blood of too many innocent little lambs. It's been tragic, too, for Evers, because she has struggled for decades to climb out of the deepest, darkest pit of psychosis.

Evers said in a 1983 deposition that she had her first hallucination during childbirth in 1977.

In one hallucination a nurse congratulated her for giving birth to twins.

"And I said, 'What? I just had one baby,' and then she said, 'Oh my God, you don't know.' And then she walked out of the room."

She said she saw three doctors in the delivery room, and they wanted to give her an injection. They said: "Mary, we've got to give you a shot of LSD to see if you're the true mother of Christ."

"And I said, "Please don't do this to me."

She said she saw vibrant colors, saw their faces get really big, and then really small. "It was just like LSD... Well, I never had LSD, but it's like the movies in school that they show you about LSD."

"We're going to give one of the babies to Joseph," one of the doctors said. You married the wrong man."

She said she dreamed that a man took her to Israel and married her. She said a cloud also talked to her. The cloud said, "Mary, mother of Christ, is that really you in a halter top?"

She said she later went home and burned all of her "sinful clothes."

She said a therapist later told her that she could have been under the influence of child-birth drugs. She was treated with anti-psychotic drugs for her mental illness.

A year after drowning her children she was found not guilty by reason of insanity and sent to Florida State Hospital for the criminally insane. For years she has tried, with the help of hospital staff, to move into a step-down facility, a halfway house, or given extended furloughs, almost always with negative results.

In 1992, her ex-husband told the court he would be in fear of his family's safety if she was released. She was allowed an overnight leave in 1996 to be with her new husband, a former patient. But Circuit Judge Mark Hill, observing that her behavior was "very, very inconsistent" was reluctant to grant more freedom. Hill kept up with her status reports. He noted that she would be fine and then quickly "decompensate," as her caregivers put it. "I remember a few years ago when she decompensated right before a hearing and tried to saw her arm off," he said (*Sentinel*, March 27, 1997).

The term decompensate refers to an increase in symptoms and a decrease in normal functioning.

In April of 2013, I attended a hearing for Evers and was stunned to hear something I thought I would never hear.

"I cannot, in good conscience, say that she still meets the criteria for involuntary hospitalization," Assistant State Attorney Bill Gross told Judge Hill.

Hill thanked Gross for his candor, and for the first time in 33 years the two of them and Evers' lawyer set about devising a plan to move her to a step-down facility in Miami.

Psychologists and a psychiatrist testified that she had been compliant about taking her medications for the past nine years, and they assured the court that the facility in Miami had sufficient security.

They described her condition as borderline personality disorder and schizoaffective disorder. Borderline personality patients feel worthless and are prone to severe mood swings, outbursts, and impulsiveness. Schizoaffective disorder is a combination of schizophrenia, marked by delusions and hallucinations, and some other disorder, which in Evers' case includes depression. It affects each patient differently.

She also suffered from physical problems. She arrived in the courtroom in a wheelchair with a chain connecting handcuffs to her ankle chains. She needs a knee replacement, her doctors said.

Elizabeth McMahon, a Ph.D. psychologist, discounted the idea that Evers would ever be a threat to other children. She suffered from a religious-based delusional system, she said. People who suffer from this kind of psychosis harm their own children, not others.

"This is a very unique syndrome," said the longtime mental health expert. She was a key defense mental health expert for vampire cult leader, Rod Ferrell.

The most famous similar case is that of Andrea Yates of Texas. She drowned her five young children in the bathtub in 2001 "to keep them from going to hell." She was convicted of capital murder in 2002, but she was acquitted in 2006 when jurors found her not guilty by reason of insanity.

McMahon said Evers would do well in the structured environment of a treatment center, including coming to grips with her past.

"A part of therapy is, 'I have an illness.' She is very aware of how different she is now. There is grieving—anybody would be distraught. She feels guilty. She knows she was psychotic but still realizes, 'I did it,'" McMahon said.

In her 1983 deposition, Evers said she would like to get married again but did not want to have any more children. She had a tubal ligation after her last child was born.

"I don't think I could handle giving them a bath because I would always remember what happened …."

Finding a defendant not guilty by reason of insanity is very unusual. In Florida, like most states, it depends upon whether the person knew what they were doing was wrong. Using an outrageous example, the state could not try someone for stabbing someone to death if the attacker was so delusional he thought he was peeling an apple, or that he was Napoleon fending off British soldiers.

Once found not guilty by reason of insanity, the person cannot later be tried for murder. In theory, anyway, they could be granted a conditional or full release back into society once treated.

Florida authorizes involuntary hospitalization if a person is a danger to himself or to others. In a criminal case, a court can order a person to be held until he is competent to go to trial.

Sometimes, it comes down to legal hair-splitting. Several years ago, a 22-year-old man took a hostage at knifepoint during a convenience store robbery. A judge ruled that he wasn't crazy, even when he yelled at the cop: "Shoot me or I'll kill him."

The previously convicted felon was just violating his probation, the court decided.

This decision was reached even after it was learned that he had recently been released from a mental hospital in St. Petersburg after taking drugs and claiming people were reading his mind. He said he called his social worker to demand money but was refused. He said he wanted the money to buy a gun.

In Orlando, a woman stood in a busy intersection and yelled to motorists: "Hit me!" Was she crazy? We'll never know. She was hit and killed by a passing car.

Then, there was Anna Tracy, 45, who stabbed her husband to death, smeared bloody hearts on his chest, and scrawled a message on his body with a black felt-tip marker.

I wasn't on the cop beat that day, but my curiosity was off the charts. "I have to know what she wrote," I told the reporter assigned to story. "Do you mind if I call someone I know in Major Crimes?"

After making a quick call, I found out that she had written, "I love you."

"Now, we've got a story," I exclaimed.

She was not legally insane, as it turned out. She was charged with first-degree murder and sentenced to life in prison.

**

Sometimes people can see trouble coming but are helpless to stop it.

Neighbors in the little town of Umatilla were wary of David and Katy Gershon's 36-year-old son, Abraham. They knew there had been trouble in the past, with Abraham trashing the house before his parents kicked him out. He was in a mental hospital for years before being put into a nursing home in Leesburg. His parents had been picking him up for weekend visits.

But on Sept. 25, 1995, Abraham notified the manager of the nursing home that he would not be returning. He said his parents had gone to Canada and he was watching their house. Social workers called the house several times. When they did not get an answer, they went to the house with a sheriff's deputy.

The authorities realized immediately that something had gone horribly wrong. The couple's recreation vehicle was parked in the driveway, its windows smashed out. Even worse, there was a "foul odor" coming from inside the house

It was there that they found Gershon's dead parents stuffed inside a closet. A bloody hammer was nearby. Abraham was in another room. Deputies shouted for him to come out. He shouted that he had done nothing wrong, and then demanded that they shoot him. Instead, they took him into custody.

Like Evers, he was sent to the Florida State Hospital in Chattahoochee. In November of that year, he was found to be incompetent to help his defense team prepare for a murder trial. By May of 1996 he was adjudged to be fit for trial, then he wasn't, and so the pattern began.

In 2005, he was found not guilty by reason of insanity.

***

Sometimes a mad man can be taken off the streets before he harms someone.

There was the 19-year-old man, for example, who liked the Freddy Krueger horror movie character just a little too much.

He was charged with breaking into a woman's house and handing her a note that read: "The world is dimming before your very eyes. You will see that tonight you will die. FREDDY."

The woman said he then reached behind his back and brandished a heavy-duty work glove with steak knives attached to the fingers and began choking her.

Authorities released him to an outpatient treatment facility in New Jersey.

***

In 1999, the Jordan family awoke at 4 a.m. to the sound of gunfire and hell on earth. Unlike many people who wake up to find armed intruders in their home, no one had broken in, and this was no stranger.

Lake sheriff's deputies described Christina Jordan, 34, as "wild" and "enraged" when they arrived (*Sentinel,* May 7, 1999). She was certainly wild when she shot her sister, Patricia Jordan, 36, several times while she slept.

After shooting her sister, she stormed into her parents' bedroom where she struggled with her father, Jim, 59, before shooting him in the abdomen with her .380-caliber semi-automatic handgun. Patricia's teenage son and her mother managed to subdue her and call 911.

While deputies arrived and were trying to help the shooting victims, Christina struggled with a law enforcement officer and tried to take his gun, a sheriff's spokesman said.

Jim Jordan would recover from his wounds. Christina's sister died of her wounds at the scene.

Christina was under the care of a psychiatrist for depression, her mother, Genevieve, told investigators. Detectives also found a variety of pills and empty bottles including Paxil, which is prescribed for depression, Depakote for seizures, Zoloft for panic disorder, and Ultram, a pain medication that can cause seizures if abused. She had apparently also taken Soloxine, a thyroid medicine prescribed for the family dog. Investigators also found a Baclofen bottle (a muscle relaxer). Detectives also either found pills or bottles that held Amitripyline, an antidepressant, Skelaxin, another muscle relaxer, and an empty bottle of phenytoin sodium, an anticonvulsant drug.

Investigators also found an instruction manual for the gun and additional ammunition.

Detectives were at a loss to discover a motive. The sisters lived together in nearby Tavares with Patricia's son. Christina arrived at her parents' home at about 11:30 p.m.

Five years earlier she had been charged with aggravated battery-domestic violence in which a man was attacked with a knife.

No one—not a doctor, pharmacist, or chemist—tried to guess what the effects would be for a person taking all of the drugs at the same time, if that is what she did.

She vomited pills after she was arrested, and she was taken to the hospital where her stomach was pumped.

In 2003, she was found to be competent. She pleaded guilty to second-degree murder and attempted murder. She was sentenced to 20 years in prison, but with credit for time served in jail and other stipulations it ended up amounting to 20 years' probation. She was also ordered not to have contact with her parents unless they requested it.

***

Even judges sometimes have a hard time deciding whether a person is insane.

The late Lake County Judge Richard "Red" Boylston used to regularly visit the Lake Correctional Institute state prison to check on prisoners.

Guards would wear thick leather gloves and arm coverings while glassy-eyed prisoners would sit, wearing only a sheet, facing the judge and doctors who might be testifying. Some of the men were forced to wear masks so they could not bite anyone. Frequently, the men refused to take their psychotropic drugs.

One man was especially intelligent, the judge noted. He pointed out that he was entitled to a hearing. The judge agreed he was.

"Your honor, I talk to my mother and my grandmother every day, and they say I don't have to take my medicine," he said (*Sentinel*, Aug. 1, 1999).

After he left, the judge learned that the man had killed his mother and grandmother.

***

One of the strangest cases I helped cover involved the 2002 nationally publicized case of a woman who was diagnosed with 12 different personalities in a rare condition known as dissociative identity disorder. Personalities ranged from a streetwise, in-your-face character named Vanessa, to a motherly figure. The illness was similar to that of a woman that Sally Field depicted in the movie *Sybil,* who allegedly had had 16 personalities.

The issue in the 2002 case was her psychotherapist in Volusia County. She claimed that Dr. Ronald Malave, 44, took advantage of one of her personalities, a "16-year-old" sex-crazed girl named Bridgett. She said she would switch personalities in the midst of a sex act to find that he was having sex with her. The psychiatrist was charged with having sex with a patient, a felony.

She said it happened more than two dozen times over a span of five years. She called the experience of switching from one personality to another "losing time," or when she "comes to herself." Usually, she had no memory of the other personality. "This is every good doctor's worst nightmare," his attorney, Chandler Muller, said (*Sentinel,* April 14, 2002). He said sometimes very sick patients become obsessive about their doctor.

The 41-year-old woman had had a horrific upbringing, with her being sexually abused by her father starting at age 4, and witnessing her dad hitting someone in the head with a machete. She heard voices in kindergarten, suffered from narcolepsy, bulimia, and self-mutilation.

Defense attorneys tried to keep the woman from testifying. She was "incompetent," they said. The judge, however, ruled that she could testify.

In their questions, defense attorneys accused her of demanding $25,000 from the doctor one time, and $5,000 another time. She denied it.

She also said she had no memory of posing as a student journalist while acting out as another personality and asking Malave's son to take her to see the movie *Eyes Wide Shut*, something that reportedly angered Dr. Malave.

"If I did, I'm very, very sorry because I would never do that as myself," she testified (*Sentinel,* April 20, 2002).

Twice, she apparently slipped into another persona while on the stand.

"How do you do?" she said, seductively to Muller.

"Who am I talking to?" the attorney asked, and then she snapped out of it.

Sometimes she held her head in her hands. She said she was trying not to hear other voices talking to her.

But the really damning evidence were panties she said she hid beneath her bed or in a safety deposit box that had traces of semen that were a genetic match for Dr. Malave.

The defense's theory was that she somehow got the samples by rooting through his trash and transferring the genetic material to her clothing. She was a former medical assistant with experience in handling such samples, they noted.

Malave's wife testified that the woman, whose name was never publicized in *Sentinel* stories, was stalking the family, making harassing phone calls, and sending inappropriate notes and other materials to their home.

Malave took the stand to deny that he had ever had sex with her or any other patient. He said he always tried to make "Bridgett" understand doctor-patient boundaries. Sometimes she tried to make it like a daughter-father relationship, he said.

The defense also called forensic psychiatrist Dr. Barbara Stein to discuss another symptom: borderline personality. These patients are easily manipulated and fearful of being abandoned, she said.

"They have no sense of self. They create a fantasy life. They put someone on a pedestal and the next minute they're the devil," she testified (*Sentinel*, April 24, 2002).

The courtroom was packed with Malave's family when the jury came back with the verdict. Malave wept when the clerk said, "not guilty," and so did his wife as they embraced in a joyous hug. The crowd hollered. The woman sobbed, as a psychologist and lawyers escorted her out of the courtroom.

She had no better luck later in her malpractice lawsuit against him. It was dismissed after a hearing.

"I'm overcome by emotion right now," said Malave after the criminal trial. "I think justice was served here today. I'm hoping the state of Florida will give me a chance to help people again."

He may have been acquitted by a jury, but the Medical Board was still troubled by the allegations. His license was revoked in Florida.

Prosecutor Raul Zambrano was philosophical. He knew it was going to be tough case.

"This isn't L.A. or Hollywood, or a made-for-TV movie. Keep your eye on reality," he had warned the jury.

"I have a victim who loses time and can't account for time. I believe her and I'm proud of her," he said after the verdict was read (*Sentinel,* April 26, 2002).

***

I don't know whatever happened to "Bridgett." It would be nice to think that she's down to one personality now and that personality is a good one.

Evers was eventually moved to a step-down facility.

Hopefully "Freddy" is doing better in New Jersey.

His story was encouraging to some native Floridians who long for the good old days before air-conditioning and Interstate highways encouraged everyone north of the Mason-Dixie line to come to Florida. At least "Freddy" left on a one-way ticket. Most crazy Northerners come to Florida and stay.

Chapter 18

Baby-face killers

It was a brewing, perfect storm. Not only were the middle school students bouncing off the walls with their hormone overload and raucous, insult-packed jeers, but a troubled kid with a 9 mm semi-automatic handgun was about to confront his loud-mouth tormentor. The two began shouting obscenities at each other when the 14-year-old pulled the gun out of his waistband and started shooting.

About 300 terrified students started running. Teachers called for students to get into their classrooms, and Keith Johnson kept advancing, firing 13 shots as he stepped closer to the 13-year-old, now helpless and dying in a pool of blood on the ground.

Johnson's defense lawyers said he was in fear for his life. A psychiatrist said he was the victim of "battered child syndrome."

Prosecutors succeeded in keeping from jurors many facts about the 13-year-old shooting victim's behavior, which included "everything from hitting students to mooning someone on a bus, some pretty outrageous behavior," the chief assistant state attorney conceded.

But was Johnson really in fear for his life?

Some people called Joey Summerall "a wimp," a kid that was rowdy but all talk. A few even thought they were friends and were joking when they made verbal jabs. Others, however, said Joey's comments cut to the quick and that Johnson took them seriously.

It would be up to the jury to decide. Prosecutors decided to try him as an adult. If tried as a juvenile, he might serve as few as three years in confinement. If convicted of first-degree murder as an adult, the young teen would face life in prison with no chance of parole.

The slaying in 1995, one of the first in a deadly string of school shootings that still rock the nation, shook Lake County to its core. If kids are not safe at school, parents thought, they are not safe anywhere.

It wasn't just the clash between the two Tavares Middle School students that ignited a firestorm. Johnson's life was unraveling in the days leading up to the shooting.

His father, who had been absent for 10 years, came back to the family but remained emotionally distant with his son.

Keith, who had near-perfect attendance and good grades in elementary school, became defiant in middle school. The dean of students confiscated banned items from him like "gangsta" bandanas and sunglasses and ordered him to hitch up his baggy pants. Classmates said he had a fascination with gangs, especially Folk Nation, though there was no evidence that he was a member. Joey used to provoke him by flashing the gang sign—a pitchfork—an act of disrespect if you are not a member of the gang.

Coach Sonny Walters said the once quiet and respectful Johnson had become surly.

"He just had an attitude [of] 'I don't care' right before the shooting, just a couple of days before (*Sentinel,* April 21, 1996)."

Two weeks earlier he stole his mother's Jeep Cherokee and drove it to New York with his girlfriend. His mother slapped him in the face for the first time in his life and kicked him out of the house. A family friend, Chuck Thomas, offered to let him stay with him.

Thomas was confined to a wheelchair, the victim of a shooting in 1991.

On the day of the shooting, Sept. 29, 1995, Johnson removed an unloaded, holstered 9 mm handgun from beneath Thomas' pillow when Thomas went to the bathroom. Johnson then unlocked a cabinet where a magazine loaded with shells was stashed. He threw the holster on the bed, covered it with a pillow, and left for school with the handgun in his backpack.

On the bus, Johnson pointed his finger at a boy at the front of the bus like a gun and said, "Pop! Pop!"

On the ride to school, he talked to friends about having to shoot someone and asked the boys who they would like to see killed. He named five students, including Joey.

"I'm just joking. I ain't got a gun," he said.

At school, students asked Joey if he knew Johnson was coming for him.

"Yeah, I've already heard that he wants to kill me and that he has a gun," he said. Then, he laughed.

It was picture day at Tavares Middle and Joey made his trip to the school library for his picture.

"He was just very, very solemn and quiet, which was very, very unlike Joey," a cafeteria worker noted.

Moments later, the two boys faced each other under a covered walkway, argued, and began using profanity.

A girl just two feet away said she heard Johnson say, "Here I go," and he began firing.

"There was a look of shock on his face like it just hit him, what he'd done. It wasn't anger. It was like he was in slow motion trying to take off and didn't know what to do (April 21, 1996)," a teacher said.

He ran to a nearby field but was quickly captured. His parents were called but they waived their right to sit in on questioning by Tavares Police Officer David Myers and State Attorney Investigator Pat Kicklighter.

DM: "Have you ever taken a gun to school before?"

KJ: "No."

DM: "What made today so different? Why did you take it today?"

KJ: "Because I knew he would start running his mouth to me again."

DM: "But he had run his mouth to you before, you never took it in there before, why did you do it today? What had he said? What happened between you all that got you so aggravated?"

KJ: "What he did?"

DM: "Yeah."

KJ: "He just [sic] running his mouth."

It was part one of a damning statement that would come back to haunt him. The second part came within a few moments.

PK: "Do you have any remorse for what you have done?"

KJ: "Have any what?"

PK: "Remorse."

KJ: "What's that?"

PK: "What does that mean? Do you feel sorry for what you have done now?"

KJ: "Yeah. Because I could have just walked away."

Defense lawyers tried but failed to keep the videotaped confession out of the trial. Nor could their mental health experts legitimately claim that he was not guilty by reason of insanity.

However, Dr. Wade C. Myers, a professor at the University of Florida, was going to present a defense labeled "self-defense battered-child syndrome."

Myers cited the incendiary family dynamics and told jurors that Johnson believed his life was in danger. He said Joey had tried to pick a fight 20 to 30 times.

"The day before the shooting, Joey said, 'Me and my boys will kill you at school tomorrow,'" Myers testified, quoting Johnson (*Sentinel*, May 2, 1996).

Prosecutor Ric Ridgway began unraveling Myers' theory one thread at a time.

It was the first time the "battered-child syndrome" was trotted out in a juvenile-on-juvenile crime.

The syndrome was identified by a pediatrician in the 1960s to describe physical, not emotional injuries, and the victims were younger than 3 years old.

"Keith Johnson is not under 3, is he doctor?" the chief assistant state attorney asked.

The description of the syndrome was later expanded to include psychological trauma at the hands of a parent, much like the "battered-spouse syndrome," in which the battered spouse harms the abuser.

The syndrome's symptoms were described as withdrawal, psychological "numbing," "hyper-vigilance," and a fear of imminent danger. But Myers conceded that the so-called syndrome was not listed in the *Diagnostic and Statistical Manual of Mental Disorders*, a kind of bible of the American Psychiatric Association.

Ridgway asked if there were other disorders at hand, all the while chipping away at the defense claim that Johnson was in fear for his life.

"The boys traded insults, and there was only one fight, isn't that right?"

Ridgway leafed through the psychiatrist's report, calling attention to a condition known as "adjustment disorder."

Symptoms are "mixed emotions, anger mixed with depression. It is common and it is caused by stressors.

Ridgway also led Myers to talk about "displaced anger."

"It's like when you're mad at your boss but you go home and kick the cat," Myers said.

Ridgway also brought up "malingering," which is basically faking a mental illness.

Myers said Johnson was not lying.

Ridgway also brought up Myers' own research about adolescents who killed other people. In each case, "conduct disorder" was present. Teens had used a weapon, had stolen something without confronting the victim, and had run away from home—which is what Johnson did.

Ridgway, for the most part, fended off attempts by Myers to discuss Joey's behavior. When defense witnesses described Joey as a "bully," he got them to concede that the sparring was verbal.

The day before, prosecution witnesses testified about premeditation. One boy had traded shirts with Johnson on the bus. Johnson then wanted his own shirt back.

When the friend asked why, Johnson replied: "Because I'm going to jail for murder one."

The day before the shooting, one teen testified, Johnson mentioned Joey's name and said he "wanted to blow his head off (*Sentinel,* May 1, 1996)."

After weighing the evidence, the jury announced its decision: First-degree murder.

It was a crushing blow for Johnson's mother, Julie, who sobbed in the courtroom while Joey's family sat silently, swamped in their own grief.

Circuit Judge Don Briggs sentenced Johnson to the only sentence he could legally impose: Life in prison. He looked down from the bench at the now 15-year-old and said he could have been convicted of robbery, too, "because you have robbed this community of its innocence (*Sentinel,* May 3, 1996)."

Like all reporters, I had worked hard to establish a rapport with Julie Johnson during the week. She had been a classmate of my wife's in nursing school, but I didn't press her. I told her I would be ready when she wanted to talk. She was not ready to talk in the courthouse. It was not until she walked out into the parking lot and was surrounded by TV reporters, camera lights blazing, that she began to speak. I ran up to the mob just in time to hear her say what was on her heart.

"Next to my son, the justice system, the school system, and I should have all been tried for that crime," she said.

Ridgway was also surrounded, pinned up against his car by TV reporters eager for a sound bite. "Are you happy with the verdict?" one reporter asked.

"What is there to be happy about?" A 15-year-old was on his way to prison for the rest of his life and another child was dead, he said.

It was a rare moment of agreement between prosecutors and defenders.

"A double tragedy," said Public Defender Howard "Skip" Babb Jr. (*Sentinel*, May 4, 1996).

It certainly was a hard blow for the Summerall family, already reeling from the death of Joey's young cousin to a traffic accident.

Joey's mother, Diane Summerall, struggled to find the words to express her overwhelming feelings of frustration, guilt, rationalization, and loss in a deposition. She said she was so exasperated at one point she threatened to put Joey into a boy's home.

"At one time he ... was playing too much, getting suspended, getting referrals, and giving them to [his] grandmother and wouldn't tell me about them, and it was just getting, just .... My life might have something to do with it and just everything clogged up as one. It didn't have to be him so much."

"What would your life have had to do with it?" the interviewer asked.

"Well, life … my life has a lot to do with it. Raising kids, a single parent raising kids, trying to work and keep a roof over their heads, sometimes it get[s] hard and we don't always take action the right way. We don't always do things. Sometimes you get frustrated and don't know which way to turn. You get frustrated, you know. You know, it ain't no … I'm not perfect. I try to do the best that I can do and that's all I can do, and I did the best that I can do."

As Judge Briggs noted during sentencing, once innocence is lost it is gone forever. However, Lake County was not as innocent as everyone thought.

A year later, the Lake section of the *Sentinel* featured an older-looking Keith Johnson showing off his new tattoos that he had obtained in prison.

"I know why I did it: Because he was going to kill me the next day at school," he said in the accompanying interview," (Sept. 29, 1996). Johnson claimed he was walking with some friends near the mall when someone—presumably Joey—shot at him from a passing car, "so I thought he was serious."

In an appeal for a new trial in 2001, Johnson claimed Joey shouted from the car that night: "You're dead at school tomorrow, White Cracker!"

Racial slurs and taunts about each other's mother were common between the two.

But the huge, bold headline over the page read: "Lake schools No. 1 in violence."

Lake County led all 67 counties in the state for the rate of violence per 1,000 students, and ranked third behind huge counties like Dade in the sheer number of violent incidents, according to state education officials.

Lake school officials were stunned and vowed to get a handle on the problem.

"This is a real gut kick," said Kyleen Fischer, chairwoman of the school board. She described the finding as an "emergency" and top priority. The superintendent of schools said he couldn't help but think the shooting was a one-term incident that was unlikely to happen again (*Sentinel,* Sept. 29, 1996).

Stern warnings, promises to parents, metal detectors and other safeguards popped up in schools.

Kids were told: If you see a gun or hear someone talk about committing violence, tell an adult.

If anything positive came out of the tragedy, anything at all, it was that new conversations were taking place between parents and their kids.

The photo of Johnson showing off his prison tattoos led to at least one critical letter to the editor.

"Does this image help to present to our impressionable young people in Lake County the dire consequences of aggressive, violent behavior? I think not! Instead, it panders to the Hollywood formula of emulating the movie *Natural Born Killers.*"

The letter writer, who identified himself as a pastor, praised the article but said the Lake edition, where the photo appeared, should have published a photo of Johnson behind bars "or staring out through the razor wire … (*Sentinel*, Oct. 16, 1996)."

I had no part in choosing the photograph. I hadn't written the follow-up article. To me, it showed the sharp contrast between a boy and a wannabe man displaying his tattoos, but it did sharpen the debate over teen violence.

The testimony of psychological experts had also raised some eyebrows, especially when Johnson's expert appeared to stretch a syndrome to fit Johnson's case.

The public, and I think many jurors, bristle at the idea that psychological "mumbo jumbo" might become an excuse for people not taking personal responsibility.

I understand the process. Sometimes it is all that a defense team has in its bag of tricks.

Authorities doubted Johnson's stories, including the one he told in his appeal. No one could dispute one thing he said, however: "I wish it never happened."

***

Sometimes parents are put into a dilemma so horrible it is beyond belief.

Patrick Boykin, Sr. and his wife Helena lost their 13-year-old daughter, Constance, to a homicide in 1999. If the killer, who was 12, was tried as an adult and found guilty of first-degree murder, the punishment would be life in prison.

But the parents begged the state not to impose that penalty because if that happened, they would lose their son, too. Patrick, Jr. is the one who killed Constance.

Kids in the little town of Minneola were hustling to get ready for school on Jan. 25, 1999, and parents were rushing out the door to get to work.

Dispatchers at the Lake County Sheriff's Office were handling the usual radio chatter about accidents and cars bunching up on U.S. Highway 27 headed toward Florida's Turnpike and Orlando. Normalcy ended at 7:39 a.m., when the 12-year-old called 911.

The slight-built child was standing outside when the first patrol car arrived.

"I shot my sister," he told the deputy. "I was depressed."

Inside, his sister was found with her head down in a crouched position. She was completely clothed but had a black shoe on her left foot and a white shoe on the right. She had been shot four times—three times in the back and once in the head.

Patrick led deputies to his parents' bedroom where he had placed the nine-shot .22-caliber revolver on top of a file cabinet. There were four spent shell casings in the cylinder and five live rounds.

Patrick said he had gotten the gun from a shoe box in his parents' closet after they left for work. He said he loaded it with shells in the shoe box and then walked into the kitchen. He said he shot her at least twice without saying anything to her. He said she looked at him and said, "I love you."

He said that before getting the gun he heard "something like the devil's voice." The voice kept saying, "Shoot her. Shoot her."

After his sister told him he loved him, the voice went away, he said.

He admitted being jealous of her sometimes, but he said he did love her.

One of the deputies searched his bedroom.

"I located a paperback book titled *Screaming Skull* and a magazine in the defendant's desk drawer. The magazine depicted pictures of women posed in similar positions as the victim was found, holding handguns."

The deputy also found a butcher knife under his mattress.

Within minutes of their arrival, a girl walked up and identified herself as Constance's best friend. As she left and walked past the patrol car, Patrick stuck out his finger like a gun and pointed to the house.

Later, deputies interviewed the girl at her middle school. She told investigators that the siblings were always fighting but not in normal brother-sister battles.

"She said they would pull hair and bite each other. She stated approximately six months ago, Constance told her that P.J. had pulled a knife on her and put it to her throat," the investigator noted in her report.

Another student said "P.J.," as his friends called him, told other kids that he was going "to kill my sister."

Prosecutors were moved by the Boykin family tragedy. Unlike so many cases where children are practically thrown away by their parents, this hard-working middle-class couple was driven to do anything they could for their kids.

Constance was a popular, rising-star basketball player. P.J. liked sports, video games and computers, and he had a girlfriend.

He was doing fine in school until nine weeks before the shooting. That's when he started saying that he "didn't care" and his grades began sliding downward.

Prosecutors took the thorny case to the grand jury, which published its report on Feb.5, 1999.

"We have carefully considered the nature of the crime as the evidence reveals it and the alternatives available in both the Department of Juvenile Justice and the Department of Corrections to deal with a child of Patrick Boykin's situation should he be convicted of the crime charged or some lesser offense.

"Our determination to charge Patrick Boykin as an adult in this case is based upon the nature of the crime, the possible consequences in the juvenile or adult system, and our concern as to what message would be sent to the children of this community should this crime not be treated in a serious manner.

"We know that, as charged, Patrick Boykin faces life in an adult prison. Our indictment should not be taken as an endorsement of *this* sentence in *this* case. We have attempted to balance our concern for public safety, the severity of the offense and the alternatives that can be available by a blending of adult and juvenile sanctions, as opposed to juvenile sanctions alone.

"We have declined to hear from a variety of character and mental health witnesses which were made available to us by Patrick Boykin's attorneys. We have done so because we understand that it is not our responsibility to try this case as to mental health issues or to pass sentence upon Patrick Boykin. We accept that this was by all appearances a good family in which something went terribly wrong. We ask that the court system try to resolve the very compelling issues of the child's age and the consequences of his actions that exist in this case. We strongly recommend that there should be rehabilitative opportunities for Patrick Boykin, but also believe that there should be structure for control and punishment for him as well.

"Our sympathy goes out to the Boykin family and all of those who have been deeply touched by this case.

"By this indictment and presentment, we hope to achieve justice tempered by mercy."

Then, in an unprecedented step, it asked that the presentment be published "in its entirety by news organizations so that our position will not be misunderstood."

Of course, grand juries have no power to make a news organization publish anything, but the message was clear: It did not want to be "misunderstood."

But was such a blending of juvenile, adult, and rehabilitative sanctions even legally possible? And would the courts go along with it?

Clearly, the State Attorney's Office thought so, or it would not have planted the idea in the minds of the grand jurors. The parents, who were both the parents of the defendant and the victim, would certainly go along with it, considering the alternative.

The idea of sentencing a 12-year-old to life in prison with no chance of parole was troubling to the panel, and troubling to the justices of the U.S. Supreme Court, as it turns out. In 2012, the high court ruled 5-4 against mandatory life sentences for juveniles with no chance of parole, saying such sentences were a violation of defendants' Eighth Amendment right against cruel and unusual punishment.

"A judge or jury must have the opportunity to consider mitigating circumstances before imposing the harshest possible penalty for juveniles," wrote Justice Eleana Kagan in the majority opinion (csmmonitor.com, June 25, 2012).

Circuit Judge Don Briggs, citing a district court ruling, said that the ruling has no effect on a handful of defendants from Lake County already serving life terms, including vampire cult killers Rod Ferrell and Howard Anderson.

As it turned out, the courts did give Ferrell, Anderson, and others—including Keith Johnson—a chance for a rehearing. Johnson is still awaiting his second chance.

Boykin's lawyers talked about mitigating circumstances. In a hearing to determine if he was competent to even go to trial, experts testified that Boykin sometimes heard soothing voices he attributed to Jesus. Booming voices were Satan's, he believed, and high-pitched voices were those of angels.

He said he wasn't angry with his sister the morning he shot her, and he stopped hearing a voice to shoot her after he "snapped out of it," and called 911.

That is evidence of brain damage, psychologist Robert Berland, Ph.D., said in his sworn testimony. When Patrick was 2, he drank a small amount of charcoal lighter fluid and inhaled some of the hydrocarbons, damaging his lungs, Berland said, citing medical records.

When Patrick was in the back of the patrol car and an officer gave him a soft drink, Boykin became excited when the bottle cap showed that he had won a free drink. It was as if the shooting had never occurred, Berland concluded.

There was other evidence of problems: a long history of headaches, and he wet the bed until he was 10. Once, when his parents took him to the hospital for headaches, he lost consciousness.

Sometimes he thought bugs were crawling on him or believed someone was poisoning his food.

The night before the shooting he had been whipped with a belt after being caught with an adult pornographic video.

Patrick said he had been spanked 100 times overall by his mother and about 30 by his dad. Dr. Wade Myers described the treatment as "harsh," and said it caused Patrick to be depressed *(Sentinel,* Aug. 22, 1999).

Lake County Judge Richard Boylston ruled that Boykin was incompetent for trial and ordered him to be sent to a mental health facility for treatment.

In April 2001, Boykin, by now 14 years old, was still charged with first-degree murder but was sentenced to nine to 12 months at a juvenile detention center on a lesser charge of using a firearm during a felony. Lawyers were told to revisit the murder charge later in a possible settlement agreement.

"Hopefully, this is the first step in a just sentence," said Assistant State Attorney Bill Gross.

Defense attorney John Spivey said, "I think he's had a marked improvement."

In 2002, he was allowed to plead guilty to the lesser murder charge of manslaughter with a firearm and was sentenced to two years of community control, a higher level of probation.

The following year, he was released from house arrest and allowed to attend the area high school under normal probation.

"He has no psychiatric problems to speak of at all," Gross said (*Sentinel*, Oct. 31, 2003).

Patrick's parents refused to talk to reporters.

It appeared that the grand jury's hope for "justice tempered by mercy" was achieved.

***

The uneasy feeling started when Dan and Faith Nawara tried to call home but didn't get an answer. When they walked up to their front door on July 5, 1993, their hearts sank when they saw the note from their 14-year-old son saying that he "had done something wrong, the babies were alright, but Tammi wasn't." The note said he had gone to the police station.

They drove to the Fruitland Park police station nearby to find cops drinking coffee. When they identified themselves and showed the note, one of the officers said, "Yeah, we got a call about that."

The parents headed back home with a patrol car following them.

On the way back to the house, Faith said, "That looks like Jason." Both cars stopped. Police put him in the back of the squad car.

When they got to the home, Faith ran to where her stepson, Jason, was sitting in the back of the patrol car.

"What happened?" she said.

"Tammi's in your room," he said.

Dan went inside with police officers while another held back the panicked, shaking mother. She continued to try and find out what was going on.

"What happened? What happened?" she asked.

"I can't talk about it," Jason said, and a police officer walked over and shut the car door.

The men rushed through the living room to the master bedroom. Jason had indeed done "something wrong."

Ten-year-old Tammi Peck was lying on her back on the floor, nude, her ankles crossed, her left arm across her chest.

There were pools of blood on the carpet, on a rumpled bed sheet, and on her face. There were also knotted, blood-stained sections of cut telephone cords. Near the bed on the floor was a lever-action .22-caliber rifle. They also found a bloodied T-shirt and a pair of panties that had apparently been cut off her body. A jar of petroleum jelly was found on the second shelf of a nightstand.

An evidence technician also spotted two spent shell casings in the living room and one in the dining room. A spent round was found in carpeting near her head.

Faith and Dan Nawara were stunned. Dan, a former pastor, was principal of a Christian school in Leesburg. Faith worked in the office. They had two children between them, one was about to turn 3, the other was almost 4 years old.

Tammi was Faith's daughter from a previous marriage. Jason was Dan's.

"I've had Jason now for two to two-and-a-half years. I've never seen anything. I mean, never anything that showed any kind of violent behavior or anything," she told Assistant State Attorney Bill Gross in a taped interview on July 13.

"I was the best mother to Jason I could be," she said. "I have three children of my own. I cannot tell you that I loved Jason more or Jason less. I can only tell you it's a different kind of love."

Jason's mother got him every other weekend like clockwork.

Tammi had never complained of any kind of sexual abuse or displayed any behavior that indicated that she knew too much for her age, Faith said.

"If there would have been any doubt or any of that whatsoever, it would have been taken care of immediately," she said.

"... that's why it's so hard and so shocking about any of this that ... our family was a normal family," she said.

She said the tragedy put her and her husband "in a horrible position."

She added: "... we're not only in this tragedy with Tammi, but we're in this [with Jason, too]."

Then, she said: "If there is hard evidence or facts proving that this was not an accident, I want what is fair. Do you understand what I'm saying? I am not, I mean, I can see that obviously I ... you're not dealing with a mother that, well, I've lost one child ... somebody said the other day, well, you've just ... you'll protect this one. That's not true. I want what's fair, you know. At that same time, you've got to realize that I've lived with this child for two years ...."

She explained that Jason had shown nothing but respect toward her.

"… all we can think of, as parents, is this had to be a horrible accident somehow."

Faith Nawara was still reeling when 250 people packed the Leesburg Tabernacle Church, filling it with flowers and tears.

The pastor called her the "sweetheart of the church, a kid with a quick smile who loved to cut up."

"Tammi is with Jesus," he said to the sobbing crowd.

One mourner said she felt sorry for the family. "They lost two kids."

Tammi's white casket, trimmed in pink, was surrounded by a swarm of flowers. She was laid to rest wearing a flowery dress, a single white rose in her hands, and a pink doll at her side.

The picture of Tammi clinging to childhood even in death was even more disturbing when the state added a rape charge to the murder charge that Jason was already facing. The FBI laboratory found that he had used some type of object to violate her rectum.

Jason's friends told authorities that he hated his stepsister and said he wanted to kill her.

On May 2, 1994, lawyers picked a jury of 12. On May 5, on the third day of his trial, he spent 25 minutes in front of the courtroom with his father, stepmother, and his mother, Jill Nawara, before entering a surprise guilty plea. Judge Briggs sentenced him to 50 years in prison on a charge of second-degree murder and sexual battery. He was too young to be executed, the high court had already decided, but not too young to spend his life in prison.

"It's all right," he told his mother while hugging her and fighting back tears.

"I never wanted this to go to trial," he told the *Sentinel* in a phone interview. "I never wanted to put my family through it. I didn't want to go through it."

"I am satisfied," Faith said.

"We don't feel like anybody won," said Jill's brother, Bruce Lovett. "Tammi Peck sure didn't win anything, and Jason didn't win either."

It was a loss for everyone. It was a double loss of innocence for the Nawara family. The shocking case also led to the feeling by the public that Lake County was losing its innocence, a fact that Judge Briggs would point out two years later while sentencing Keith Johnson to life in prison.

***

Paisley, a peaceful-looking rural neighborhood on the edge of the Ocala National Forest was terrorized by a band of young, local toughs in 1999. The teens, including the son of sheriff's deputies, smashed mailboxes, yelled obscenities, and would lie down in the road so cars couldn't pass.

They regularly gathered beneath a tree near a telephone cable box that was painted with the words: "SATAN WUZ HERE."

"One day, I went out and someone had smashed a plastic chair I had in the yard," one resident said. "And I saw this kid, and I said, 'Hey, how are you?' And he said, 'The same thing that happened to that chair is what's going to happen to you.'"

He said the youth then threatened to burn his house down.

"The other night I woke up screaming. I had a nightmare that the house was on fire, and I couldn't move," he told authorities.

Finally, after months of torment, the 73-year-old man whacked the 16-year-old youth in the leg with a stick, then struck him in his face.

"I broke the boy's jaw. I feel bad about that. But I just couldn't take it anymore (*Sentinel,* March 21, 1999)."

The retiree was charged with aggravated battery.

He soon joined some of his other neighbors, including a 55-year-old woman, who put their homes up for sale.

"You get to be 73 and you think you're going to settle down and have some peace," he said, shaking his head.

After writing this story, I went to see Sheriff George Knupp personally, in part because of the allegation about the son of deputy sheriffs, who reportedly taunted, "You can't touch me!"

Within minutes, he summoned some of his top aides into the office and ordered a task force to get out to the neighborhood to put a stop to the terror. I wasn't kidding myself. He wasn't calling out the troops because Frank Stanfield had called his attention to the problem. I was representing the *Orlando Sentinel* and thousands of readers.

Things seemed to settle down afterward, at least for a time.

The stressed out 73-year-old man was later charged with felony battery, but prosecutors dropped all charges after the man entered a pretrial intervention program and agreed to serve 50 hours of community service.

There was no word on what happened to the punk or to the prospective home sales.

The man from Paisley was not the only one to strike back.

There was a similar confrontation in 1997 between a band of teens and a 54-year-old man in a poor mobile home community called Pine Lakes.

I once had a court official jokingly tell me that if a fighter jet dropped a guided "smart bomb" on Pine Lakes the state could lay off about a half dozen public defenders, and prosecutors, and a handful of sheriff's deputies.

Stretched along State Road 44 just west of the Volusia County line, the community's most striking features are beat up mobile homes and a honky-tonk across the road.

Government services were sparse at the time. Instead of normal trash pickup, for example, a girl suffered severe burns from an exploding aerosol can while burning trash in her yard.

Unlike the Paisley man, who hit a teen with a stick, the Pine Lakes man fired a .357 Magnum bullet into a 17-year-old's leg.

The man said the 17-year-old and nine other kids had threatened to set his house on fire a few weeks earlier. On the night of the shooting, he said the kids stood outside his home and yelled: "Come on old man, it's time."

He said he walked outside with the handgun just to scare them off but fired the weapon when one of the teens charged him.

The kid said he and four friends were just walking past when the man came out and yelled: "You want trouble? Wait right there. I've got something for you, you punk kid."

"I said, 'What have you got? What have you got? Then I saw the flame. He shot me (*Sentinel*, April 16, 1997)!"

The man was charged with aggravated battery with a firearm.

If the kid was surprised when the man shot him, he was even more surprised when the man went on trial and a six-member jury found him not guilty.

The kid, who was limping, was angry. His parents were angry. The prosecutor was probably angry. They never like to lose. The man was relieved. After everyone left the courtroom, however, deputies gave him a friendly piece of advice: Move someplace else because those kids will be back.

***

Lady Lake residents were fed up with a kid they called a one-man crime wave, but they managed to have their voices heard in a meeting with a state House representative, prosecutors, and a sheriff's detective.

He had a long history of arrests, including setting one kid's feet on fire with a match and lighter fluid. He would be arrested on juvenile charges only to be quickly released and be seen riding his bicycle with a big boom box on his shoulder.

The problem was, prosecutors said, was that there were precious few beds in juvenile detention and so many cases that the kids were placed on probation or house arrest, often with predictable results.

"We're going to try and find out what's not working with juvenile laws," said Rep. Everett Kelly, D-Lady Lake. "I most assuredly am going to make every attempt to toughen the laws because we don't seem to be gaining much ground on juvenile crimes (*Sentinel,* Oct. 11, 1996).

By the time the group met, State Attorney Brad King made sure that Steven Dominique "Nicky" Peachey would be charged as an adult. Peachey was facing four counts of burglary of a vehicle, seven counts of dealing in stolen property, one count of burglary of a structure, three counts of burglary to a dwelling, four counts of grand theft, one count of possession of a firearm by a delinquent, and one count of petty theft.

That's really sad for a 17-year-old," said one neighbor, "but that child is truly feared."

Chief Assistant State Attorney Ric Ridgway was quoted in the *Sentinel* story as saying: "What these people are describing is not unique to this kid. There are more kids than they [Department of Juvenile Justice] have programs or [jail] room to handle."

In the end, Peachey negotiated a plea and pleaded no contest to five charges. He was sentenced to 13 years in prison.

I don't know what, if any, changes were made to the law that year but the only real change that has emerged over the years has been the growing trend of trying juveniles as adults. The Legislature has given the state attorneys the power to make that decision. That, and the ever- increasing number of tough mandatory sentences, has helped clean up the streets, but at the high cost of warehousing young people in prisons.

In DJJ'S defense, "they're still being asked to carry five gallons of water in a two-gallon bucket," Ridgway said.

"It puts a lot of pressure on prosecutors," said Ridgway in interview for this book 17 years later.

"Say you have a kid who has committed some serious crimes, not murder or [armed] robbery but he has broken into some homes and stolen some guns. He hasn't used the guns, but the guns are now out on the street. Well, the most he could get as a juvenile would be two years. If he's treated as an adult, that's life. That's a big difference.

"It's OK if he pleads to that [two years] but if he is tried as an adult and is convicted, [life] may be the only sentence possible."

***

Sometimes it's a kid's arrogance that gets him in trouble.

Circuit Judge Mark Hill imposed a three-year prison sentence on a 16-year-old A-B honor roll student who participated in an armed robbery just to prove to his friends that he could do it.

"You're supposed to be a good student and one of the more intelligent people," the judge said.

"I need to send a message to your school that this is not a game. I'm doing this to save other children (*Sentinel*, Jan 8, 1999)."

Defense attorneys tried to convince the judge to sentence the teen to a year in the county jail, which had a school for juveniles, but the victim's testimony led to a tougher sentence.

The woman, who was a clerk at a convenience store, said she thought she was going to die. She said she had nightmares.

An 18-year-old man pulled a .25-caliber handgun and pointed it at her head. The 16-year-old flashed a realistic-looking weapon, but it was actually a BB gun.

***

Brutality is not limited to teenagers, but in some cases their complete lack of empathy is as shocking as the crime itself.

Unlike many crimes in one neighborhood filled with resentment and suspicion of cops, no one was saying, "I don't know nothin'" when two teens broke into the home of a wheelchair-bound 63-year-old man.

Joseph Dillon was minding his own business and sitting in his wheelchair when the two young thugs walked into his home and one of them pulled out a .25-caliber handgun and demanded money.

"Fellow, I don't have no money. I'm living on disability," Dillon said. "Where do you think I get money from (*Sentinel,* April 21, 1999)?"

He told investigators: "They told me, "You hide money in this house. You'd better tell me where it's at or I'm going to blow your brains out."

"I told them, 'You might as well go ahead and squeeze the trigger, because I don't have any money."

He said one of the teens grabbed him by the hand and threw him on the floor. The impact dislocated his shoulder.

The teens found $240 in an envelope he had set aside to pay his utility bill. They also took a gold watch, a knife, and two handguns.

They smashed a portable phone and cut the cord from another and used the wire to tie his hands behind his back.

The two kicked him in the side as they left.

He was on the floor for about an hour before a friend found him and called police. When a cop started to untie his wrists, he stopped the officer and said: "No, go to your car and get your camera and take my picture. If these fellas get caught, I want the world to see what they've done to me."

The world didn't see the photos, but a judge did. They pleaded guilty, and despite their families pleading for leniency, the judge sentenced the pair to six years in prison. It could have been worse. They could have been sentenced up to 30 years.

***

When an alarm tipped the sheriff's office about a break-in at Lake Square Mall at 4:30 a.m., two deputies stood outside an employee's entrance door and caught the culprit walking out. But that wasn't the big surprise. The real surprise was the thief's age—14—and the actions he had taken leading up to his arrest.

The middle school student, who had just had his 14th birthday, slipped out of his house at 2:45 a.m. He broke into a car upholstery shop where he stole $40 cash and found a car with the keys in the parking lot.

He stole the car, and then switched license plates with a car at a nearby shop.

He drove the car a couple of laps around the mall, then rammed the car into the glass paneled entrance to a J.C. Penney store. He backed up and parked the car behind a nearby shopping center. He went into the store and began looking for a jacket he had spotted earlier, but it was too dark to see so he went to the jewelry department and stole items there.

He left when he heard a security guard coming.

He told deputies he heard "a voice" telling him to break into the store.

"I think it was just an excuse he was trying to use," a detective said (*Sentinel,* Nov. 19, 1997).

***

Vandalism is always an attractive idea for ugly minds. But when vandals broke into South Sumter High School in Bushnell, smashing every TV, computer, window, and destroying books, they outdid themselves by racking up $400,000 in damages. And that was 1994 dollars.

They spray-painted racial slogans on walls such as "Black Power," "White Trash," and "Blacks Rule" to throw authorities off the track, but it didn't work.

One official noted, "When's the last time you heard the phrase 'Black power' (*Sentinel,* Nov. 23, 1994)?"

People young and old volunteered to clean up the mess.

Three teens were arrested shortly after the spree.

"They *are former* students," said Schools Superintendent Preston Morgan. Two were 18 years old. One was 16.

What kind of former students? "Meatheads" and "troublemakers," Morgan said (*Sentinel,* Nov. 29, 1994).

The 18-year-olds were sentenced to 38 months in prison. It was unclear what punishment was meted out to the juvenile.

***

"Nine-one-one, do you need police, fire, or an ambulance?"

"My friend found my dad's gun," the kid told the 911 dispatcher, then gave his name, address, and his dad's name. In fact, he gave his dad's name a couple of times, possibly thinking that the dispatcher might even know his dad. After all, his father was the gun safety officer for the Lake County Sheriff's Office.

Unfortunately, it was too late for safety on June 23, 1995. One temptation, one miscalculation, and one stupid act changed the life of one boy forever and ended the life of another.

"My friend, my friend found my dad's gun, you know. And he shot himself in the head. There's blood everywhere," he said. "I swear I didn't do it."

"Oh, don't worry about that right now, OK? We just need to get an ambulance there, OK?"

"Am I going to get in trouble for this?"

"Honey, don't worry about that right now. OK? We're doing ... need to get the ambulance out there to him."

No ambulance crew in the world could have saved 13-year-old David Jones. Rescue workers found him sitting in a recliner in the family room with a bullet hole over his left eye. A stainless-steel semi-automatic handgun was lying on top of his abdomen on his right side, just above his right hand.

He had a slight pulse. Hours later his parents gave consent for his organs to be donated.

"We didn't want our son's life to be lost in vain," said David's father, Richard. "That was our son's last gift (*Sentinel,* June 25, 1995)."

The shooting immediately put the sheriff's trainer on the spot. The department's official position was that gun owners should keep their guns under lock and key—preferably unloaded.

"There's a natural curiosity with kids and guns, and guns are a dangerous thing to be curious about," said Sheriff's spokesman Lt. Chris Daniels after the shooting.

In Florida, a gun owner can be charged with culpable negligence, a third-degree felony, if a child kills someone with an accessible, loaded firearm. Investigators immediately wondered: Was the sheriff's deputy guilty of that crime?

The deputy told prosecutor Ric Ridgeway in a taped interview on June 29, 1995, that he had a flood of emotions when he saw an ambulance leaving his neighborhood.

"As we pulled up coming down Vine Street, I saw Mrs. Lawrence, who's our neighbor across the street, and John (not his real name) sitting in a lawn chair. And I just remember a big sigh of relief that, that it was not John. And I was pissed off. And then, to be quite honest, I was very upset. I didn't want to get close to him [inaudible] at that time .... And then I got up and walked over to John."

The deputy said he thanked his neighbors for their kindness and apologized to one neighbor for not coming over right away.

"I still regret that today. I hugged him," he said of his son.

He said he reminded his son that no one was allowed to come into the house while he and his mother were away.

It was one of the few times the couple had allowed him to stay at home by himself. Occasionally his 14-year-old niece came over to keep an eye on him.

The deputy said he normally kept the .45-caliber semi-automatic handgun in a gun safe in the garage but he had taken it out the night before to get the serial number so he could order a part. A friend came over and the deputy showed the gun to his friend. He said he removed the magazine, or "clip," and then removed all eight rounds in the magazine and placed the bullets on the breakfast bar. Later, he put the gun on top of the refrigerator—unloaded—thinking that he would put it back in the safe, but he was tired, forgot about it, and went to bed.

There was a second magazine, loaded with eight rounds and a separate live round, stored in a clay pot near his police scanner, he said.

One of the first people to reach the house on the afternoon of the shooting was the deputy's friend, Chuck Johnson, a former sheriff's deputy who had become a lawyer.

Johnson put father and son in his pickup truck.

"I sat John in the seat," the deputy said. "I kneeled between his legs. And I asked him, I said, 'John, what happened?'

"He told me that he had let David into the house. And I said, 'Why did you do that? You know no one is allowed in the house.'

"He said he'd been riding his bike. He wanted a drink of water. He said while David was getting the water, he went out back to feed the dogs because he hadn't fed and watered the dogs that day. He heard a gunshot, and he ran back into the house.

"I became very upset with him. I said, 'John [inaudible] there wasn't a loaded weapon in the house. It couldn't have happened that way.' I said, 'Tell me the truth. I'm your father. I might get upset with you, but I love you. And tell me the truth. I need to know the truth, John.'

"At that time, he said that David came to the house, came to the front door. John would not let him in. He asked about three or four times to come into the house. And John finally let him into the house."

John told his father that he left David for three or four minutes to take care of the dogs and when he came back in, he saw David standing by the refrigerator with the gun in his hand.

"I said, 'Where did he get the pistol from?' At that time, I realized that I had left the pistol [inaudible]. I told him, 'John, it couldn't happen. The gun was empty.' I said I unloaded the weapon. I put an empty magazine in it.

"He said he had taken the gun from David. He told David that he's not allowed to be in the house. He's not allowed to have ... and John isn't allowed to handle any weapons."

John told him that he took the weapon from David, stepped into the laundry room, and opened the door to the garage. He pulled the magazine out and placed the gun on the washing machine.

"And he said that there was a live magazine in it."

The boy's story was confusing both to the deputy and to investigators, but what was clear was that there was some manipulation of the weapon, and the gun was moved into the den.

The boy claimed he was pointing the gun at the floor, not at his friend.

"He said the muzzle flew up in the air. He didn't understand. He said … that he had emptied it. I said, 'John did you check the chamber?'

"And he said, 'No, Daddy, I didn't check the chamber.'"

There was another mystery, too. When David was taken to the hospital doctors found an unspent 9 mm round in the back of his throat.

"… I specifically asked John. I said, 'John were you trying to play Superman, you know, catch the bullet?' I said, 'Tell the truth, John. Did you point the weapon at him?' And he swears that he was pointing it at the ground.'"

The family hired veteran criminal defense attorney Jeffrey Pfister to defend their son, who was charged with armed manslaughter as a juvenile.

Pfister argued that the case should be dropped. It was an accident, he said.

"They were good friends; there was no animosity between them (*Sentinel*, Nov. 3, 1995)."

Ridgway pointed out that John changed his story three times and there were still questions.

Circuit Judge Jerry Lockett agreed. "This case is too important to turn on this motion."

As for the possibility of a culpable negligence charge, Ridgway told State Attorney Brad King that John probably loaded the weapon.

He also noted: "It appears there is a defect in the statute in that no prohibition exists for leaving an unloaded firearm, and ammunition to fit it, unsecured (Memorandum, Sept. 13, 1995)."

In December, court officials met again. One suggestion was to send John to a juvenile camp with counseling or halfway house. Another idea involved a plea bargain with a sentence of withholding adjudication of guilt. That would seal the record, which was a juvenile case anyway.

But that idea was tossed too. The charge was too serious. Another problem was that the case had already been heavily publicized locally. But the real question was: Would it look like a cover-up or slap on the wrist because of the dad's position with the Sheriff's Office? Or would it look like one police department doing a favor for another?

Trial was set for late January, 1996. Nerves were rubbed raw for both families.

"Their son is not responsible," said David's mother, Nancy. "They were just two teen-age boys doing what other boys would do—investigating a gun. Thirteen-year-olds make mistakes (*Sentinel*, Jan. 28, 1996)."

She said John's parents should be held accountable, and she said she was disappointed in the gun law.

She was also upset at the yawning silence that separated the two families that seemed to her to be a sign of disrespect or a lack of caring.

"We need to sit down and say, 'Look, this was a bad accident. But when they say nothing, and let the attorneys talk ....'"

She said she hoped the trial set for Jan. 29 would help heal the hurt.

"I hope so, but maybe not. May 14th is David's birthday. Then it will be the anniversary of his death. My son is never going to be with us again."

The deputy testified that the gun was unloaded when he left it on top of the refrigerator. He said it was a house rule never to leave a round in the chamber when a gun was brought into the house.

Pfister suggested that David might have loaded the weapon when John was outside feeding the dogs. Ridgway disagreed. Why would David load the gun, pretend he had not seen it, then sit in the recliner and allow what he knew was a loaded gun to be pointed at him?

As for the unspent bullet in David's throat, that indicated some "horseplay," Pfister said (*Sentinel*, Jan. 30, 1996). Physicians theorized that he swallowed the bullet after being shot in the face.

Lockett said he needed time to reflect before making a ruling. In an unprecedented move, he took custody of the firearm so he could get a better understanding of how it operated.

The next day, the judge found John guilty of manslaughter and sentenced him to a juvenile justice wilderness camp with counseling.

It was "another horrible tragedy in Lake County," he said (Feb. 1, 1996).

He ruled that John pointed the weapon at David and pulled the trigger but did not know the gun was loaded.

"It saddens me for you that you have to make this decision," the deputy told the judge.

David Jones' father asked for a mixture of compassion and punishment for his son's killer.

"After reading John's statements, it occurred to me that John was more concerned about whatever action his parents might take, especially his father, than in taking another person's life," he said.

Life had become an unimaginable hell for his family, he said.

"It's a tragedy so severe that unless you go through it you can't comprehend it. I'll never see my son grow up. I'll never have a grandson by him."

He also said, "My son was a very strong young man. One of the things he valued was friendship. He held John in high regard." He said David would have wanted compassion for his friend.

Ridgway, who said he couldn't remember a tougher case in18 years, recommended a 4, a mid-range punishment, on a juvenile justice scale of 1 to 10.

Higher level facilities were filled with "career criminals," he said.

There was no hesitation for the deputy to hug his son on the day of sentencing. John wept on his dad's shoulder. His mother, nerves frayed to the maximum, snapped at a news photographer: "Go away! Can't you see we've been tortured enough?"

The judge ordered that the boy have no contact with guns and ordered him confined to house arrest until an opening came up in a camp.

He then took the unusual step of urging the parents to get together to "share their grief." He said he knew there might be pending lawsuits but said attorneys should put their "lawyering" aside, at least for a time, to allow for some healing.

***

Why is there so much juvenile violence? And what can be done about it?

In dealing with the Keith Johnson middle school tragedy, I interviewed an expert who said many video games and movies were causing a "toxic addiction" to violence.

That might sound like a pat answer by a hip-pocket philosopher or editorial writer, but retired Army Lt. Col. Dave Grossman had taught at the U.S. Military Academy at West Point, wrote a scholarly book called *On Killing,* and helped counsel students and teachers in his hometown of Jonesboro, Ark., after a kid opened fire on students in that city. He was also a prosecution consultant in the Oklahoma City bombing trial of Timothy McVeigh, and he analyzed the school shooting in Paducah, Ky., that left three dead and five others wounded.

The 15-year-old shooter in Kentucky hit eight out of eight moving targets and barely moved his hands, yet he had never fired a handgun in his life.

"He was shooting at a screen," Grossman said. Some killers are addicted to "point-and-shoot games."

Computer simulation is so effective it has now become a major part of training for the military.

Grossman was brought in to discuss his findings by the Lake County School Board. He was asked who is to blame.

Some say there has to be personal accountability. Some say it is society's fault, mental illness, sin, or the guns themselves.

"There's enough blame to go around for everybody (*Sentinel,* April 3, 1999)," Grossman said.

***

One of the saddest things I ever witnessed was the outrageous behavior of a student when I was a teacher in a public middle school. Kids of that age, though half out of their minds with puberty and incessant blathering, can usually be controlled with appropriate discipline or even "the look," an evil-eye trick favored by teachers, moms, and married women everywhere. That was not the case with this kid, however. He would stare back with cold steel eyes as if he wanted to kill you.

He was a constant discipline problem and went out of his way not to do his schoolwork. One day he was gone, and when I found out he had moved to Texas I wasn't unhappy. A few days later, he was back.

"His dad didn't want him," the guidance counselor said.

No further explanation was necessary.

Chapter 19

Love hurts

Jolene Fisher was nervous when she walked through the door of her grandparents' darkened home. She was frightened when the door slammed behind her, petrified when she saw the glint of a knife blade, and was sure she was going to die when she realized that the man slashing her was the man who had once sworn to love and protect her.

Friends, family—virtually everyone, in fact—were stunned by the ferocity, and the fact that both Jolene, 21, and her 30-year-old estranged husband, Tony, survived.

Jolene had moved out of the home she shared with her husband and into her grandparents' home in a quiet, middle-class neighborhood in Eustis. She was afraid of Tony, and for good reason.

Between 1 p.m. on May 18, 1996, and 2 p.m. the next day, he had made a dozen threatening phone calls. In one call, he threatened to cut her head off with an ax. In another, he threatened to come over with a shotgun and shoot a friend of hers.

He had an ugly, violent past. Six years earlier he had jumped through a plate-glass window while armed with a sawed-off shotgun and dragged a woman out of her apartment.

"You're dead," he shouted, but a juvenile grabbed another shotgun and fired at his feet. He was charged with

13 crimes in that incident and went to prison for three years (*Sentinel,* May 22, 1996).

Jolene had come home on May 21 with a friend. As soon as she walked in, the door slammed behind her, leaving her friend outside. The friend ran next door for help.

"She was screaming that he would kill her," said neighbor, Jack Keck, who called police and rushed next door to help (*Sentinel*, May 22, 1996).

"I picked up a cast-iron dog doorstop and smashed the glass out," Keck said after first trying to smash the double-pane glass with a stick.

Keck thought she was being beaten.

"But when I went inside, there was blood everywhere. I had been to Vietnam, but I had never seen anything like that before."

By the time police arrived, Fisher had locked the bedroom door, but Tony had entered the room and was holding a nine-inch filet knife to her throat. He had struck her face several times with the pistol. He had cut his own throat.

Because they could not shoot without hitting Jolene, officers had to use pepper spray to free her.

She suffered a punctured lung, a lacerated liver, and had knife wounds down to the bones in her arms, and neck wounds. The worst injuries were to her hands, which she had used to block the knife blade as he tried repeatedly to cut her throat.

"Tendons were diced," said Jolene's grandmother, Yvonne McQueen. McQueen, who rushed home from a trip out of state, said, "I've never seen anything like it."

"I have seen the face of evil," McQueen said, after seeing the blood spilled in her home (*Sentinel,* June 2, 1996)."

Tony Fisher survived, despite cutting his carotid artery and esophagus. Even after police used pepper spray, he was too violent to be airlifted to a hospital.

Police said he broke into the home through a rear sliding-glass door after arming himself with a knife, a shotgun, and a .357-Magnum handgun.

Keck refused to call himself a hero.

"I just did what I had to do (May 22, 1996)."

She would have other guardian angels in her life, too.

Two days after being taken to the hospital, plastic surgeon Dr. Peter Marzek spent 10 hours putting sutures into her damaged tissue, tendons, and nerves, alternating between using a microscope and high-tech magnifying glasses called loupes. Nerve endings are one-quarter the size of a human hair; tendons are about a quarter-inch wide.

She would undergo more surgery two days later—more than 20 hours in all—to repair deep gashes on the back of her hand and cuts across the inside of her fingers. At one point, she grabbed the blade to keep it from reaching her throat.

"She probably had between 300 and 400 stitches, internally and externally," he said (*Sentinel,* July 13, 1997).

To keep her hand from becoming immobile from scar tissue, he installed a motion machine on her hand to make sure the hand would tense up and relax continually.

The surgery and months of assistance by physical therapist Pam Smith helped tremendously. She still had no feeling in her fingertips, however, and faced a long road of recovery.

But after initially referring to herself in the third person, and in words that sounded like headlines, she was regaining her strength and her confidence. The right-hander could hold a cup in her right hand and sip from it and could almost make a tight fist.

"Even my anesthesiologist said, 'You'll never use your hand again.'"

Yet, she dreamed of becoming a veterinarian, working with computers, or becoming a nurse.

She had the strong love and support of her family.

"She's a fighter. She is my hero," her grandmother said.

If she had not proved it the day she fought for her life, she proved it the day Tony Fisher was sentenced after pleading guilty to attempted murder and armed burglary.

He bowed his head and braced for a firestorm of anger. Instead, he faced a strong, confident woman who had learned what so few others had discovered.

"Technically, I'm a victim, but victims are buried. Survivors thrive," she told him before he was led off to serve 18 years in prison and 10 years' probation (*Sentinel*, Feb. 4, 1997).

***

One of the victims Jolene could have been referring to was 25-year-old Manuela "Mandy" Forbes, who was beaten to death by her boyfriend in 1994 and stuffed into a refrigerator.

Corey E. Brown, 22, said it was an "accident," which it was, *if* knocking your girlfriend to the floor and hitting her in the head with a brick at least three times after accusing her of infidelity can be considered an accident.

What he meant, of course, was that he didn't intend to kill her. That's what he claimed, anyway.

"He said she was screaming, and he just wanted her to be quiet," said Clermont Police Detective Danny Cheatham (*Sentinel,* April 15, 1994).

After killing her shortly after midnight, he put her in their bed and slept beside her. The next morning, he put her body in a closet and called a friend for help.

Together, the two geniuses decided to swap her bloody shirt for a clean one and got rid of the bloody brick and rags. The friend then suggested they stuff her into the refrigerator. They removed the food and the shelves, leaving only the condiments inside the door shelves, and folded her into the fetal position. Their fuzzy plan, Cheatham said, was to bury her in a remote cemetery somewhere.

In the meantime, Brown went to work at his grocery store job, apparently unaffected by what he had done, employees said later.

The two men decided they needed another helper, so they called another friend. But when that man realized what was going on, he made an excuse to leave and went straight to the police.

When Forbes' mother arrived in Central Florida from Germany she wept and said her worst fears had been realized.

"Her mother was thousands of miles away, on the other side of the world, and she still knew," Cheatham said.

Tragically, Forbes recognized the danger and left Brown, but she kept coming back.

Once, she had Cheatham stand watch while she took her things out of the apartment.

"The last thing she said to me was, 'If you see Corey, tell him I'm not coming back. And tell him not to come looking for me,'" Cheatham said (*Sentinel,* April 16, 1994).

That was in February. Brown had beaten her in October, yanking her out of a woman's apartment, slapping her, throwing her up against the wall, and kicking her in the head. She was taken to a hospital and treated for her injuries, which included a broken nose. He was charged with battery, paid a $250 fine, and ordered to take an anger management class.

She moved in with another friend, a woman whose mother had been killed in a domestic violence incident.

"Plenty of times my mom left, but just like Mandy, she kept going back and going back," the woman said (*Sentinel,* April 16). The friend said Brown had a way of sweet-talking Forbes in a "poetic, soft-spoken way."

"I told her the next time I saw her it would probably be in a coffin," the woman said. "But she never listened."

Domestic violence shelter operators say it is a familiar story. Often the abuser seems genuinely remorseful and promises never to do it again. Often, the woman is afraid because she does not have any money or a place to stay, has children, wants to salvage a long-term relationship, or might even be advised by well-intentioned clergy to stay in the marriage.

Forbes knew the danger.

She had obtained an anti-harassment court order after he stalked her in the parking lot of a fast-food restaurant where she worked at a second job. The restaurant also took out a trespass order against Brown. She also complained of trouble at her primary job in food service at a nursing home.

"I am seriously afraid, scared of this man and what he might do to me or the people who are trying to help me," she said in a written statement to police.

Brown won't be hurting any woman any time soon. He pleaded guilty to second-degree murder and was sentenced to 50 years in prison.

***

One of the most bizarre and controversial cases involved a law enforcement officer who was accused of battering his wife after she was found in her home with a broken collarbone and 80 percent of her body covered with bruises.

The problem for prosecutors, was that she said she couldn't remember how she got the injuries. She also did not want her husband to be charged with domestic violence, which is not unusual. But her struggles with mental illness and overdosing on pills, plus her husband's insistence that he was innocent did not convince investigators, and the case created a legal showdown and a mess of a case for prosecutors.

Pamela Baker, 44, stared at the police photographer on Sept. 14, 1997, her face looking like a black and blue human punching bag, complete with a shiner under one eye. Other 8-by-10 color photos show huge black splotches on her buttocks, yellow contusions, and cuts and scrapes all over her body.

"I've seen dead people who haven't looked this bad," Assistant State Attorney Sue Purdy told me (*Sentinel,* May 26, 1998).

When her daughter couldn't reach her mother on the phone on that day, she asked her aunt to check on her. Jean McDaniel found her sister lying nude on the bed, the house completely trashed, with food yanked out of the refrigerator and dropped on the floor, a table overturned, a laundry basket turned upside down, and plants knocked over.

McDaniel had seen it before but not quite this bad, she would later remark. Once, her sister was so overdosed on pills she fell asleep at the dining room table. Baker said she had a mental condition known as bipolar disorder, formerly known as manic depression, and was using a fistful of prescription drugs to fight the symptoms, including a tranquilizer, antidepressant, and anti-seizure medicines, and was also taking pills for hypertension.

Jesse Baker said he had locked himself in the bedroom while she went on a rampage and demanded an unlimited use of pills.

He said he went on to work the next morning after putting her to bed. He said he did not notice her dislocated shoulder, only some red spots on her body where she had injured herself.

When Pamela's niece learned of the injuries, she took her aunt to the hospital. Medical staff there called the Lake County Sheriff's Office.

"What's wrong with your shoulder?" Investigator Vaneese Schreiber asked.

"It's dislocated. It pulled away from my shoulder."

"How did that happen, Pam?"

"I don't know."

"How do you think it happened?"

"The only thing I can think of is, I fell and that, you know. I don't know."

"How did you get covered in all the bruises that you have?"

"Right, I ... don't know."

"Is it possible that somebody did this to you?"

"It's possible."

"Who could it have been?"

"Well, the only person around me was my husband."

"So, it could have been Jesse?"

"Yes."

"What kind of person is Jesse?"

"A very loving, giving, kind person."

"Does he have a mean side to him?"

"Not that I've ever seen."

She also told the investigator that she didn't want her husband to lose his job, and she didn't want to end up "a bag lady."

When Baker arrived at the hospital to see her, he was arrested by sheriff's deputies. She stayed in the hospital for seven days. He was fired from his 20-year job with the state game and fish commission where he was a sergeant and law enforcement officer.

He was charged with aggravated battery domestic violence and was ordered to stay away from his wife. The trial was delayed, not once but twice.

Then, in an unheard of move, Pamela Baker sued the State Attorney's Office, saying the order violated her Constitutional rights. The suit also stated that their 18-year marriage was "a relationship of love and devotion. Pamela Baker is unaware of any time during any point in her marriage to Jesse Baker that he has ever assaulted, hit, slapped, or in any way physically harmed [her] ...."

Through her attorney, she admitted in the suit that she had suffered from the effects of bipolar disorder for 20 years and had been taking prescription drugs to combat the symptoms.

"During the period of her marriage … [she] has, on more than one occasion, become intoxicated through use of prescription drugs; and has, at times, been unable to control her use of prescription drugs and her actions when under the influence of prescription drugs and incapacitated by her physical and psychological disorders."

She said she had never asked the state to intervene on her behalf, that her husband never harmed her and that she was sure her injuries were self-inflicted. She said she had a right to privacy and "freedom from government intrusion."

A judge dismissed the suit, but the couple was allowed to reunite.

"It's been a living hell," a relieved Jesse Baker said (*Sentinel,* June 5, 1998).

Pamela Baker said her doctors changed her prescriptions.

The State Attorney's Office always maintained that they were right to bring charges against Jesse, even if his wife didn't want to press the issue.

"If the law of the state of Florida says we have to wait to prosecute until the victim complains, we will be operating under radically different laws than the rest of the country," said Ric Ridgway, the chief assistant state attorney (*Sentinel,* Nov. 15, 1997).

He said his office recently had a case where the victim testified for the defense, despite witnesses testifying that they saw the attack taking place outside a store.

"We don't have to wait until someone is dead to act," Ridgway said.

Prosecutors and investigators are not the only ones who see misplaced loyalty.

"I've had women waiting at the door of the jail begging me to release their husband without bond," said Circuit Judge Mark Hill (*Sentinel,* Oct. 25, 1998).

One victim especially stood out in his mind. She had a black eye and a nose so severely broken it was pushed to the side of her face.

"Ma'am, you need attention first," he said, referring to medical aid. Then, he told her she needed to get some counseling. He had no authority to order her to get it, but hopefully she took the advice.

Prosecutors offered the 40-year-old Jesse Baker a plea deal: Take an anger management class and accept probation and there would be no trial. He refused. He told his lawyer, James Hope, that he was willing to risk being sent to prison for up to five years rather than admit to a crime he did not commit.

"I've got to win," Hope told me on the eve of the trial.

Hope, a brilliant, persuasive lawyer, laid it out for the six-member jury. He said there were "two Pam Bakers." One was alert with a normal IQ, and the other is a woman who is frequently overdosed and who has heard her dead brother's voice for 15 years.

He said she slit her wrist at age 15, said she once jumped out of a third-story window, and had recently put a gun in her mouth but couldn't figure out how to manipulate the gun's tricky trigger mechanism.

Purdy, a smart, fiery, hard-working, tough-as-nails prosecutor who hates domestic violence, promised jurors they would hear relatives say they overheard damning statements by Jesse. In one case, Purdy said a relative overheard Jesse say: "Tell 'em I did it. Just tell 'em I did it."

Pamela then reportedly said: "You know you did it!"

On Sept. 11, 1997, just days before Baker was hospitalized, her nephew drove her home because she was "a little intoxicated," Purdy told jurors.

He woke Jesse, who asked: "Did she kill herself?"

When the nephew said no, Jesse said, "I wish she had (*Sentinel*, Oct. 26, 1998)."

Later, however, the nephew testified that because the conversation happened more than a year ago, he could not remember exactly what was said.

Baker's sister also testified about finding her injured sister and her saying, "I fell a bunch of times."

The next day Jesse took the stand.

"I am absolutely not guilty of causing these injuries to my wife. That's a fact," he testified (*Sentinel,* Oct. 29, 1998).

He talked about her wild mood swings, hyperactivity, sleeplessness, and deep depression. He testified that she had once been injured in a car accident.

He also talked about her demanding pills the night she was injured. She was addicted to Xanax, he said.

"That was her favorite. That's the one that gave her the high."

He said he had to get up early the next morning, so he locked himself in the bedroom. He said he could hear her dump the contents of her purse, tear open cabinets and drawers, and could hear her stumbling over furniture. The next morning, he said he found her nude on the floor in front of the refrigerator near broken eggs and other food. He said he picked her up and put her in bed and went to work.

He said he didn't want to take her to the hospital because "all they have done in the past is give her more pills and increase my insurance bill."

Purdy, during cross-examination, pointed out that Pamela suffered from life-threatening seizures.

"Were you not concerned enough to call 911?" she asked.

She also accused him of not doing anything to help her with her drug addiction.

"I allowed her to go to the same doctor and he kept prescribing the same medicine," he admitted. He did say she was once "warehoused in a zombie-eyed state" in a mental hospital until he insisted that she be released.

Hope lit into Investigator Schreiber, who said she viewed Pamela Baker's self-inflicted injury story as "an excuse." He accused her of taking advantage of "a mentally feeble" and "pitiful, drugged-up woman."

Another sheriff's deputy testified that when he talked to Pamela at the hospital, "She did not understand what happened; that he had never beat her like this before."

Hope also criticized hospital employees who speculated that some marks looked like they had been caused by a boot or a belt buckle. They had been conditioned to believe that's what they were seeing, he told jurors.

After closing arguments, the jury came back with a verdict after only 1½ hours: Not guilty.

"All they [prosecutors] had were pictures," an alternate juror said *(Sentinel,* Oct. 30, 1998).

"I'm very glad it's over," Pamela Baker said. "It's been a long year."

Jesse Baker, whose facial muscles had been bunched into a knot, felt his whole body relax.

"I'm glad this part is over with," he said. "Now I'm hoping the Game and Fish Commission does the right thing and gives me my job back."

The front page of the Lake section of the *Sentinel* the next day featured a huge photo of the Bakers kissing each other in the courtroom. It could have been a wedding photo.

Less than two years later, she was dead. She was only 45 years old.

The autopsy would list her death as natural, the "result of an idiopathic ventricular arrhythmia, possibly associated with myocardial fibrosis." Idiopathic refers to a spontaneous event from an unknown source. Fibrosis refers to the stiffening of heart muscles, interfering with the muscles' ability to contract. Arrhythmia is an irregular, out-of-synch heartbeat.

Lab workers found traces of cyclobenzaprine in her body, which is an ingredient in muscle relaxers, and thioridazine, a drug prescribed for the treatment of schizophrenia.

Rx List, an Internet drug listing resource, notes that thioridazine has been associated with some kinds of arrhythmia and sudden death. It should only be prescribed for patients who are unable to take other kinds of prescribed drugs aimed at treating the mental disorder (rxlist.com/thioridazine-drug.htm).

***

Many cases are similar to the Fisher case, with the man thinking, "If I can't have her, no one will."

Christopher Ronson was such a man.

On April 20, 2008, he called a friend at 9:30 p.m. to say that his 39-year-old estranged wife, Laura Lynn, had gone out with another man.

The friend offered some good advice: Let it go. Move on.

Ronson called back a half hour later, however, to say he had done "something he was not going to like (*Star-Banner*, June 4, 2008)."

He had shot her and her friend, Michael Bubnow, 32, in the parking lot of the Chili's restaurant in Ocala. Now, he said, he was going to kill himself.

Ronson, 39, took off for the nearby entrance ramp to Interstate 75, heading west on an agonizing, tragic journey and making a series of phone calls as he went.

One of the first calls was to his children, ages 12 and 15.

"I did something really bad," he said, "I shot and killed your mother and the guy. Call your grandparents and have them come and pick you up." He ended the conversation by saying, "I love you. I'm next. I'll never see you again."

Restaurant workers and a police officer tried to help the shooting victims. Laura was dead, but Bubnow was alive and was able to identify his attacker. Ronson had confronted the couple inside the restaurant, he said, and then left. As the couple came out of the restaurant they were about to get into her Jeep when he appeared, and they exchanged a few words. Then, he started shooting.

Hours later, Ocala Police Detective Sgt. Chais Maier managed to get Ronson on his cell phone. Ronson asked if anyone was hurt. He said he had been under psychiatric care, was on medication, and wasn't sure what he had done. Maier told him that his wife had died, but he wasn't sure about Bubnow. Ronson said he had never hurt his wife. He told Maier that he said goodbye to his children and that he was going to kill himself.

The next evening, Maier got a call from Ronson's father, Robert. Ronson said he had spoken to his son at 9:45 p.m. He was near Houston, Texas, and he was "making suicide threats because he could not live with the consequences."

At about midnight, Walker County, Texas, deputies called Ocala police to tell them that Ronson had indeed committed suicide just off Interstate 45 with a .45-caliber handgun.

It is hard to fathom what's going on in people's heads. It's not clear from police records if Ronson was really under psychiatric care, but he wasn't thinking of his children when he killed their mother or the harm he was causing her friend.

Ronson left a note, saying he wanted his ashes to be spread in Lake Ontario, near his birthplace. He said he loved his children. They were the thing he lived for, he said, adding that he was sorry he wasn't stronger. The letter also talked about his love for his father, and that he wanted the children to live with his wife's parents.

"It's a sad chapter," said Laura's mother, Carol L. Fairclough, who said the children were "managing."

Bubnow's family told reporters that a bullet lodged near his spine caused him to be paralyzed for life.

***

Sometimes it's a cheating woman's husband who gets killed.

That's what happened when a 48-year-old man was gunned down by his wife's former lover after his wife broke off the affair.

The husband, who was the father of two teenage daughters, knew about the affair. He and his wife were trying to repair their marriage, sheriff's deputies said.

He was at his job at a hospital in Eustis when his wife called him to say she just passed her former boss and lover on the road. She said she was afraid he was heading to their home. The husband called a neighbor and learned that a car was in his driveway. He told a coworker to call the sheriff's office to report a trespasser and then drove to his house.

By the time he arrived, the 54-year-old Orlando businessman had broken into his home. About a minute later, the businessman shot the husband two times with a large-caliber handgun, then sat down on a couch in the living room and shot himself to death.

Investigators found intimate photos of the businessman and the woman that the man had brought to the home. No one knows what the two men said to each other.

"The only two who can tell us what really happened are gone," said sheriff's Lt. Cecil Garrett (*Sentinel,* Oct. 2, 1999).

***

Sometimes children are on the front lines in their parents' battles.

One man was arrested in 2001 and charged with aggravated battery with a motor vehicle and child abuse when he rammed his pickup truck into a flatbed truck driven by another man. There were kids in the pickup. Witnesses said the man loaded the kids into a Camaro that stopped at the crash site in a parking lot.

It was complicated. The officer's arrest report, written in what I call "police speak," said: "I spoke with the victim who stated that he is now intimate with the driver of the Camaro, which is the ex-girlfriend of the defendant and mother to the two children involved. The victim did not wish to make a written statement at this time. He did state that he has been a lifelong acquaintance."

One loser rammed his car into his girlfriend's vehicle when she said no to his marriage proposal (*Sentinel*, July 4, 1997). After the 57-year-old woman got into her car with her 3-year-old grandson, he kicked the car and smashed the mirror on the driver's door. When she drove off, he rammed the rear of her car with his vehicle.

Earlier in the month, he got into a fight with the woman's ex-husband. He sprayed the ex- with pepper spray but apparently ended up losing the fight anyway, suffering broken ribs and a lacerated liver. The ex- was charged with aggravated assault and battery in that battle. The man was charged with domestic violence battery and criminal mischief in the jilted lover spat.

Sadly, police reports are filled with instances of men hitting children that are being held in their mother's arms or striking kids who are trying to protect their moms. Sometimes children become witnesses to abuse so frequent and so unrelenting that they tend to think it is normal behavior, especially when drugs and alcohol are added to the mix.

In one case, a couple's 5-year-old son was forced to testify against his father.

When Oscar Murrillo took his wife, Lisa, to a hospital in Ocala with a stab wound to her chest, she told doctors she had been attacked in a Kmart parking lot by a black man who tried to steal her purse. The attack had happened in the Marion County town of Belleview, about 10 miles south of

Ocala, she said. Murillo told doctors he didn't see the attack because he was strapping his children in the car.

But the next day, she told detectives that her husband had stabbed her inside her car at a Kmart parking lot in Leesburg, 30 miles away.

She said she was tired of arguing with him and just wanted to drop him off at his pickup truck when she reached for the ignition key and felt the sharp blade of a knife being plunged into her chest.

"You stabbed me!" she exclaimed.

"I know I did," he said (*Sentinel*, Jan. 8, 1999).

He became enraged when she told him she was going to take their three children and move in with her mother for a while.

"If I can't have you, no one can," he told her (*Sentinel*, Jan. 6, 1999).

"I'm going to kill your three kids in front of you, then I'm going to kill you," she quoted him as saying.

The children began crying and she begged him not to hurt the children. She promised to go home with him if he took her to the hospital. She also promised to go along with her husband's robbery story.

She said he put her in the back seat, where she pulled the knife out of her chest. She was stabbed twice and suffered a collapsed lung in the attack.

Murrillo, 29, was charged with aggravated battery with a deadly weapon. When the trial began, Murrillo claimed his wife had filed a false police report about a rape in Miami, but Circuit Judge Jerry Lockett wouldn't allow the jury to hear the allegation. Assistant State Attorney Hugh Bass said it was not relevant to the stabbing case.

Lisa Murrillo told her story in court, and so did the couple's 5-year-old son.

"Is Oscar your daddy?" defense attorney Henry Ferro asked the little boy.

"Nope, not no more, 'cause he did something bad."

Ferro told jurors the boy had been "programmed," but the jurors took note.

Ferro disputed Lisa's story, saying there were inconsistencies, and said she was bowing to her family's pressure to leave him, so she made up a story to get rid of him.

She denied it. "It was even hard to tell police about this," she said.

The couple married when she became pregnant at 14. In 1997, he had been placed on probation for beating her with a belt.

She described him as a jealous, controlling man. Sometimes their battles were pushing and shoving matches. Sometimes they ended in fist fights, she said.

Murrillo, who was from Honduras, did not testify but after the jury found him guilty, he told the judge through an interpreter: "The thing that happened to my wife, I did not do it."

His wife was lying, he said at his sentencing. "She has her motives for doing it. Only she and God know it (*Sentinel*, July 15, 1999).

The standard sentence was 7 ½ years but Lockett imposed a term of 12 ½ years. A domestic violence law allowed for enhanced sentencing if the attack is witnessed by children and if the injuries are life threatening.

***

One woman's ordeal, which unfortunately is not that unusual, began when her man started mixing drugs and alcohol, in this case marijuana, whiskey, and crack cocaine, she said in a police report.

She had recently put one child up for adoption but was pregnant again, and the man was giving her an earful about it. He began calling her names and accusing her of not caring about the 5-year-old daughter they had together.

"When I didn't let that unnerve me, he started to get upset and threw lighters at me. My daughter woke up and witnessed him choke me in the bedroom."

He demanded sex. She refused and told him to get out. She said he hit her in the head with his fist.

"I then started screaming for help," she said in the Lady Lake police report.

She told her daughter to run for help, but the child was too frightened to go outside. "She is only 5 and scared of the boogie man," she said.

She said he let her get as far as the living room but began slamming her into the wall.

"… our daughter started pulling his hair, yelling: 'Let my mommy go!' He just kept pounding me into whatever was the nearest thing. I got free somehow and went to go out of the front door and he got a hold me and started slamming my face into the ceramic tile in the kitchen."

The whole time, she said, he was screaming at her, calling her names, and saying he was going to kill her.

"I somehow made it to the front door and ran like hell to the neighbors …," she said.

Police found clumps of hair and blood in the house, as well as crack pipes and other evidence. She concluded her statement by saying that he also "tried to hold me down in the [bath] water and drown me. I just kept fighting and thinking of my daughter. That was the most scariest thing that has ever happened in my life," she said.

"I am willing to press charges to the fullest."

Another woman who had had enough begged a judge to send her boyfriend to prison and throw away the key.

He had set her on fire in what the prosecutor called an act of "malicious torture" so heinous the Legislature had not even passed a law to classify the crime.

Even then she had mixed feelings.

"Some parts of me are still in love with him," the 32-year-old woman said of James E. Lyons. "But there is a monster inside there. He needs to be stopped," she told Circuit Judge Hale Stancil in the Sumter County courtroom (*Sentinel,* Feb.17, 2000).

She had initially gone along with Lyons' story about someone driving up and throwing a gasoline bomb at her. In fact, she said, the two were inside the home they shared and smoking crack cocaine when he doused her with gas and lit two matches, then blew them out before striking a third that set her ablaze. She suffered second- and third-degree burns.

Lyons said she had no credibility, that she faced charges of prostitution, grand theft, and criminal mischief.

Lyons' attorney sought a sentence of 30 to 40 years, but the judge imposed a life sentence, based in part, on his previous record.

He had just gotten out of prison for tying his then-girlfriend to an overturned couch and leaving for eight hours while their baby sat helplessly in a car seat in the middle of the room.

***

A lot of people reading these two women's accounts will probably heave a sigh of relief and thank their lucky stars they are not trapped in poverty, have not been forced to give up a child for adoption, and in the Lyons case, are not ensnared in substance abuse and alleged criminal behavior. But domestic violence crosses every social, ethnic, religious, and economic line.

That fact, and the fact that no one really knows what goes on in people's private lives, shook people in Ocala to the core in October 2003 when one of the most respected women in the community was slain by her husband.

Even sheriff's deputies were shocked when they raced to a private airstrip community to find a hangar on fire and a bloody man and his wife lying on an American flag on their adjoining home's patio.

After hearing several explosions in the hangars, the deputies ran across the yard to wait for the paramedics. Cheryl Deamer-Boykin had been shot in the head but was still alive. Her husband, Mark, who had called 911, was dead from a self-inflicted gunshot wound. A deer rifle and box of ammo was nearby.

Colleagues at West Marion Community Hospital where she was the administrator were stunned. They used such words as "splendid person, wonderful human being and great leader" to describe her, and many joined family at her bedside to pray and hope for her recovery *(Star-Banner,* Oct. 16, 2003).

Neighbors were also shocked.

"It's the last place you would expect something like this would happen," said one man. "They were mighty fine people ... mighty fine people."

"We walked with them in the mornings, and we never heard them at each other's throat or anything like that," said another resident of Leeward Air Ranch. The couple said Mark Boykin always volunteered to barbecue at community events and took good care of his lawn.

The truth was that things were far from perfect. In fact, Mark Boykin's life was spinning out of control. The day before the shooting a neighbor was reportedly at the home helping Cheryl pack her husband's belongings. She told a friend on Oct. 8 that he had been abusive, and she had told him to leave. Married for 12 years, he had apparently been unemployed as a stockbroker for some time.

A more complete picture became known when detectives found three letters written by Mark Boykin addressed to four people.

In a four-paragraph letter dated Sept. 23, he ranted about what he called his wife's "God complex." He accused her of being violent and of feeling threatened financially *(Star-Banner,* Oct. 16, 2003).

At the end of the typed letter, which was mailed to a hospital official where she worked, he wrote the following in bold, capital letters: "ONLY SUCKERS TAKE IT! REAL PEOPLE ANNIHILATE THE BASTARDS!"

A second letter was sent to a fishing tackle store. In that letter he claimed to have a terminal illness and asked them to sell his fishing rods to one of their good friends at a bargain price.

The third letter was placed inside the Boykins' cat carrier with their cat "Squeakers" and was set outside a neighbor's home on the morning of the shooting.

The couple, who were on their way to the Boykins' home, didn't discover the note until later. He claimed that his wife was planning to destroy him financially and that he could not take it anymore. He ended with, "be kind to each other. You are all you have." Much love, Mark."

Pat Gabriel, a longtime friend of Cheryl's, said Mark Boykin's allegations were not true.

"Far from it," she said. "Cheryl is nowhere near what Mark is trying to paint her to be. In the time I've known her, Cheryl is a gentle, kind, compassionate and sensitive woman."

She managed to cling to life until Oct. 22—13 days after the shooting. She died surrounded by friends and family. She was 46 years old.

Gabriel reflected on Cheryl's and Mark Boykin's life. "It looks like [he] was suffering from some serious mental health problems," she said. "It's a sad, sad, terrible tragedy. Maybe we all need to learn more about depression and suicide so we can stop this from happening (*Star-Banner*, Oct. 23, 2003)."

Her death did bring attention to the tragic problem, but if the public's awareness went up a notch with her murder, the issue gained even more focus with a shocking slaying that forced police to change the way they operated.

Debra Allen Vazquez, 50, was desperately trying to get away from her husband, Jose, on July 4, 2004. Witnesses say they saw the couple arguing near a Wal-Mart parking lot on that Sunday afternoon when she drove away in her car. He jumped into his pickup truck and rammed her car, trying to get her to stop.

She drove to the Ocala Police Department in the heart of the city on U.S. Highway 27-441. He punched her and tried to drag her out of her car as she kicked him and tried to fight back.

"I started to drive over there to break them up," said a witness who refused to give his name. "Then I saw that he had a shotgun and he shot her. He took her over to the side of the building and then got back into his car (*Star-Banner*, July 5, 2004)."

Jose shot her twice with his 12-gauge shotgun, once in the hand and once in the chest.

One woman walked over to her to comfort her in her final moments and to ask her if Jesus was her savior.

"I pray she could hear and take some comfort," she said.

He drove to a community 10 miles away, and with the engine running in his pickup truck, turned the gun on himself and shot himself to death.

The couple's 8-month-old grandson was found sitting in her car unharmed.

The public was perplexed, then outraged. How could this happen in a police department parking lot? Where were the cops?

The station, as it turned out, was unmanned. Everyone was out on patrol.

Once again, the community had lost a beloved, valued figure in the community. Vazquez was an award-winning associate communications professor at Central Florida Community College and a poet, respected by students and faculty alike.

People writing letters to the editor were aghast. One woman said Vazquez was doing what everyone should do when they are in danger: Seek help from police, but the police were not there for her. The police chief announced that someone would soon be at the station around the clock.

One witness said it wouldn't have made any difference.

After the shooting, Jose Vazquez had driven to a friend's home in Summerfield. The friend had been keeping some of his guns for about a month because of a "family problem," as he put it.

Jose had been to the friend's house earlier. He told him that he needed his shotgun to kill an animal "that had killed several of his farm animals." When he went back for a second time, he said he needed more ammunition. He seemed "nervous" and "hurried," the friend said. Then, as he was about to leave, Vazquez said: "Pray for me, I just killed my wife in front of the police, I've done a terrible thing (*Star-Banner*, July 7, 2004)."

Vazquez then drove away. His friend called 911. Deputies and officers found Vazquez dead in his truck nearby.

Friends and family said Jose was undergoing psychiatric care and was taking several medications, including Xanax.

Debra had taken shelter with one of her coworkers, but Vazquez's daughter said Jose had recently returned from Puerto Rico with $20,000 and plans to hire a hit man to "knock her off'" because she was helping Debra.

Debra and her friend were told they could get a protective restraining order. They never did. Court orders can be effective, but they are no guarantee of safety.

Court records indicated that the couple agreed in separate documents that their 31-year marriage was "irretrievably broken."

Friends, students, and coworkers mourned her loss. Students respected her, teachers said, because she challenged them.

One of her fellow teachers read a passage she had written about herself.

"I teach because I love language and I love people," she wrote. "My profession came to me gradually... I discovered I had an innate ability to get to the essence of the matter at hand.... Life should consist of learning until the day our brain no longer responds (*Star-Banner*, July 10, 2004)."

It's hard to imagine anything positive coming out of such a tragedy, but the slaying of the two professional women, plus a rash of other domestic violence murders, stirred Marion County residents into self-examination and action.

Marion County suffered seven domestic violence homicides in 2004—the eighth highest rate among Florida's 67 counties, according to the Florida Department of Law Enforcement (*Star-Banner*, Jan. 25, 2006).

The *Star-Banner* was filled with articles, editorials, and letters focusing on the problem. Groups were formed, seminars planned, and money was raised to build a new wing on the Domestic Violence/Sexual Assault Center in Ocala.

"If the community were to stand together and stand up and say we're not going to tolerate this kind of behavior, it may go further. We may be able to decrease the incidences of domestic violence," said Cathy Paris, executive director of the Women In Need Network. "Education and awareness are the most important things. If we all team up and network together, then we can actually be more productive and benefit our community," she said (*Star-Banner*, July 10, 2004).

"We want to have a place where the women feel comfortable to work on their problems, to make a difference, and won't go back home and be murdered," said abuse center director Dr. Judy Wilson, while announcing the 3,315 square-foot expansion. "It gives the women hope to not stay in a lethal situation (*Star-Banner*, Jan. 25, 2006)."

Shelters are a sad fact of life for a lot of women and children. One out of every four women and one out of nine men in the U.S. are victims of domestic abuse at some point in their lives, according to the Centers for Disease Control and Prevention (familydoctor.org).

Why do some men abuse their wives and girlfriends? They consider women and children to be their property, to be dealt with any way they choose, according to a former shelter operator I interviewed in1998.

Abusers can be extremely controlling, hypersensitive to perceived threats, wildly jealous, and manipulative.

The most dangerous time is when a woman tries to leave. Shelter operators urge victims to plan their escape carefully, hide money, and create an escape kit.

It's not just physical trauma that victims have to worry about. Psychological damage can be severe, including the effects on children.

Victims can suffer depression, anxiety, panic attacks, substance abuse, and post-traumatic stress disorder.

Children can have developmental problems, psychiatric disorders, school issues, engage in abusive behavior, and have low self-esteem, according to the American Pediatric Association. Kids sometimes mimic the destructive behavior they see at home.

"I've seen children beating their mothers," said another shelter operator.

Chapter 20

Dead man talking

"It is a capital mistake to theorize before one has data. Insensibly one begins to twist facts to suit theories, instead of theories to suit facts." --
Sherlock Holmes, "A Scandal in Bohemia."

"I thought you might want to know," my source said on the phone. "The Mount Dora Police Department has classified a homicide as a natural. That's not right. This is murder."

He had my attention when he said, "Mount Dora," let alone "murder." The little town that prides itself on its annual art festival and looking like a movie set for an MGM musical, was reeling from series of violent attacks, including that of an elderly man whose throat was cut during a home invasion robbery, a woman hospitalized after another home invasion, and an attack on a woman walking down the street. Now, a man found dead in his home may have been suffocated by an armed intruder.

There were obvious clues that were overlooked in the newest incident, said my source, who insisted on remaining anonymous.

A neighbor found Robert Terrell's body kneeling next to a daybed on Dec. 30, 1998, his arms outstretched toward a pillow. A knife was lying on the floor near the 85-year-old.

Police found his wallet, but there was no money in it, and he usually carried about $100. There was also broken glass near the door and signs that a doorjamb had been damaged so severely the door could no longer be shut tight. The most obvious red flag of all, however, was that the phone line had been cut.

Then, there were the rumors; rumors that one of the suspects in the case of an elderly man whose throat had been cut, had bragged of "suffocating an old man" in another robbery.

If it was a murder that was classified as a natural death, it was, at best, gross incompetence. The worst scenario was that the cops, who were feeling the heat from a series of unsolved cases, were trying to sweep it under the rug.

The turmoil that surrounded the police department began on Dec. 28, 1998. That's when race walker Frances Meli was stabbed and slashed by a robber while she was exercising at dusk three blocks from the police department. She screamed for help, but not before the attacker managed to slice an artery near her heart, stabbed her in the leg, and cut her spleen, which had had to be removed.

The attack on Meli, who was a civic leader, shocked and angered residents.

"We're afraid, but we're not going to stand for this," one woman said at a rally that drew more than 200 people, including the mayor (*Sentinel*, Jan. 3, 1999).

"We're concerned about the type of crimes becoming more violent and frequent," said a friend of Meli's.

In a less-publicized case, another woman was robbed in her home on Dec. 13. The man who robbed 71-year-old Nellie Poole held a knife to her throat.

Poole suffered heart issues after the robbery. While recovering in the hospital, someone set fire to her house.

It was while she was in the hospital that she told her daughter that she recognized her attacker in a TV news report about another Mount Dora attack. The robber who attacked her had been arrested in the home invasion and murder of Billy Simpson, a church deacon. Simpson had been beaten and his throat cut in a home invasion on Jan. 18.

Police, who were roundly criticized for failing to make an arrest in the Meli and Poole cases, acted quickly in the Simpson case because the case unfolded before their very eyes.

They were called to the modest home of the 84-year-old retired insurance salesman at 11 p.m. after Simpson's next-door neighbor saw someone using a flashlight inside the house. She also heard someone say, "Hurry, hurry, faster, faster."

She then saw some young men ride away on bicycles and two others stealing Simpson's grey 1995 Oldsmobile.

At 11:50 p.m., an officer spotted Terrell A. "Bossy" Manor, 16, riding a bicycle. The officer demanded that Manor stop and tell him where he had been for the past hour.

"Why should I?" he asked.

"Because I said so!" the cop replied. He told him he was investigating an incident involving juveniles and bicycles. As he was getting out of the car, the officer saw Manor reach into his pocket and throw something into knee-high grass.

The cop asked him what he had thrown.

"It was nothing, man!" Manor replied, but with another officer keeping an eye on Manor, the cop searched for three or four minutes and found a set of keys.

Officers took Manor and the keys to Simpson's house where they used one of the keys to unlock a padlock on a shed in the back yard. Police soon found Simpson's car abandoned in a field. The keys on the ring also unlocked and started the car.

Manor claimed he found the keys. Asked why he threw them, he said: "I thought you were looking for keys. I don't know why. I just had a feeling."

It wasn't long before officers found Antony Lillie, 18, and Anthony L. Conyers, 14, who went by the street name of "Tony Woods," sitting in a car.

"You've got the wrong [n-word]," Conyers shouted. But it didn't take long for Conyers to admit that he had been inside the murder home with the others.

Police said the teens picked Simpson to be their victim because "they wanted to do an elderly person (*Sentinel*, Jan. 19, 1999)."

Despite the arrests, city residents were not yet able to breathe a sigh of relief. The suspected knife-wielding ringleader, Roosevelt "Red" Hackney, 19, was nowhere to be found. Hackney was a young man with a much older person's rap sheet, including a charge of threatening to kill a police officer.

Hackney initially looked like a good fit for the Simpson and Meli crimes. For one thing, a composite sketch of Meli's attacker resembled his mug shot.

"He's running but he's not going to outrun us," Mount Dora Investigator Guy Dailey said.

Manor told police the teens hatched the plan in a game room in town. Hackney said he knew of an elderly man who lived alone and told the teens they could each expect to get $100.

"Roosevelt said, 'If someone comes out, we are going to have to kill him,'" Manor said. "He said that before we went in. The rest of us didn't agree with that. Roosevelt laughed and said he didn't care."

Simpson came out of his bedroom and exclaimed: "What are you doing?" He then began to struggle with them, Manor said.

"Roosevelt hit him with his fists and started kicking him and said, 'I'm not gonna get caught.'"

Hackney stole a VCR and rode off on his bicycle. Manor drove the car.

Police went to Hackney's home the next day. He was gone but officers found Simpson's stolen VCR and a radio/cassette player.

Manor's story surrounding the Simpson murder would be refuted by others, including Hackney. No wonder, since he kept changing his story. After denying that he had found the keys and had not entered the house, he claimed to have taken the car after it was ditched behind some apartments. Then, he admitted taking the car at the crime scene. He said he took the keys from the kitchen counter. He finally admitted to driving the car. He then said, "I kicked the door in. I was the second one in the house."

Police said he also lied about his companions, initially giving cops the names of people from Orlando.

Hackney was arrested a short time after the Simpson murder in Miami.

But if Manor was blaming Hackney for killing Simpson, he was taking all the credit for Terrell's slaying when he flashed a wad of cash and bragged to kids that he had "suffocated" a man in a different robbery.

The cops heard rumors of the bragging too, including veteran Lake County sheriff's detective Ken Adams. Adams would soon write in a report that he had received a phone call from "an unknown person" listing the suspicious clues ignored by police at Terrell's house and the suffocation rumor. He contacted an investigator with the Mount Dora Police Department. That investigator had heard the rumor, too, but it wasn't his case. He referred him to Dailey.

Dailey said he did not learn of the cut phone line until a day or two after Terrell's death. He said there was no obvious sign of a robbery. The house was not "tossed," with drawers pulled out and things dumped on the floor. He was aware of broken jalousie glass in the door, but he said Terrell's girlfriend, Gwendolyn Manning, said Terrell might have broken it himself. He was suffering some early form of dementia and may have locked himself out accidentally. He was not aware that another door was open in the house.

It was Manning—not police—who found the cut phone line, and it was Manning who raised questions about money missing in Terrell's wallet. She also found an empty bank envelope.

A neighbor told Adams that Terrell asked for change for a $5 shortly before the attack. He had several bills in his wallet. Friends said he generally kept $100 on hand.

Adams, with permission of one of Terrell's neighbors, who served as a kind of caretaker for the property, looked around the house. He viewed the broken glass around the door handle, the damaged wooden door frame, and cut phone line as obvious signs of a break-in.

Adams relayed his concerns to Assistant State Attorney Bill Gross and Medical Examiner Dr. Janet Pillow, according to a deposition. Both agreed the body should be exhumed and a thorough autopsy performed.

Police had not even relayed any information to the medical examiner's office that would have resulted in a full autopsy. Pathologists had been told that Terrell had a heart condition, which was true, so they had only performed an external examination. There were no obvious signs of trauma, and he was elderly, so he was released to a funeral home, embalmed, and buried.

At first, the sheriff's office offered its help to Mount Dora, including the use of its crime scene technicians. Soon, however, the sheriff announced it was taking over the case.

Adams asked Mount Dora officers for all the information they had in the Terrell investigation. They handed him a single page "Unattended Death" report that said virtually nothing, except that Terrell was known to have had a bad heart.

At the time, I wasn't having an easy time dealing with Mount Dora police myself, and I wasn't the only reporter having trouble. One lieutenant in particular delighted in abusing reporters, withholding information, and just being as arrogant as possible. I can understand not liking reporters. We are generally about as welcome as death at a birthday party, but Florida's public records laws are strict and straightforward.

"I did not notice anything unusual throughout the residence," wrote Officer Keith Flanary, the first officer on the scene, in his skimpy report. "The items in the room did not appear to be disturbance (sic) and nothing appeared to be missing. Due to my experience of investigating burglaries, it appeared that a burglary did not occur at the residence."

He did not say how much experience he had.

But whole thing looked fishy to the sheriff's office. One crime scene photo showed a knife on the floor near Terrell's body. Another showed that the knife had been removed.

"What is this?" Adams wondered after seeing the photos.

The first officer on the scene later said he kicked the knife out of the way "for officer safety."

It wasn't clear how "officer safety" was involved. Did the officers think the dead man was going to stab them?

Dailey said in a deposition that he was "a little bit curious" about the knife, but he said there was no sign of trauma. "… there wasn't a cut, a scratch, a scrape, nothing."

Manning, who described herself as Terrell's "lady friend" of eight years, was anything but satisfied with the police work and said so in a letter to prosecutor Bill Gross on Feb. 23, 1999.

"I ask you—or anyone who *really* cares—if they had a loved one who died and there was a *great* possibility that their loved one was murdered, would they want the person(s) responsible for their death to get away with killing them? The answer to this question is *no* (her emphasis)!"

She also wrote: "I have seen a picture of the knife that was found beside Bob's body. Although I had visited his home and cooked in his kitchen *many* times, I have *never* seen that knife there (her emphasis)."

Because police wrote the death off as natural, they did not process the knife for evidence. In fact, someone put it into a kitchen drawer. When Terrell's relatives came and took some of his belongings, a sister from Alabama took the knife, along with some other items. When she learned that the knife might be important to the investigation, she mailed it to Manning, who then gave it to Adams.

As for the kneeling position his body was in, police figured he was "praying" when he died.

"It was just weird," Adams said. To him, it looked like Terrell might have been trying to resist someone placing the pillow over his face.

Nor were sheriff's investigators buying the idea that Terrell locked himself out. A neighbor had taken Terrell to a grocery store the day before and brought him back home. There was no damage to the door. In fact, Terrell had to use a key to get in, the neighbor said.

The cut phone line was the clincher, however. Dailey said in deposition that he thought the cut phone line was "a little odd."

Manning acknowledged that Terrell had a little bit of dementia, but nothing on any scale that would result in him cutting his own phone line.

There was also just plain old sloppiness during the investigation. Police, for example, did not bother to check with Terrell's neighbors.

"I asked them if they found any money," Adams said in an interview for this book.

"Well, he had no money," they said.

"I said he had about $100 on him."

"How do you know that?"

"Because a neighbor told me," Adams replied.

Nor had Mount Dora police checked into the suffocation rumors.

"I heard that, too," one officer admitted.

Sheriff's investigators tracked down kids in the neighborhood to see if they could verify the reports. One youth said he was hanging around a basketball court when "Bossy" Manor walked up.

"He came up, he was like, he showed us a whole bunch of money and he was like, 'I smothered the dude down the road.'

"I thought he was joking around. Then he started pulling out money and all that kind of stuff," he said in a deposition.

Mount Dora Police officers interviewed Manor concerning Terrell's death.

Manor, who had done some odd jobs for Terrell in the past, admitted going to the house on Dec. 29. He said they ate watermelon and drank some beer. He said he left and came back later and found Terrell dead. He didn't call police, he said, because he was "scared."

Dailey would recall in a deposition that he figured Manor was lying to him.

A: "Well, he told me a couple of things and I was pretty impressed, you know. One, because I can't do it. He told me that when he went to see Mr. Terrell, that he visits him all the time, and you know, they're friends, that they sit down. And that Mr. Terrell drank a whole beer in one gulp, and I was impressed."

Q: "For an 85-year-old man."

A: A can of beer, yeah. That was pretty impressive, and I go, 'Wow.' But not only that, but that Terrell drank beer with him.

Q: "Oh, with a minor?"

A: That he gave Bossy a beer, too. And later on, I talked with Ms. Manning again. She said yes, he would drink a beer, you know, when the boys were there. There's no way he could chug a beer."

For one thing, he didn't allow himself to get drunk. Besides, he couldn't chug a beer if he wanted to. It would "back up on him," she explained.

Not only was Manning pushing for authorities to find out who killed her friend, but she was a keen observer, too.

When Adams conducted a taped interview with her three months after the homicide, she recalled seeing Terrell's watermelon in the refrigerator—still wrapped and uneaten.

Manning was sweet-natured and soft-spoken, but she was nobody's fool. A member of the Eustis City Council, she knew how things worked and she knew how to get things done.

"She was frequently quoted in the news," Dailey said in a deposition. "I know that there was communication between her and the chief, and the chief and the lieutenant. And she's the only one that really knows how many people she contacted to kind of push things."

She was, in fact, more interested in getting Terrell's body exhumed than his own family.

"There are too many unanswered questions, too many things found amiss," Manning told me (*Sentinel*, March 24, 1999). "I couldn't be at peace with it. I never believed Bob died of a heart attack."

For one thing, he had been healthy recently, she said, thanks to his medications and the defibrillator.

Adams said in his deposition that he talked to one of Terrell's brothers, who believed that the Mount Dora Police had not done anything to investigate his brother's death as a homicide. But his position was that authorities should let his brother rest in peace.

"… I prefer not to disturb him," he said in a letter to Dailey. "He's resting. If you dig him up, they will only … chop him all to pieces and put him back in his box all cut up."

Meanwhile, news stories by me and police reporter Karin Meadows, which included Manning's outrage, and the *Sentinel's* columnists and editorial writers, were pushing the state to dig up the body.

"This is not something we do every day," a harassed prosecutor told me. "There are procedures for this kind of thing."

Because Terrell and Manning were not married, permission to dig up the body had to come from Terrell's family. Fortunately, another brother was willing to give permission and a judge wrote a court order for disinterment.

On March 23, 1999, a funeral home opened the grave and Terrell's remains were taken to the Medical Examiner's Office. Adams and a sheriff's evidence technician watched Dr. Pillow perform the autopsy. No one from Mount Dora was present.

She removed the pacemaker from Terrell's body, which was then taken to the medical center where it had been installed.

She also removed fibers found in Terrell's nose, in an effort to compare them to the pillow found near his body. For the sake of thoroughness, Adams also talked to the funeral home to see if the fibers could have come from the embalming process.

The next day, the funeral home picked up the body and reburied it in Edgewood Cemetery in Mount Dora.

In early May, a grand jury was convened. The panel questioned Dailey, Adams, Dr. Pillow, and Manning. Pillow's ruling this time on the cause of death was "probable homicide."

Pillow has since moved out of the area. Medical examiner records are unclear, with some possibly even missing, so it is not entirely clear how the pathologist arrived at her finding, but her report helped push the case to the forefront.

Manor was indicted on charges of first-degree murder, burglary, and robbery.

Manning was happy with the panel's findings and glad she did not give up, though there were times when she doubted the case would ever be investigated seriously, especially when the police department wrote "HEART ATTACK" on the case file and did not bother to tell the medical examiner's office of any suspicious circumstances.

"I just believe in justice and the system," she said (*Sentinel,* May 6, 1999).

Sheriff George Knupp said he felt like his department had to take the case away from Mount Dora.

"The public sentiment was that nothing was being done. I felt like I needed to jump in and do something about it."

It wasn't just public sentiment. Nellie Poole's family was irate, too. Police never bothered to talk to her in the hospital, despite telling her family she recognized her Dec. 13 attacker in the TV news report. She died on Feb. 26.

"If they had pursued my mother's robbery as diligently as Mr. Simpson, maybe Mr. Simpson's life would have been spared," said Poole's daughter, Estella Crummer (*Sentinel,* March 14, 1999).

Mount Dora, sitting atop an angry beehive of public backlash, finally added its name to the list of agencies wanting the body exhumed. The city agreed to foot the bill for all expenses except the autopsy, which the county funded.

Despite the investigative victories, prosecutor Bill Gross wasn't looking forward to going to trial in the Simpson case. For one thing, the teens were telling conflicting stories.

That's common in these types of cases," Gross said, "people pointing the finger at the other guy, but we were pretty confident that we could place the knife in Manor's hands."

Hackney denied killing Simpson. "I seen Bossy cut the man's throat," he told investigators.

Conyers denied killing the man.

One of the teens said Manor had purchased the long, curved-bladed knife at a flea market.

There were other witnesses in the case who shed light on what happened.

Conyers' sister said she saw Manor come to her house to change shirts, even though her brother's shirt did not fit Manor. She later identified the shirt for police so they could test it for blood.

There were other breaks. An investigator talking to another teen, Reggie Conley, about an unrelated case testified in a deposition that Manor suddenly started blurting out information about the Simpson murder.

Conley said he had talked to Hackney and Manor before the slaying at 8:30 p.m. that evening.

"Bossy told me they was gonna do a 'lick,'" referring to a slaying or a robbery. They asked him if he wanted to come along. He said no.

He later saw the teens, along with Conyers and Lillie, in the dead man's stolen car. They were wearing gloves, he said, and they threw the gloves in the woods behind a friend's house.

The teens boasted that they had robbed someone.

"Bossy told me he killed the insurance man, Mr. Simpson, because he looked him in the face. Tony Conyers held his knees in the man's back, held his head up, and Bossy slit the man's throat. They told me that Tony Lillie, Tony Conyers, and Bossy beat the man. They beat the man down and killed him and stuff. They said Roosevelt was outside."

But the biggest problem the prosecutor faced in both the Terrell and Simpson cases came from his official witnesses: Mount Dora police officers.

In the Simpson case, for example, sheriff's evidence technicians were sent to help Mount Dora officers recover stolen items from Hackney's home. Crime scene technicians were using gloves to protect any possible fingerprint evidence. "You don't need to do that," one Mount Dora officer said, and began picking things up with his bare hands.

Gross later asked Mount Dora police if there was a tape inside the cassette player that belonged to Simpson. A Phil Coulter tape had been a favorite of Simpson's late wife. It was indeed inside the player. "They hadn't even looked," Gross said.

Gross decided to try his luck by trying Conyers first. He was especially hopeful because he was so young (14 at the time of the crime), and he didn't come with a long criminal record.

Gross was also hoping to use some sentencing leverage with the young man. If convicted of first-degree murder, he would be sentenced to a mandatory term of life in prison with no chance of parole. Anyone convicted of burglary when someone is murdered during the burglary is guilty of felony murder. But Conyers refused to take a plea deal and went to trial.

Gross was also frustrated by Reginald Conley, who had seen the teens in the dead man's stolen car and heard them boasting.

"I knew how hard it was going to be for him to testify against his buddies," Gross said, "so I went to the jail, where he was held on some charge, and talked to him about what he saw and what he was going to say, until he was good to go. The next day he came down with a case of amnesia. I was so mad. It was one of the most frustrating things …. He kept saying, 'I don't remember that.' I said, 'Well, you remembered it last night!'"

Conyers took the stand in his own defense and said that he didn't know his friends were planning to burglarize Simpson's home. He said he entered the home briefly because he was "curious *(Sentinel, Aug. 9, 2001)*."

Initially he had told police that he and Manor stood outside the house while the others went inside. During the trial, he said Manor was inside.

Gross asked: "Bossy did kill that man, didn't he?"

"I'm not sure who did it, sir," Conyers replied.

Defense attorney James Hope, in his closing argument, criticized the state's "lack of meaningful evidence." He also said: "There is no crime called felony-being-there."

He described Conyers as "an eighth-grade tag-along ... following the wrong crowd, yes, but an aid and abettor, no."

When the jury went out to deliberate the fate of Conyers, Gross told the defense attorney that he would somehow, "by hook or crook," get Conyers' sentence reduced if he would testify against the others—even if he was convicted of first-degree murder.

Conyers agreed to the deal.

Members of the jury, some with tears in their eyes, found him guilty.

His sister Anthonette, 18, sobbed in the courtroom.

"I don't feel like it was right," she said later. "He wouldn't have done that. I think he [thought] he had a chance. He was at the wrong place at the wrong time (*Sentinel,* Aug. 10, 2001)."

"It's a tragedy because this kid is facing the rest of his life behind bars," Gross said. "It's extremely harsh ... for a kid," he added.

But in his closing argument, Gross noted there was a reason the Legislature passed such a tough law calling for maximum punishment for home invasions. "They were basically saying, "Don't do this anymore."

In an interview for this book, Gross said: "After the trial, I brought a guy in from Orlando and paid him $500 to do a polygraph. He called me up and said the kid refused to take the test. I was so angry. I tried everything I could to help him. By that time, I was just over it."

The judge imposed a life sentence on Conyers six months later.

Even without the threat of Conyers testifying against them, the others suddenly were interested in taking plea deals. Lillie, however, was so mentally challenged a judge ruled he was incompetent to aid his lawyers in his defense.

He was sent to a mental hospital and later released to the care of his mother.

Manor also agreed to a plea of second-degree murder for both murders and was sentenced to 50 years in prison.

Hackney pleaded guilty to principal to second degree murder, along with the burglary and robbery charges. He was sentenced to 25 years in prison and 10 years' probation. He also pleaded no contest to aggravated battery and attempted robbery with a deadly weapon and attempted armed kidnapping in the stabbing of race walker Meli. He received a 15-year prison sentence in that case, to run concurrently with the Simpson slayings.

By March, Mount Dora's city manager decided it was time for a change and announced the firing of the police chief.

She said the change was not prompted by the recent rash of violent crimes but, in a rhetorical leap that only bureaucrats can achieve, said he should have done more to calm the fears of citizens.

"It is time for the city to have a leader who wants to be there 100 percent, who is proactive, progressive, and exudes confidence," Bernice Brinson said. "The leader of the department needs a vision and has to express it to his subordinates and the community (*Sentinel*, March 10, 1999)."

She said some officers felt that he was indifferent and no longer cared about the job.

"I feel like I was a scapegoat for new, high-profile crimes," the chief said later (*Sentinel,* March 28, 1999). He insisted that people enjoyed working for him.

What the city manager did not share with everyone was that the chief had been having a meltdown.

In July, the former chief wrote to her and told her he was applying for disability retirement from the Police Retirement Board. He said he had also applied for Social Security disability.

He said he made the mistake of being "married to the job."

"The stress of working for Mount Dora has cost me so much," he wrote. "I lost my wife, lost my job, lost my steady income, lost my reputation, lost my friends, lost my associates, lost my co-workers, and even lost my sanity."

The 48-year-old man also lost his girlfriend of two months in February. She filed a complaint in court claiming he was stalking her.

The 30-year-old woman, who was a member of a prestigious art group, said he never threatened her but described him as "a desperate man" and said she was "deeply concerned" for her safety.

The newly fired chief denied any wrongdoing. "I don't know why she is doing this. I feel like my whole world is crashing down (*Sentinel*, March 12, 1999)."

He told his side of the story to prosecutors. At a hearing, a judge rejected her request for a permanent protective injunction against him but told him to stay away.

"No calling, no writing, no contact, no saying hello, no nothing," the judge told him (*Sentinel,* March 25, 1999).

"I'd like to wake up and realize that this has been a nightmare," the 19-year-employee had said just two weeks earlier. "My reputation is completely ruined, and I've been fired."

The city eventually hired top Orlando homicide officer Randy Scoggins as chief.

Looking back, it is still hard to believe how police officers could miss so many signs.

"A lot of people didn't see a lot of things," Adams said.

There was, for example, the neighbor, Andrew Watson, who went to Terrell's house looking for him when Manning couldn't reach Terrell on the phone.

Watson did not get a response to knocking on the door and ringing the doorbell.

"He said that he entered the house and called for Mr. Terrell and got no response," Adams noted in his report. "He said that he checked the house and walked to the family room and looked to his right and did not see the victim. Mr. Watson said he did not look to the left side of the room."

He went home and called Manning, who urged him to go back and check outside. When he went back inside, he looked to the left, saw Terrell's body and called 911.

"One elderly man checking on another," Adams reflected.

"I think they were overwhelmed," Adams said recently of Mount Dora police in his characteristic gentlemanly way. "They were probably stressed and didn't want to have to deal with anything else."

"I was so glad I could settle that case," Gross said of Terrell's suffocation.

"There were so many problems with that case. For one thing I would have had to call a bunch of police officers liars."

For me, as a journalist, writing stories that prompted the exhumation of a homicide victim and pursuit of the killer by the authorities, it was a chance to set the record straight, to make things right for an elderly man who was murdered in his own home.

Chapter 21

Senseless

"Jesus, get these demons out of our house!" the wife of the retired preacher shouted in a desperate prayer, but the evil that was about to claim her and her husband's life kept coming (*Sentinel*, June 25, 2000). Within minutes, a quiet farmhouse on the edge of a tiny town was turned into house of murder, blood, and horror.

When law enforcement officers arrived, they found 71-year-old Lindsey Croft dead and sitting upright on a couch with 19 stab wounds to his head and five to his torso. Lucille Croft, 67, had suffered multiple stab wounds, including several defensive wounds. Two knives were protruding from the back of her head.

The first inkling of trouble in Center Hill came in the form of a hysterical woman on the phone with a 911 dispatcher.

"He killed those two people!" screamed Judy Brigham. "He stole all my money!" she added in the 8:45 p.m. call (*Sentinel*, Jan. 22, 2000).

Brigham explained that she was talking about two separate incidents. In the second, Richard S. Boone, Jr., 18, came to her house with her son, Scott, 18. Boone attacked her husband and stole her purse containing $1,300 she had set aside for rent.

In the first incident, Scott Brigham said he and Boone were in a car that broke down, so they walked to the Croft house so they could use the phone to call for a ride.

Lindsey Croft, who sold cattle at a local market, knew Boone because the young man worked there.

Shortly after asking to use the phone, however, "something snapped" in Boone, said Center Hill Police Chief Steve Allen. The two teens took the Crofts' 1995 Grand Mercury Marquis and drove to Brigham's house. After Boone took Judy Brigham's purse, he drove off in the Crofts' car.

Sumter County Sheriff's deputies arrested Scott and took him to the site of what they called a "frenzied" killing.

Sumter deputies called the Lake County Sheriff's Office to say that Boone might be headed to a poor, drug-infested community in that county called Stuckey.

Deputies found the stolen car just outside of Stuckey. It had left the road, overturned, and ended up five rows deep in an orange grove. As they approached a local drug hideout, Boone walked out and surrendered.

Center Hill, population 900, was stunned, both by the horrific violence and the loss of the Crofts.

"There's just no reason for the killing—that's what gets me," said Gary Sutton, a member of the church that Croft was serving. "They were good people (*Sentinel*, Jan. 24, 2000).

Friends said the couple would have given the two young men their car if they had asked for it.

In Ohio, friends said he gave a needy family his grocery money, figuring they needed it more than he did.

"I guess he went hungry for the next couple of days, but it didn't matter to him," the friend said.

He didn't collect his pay at the little church he was serving temporarily so the church could pay its utility bills.

The slayings also shocked Boone's father.

"He had to be on something," Richard Boone, Sr. said. "This is not the Ricky I know. He snapped (*Sentinel*, Jan. 23, 2000)."

He visited Lucille's family, the Huetts, to apologize for his son's actions.

"This is a terrible tragedy. I'm just so sorry for that family," he said.

In November 1999, a judge signed an order committing Ricky to a mental hospital for drug treatment.

Boone, Sr. wrote a letter to the judge.

"I thought it would help him. It lasted awhile, but now he's 18, and he's back on these drugs so bad that he stays out to all hours, blows his money on drugs and is broke the morning after pay day. He's ... stealing things such as stereo, money and speakers from our house and from his grandparents' house, and Lord knows who else, to supply his needs (*Sentinel*, March 9, 2000)."

He said family members tried to talk to him.

"He needs professional help before he either gets killed by those people who supply him, or he kills himself."

Ricky told cops that it was Brigham's idea to steal the Crofts' car and he handed him an empty wine cooler bottle to strike Lindsey Croft in the head.

Authorities believed Brigham's version, however. Evidence technicians could find no blood on Brigham's hands or clothing.

Prosecutors dropped the charges against Brigham.

Over a year later, Ricky, his face contorted in tears, pleaded guilty. His father wept, too.

"I'm so terribly sorry this happened," Boone, Sr. said as he turned to the Crofts' grief-stricken family sitting in the courtroom (*Sentinel*, Feb. 8, 2001).

The Crofts' son, Dale, addressed the court.

"I'm sad for his family—they lost too. They lost their son. I'm sad for Ricky because he threw his life away. He destroyed the hopes and dreams most young people have."

Croft, who was a part-time preacher, also spoke about his parents.

"Their purpose and mission was to help others. That night, they were killed trying to help."

Afterward, he said the family was not interested in the state seeking the death penalty, saying "it wouldn't change a thing." Besides," he said, "we need to get on with our lives."

Death penalty cases are ensnared in red tape and years of appeals, he noted.

"I knew from the beginning that there was no way to get justice. I lost my mom and dad. He only has one life to give. There's no way that would be enough."

His brother, Randy, did not agree.

"The only justice is to take him out behind the house and shoot him in the head," he said.

***

Sure, the mind of a criminal is a dark place. The thought process, such as it is, is inevitably based on selfishness, greed, lust, or old-fashioned coveting.

But shouldn't there be *some* logic? Shouldn't their half-baked schemes make even a little sense?

Apparently not, if you decide to try to hire a hit man to kill a judge who has sentenced you to three years in prison, and you think you should get probation, despite getting breaks and violating probation in the past.

Such was the case of Julienne Massad Williams, 30, who not only wanted to strike out at the judge, but also two witnesses who testified against her.

Circuit Judge Jerry Lockett was mystified when interviewed after Williams was arrested and charged with solicitation to commit murder on Jan. 12, 1996.

"What would she gain if I'm killed?" he wondered. "She'd still go to prison. There's no logic to this, no reason (*Sentinel*, Jan. 13, 1996)."

Williams essentially told me the same thing in a jail interview.

"I would not have done this. There's no reason," she said.

The judge had given her a break by deferring her sentence after being told she was having problems with her 4 ½ month pregnancy, and she had an upcoming civil trial. She used the break to try and hire a hit man, investigators said.

Her reasons were clear in her mind, Assistant State Attorney Hugh Bass said: "Revenge and obsession."

It was an ugly case. The chief witness against her was a longtime confidential informant and drug user who pretended to be a hit man who had been "raised by the Mafia" and had ties to bikers.

Lake County Sheriff's investigators played taped conversations in which the two talked in code. For example, one conversation had the informant talking about messing up "the locksmith on the 18th hole (*Sentinel*, Aug. 28, 1996)."

Lockett lived on a golf course. In another conversation Williams wondered if the judge could be bribed. The informant instead talked about killing the judge.

"I'm not sure that's going to do me any good," she replied.

Prosecutors also pointed to her comment: "I'll tell you what. I want to see it done myself (*Sentinel*, Aug. 25, 1996)."

On the stand, the man, who said he was a disabled Vietnam War veteran, claimed he went to sheriff's deputies right away after pretending to be a hit man because he was "just doing the American thing."

Defense attorney Alan Shuminer, however, pointed out that he earned $1,500 for 24 hours work. With his questions, he led the informant through a tangle of contradicting stories about agencies he had worked for. One case was a homicide in Lake County. The man testified that he could not remember a lot of names and other details. Shuminer also got the man to admit that he had been taking drugs until recently.

Jurors also heard from a former prison friend of Julienne's, who said Williams wanted to put a bomb "under Judge Lockett's chair."

Williams also told her that she had paid the "hit man" $800 for a sniper rifle. She testified that she wanted the two witnesses against her in her drug case to be killed, too.

Williams was angry, she said, because "she only violated [probation] on a technicality" and should have been sentenced to community control or house arrest so she could take care of her children (*Sentinel*, Aug. 29, 1996).

Defense attorney Chris Lyons ripped into her testimony, and managed to get her to say that she had so many felony convictions she couldn't remember how many there had been. There were 36, not 25 as she had estimated.

Lyons called her "the most decorated felon to ever testify in this courthouse (*Sentinel*, Aug. 30, 1996)."

Shuminer told jurors the male informant was "an out-and-out fabricator, prevaricator, and fibber. He lied every second he was up there."

Defense attorneys did not call any witnesses and they did not put Williams on the stand. After deliberating for four hours, jurors came back with a guilty verdict.

"They believed the crook," said her mother, Pastora Massad, a prominent lay leader at a Catholic church.

Two of Williams' children were in the courtroom when the verdict was announced, and they sobbed as they sat beside their father and grandmother.

The trial judge, who had been brought in from another circuit, would soon announce the biggest blow of all—a 50-year prison sentence.

Williams appealed.

"I would have hoped you might have wondered why I was stalling the informant, why I wouldn't show him where Mr. Lockett lived," she wrote to Judge Uriel Blount.

"I am really very sorry. I would ask you if you ever see Mr. Lockett, to tell him I am sorry and embarrassed for what I've put him through. But most of all, I hurt for what I've done to my family," she wrote (*Sentinel*, May 27, 1998).

It didn't help, nor did a motion asking for a reduced sentence.

"Being a habitual offender who seeks to have the judge killed does not lend itself to a lenient sentence or to the mercy of the court," Senior Judge E.L. Eastmoore wrote in his ruling.

***

The two college students were packing up their campsite when the young stranger walked up and asked them how to get to a hiking trail.

It was not unusual to encounter other people, even in the sparsely populated 380,000-acre Ocala National Forest. They chatted for five or 10 minutes, and then the young man left.

But what Amber Peck and John Parker didn't know, was that the young man, 19-year-old Leo Boatman, was crouching behind a tree just up the trail with an AK-47 rifle and, that he was preparing to kill them for no apparent reason.

Five days after the two 29-year-old Santa Fe Community College students were supposed to return home on Jan. 4, 2006, family members discovered their bodies in the Juniper Springs area of the vast forest.

Thanks to a tip from a man who remembered picking up Boatman in his car, Marion County sheriff's investigators tracked down Boatman.

The story became more bizarre by the minute. Boatman, they learned, had told a 20-year-old acquaintance, Briana Ryan, that he wanted to be a serial killer.

"I wouldn't kill a bum, because they would have nothing to lose. I went out there and came across two preppy kids and killed them." (*Star-Banner*, Jan. 15, 2006).

The 19-year-old was simmering with rage against his friends, his family, and against life itself.

He was born in an insane asylum where his mother was a patient. His mother, who had a long history of mental illness, may have become pregnant while in the institution. When she wasn't hospitalized, she was binge drinking and taking drugs. The court ordered his grandmother to take care of him, but she frequently took him back to his mother. He was often bounced from one house to another.

His mother died when he was 8 when she passed out and drowned in a ditch. He was placed in foster care, where he was sometimes physically abused.

When he was 12, he was placed in juvenile detention after committing various crimes.

At 15, he head-butted a teacher, stole prescription drugs, punched a 7-month pregnant woman on the shoulder, and threatened to kill her and her baby.

A year earlier he was caught in a sexually compromising position with another juvenile.

At age 19, he was released and staying with his uncle, Victor Boatman, in Largo. Victor thought Leo was on the right track because he had enrolled at a community college in St. Petersburg.

The event that set off the murderous explosion was an accident in which he wrecked his new motorcycle. His friends laughed at him.

Already enraged at his family, he stole a friend's AK-47, boarded a bus, and headed 100 miles north to the forest.

It was there that he met the two 26-year-old college "preppy kids." He couldn't have been more wrong.

Parker had served as a Marine in Afghanistan. He loved the outdoors, plants and flowers and wanted to become a forest ranger. His favorite place was Hidden Lake, the spot where he was killed. He had taken his 8-year-old daughter there recently.

"He was a wonderful father. He was always trying to teach her something—not like school-type lessons, lessons in life, life skills, wilderness skills, survival skills," said his sister, Bethany Parker (*Star-Banner*, Jan. 15, 2006).

"He just loved that place, and he wanted everybody to see it. It's high and it's gorgeous."

Peck and Parker were not in a romantic relationship. She was the only other student who signed up for the field trip.

Peck's parents, however, would later tell reporters that Amber, who had recently broken up with her boyfriend, had a bit of a "crush" on Parker.

She had a lot of keen interests, including gymnastics, drama, hockey, and swing dancing, but her greatest love was animals, said her brother David, at her memorial service.

"When she was little, we'd take her to the zoo. She'd say, 'They shouldn't cage those animals, Mom.'"

Then, she would cry.

She was "a beautiful child of God," he said.

She was about to go to Australia to study zoology on a scholarship.

She kept a scrapbook but it wasn't just a keepsake of her own life. For some reason it included newspaper clippings about a horrific murder in Michigan, in which 23-year-old Rose Larner was killed and mutilated. It included information about the 1997 conviction of John P. Ortiz-Kehoe. Peck didn't even know the victim.

"She cried for this girl," said her mother, Glenda Peck. "It just touched her so much that anybody would do that to a girl."

Faced with the prospect that he might face the death penalty, Boatman pleaded guilty in exchange for two life sentences with no chance of parole.

"There is nothing I can say that justifies what I did," Boatman told the court. "I can't offer any explanation for what I did 'cause there is none. All I can offer is my sincere apologies. I'm sorry, and one day I hope I am forgiven (*Star-Banner*, July 31, 2007)."

State Attorney Brad King said he would have been "more inclined" to seek the death penalty but accepted the plea deal because it was the wish of the families.

Peck and Parker never got a chance to live out their dreams, but at least one investigator theorized that Boatman selfishly carried out his plan.

"I really think he was fulfilling his dream," said Marion County sheriff's Capt. Dennis Strow. "And he was a serial killer in the making (Jan. 15, 2006)."

***

What kind of punishment should a judge impose on a man who is already serving a life sentence when he kills a fellow prisoner? Would yet another life sentence be meaningful?

What if the man tells a judge that he wants to be executed? Would putting him to death be a punishment or a reward?

These are just some of the questions that swirled around like evil spirits in a case that involved drug dealing, homemade weapons, and thievery—all within the confines of a prison's walls.

It was not exactly a whodunit. There were more than 100 witnesses to the slaying, but many were being treated for severe psychological disorders, including schizophrenia.

The tragedy began unfolding on Dec. 20, 1998, at Lake Correctional Institution when a man named Lawrence Wood burst into the state prison's day room, unplugged the TV, and told everyone that someone had broken into his locker and stolen some of his belongings. He demanded that the missing items be returned.

Wood's roommate, Allen Cox, 37, had also been victimized, and he was especially outraged. He vowed to kill the thief and offered a $50 reward.

The theft went right to the heart of his business—dealing drugs—because the thief stole $500 cash, not only a hefty profit but highly prized prison contraband.

"I'd rather do time on death row with a TV than have people breakin' into my house," he exclaimed (*Sentinel*, March 3, 2000).

The next day a prisoner told Cox the thief was a 25-year-old convicted burglar named Thomas Baker.

Prisoners were milling around a recreation area at lunchtime when Cox pounced on Baker, straddled him, and began "punching down" on his victim, who curled up in a defensive fetal position.

"I ain't got it!" Baker screamed.

Cox said the beating "wasn't good enough."

"Then he went in his waistband, and he pulled out something and he stabbed him like four or five times," a prisoner said in a sworn statement.

The "something" was a homemade knife called a "shank" that had been fashioned out of a stolen welding rod, its point sharpened against concrete or a metal bed frame, its handle crafted from a carefully wrapped wad of tape.

When Cox finally released him, Baker ran to a nearby building where he told a guard he had been stabbed.

"Please don't let me die," he pleaded, but he did die an excruciating death as the result of a punctured lung.

Before he died, Baker implicated Cox's roommate, Wood. Cox announced that he had "one more … to get."

The first person he spoke to was another prisoner, Donnie Cox.

"If I find out you've got my money, I'll kill you, too," according to court records.

The case gave me a rare opportunity to write about life—and death—behind bars.

How can a prisoner, for example, not only sell drugs but keep a wad of cash hidden from guards?

"Any warden who says there are no drugs in his prison is either lying or doesn't know what's going on," James Upchurch, chief of the Bureau of Security Operations for the Florida Department of Corrections told me in an interview (*Sentinel*, March 5, 2000).

Visitors smuggle drugs into prisons, especially when prisoners are allowed to hug their family members in contact visits. Sometimes, confederates toss drugs over the fence.

LCI is one of a handful of mental health treatment facilities within the state prison system. Prisoners often swap or sell their own prescription medicines, plus they make a homemade alcoholic brew called "buck" out of yeast smuggled out of the kitchen.

"We treat yeast like a narcotic," Upchurch told me.

I wanted to know even more. When I learned the public defender's office wanted to take jurors to the prison to see the scene of the crime, I told Circuit Judge T. Michael Johnson that the press would have to go too.

"Let me call the prison," he said. Within minutes he said, "Well, that's out." No one would be visiting the prison. The last thing wardens want is to have reporters wandering around their facilities. Nor do they want any other citizens gawking at the barren surroundings inside the razor wire. Not only is it a potential safety hazard but prison managers loathe any change that might excite prisoners. The ideal environment, they believe, is routine—forever.

There was nothing routine about Cox's life.

A native of Kentucky, he grew up feeling "unwanted, unloved and worthless," defense attorneys said (*Sentinel*, June 18, 2000).

His mother was a state witness against him at his trial. When he was a child, she "dumped him like a dog" in the road when she turned him over to his father, said Chief Assistant Public Defender Bill Stone. "She said, 'Don't come back or I'll kill you (*Sentinel*, June 30, 2000).'"

There were stories about Cox's father waking up to finding his wife standing over him with a butcher knife, cruel beatings when he was a child, and other nightmarish tales.

The defense also claimed that Cox was never taught or developed a moral code.

Assistant State Attorney Bill Gross pointed out that Cox's mother was forced by the state to testify against her son, and she tried to soften the blow with her testimony.

His sister was a defense death penalty mitigation witness in his murder trial. She offered a stereotype hillbilly defense when she pointed to a family tree with too few branches. The defense claimed that "two pairs of the defendant's great-grandparents were brother and sister, meaning that 'there wasn't a whole lot of diversity in his gene pool,'" according to court records.

Yet, Gross pointed out, the sister and others in her family turned out just fine. She had a normal life, graduated with honors from college, and had no criminal past.

Jurors were not allowed to hear about Cox's criminal past because it would be "too inflammatory," including the reason he was serving a life sentence.

According to court records, he went into a South Florida convenience store with a T-shirt over his face. When the 50-year-old store clerk started to open the register, he said he wasn't there for money. He grabbed her and threw her over a concrete wall, breaking her hip, and then proceeded to rape her while she was lying on a mound of fire ants.

A few days earlier, he stuck a gun in the face of two women he worked with and robbed them.

He was also convicted of breaking into a home. When he was confronted by the homeowner, he struck the man's head with a piece of office equipment.

What jurors did see, however, was a parade of colorful prisoners who testified against Cox.

One flamboyant character was nicknamed "Dancing Willie." He was taking heavy-duty psychotropic drugs to control his delusional behavior.

"Are you having any hallucinations now Willie?" Stone asked, with the proper amount of indignation for the jury's benefit.

At one point, defense attorneys tried to pin the blame on another prisoner. Cox claimed Vincent Maynard accidentally stabbed Baker while he was trying to stab him.

"I can't understand you doing this to me," Maynard said as he looked at Cox from the witness stand.

Jurors would have been interested to learn Maynard's past had they been allowed to hear it. He was serving time as a habitual violent offender after hitting an Outlaws motorcycle gang member with a pipe, beating, and kicking him, and biting off his nose after the biker beat up Maynard's girlfriend.

Gross insisted that Maynard's past was irrelevant.

The defense also argued that the prison was liable because it did not protect Baker. Judge Johnson did not allow that novel approach, however.

Gross described the defense case as "foolishness and fallacies (*Sentinel,* March 15, 2000)."

In the end, jurors took only 2 ½ hours to decide that Cox was the killer. Their only question was whether the homemade knife was the actual murder weapon. Cox ditched the knife after the attack. Jurors requested a ruler and a copy of the medical examiner's report.

Gross conceded that the knife that was found could have been a decoy of some sort.

"We'll never know for sure," he said.

When a majority of jurors recommended the death penalty, Cox wrote a surprising letter to the judge.

"I want you to go along with the jury's recommendation and send me to death row," he wrote (*Sentinel*, July 7, 2000).

He said he was sure he would get a new trial. "But if I don't, and they carry out my death sentence, the way I see it, I don't want to die an old man in prison. They will be doing me a favor if they give me a shot and put me to sleep," he said.

"Do you remember one of the jurors saying she would rather die than to spend the rest of her life in prison? Well, she hit the nail right on the head. That's how I feel, and I hope you will grant my request to follow the jury's recommendation."

He would get his wish. The jury recommended death in a 10-2 vote.

Johnson said Cox forced him into making "the most difficult decision as a judge and as a human being." He ruled that Cox was guilty of four aggravating circumstances: Cox was imprisoned at the time; he had prior violent felonies; the crime was heinous, atrocious, and cruel; and it was cold, calculated, and premeditated.

Mitigating evidence was weak if not fake, the judge ruled, including the idea that he was not taught a moral code. He certainly was instructed on rules and regulations in his many trips to prison, he noted.

"He knows what society expects of him; he just doesn't care to comply," Johnson noted in his sentencing order.

Stone blasted the state's decision to seek the death penalty. He called it an "example of dishonest prosecutorial authority." The state was gunning for his client with a death sentence because of the severity of the rape case, he said.

Gross said the argument was ridiculous.

"What were we supposed to? Pat him on the back and send him on his way?"

***

I suppose in a way that every chapter in this book could be entitled "Senseless." By normal standards of morality, common sense, decency, and even common courtesy, crime violates our sensibilities. But some crimes are especially cruel and heinous.

Take the case of the 29-year-old man who threw a 30-pound television set at his 81-year-old grandmother, then hit her three more times before going through her pocketbook and taking $30 and her car. Three days later, the Florida man pulled up behind a police officer in Virginia, got out, and confessed that he had "killed" someone in Florida. Yet when police in Eustis went to her house, they found her covered in blood but alive.

A doctor testified at the man's attempted murder trial that she had lost one third of her blood and suffered dehydration and hypothermia. A fingertip crushed by the TV had to be amputated. Her ribs were so bruised she could not take a deep breath.

Before hitting her with the TV, Tony Harrell said he punched her three times in the chest with his fists.

"It's her fault—she has put me through so much (*Sentinel,* 10-23-1996)."

He said she hit him on the arm.

"I told him he needed to take a bath," she testified.

He claimed he couldn't stop himself. The state stepped in to help him with control by sentencing him to nine years in prison.

***

Unarmed security guards and bouncers are shot while trying to maintain order and protect property, pizza delivery drivers are killed for a handful of change, a car, and hot bread.

In 1995, a man was shot to death for dancing with another man's girlfriend at a bar.

Witnesses testified the following year that Thaddeus Richardson tried to ask for forgiveness, saying he didn't know the woman was Perry Omar Buckner's girlfriend.

"Ain't a thing you can explain," the 18-year-old said. As the two began fighting for control of the gun, it went off twice, striking Richardson (*Sentinel*, June 6, 1996).

"Oh, God! Somebody help me," Richardson shouted (*Sentinel*, April 17, 1998).

"You ain't had enough?" Buckner said. He then walked over and pumped three more .22-caliber rounds into the helpless man.

Buckner fled. The gun was never found.

Buckner was found guilty of first-degree murder and sentenced to death, because among other reasons, the crime was ruled heinous, atrocious, and cruel.

Circuit Judge John W. Booth said the young church musician "suffered great pain and extreme mental torture during the last 10 minutes of his life."

The Florida Supreme Court disagreed and changed the sentence to life in prison.

But the most senseless crime ever committed was the carjacking of a young widow, who was raped, shot, and left for dead, and her two young daughters murdered.

Dorothy Lewis was minding her own business on Super Bowl weekend 1993 when she went to the grocery store to pick up a few items for a church luncheon the next day. She went with her two young daughters, Jamilya, 7, and Jasmine, 3.

When she came out of the store, 14-year-old Alphonza Smalls lifted his shirt to show he had a gun.

"Get in the car and don't say a word," he said.

Richard Henyard, 18, was also involved.

She told them to take the car, just leave them alone. They refused but promised "… if you just do what we tell you to do, you won't get hurt."

The girls started crying. She started praying.

"This ain't Jesus doing this," Henyard sneered. "This is Satan doing this."

Dorothy and the children were driven to an isolated area where she was assaulted by both teens on the trunk of the car. She begged them not to rape her, especially in front of the children. She grabbed the gun at one point, but it was wrestled away from her. She was then told to go sit on the ground.

She protested, reminding them that they promised not to harm her and the girls. Henyard then shot her in the knee.

"And then he started coming like closer toward me aiming the gun and that's when I started fighting back and I just remember just fighting, look like all three of us you know, was fighting and I don't remember any more shots," she said, adding that she was "swinging like a wildcat."

One shot from the stolen .22-caliber pistol grazed her neck, an intensely painful wound that caused problems for months. One shot went into her mouth, blasting out teeth and hitting the base of her tongue. But the one that should have killed her went right between her eyes.

When she came to hours later, the car was gone and so were the girls. Despite her injuries, she was able to start walking down the desolate road to seek help. Every time a car passed by, she hid behind brush, thinking the teens had come back to make sure they finished the job.

She finally found a house where someone could call police.

The children were found hours later, shot and dumped like discarded dolls behind a barbed wire fence.

The story didn't end there, of course. In fact, I didn't cover the crime or the two murder trials. It was only later, when I covered some of the appeals, that I got my first impression of Dorothy.

In spite of all that had happened to her, and losing her two beautiful children, I was struck by the peace, composure, and dignity that she possessed. Where did this peace come from, I wondered?

Years later, Dorothy and I would be brought together to team up on the book, *Unbroken: The Dorothy Lewis Story.*

It is called *Unbroken* because her Christian faith remains unbroken, and because of that, she has been able to rebuild her life and be stronger than ever.

I can't begin to detail everything about Dorothy's story in *Vampires,* so I strongly urge you to check out her story in *Unbroken*, but here is just a sample of what she wrote in an introductory chapter: "Even though I was faced with a mother's worst nightmare, He never left me, and God is still carrying me through it. The word of God says, "We often suffer, but we are never crushed. Even when we don't know what to do, we never give up. In times of trouble, God is with us, and when we are knocked down, we get up again (2 Corin. 4:8-9 CEV)."

The day after the shooting, Henyard, in the most brazen, idiotic stunt, went to the Eustis Police Department and tried to blame Smalls and another teen in hopes of getting a $1,000 reward. While spinning his story, a detective noticed something on Henyard's tennis shoe and white socks.

"There's some [expletive] blood on your socks," Bud Hart exclaimed, adding that he saw blood on his shoes, too.

"How you know that ain't no ketchup stain?" Henyard replied.

"We'll find out," said Robert A. O'Connor," an FDLE investigator who had been questioning Henyard.

"Two dead babies," Hart said (*Unbroken*, page 63).

Henyard was sentenced to death. He died of lethal injection in 2008. Smalls is serving a life sentence without possibility of parole.

Years later, I asked former Chief Assistant Public Defender T. Michael Johnson why Henyard did not just take the car and spare Dorothy and her children?

"If he were here today, he couldn't explain it," Johnson said (*Unbroken*, page 160).

Before he committed the carjacking, he bragged to his hoodlum friends that he wanted to take a car and put someone in the trunk before killing them. Could the tragedy have been avoided if someone had tipped police ahead of time?

Johnson didn't think so, especially in that group.

"It's a lifestyle, they all have guns. And it's worse now."

In other words, things are more senseless than ever.

Chapter 22

Death knell for newspapers?

It's hard to slip anything past reporters and editors—at least the good ones. After all, it's their job to stay on top of things and to sift the truth from politicians, crooks, lawyers, and PR flacks. So, when the editor of the *Ocala Star-Banner* started rearranging the furniture in the newsroom in 2008, everyone knew something was going down.

One of the changes came when maintenance people started hanging computer monitors and TV sets from the ceiling. The idea was to remind everyone of the importance of creating and working in a "digital newsroom."

We already knew the importance. We were updating the updates on the website and had been for some time. Many of the younger journalists realized the importance years before the editors and publishers. Newspapers were late jumping into the digital age and often floundered when they did. One former reporter told me that it was not until the mid- to later 1990s that she had Internet access on her computer. Only two computers at the *Daytona Beach News Journal* were hooked up because management didn't want reporters and editors to be "distracted."

Once it became apparent that newspapers would have to take the plunge, folks who make their living sitting around conference tables couldn't agree on the details. Newspaper subscribers and single-issue readers pay. Newspaper ads can be sold based on size, frequency, position, color, day, and section. What about the online versions? What about classifieds? Newspapers have to abide by an independent auditor's rules on circulation counts to reassure advertisers. But because Web sites can count page "hits," advertisers can be especially picky, plus, they no longer have to deal with a monopoly. Retailers and others have websites, too.

New technology, a dismal economy, a shakeup of media companies and distrust by the public created upheaval in newspapers and in the news business itself.

"The stock was once $50 a share, now it's down to $4," a former *Times* reporter was quoted as saying at a stockholders meeting (May 1, 2013, bostonherald.com). His big question for the directors was: What are the executives doing to hold down the costs, including their own compensation? It's not just about holding down costs, of course, but reducing debt and raising cash (on June 16, 2021, the stock was listed at $40.55).

In December 2011, the New York Times Co. announced it was selling its 16 regional papers, including *the Star-Banner*, to Halifax Media Holdings of Daytona Beach for $143 million in cash.

Arthur Sulzberger, Jr., chairman, said the sale would "enable The New York Times Company to continue our transformation to a digitally focused, multiplatform media company."

Ken Doctor, a media and publishing analyst at Outsell Inc., said the price was "incredibly low."

"That's saying basically each title is worth about $10 million" on average, he said, "which is just breathtaking when you consider what kinds of profit machines these newspapers used to be."

The story said the Regional Media Group accounted for 11 percent of the company's $2.4 billion in revenue in 2010. The group's advertising revenue fell 8.2 percent at that time to $177 million, according to the Times 2010 annual report (mediadecoder.blogs.nytimes.com/2011/12/27).

Doctor said the sale of the regional papers would allow the Times Co. to decide what it wanted to do with *The Boston Globe.*

What it wanted to do, of course, was to unload it, which it did in August 2013 by selling it to John W. Henry, principal owner of the Boston Red Sox, for $70 million.

The New York Times said in its story on the sale that it was part of the company's "latest move to shed assets and focus more on its core brand (NYTimes.com., Aug. 3, 2013)."

The company was also selling its other New England media properties to Henry.

The article conceded that the sale represented "a staggering drop in value for *The Globe.*" The Times bought the paper for $1.1 billion in 1993.

The paper lost readers to the Internet and revenues dropped like a rock.

The sale fit into a sickening pattern of decline. In April 2012, Philadelphia's newspapers sold for $55 million after selling for $515 million in 2006. In October, *The Tampa Tribune* sold for $9.5 million, the *Times* article noted.

In 2016, *The Tampa Bay Times* purchased the *Tampa Tribune* and shuttered its doors.

New Media Investment Group Inc., which listed GateHouse Media LLC as a subsidiary, purchased Halifax in 2015 for $280 million.

In 2019, GateHouse would buy Gannett for $1.1 billion, making it the largest newspaper chain in the country.

"In an interview with The Associated Press, executives of the combined company, which will keep the Gannett name, acknowledged there will be layoffs — the company has committed to cutting $300 million in annual costs," (MarketWatch, Nov. 19, 2019).

"Current Gannett CEO Paul Bascobert said front-line reporters are 'the last place we want to touch' when it comes to job cuts. He cited 'duplication of management' and potential excess costs in financial, printing, and advertising divisions as opportunities to reduce costs, and said the company will further centralize editing and newspaper and web design functions."

In 2013, Amazon founder Jeff Bezos purchased *The Washington Post* for $250 million in cash, ending the Graham family's reign over the legendary paper after four generations.

The Washington Post story included this admission: "... for much of the past decade, *The Post* has been unable to escape the financial turmoil that has engulfed newspapers and other 'legacy' media organizations. The rise of the Internet and the epochal change from print to digital technology have created a massive wave of competition for traditional news companies, scattering readers and advertisers across a radically altered news and information landscape and triggering mergers, bankruptcies, and consolidation among the owners of print and broadcasting properties (washingtonpost.com., Aug. 5, 2013)."

And in another big story, the Tribune Co., which owns the *Chicago Tribune, Orlando Sentinel, L.A. Times,* and a handful of other papers, announced in July 2013 that a week after making a deal to buy 19 TV stations, it was planning to "spin off" its publishing business into a separate company (July 10, 2013, Tribune.com).

The company said it had been thinking of ways to "divest" itself of the newspapers since February. By delaying a sale until 2014, it would enable Tribune Co. to offload its newspapers while avoiding the large capital gains tax it would incur from an outright sale, the *Chicago Tribune* story said.

The article said the move, "confirms Tribune Co. CEO Peter Liguori's vision of shaping the company's future around television, thus rejecting the company's long-held belief in the power of being a media conglomerate with interests in publishing and broadcasting."

Walter Hamilton, a writer for the *Los Angeles Times,* wrote a story in December 2014, which was published on the Tribune Web site.

"In cases like this one, spinoffs are Wall Street's version of addition by subtraction," he wrote. "Because advertising revenue of Tribune's publishing unit is declining steadily, splitting off the papers could make the rest of the company more appealing to investors (latimes.com, Dec. 9, 2013)."

The company announced that the spinoff was expected to be complete by the second quarter of 2014.

The announcement follows a series of moves that once would have been unthinkable.

In 2007, real estate billionaire Sam Zell launched an $8.2 billion buyout of the Tribune Co. *Chicago Tribune* reporters Michael Oneal and Steve Mills noted in a story on Jan. 13, 2013, that the move couldn't have come at a worse time. Less than a year later, the company was plunged into bankruptcy.

"The financial crisis hit with full fury in 2008, just months after the Tribune Co. deal closed, setting off a near-collapse of the economy and freezing the credit markets, which in turn prevented Zell from selling assets to pare the debt. At the same time, the digital media revolution gained steam, drawing advertising dollars away from companies like Tribune with a vengeance (chicagotribune.com)."

In April 2009, *Orlando Magazine* ran an article by former *Sentinel* reporter Michael McLeod headlined: "Is Sam Zell digging the *Sentinel's* grave?'

The subhead read: "The maverick real estate investor earned his fortune—and the nickname "the Grave Dancer"—by capitalizing on corporate decay. In buying Tribune Company late last year, he saw another opportunity to find profit in a struggling business. But he didn't see the black hole the newspaper industry was about to fall into, made deeper by the privatized company's $13 billion of debt. For the Tribune-owned *Sentinel*, Zell's ownership has come at a hefty price: drastic cuts in staff and content."

The article included an account of the infamous meeting Zell had with *Orlando Sentinel* staffers six weeks after buying the company.

Zell, who claimed to enjoy "open kimono" communication with his staff, took a question from a staff photographer. She wanted to know if he favored lighter features about "puppy dogs" over more serious subjects, such as the war in Iraq.

He told her that her question sounded like "typical journalistic arrogance." He said he wanted to have serious stories, but he had to salvage the company's bottom line. If that means stories about puppy dogs, then OK.

The photographer, who was finished with her question, turned around to return to her seat. Thinking he was being *dissed*, Zell cursed at her under his breath. Unfortunately, it was loud enough for everyone in the room and on the Internet to hear. He later apologized, saying he sometimes liked to use profanity to wake people up to the urgency of the situation.

The company eventually did come out of bankruptcy four years after the sale was completed.

New challenges would follow.

In 2021, Tribune Publishing shareholders voted to take a $633 million offer from Alden Global Capital hedge fund.

"We remain committed to serving the community with journalism that makes a difference in our reader's lives," said Editor Julie Anderson. "Our mission inspires us every day, and that doesn't change with new owners (*Sentinel*, May 21)."

But *Sentinel* editorial writers minced no words when it decried the idea on April 2.

"Alden's history with newspaper ownership is akin to a biblical plague of locusts—it devours newspaper resources to maximize profits, leaving ruin in its wake."

It mentioned Alden's takeover of Media News Group in 2010, and the subsequent reduction of the *Denver Post's* editorial staff from 230 to 70.

Sentinel staffers had hoped that wealthy individuals might buy the paper, which has been covering Central Florida since 1876.

"Our eyes are wide open about what we are able to do today versus 10 years ago," the editorial said. "With Alden as our owner, it could get much worse."

Newspapers make money, but apparently not enough for investors hungry for more.

"As an industry, we've got barrels of whoop ass left," Jim Moroney, publisher and CEO of the *Dallas Morning News* said in 2013 (April 17, 2013, frontburner.dmagazine.com).

Other executives at the Newspaper Association of America convention talked about "reader engagement," and new products, including digital.

The *St. Augustine Record*, a small paper in North Florida that was then part of Morris Communications, advertised for a "director of audience."

The ad, which appeared on the Poynter Institute Web site, said the person "will be a leader in our transformation of the Newsroom (its capitalization) as we become a more integral and indispensable part of the lives of the local people of St. Augustine."

The company's goal, according to the ad, is to "double, triple, and quintuple the audiences we reach—or more."

The ad is filled with industry buzz words, like "growing monetized audiences through non-news content, services, or functions."

It says that it is looking for someone experienced in "consumer-facing marketing or comparable public-

and business-facing communications for development of audiences and/or revenues."

Record Publisher Delinda Fogel explained the job to me in plain English.

It's not just about writing stories for print anymore, but putting out "content" in print, digital, and mobile devices.

"How many eyeballs can we get on our Web site, Facebook, Twitter?"

It's not just news. It's important to expand the advertising base, too.

The chain's Athens, Ga., *Banner-Herald* newspaper, came out with a phone "app" with news about the University of Georgia Bulldogs sports teams.

"People in their 20s don't get their news from newspapers. A lot of them have never read a newspaper and probably never will," said Fogel, who has been in the newspaper business for more than 20 years.

A lot of people now look to social media for their news, she said.

There has been a movement lately to make social media giants like Google and Facebook pay for news content.

Not everyone is sold on the notion that the newspaper industry will survive.

Peter Thiel, a co-founder of Pay Pal, said at a conference that Twitter's 1,000 employees will have jobs a decade from now, but workers at the New York Times Co. should be worried about their future (May 1, 2013, money.cnn.com).

In the meantime, newspapers are continuing to put more emphasis on digital presentation, which is a heck of a lot cheaper to produce. In the digital world there are no multi-million-dollar printing presses, trucks, carriers, mail room workers, or clerks to answer phones and apologize for wet newspapers and failed deliveries. Technology has already pushed out many "back shop" production crews.

Top executives are getting golden parachutes to retire, but that comes with a drain of experience and knowledge.

The same holds true for line editors and reporters. It's cheaper to hire young people right out of college than it is to pay seasoned veterans, but at what cost to quality? There is also the issue of quantity, as evidenced by big, empty newsrooms. With fewer editors, there are fewer filters for errors and a smaller structure to define and enforce good judgment. There are fewer eyes watching government on all levels, and more naïve puppy dogs than junkyard dogs.

Will anyone notice? The older generation, which grew up reading some quality newspapers, might recognize the shortcomings but not the younger crowd. They may be satisfied with "news" in Twitter's 280 characters or less.

In fact, what many consider to be "news" is really celebrity gossip and glamour.

Foreign news? *Forgetaboutit*, as they say in New York. Virtually all news agencies have cut back on staffing overseas bureaus because of costs. This, despite the fact that we have thousands of troops overseas, the world economy is shaky, and the United States is threatened by terrorists, rogue states, and by strong, traditional enemies.

Reduced news coverage really shows up at the local level. When I was at the *Sentinel's* Lake County bureau I had a beat—the courts. I didn't have to cover anything else. Other reporters had their own beats: cops, county commission, city hall, or schools. By being responsible only for the court beat I could dig deep on a particular case or issue. I could cover important trials gavel-to-gavel, take time to investigate rumors about abuses, and tell compelling stories about people and how they were affected by crime.

Now, there is no *Sentinel* bureau.

Sentinel columnist Scott Maxwell once wrote about what makes newspapers great.

"We have our faults. But you'd be hard-pressed to find another outlet so dedicated to covering the issues that matter—the social issues, zoning hearings, and family concerns that aren't sexy enough for TV reports or polarizing enough for blogs (*Sentinel*, May 26, 2013)."

The *Sentinel* won one of its two Pulitzer prizes for a series of editorials that called for responsible limits on development and the environment. Taking on big-time developers was gutsy since it flew in the face of gaining potential advertising revenue. Will it be even harder to take tough stands now?

On a smaller scale, the kind of story that I wrote about the injustice of cops mishandling a homicide investigation may also be harder to do. Beat reporters develop a strong network of trustworthy sources. Being the new guy on the court beat is a steep hill to climb. Lawyers are trying to protect their clients, judges their cases, and everyone their own personal reputation. Mess up once, and you are dead in the water, but if you handle material carefully, are honest and protective of confidential sources, and use good news judgment, then you establish trust, the basis of all good relationships. However, setting up a beat system takes time and costs money.

The readers are the real losers in this new era. People need to know what's going on so they can make informed decisions in the voting booth. Unfortunately, this diminished news coverage comes at a time when government—even local government—is bigger, more impersonal, more powerful, and less accountable than ever. It is especially true for the federal government.

On Feb. 18, 2013, Jim VandeHei and Mike Allen wrote an article for Politico.com headlined, "Obama, the puppet master."

"President Barack Obama is a master at limiting, shaping, and manipulating media coverage of himself and his White House," the article began.

"Not for the reason that conservatives suspect: Namely, that a liberal press willingly and eagerly allows itself to get manipulated. Instead, the mastery mostly flows from a

White House that has taken old tricks for shaping coverage (staged leaks, friendly interviews) and put them on steroids using new ones (social media, content creation, precision targeting). And it's an equal opportunity strategy: Media across the ideological spectrum are left scrambling for access."

Meanwhile, the article said, Obama is texting, tweeting, chatting, or using some other digital maneuvering to claim that he has "the most transparent administration in history."

In fact, the government is increasingly invading citizens' privacy and stonewalling misdeeds by refusing to turn over documents and give truthful testimony to Congress.

It was a brilliant piece, though I disagree with one point. A lot of reporters and editors have been only too happy to be spokesmen for the Democratic president—which makes his digital bypass even more worrisome.

The Obama press corps has tended to act more like lap dogs than watch dogs, even in the wake of the Justice Department's heavy-handed violation of First Amendment rights in its leak probes involving the Associated Press and Fox News.

Attorney General Eric Holder told Congress he had nothing to do with his department's claiming that Fox reporter James Rosen might be involved in a crime when the Justice Department intercepted his phone records and his parents', to see who leaked information to him for a story. As it turns out, Holder signed the paperwork.

In another controversy, the Federal Communications Commission planned to monitor how news organizations gather and report the news. The agency, which licenses broadcasters (who use the public air waves), planned to do a survey to make sure the "critical information needs" of the public were being served.

Journalists pointed to the First Amendment of the Constitution which says, "Congress shall make no law respecting an establishment of religion or prohibiting the free exercise thereof; or abridging the freedom of speech, or of the press; or of the right of the people peaceably to assemble, and to petition the government for a redress of grievances."

The FCC insisted that it had "no intention" of regulating the political free speech of journalists and has "revised" its plans.

Conservative news agencies who broke the story have questioned not only the method but the intent of such a survey.

Fox News, which has consistently reported on Obama administration gaffes, including the mishandled implementation of the Affordable Care Act and the way the government responded to the deaths of a U.S. ambassador and three others in Benghazi, has been disparaged repeatedly by the president and his spokesmen, claiming they are not a "legitimate" news organization, despite leading in the cable ratings by a large margin.

Fox was also at the forefront of reporting that the IRS refused to grant tax-exempt status to conservative groups before the 2012 election, something that Obama himself called "outrageous" in May of 2013. Later, he called them "phony scandals," said there is not a "smidgen" of corruption, and blamed Fox for keeping the controversy alive.

Some Congressmen tried to attack the free speech of radio talk shows by calling for strict "fairness" rules. The most successful of these programs were conservative, most noticeably *The Rush Limbaugh Show*.

Recently, the Associated Press reported that the Trump Administration's Department of Justice secretly obtained the 2017 phone records of a CNN correspondent during a leak investigation.

"The revelation comes two weeks after *The Washington Post* disclosed that the Justice Department had last year seized phone records belonging to three of its journalists who covered the Russia investigation (CNN, May 20)."

The New York Times reported that the records of four of its reporters were also seized.

It wouldn't be the first time that politicians have tried to dampen free speech. After *The Washington Post* broke the Watergate story, associates of President Richard Nixon mounted a challenge against a Post-Newsweek TV license in Miami. I was working as a production assistant at the Post-Newsweek station in Jacksonville, and we were told: "Make sure your tax returns are accurate."

The press-government relationship is supposed to be free-wheeling and adversarial, no matter who is in office. Reporters are not there to rubber stamp a politician's agenda but to ask the hard questions that their readers and viewers would ask if they had the chance.

President Donald Trump constantly blasted what he called "fake news."

Media critic and former CBS reporter Bernie Goldberg sharply criticized the press corps in the Obama White House in his book, *A Slobbering Love Affair.* The public has lost whatever respect and trust it still had for the "Fourth Estate," Goldberg said.

CBS' Dan Rather's bogus story on alleged favoritism for young George W. Bush in the National Guard, *New York Times'* reporter Jayson Blair faking stories, and other media scandals have deepened the chasm.

Major TV networks have lost growing numbers of news show viewers to cable, talk radio, and social media. The market is divided into ideological camps and fragmented by sheer volume.Top of Form

According to a Pew Research Center poll released in March of 2013, nearly a third of all people who were polled said they had abandoned a specific news outlet "because it no longer provides the news and information they had grown accustomed to ... (Poynter.org)."

It pointed out that "... those most likely to have walked away are better educated, wealthier, and older than those who did not—in other words, they are people who tend to be most prone to consume and pay for news."

The desertion comes at a time when there are one-third fewer journalists on the job since 2000. A lot of those journalists have taken jobs in government and politics.

"This adds up to a news industry that is more undermanned and unprepared to uncover stories, dig deep into emerging ones, or to question information put into its hands."

Kathryn Quigley, a former colleague at the *Sentinel* who is now an associate professor at Rowan University in New Jersey, is more optimistic.

"Journalism will always be around but it's no longer just in paper form, and it hasn't been for some time," she said.

Quigley, who also used to work at the *Philadelphia Inquirer,* remembers the days when newspaper people did just one task. Writers and photojournalists were separate. Copy editors and layout people had distinct jobs. Today, that has changed.

"We are training students to be 'backpack journalists.' They have to shoot video, shoot pictures, write stories, write headlines, and copy edit," she said, and they have to be able to post up on social media sites.

The Boston Globe had great multi-media coverage of the Boston marathon terrorist attack, and news could be updated around the clock, Quigley noted.

Newspapers have long suffered from limitations of press deadlines. The best they can do sometimes is to refer readers to the Web page for late sports scores and developments in breaking news.

Of course, "instant news" and the competitive drive to be first can be a minefield. Once, in Ocala, the online editor was hot to post something he heard on a local radio station.

The city editor said the story should first be checked for accuracy. It was good thing we waited. The story was bogus. It doesn't just happen with smaller operations, of course. Early in the coverage of the Boston terrorist attack, CNN, eager to be first, erroneously reported that authorities had arrested a suspect early on.

The Internet is already rife with falsehood, anonymous libel, and conspiracy theories without adding to the witches' brew with an error.

"There are many, many stupid people who believe everything they read online," Quigley acknowledged, but she adds: "People still like talented, smart news people."

Occasionally the tone is wrong. Once, young staffers on Ocala.com were having too good of a time with a video about a serious topic until I pointed it out and it was pulled down. It happened because so much of the Internet is flip, fun, and fast.

Fortunately, journalism students are still being taught ethics. Quigley uses the Society of Professional Journalists code of ethics in her classes, which includes: "Distinguish between advocacy and news reporting. Analysis and commentary should be labeled and not misrepresent fact or context (SPJ.org)."

Unfortunately, the young students don't always have good media role models, especially on the Internet and on cable news.

They are also still being taught the basics, like checking so-called facts, but many lessons have to be learned through experience.

One of the oddest things is that the students don't know how to use a phone like the rest of the world. They text, Quigley said.

"From the time I was 10, I had a phone growing out of my head," she noted. "They don't even talk to each other. The only time they use one is to fight with their boyfriend or girlfriend or talk to their mom.

"A lot of them want to do interviews with e-mail and we say, 'No, you can't do that.'"

Tom Rosenstiel wrote an article for Poynter.org, on May 3, 2013, headlined "5 qualities of innovative leaders in today's media." Number five was "innovators know the essentials should not change."

He picked the brain of management theorist Peter Drucker for this section.

"For any institution, that essential purpose is 'the value you provide' to your various customers. In news, this starts with readers, viewers, and listeners, but every business has many different kinds of customers. Your value is not what you do—your practices and routines—but the value you provide to people's lives. Knowing your value—the essential service you provide—is the difference between being in the transportation business rather than the railroad business. But it's also a matter of institutional values. Many in news confuse values with practices. I have also met executives who are giving up on what distinguishes journalism from other media," he said.

"You have to be smart enough to know that you can't keep cutting content and still keep your business," said Fogel of the *St. Augustine Record.*

"You have to give them content they can't get anywhere else," she said. And in the case of a newspaper company, that's local news about the community.

Chapter 23

Dreams

Everyone dreams at night. Often, the dreams are just downright weird. The reason is that your subconscious is trying to piece together the stream of things going on in your life and attempting to make sense of it. Sometimes there is a tug of war between what you want to do on the caveman level and what you know is right. Sometimes, it's a little exciting.

Occasionally, I dream that I am filling in on a copy desk, a place where I spent many years editing stories, laying out pages, and writing headlines. In the dream, I do not have a list of stories or the pages where they are supposed to run. Nor can I get a copy of the paper. It's like one of those dreams where you are being chased or falling.

The setting was jumbled, of course. The newsroom didn't really look like the one at the *Orlando Sentinel,* yet some former colleagues were there. One editor was from the *Ocala Star-Banner.*

I started to leave when I realized that I couldn't find my zippered lunch bag. I gave up and left.

I'm not a psychiatrist, but I don't think it takes a "shrink" to figure this one out. Going back, especially to the old copy desk, would be stressful. Things have changed. The lunch bag and the mixed-up editors might have appeared because

I have left a part of me, and many friends behind in various newsrooms.

The *Sentinel* learned during the Covid pandemic that it no longer needed the big building it occupied for many years. The company had already junked its huge press, which cost $100 million in the 1980s, and reporters and editors were working remotely. The newspaper is being printed by another paper miles away.

The *Sentinel* is not the only newspaper to turn building complexes into ghost towns.

Somewhere, there is the spirit of an old teletype machine spewing out rolls of paper with alarm bells ringing. Phones are jangling, desks are littered with glue pots, X-Acto knives, and copy paper, and reporters are banging away on typewriters with cigarettes hanging out of their mouths, and cups half filled with cold, nasty coffee.

The irony is that today's news stories are tomorrow's history books. Reporters are too busy to think about that, of course, but the future sneaks up on you.

There is still a need for news and for the people who gather and report it. In fact, the need is greater than ever. The challenge is finding out how to deliver it in the quickest, fairest, clearest, most accurate, attractive, and informative way possible.

Failure is not an option. Our freedom depends upon it.

Thomas Jefferson saw more danger in the possibilities for tyranny in government than in any shortcomings and scurrilous attacks of the partisan newspapers of his day.

"The basis of our governments being the opinion of the people, the very first object should be to keep that right; and were it left to me to decide whether we should have a government without newspapers or newspapers without a government, I should not hesitate a moment to prefer the latter. But I should mean that every man should receive those papers and be capable of reading them (famguardian. org)."

You can substitute the world "news outlet" for newspapers in this, the 21st Century, if you like. The idea is still the same.

"An educated citizenry is a vital requisite for our survival as a free people, he said (Monticello.org)."

Sources

Books

Roughing It, Mark Twain, 1976, Buccaneer Books Inc., Cutchogue, N.Y. pp. 177-178.

Encarta World English Dictionary, 1999, St. Martin's Press, New York, N.Y., p. 1572.

Unbroken: The Dorothy Lewis Story, Frank Stanfield, 2011, Kingstone Publishing, Leesburg, Fla.

Without A Doubt, Marcia Clark with Teresa Carpenter, Viking, New York, N.Y., p. 380.

The Yearling, Marjorie Kinnan Rawlings, Collier MacMillan Publishers, N.Y., 1967

Magazines

National Enquirer

Orlando Magazine

Newspapers

Daily Commercial

Ocala Star-Banner

Orlando Sentinel

TV

The Mike Huckabee Show
Death Row Stories

Websites and blogs

Bostonherald.com

Chicagotribune.com

CNN.com

Dailycommercial.com

Famguardian.org

Inhumane.org/data/BPMarquardt.htm

LATimes.com

(mediadecoder.blogs.nytimes.com/2011/12/27).

Money.cnn.com

Monticello.org

Myfwc.org

Nytimes.com

Ocala.com

Orlandosentinel.com

Politico.com

Poynter.org

Quotationsbook.com

Sharkattacksurvivors.com

SPJ.org

Washingtonpost.com

Tribune.com

Acknowledgments

I would like to thank the *Orlando Sentinel*, the *Daily Commercial* and the *Ocala Star- Banner* for allowing me to quote from the many articles I am referring to in this book, and for the use of certain photographs.

I am also indebted to the people who have consented to interviews, including George Burgess, director of the Florida Program for Shark Research; Delinda Fogel, publisher of *The St. Augustine Record; and* Kathryn Quigley at Rowan University.

Recently retired Assistant State Attorney Bill Gross filled in background on a violent rampage in Mount Dora, as well as Ken Adams, an investigator in State Attorney's Office.

Seminole County Sheriff's Detective Robert Jaynes shared information on the Georgia Crews cold case.

Carla Massero was very kind to speak to me about her missing grandson, Trenton Duckett, as was Leesburg Police Maj. Steve Rockefeller.

At the risk of overlooking countless others, thanks to Circuit Judge G. Richard Singeltary, Lake County Clerk of the Circuit Courts Neil Kelly and his staff, especially Pat Widman and Terry Shafar. The same goes for Debbie Allen in the State Attorney's Office and Pat Gross in the Lake County Sheriff's Office.

Special thanks go to my family.

About the author

Frank Stanfield has been a newspaperman for 40 years, working for the *Ocala Star-Banner*, *The Orlando Sentinel*, the *Wilmington Star-News*, *Daily Commercial*, and *The Augusta Chronicle*. He is the author of *Cold Blooded: A True Crime Story of a Murderous Teenage Vampire Cult*. His first book was *Unbroken: The Dorothy Lewis Story*. He received a master's degree in journalism from the University of Georgia and a bachelor's degree in political science from the University of North Florida. He was a sergeant in the Air Force during the Vietnam era. He lives in Central Florida with his wife Jackie. They have three daughters and seven grandchildren. His website is **www.frankestanfield.com**.

Index

A

B

For More News About Frank Stanfield,
Signup For Our Newsletter:

http://wbp.bz/newsletter

Word-of-mouth is critical to an author's long-term success. If you appreciated this book please leave a review on the Amazon sales page:

http://wbp.bz/gatorsa

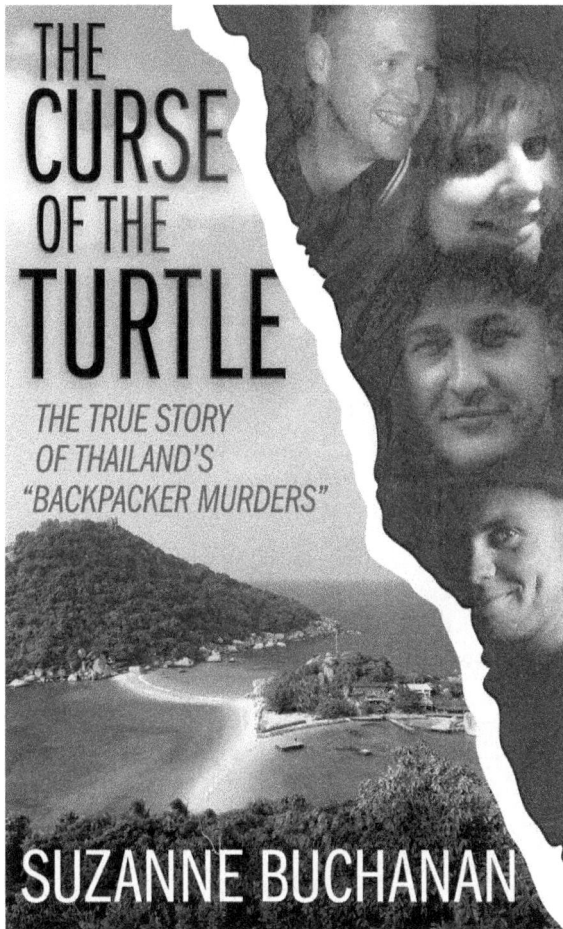

AVAILABLE FROM MIKE ROTHMILLER AND WILDBLUE PRESS!

TRUE CRIME CHRONICLES: Volume One by MIKE ROTHMILLER

http://wbp.bz/tcc1

www.ingramcontent.com/pod-product-compliance
Lightning Source LLC
Chambersburg PA
CBHW070047030426
42335CB00016B/1828